WORKER PARTICIPATION
AND THE
POLITICS OF REFORM

Labor and Social Change,
a series edited by
Paula Rayman and Carmen Sirianni

WORKER PARTICIPATION
AND THE
POLITICS OF REFORM

EDITED BY
CARMEN SIRIANNI

Temple University Press/Philadelphia

Temple University Press, Philadelphia 19122
Copyright © 1987 by Temple University. All rights reserved
Published 1987
Printed in the United States of America

The paper used in this publication
meets the minimum requirements of American National Standard for Information Sciences—
Permanence of Paper for Printed Library Materials, ANSI Z39.48-1984

Library of Congress Cataloging-in-Publication Data

Worker participation and the politics of reform.
(Labor and social change)
Includes bibliographies and index.
1. Management—Employee participation.
2. Organizational change. I. Sirianni, Carmen. II. Series.
HD5650.W645 1987   658.3'152   86-23006
ISBN 0-87722-464-1 (alk. paper)
ISBN 0-87722-465-X (pbk. : alk. paper)

CONTENTS

PREFACE

This collection of essays draws together some of the latest research on worker participation and examines not only the enormous diversity of its meanings and forms in the contemporary period but also its global character. The essays range across West and East Europe, the United States and Japan, China, and the Third World. Each of them is informed in some way by the conviction that worker participation is an eminently political phenomenon— that it is about politics and power at the level of the workplace, and that the larger context of social, political, and economic power and organization shapes what happens to participation locally. In this sense, the volume is not simply about internal workplace reforms. Nor is it a country-by-country survey of laws and institutions, but rather a collection of substantive analyses of the actual dynamics of participation and change.

My own essay, which introduces the volume, outlines some of the issues and problems of worker participation in the late twentieth century in the advanced industrial democracies. It situates participatory reform in the context of labor process debates over the past decade and examines some recent innovations and their relation to the nature of skills, the development of technology, the process of collective bargaining and union power, health and safety regulation, and work-time flexibility. Various elements of the vision of the democratization of work, which has inspired much of participatory theory over the last century, not only continue to have relevance but in some ways have found more practical resonance in the transformations we are currently witnessing.

Robert Cole's essay examines small-group innovations, such as quality circles and team organization, in three highly different societies, Japan, the United States, and Sweden, and argues for the need to focus on macropolitical and environmental factors in understanding their development and diffusion. Robert Howard and Leslie Schneider, Andrew Martin, and Giuseppe Della Rocca examine technological change and the various ways in which workers have begun to participate in the design and implementation of new systems. Howard and Schneider look at some of the most advanced examples of technology bargaining in Norway and compare these to cases in the United States. In his essay Martin examines a project in Sweden in which graphics workers from four Scandinavian countries developed new design specifications for computerized text and image processing that would upgrade the skills of workers and enhance their control over the work process. Della Rocca looks at the impact of the new technologies on participation and industrial relations in Italy, and sets the Italian experience against the background of similar developments in Scandinavia, the Federal Republic of Germany, and Britain. In his analysis of Germany, Christopher Allen examines the development of codetermination through different stages over the course of the century and focuses particularly on the problems of linking macroparticipation (in the works councils, etc.) with the newer concerns of work humanization, technological change, and work-time reduction. George Ross looks at another tradition with a very long history, namely, that of *autogestion* in France. He focuses on the revival of the *autogestionnaire* programs and slogans in the late 1960s and early 1970s and the movements that spawned them, and then traces the way that these were utilized in the political battles and realignments within the French left thereafter. The triumph of the left in 1981 led to a series of participatory reforms as part of the attempt to restructure the legal basis of industrial relations, but the more radical resonances of *autogestion* were no longer a part of that project.

The essays by Ellen Comisso, Henry Norr, and Jeanne Wilson examine the ways in which worker participation and self-management have been an essential part of the reform process in centrally planned economies. Comisso compares the self-management reforms in Yugoslavia that were able to establish a permanent political constituency for decentralized power in the economy with reforms after 1968 in Hungary. Despite the recent laws on self-management and the very innovative Enterprise Contract Work Associations within the firms, the vicissitudes of reform in Hungary have reflected the failure to establish similar kinds of political alliances within firms between workers and managers, and between managers and the ministries, which helped consolidate self-management on a decentralized basis in Yugoslavia. Henry Norr's essay examines the development of a grassroots movement for self-management in Poland in 1981 and the way in which it became part of the general strategy of Solidarity to cope with the economic crisis and the more general crisis of power in Polish society. And Jeanne Wilson looks at how participation has become part of the larger reform process in China since 1978, serving to secure political legitimation, remove operational control of the factories from party committees, and depoliticize the factories after the disruptive struggles of the Mao era.

Finally, Evelyne Huber Stephens examines the phenomenon of worker participation in three less developed capitalist countries: in Peru, where reforming military elites attempted to use Industrial Communities to undermine the unions, and in Chile and Jamaica, where participation was part of a more general democratic socialist project. In each case, the fate of participation was linked to the larger reform efforts, and relations of economic dependency set the parameters within which reformers had to operate.

I would like to express my deep appreciation to the National Endowment for the Humanities for the support received during the 1985–86 academic year that I spent at the Institute for Advanced Study in Princeton, and to participants in the Social Science Luncheon Seminar at the Institute for helpful comments on an early draft of my essay. Lucille Allsen of the School of Social Science did much of the work that made this volume come together. Members of the Social Change seminar at Empire State College also provided a welcome opportunity to discuss some of these issues. And Frank Fischer, as always, offered insight and support. The volume is dedicated to the memory of Franco Corbetta, a work reformer and friend.

WORKER PARTICIPATION
AND THE
POLITICS OF REFORM

1

WORKER PARTICIPATION IN THE LATE TWENTIETH CENTURY: SOME CRITICAL ISSUES

Carmen Sirianni

Worker participation has had a great diversity of meanings, forms, and motives over the course of the twentieth century. Many different terms are used to describe—or prescribe—workers' active involvement in decision making at work: *worker participation, industrial democracy, workers' control, self-management, workplace democracy, codetermination, employee involvement, quality of worklife (QWL),* to name just the most prominent. This diversity, of course, reflects not just different historical periods, national traditions, or academic theories but the reality of conflict and contested meanings—over the nature of work, the distribution of power, and, quite often, the future of industrial society itself. Worker participation has thus been a preeminently political phenomenon, even when disguised in apolitical or sanitized human relations terms. It has always been implicated in the conflicts of the workplace, the politics of skill and union organization, and very often in the distribution of political power in the larger social system.

This has been as true in the later part of this century as it was in the earlier decades when worker participation first achieved widespread significance as a result of mass movements for participation, resistance to scientific management, and various managerial, political, and union responses to channel protest and provide manageable structures for worker involvement in industry. As Steve Fraser has noted of this earlier period, *workers' control* and *industrial democracy* were complex metaphors, evocative yet often imprecise, with meanings that varied according to the social grammar in which they were embedded.[1] Leaders of the *Betriebsräte* in Germany or the *consigli di fabbrica* in Italy, and revolutionary theorists such as Karl Korsch and Antonio Gramsci, developed very different conceptions of the worker's role in production than the craft workers and artisans who had practiced local control for decades, or the moderate trade union leaders and corporate managers who tried to adjust in their own particular ways to demands for participation. What was industrial democracy for one afforded either too much or too little democratic power for the other.[2] In the confrontation over self-management in Poland in 1981 between Solidarity and the regime, this was again the case.[3] And as Robert Cole points out, the different terminology for small-group participation in various countries today reflects the relative balance of power and initiative of various actors. In Japan, where managers have been firmly in control of small-group innovations like quality circles all along, the terms *participation* and *industrial democracy* have seldom appeared, whereas the Swedish labor movement has possessed the industrial, political, and cultural power to shift the terms of debate toward democratization of various levels of the firm and economy. Those union leaders in the United States who have been supportive of such innovations have also stressed the theme of industrial democracy, although managers and consultants are more likely to speak of *employee involvement* and *participation*—and for some, even *participation* seems to raise more expectations than they are prepared to handle. But the unfavorable balance of industrial power for the unions has made participatory and QWL programs quite controversial and often very divisive among unionists themselves, as I will discuss below.[4]

The discourse on worker participation, at least in the West, has been informed by more general debates on democratic theory, including radical democratic critiques of capitalism and state socialism. Within the liberal tradition, the developmental model of democracy of John Stuart Mill stressed the role of participatory institutions in creating active, informed, and cooperative citizens. And democratically run producer cooperatives were viewed as potentially transforming not only the economic but the moral basis of society.[5] Various Marxist and syndicalist traditions have looked to workers' control and industrial democracy as an essential element in egalitarian social and economic transformation, and within Marxism, in particular, participation has been seen as an antidote to alienation.[6] Recent political theorists, such as Carole Patemen and Robert Dahl, drawing upon both liberal and democratic socialist theory, have argued that economic and industrial democracy is essential to a truly democratic social and political order.[7] And though normative theories of worker participation are not the focus of this volume, I have argued elsewhere that they not only have been central to the actual development of participatory reform but continue to be a crucial ingredient in the effort to expand the parameters of democratic and egalitarian thought and practice. But a normative theory of participation, one that pushes at the boundaries of a vision of democratic control in economic life, must question the division of labor at the sociotechnical level as well as the broader structures of segmented opportunity, at the same time avoiding idealizations of the one best model for participation in the varied workplaces of complex industrial societies. Normative political theories of participation have often been misleading or incomplete in this regard. Recent sociotechnical, participatory, and work-time innovations furnish us with increasingly concrete and realistic indications of what a pluralist, democratic, and egalitarian division of labor might look like, and thus provide the flesh and bones for further elaborating normative theory.[8]

A survey of the empirical development of participatory reforms in the twentieth century would show several distinct periods of relatively intense innovation, the major ones occurring during and immediately following the two world wars, and the period beginning in the mid- to late 1960s and continuing to the present.[9] Wartime political crises, and especially lost wars as in Germany twice in this century, have been particularly conducive to the development of worker-control movements and/or the institutionalization of worker representation in the governance of industry. Wartime economic mobilization also has created favorable labor-market conditions for workers to press demands for participation. In the later period beginning in the 1960s, as well, tight labor markets in many advanced industrial countries enhanced workers' ability to struggle for improvements in working conditions, and this in turn led to another wave of participatory reform.[10] A new breed of younger, more highly educated workers had come into the workforce, and many expected work to provide a source of interest, meaning, self-respect, individual rights, and equity—fertile soil in which participatory themes would grow.[11] And yet, as Cole shows, the relative degree of labor shortage was an important factor in shaping managerial responses in different countries to the problems of high turnover, absenteeism, and increasing discontent with working conditions. In Japan and Sweden serious labor shortages prompted managerial elites to experiment with small-group participatory reforms on a broad scale in order to attract and retain workers, especially in industries like autos, whereas American managers, faced with similar discontents and high turnover rates, had little motive to introduce participation because unemployment rates were relatively high and workers could more easily be replaced. As a result, despite some early showcase examples, the United States has lagged behind these and several other countries in participatory innovation, and only the challenges of international competition in the late 1970s and early 1980s have spurred greater attention in this area. And, as George Ross points out, the rise and fall of the more radical *autogestionnaire* struggles in France were also linked to changing conditions in the labor market.[12]

The later period of innovation in the West seems to be less marked by clear-cut breaks than the previous two major periods, even though workers' power in the labor market and through the political process have remained important factors in the development of reforms. As Peter Brannen notes, "whilst there are ebbs and flows, the general process is more akin to a ratchet effect: the fall back after the surge always stops at a higher level than before."[13] This may not be strictly true in terms of enhanced worker power in all cases—it is certainly questionable where participative schemes are used to undermine union power on the shop floor. But it is undoubtedly true that the forms of participation have often built upon earlier gains while becoming increasingly richer and more diverse, and have more profoundly affected the sociotechnical organization of work itself and not just representation at various levels of the firm.

Changes in international economic and political relations over the course of the century have also shaped participatory reform. In the period of World War I, movements for participation crystalized on an international scale around struggles against mass production and Taylorist rationalization, which had been given a great practical and ideological boost by wartime mobilization. By the end of the war, however, even many European unions that had been the strongest critics of Taylorism were forced to make accommodations in view of the challenge of U.S. industry and the absence of an effective international labor strategy. Older forms of craft control could no longer be effectively defended, especially in view of workers' own interests in material security and a reduction of the workday to eight hours, which were seen to be contingent on becoming competitive through the adoption of the latest mass-production techniques. Workers' control was thus redefined to accommodate many aspects of Taylorism, even when, as in the case of the Confédération Générale du Travail (CGT) in France, this accommodation was not passive but creatively expanded conceptions of democratic control in industry.[14] World War II only further reinforced the mass-production model on a global scale. By the late 1960s and early 1970s, however, a reversal of this process had become noticeable. As Robert Cole notes,[15] it was countries such as Sweden and Japan, with a heavy reliance on export industries, that experimented more quickly and extensively with participation in their quest for quality and productivity, whereas the United States, having enjoyed a leading position in international trade and a vast domestic market, showed much less concern in this area. Only with the unavoidable challenges in the international market in the late 1970s did American managers begin to look at participatory reforms as a productivity strategy. Michael Piore and Charles Sabel, in fact, trace a profound historic shift—a "second industrial divide"—which has led to the reemergence of a craft model with extensive worker participation in the late twentieth century. Various shocks in the international economy, the saturation of markets for mass-produced goods in industrial countries, and increasingly effective Third World development strategies based on mass production have helped revive flexible specialization and the craft model in a variety of industries, from specialty steel production and precision machine tools to specialty chemicals and customized textiles. The newer, more flexible technologies, such as numerical control for machine tools as well as looms, have made possible more rapid adjustment to changing markets and customized production in smaller runs. The mass-production paradigm has entered a period of crisis as a result of shifts in the international economy, even as changes in the early part of the century created the conditions for its original, if always partial, triumph. And new options are now available for reorganizing production in a way that puts a premium on flexible, participatory systems.[16]

Worker Participation and the Politics of Skill

In the remainder of this essay I will briefly discuss a number of critical issues that workplace participation schemes raise for the way we think about skills, technological development, work time, health and safety regulation, and union-management relations. Participation has added new dimensions to each of these and has raised questions that will determine the meaning of work and the future of industrial society for many years to come. That future, of course, is quite indeterminate, not only because the new technologies and their uses in the workplace are themselves still very fluid and flexible, but because the power context that shapes their development is unresolved and uncertain.

The first question is how to relate participatory innovations to the labor process debates of the past decade and a half, particularly the debate over deskilling. Braverman set the terms of the most recent debate in 1974 with his argument that, in the interests of lowering the cost of labor and securing control over the workforce, managers in capitalist (as well as state socialist) societies design the labor process to deskill work and to separate the conception from the execution of tasks. And, despite what official statistics might show, he argued further, the general trend has been in the direction of increased deskilling and degradation of work.[17] The argument was provocative, not only because it seemed to describe deskilling strategies and realities in various occupations, but because it introduced questions of power and control in the labor process in a way that had been only faintly if at all present before, particularly in the United States. Soon, however, the central theses of the deskilling argument came to be questioned, even by those more radical critics of power and skill distributions in the workplace. Among the major criticisms were that (1) the deskilling argument overestimates the power and prescience of managers to structure the labor process in a way that will yield them maximum control; (2) it underestimates the degree to which workers' struggles have themselves shaped the labor process; (3) nationwide studies of the American labor force simply do not support its contention of a deskilling trend; (4) it tends to romanticize the craft worker and the craft ideal of control and opportunity; to neglect, from a historical point of view, the differential interests of the less skilled and women workers for whom scientific management and bureaucratization often brought significant benefits; and, from a normative or ideal point of view, to misunderstand the challenges of creating a more egalitarian and democratic division of labor in a complex society where not all jobs can be reconstructed on a holistic or craft basis; and (5) it underestimates the extent to which new technologies, in order to be utilized cost effectively, depend on higher degrees of worker skill, commitment, attention, responsibility, and the capacity to keep learning, rather than on the mindless repetition of fragmented tasks separated from all planning and conception.[18]

Participatory innovations provide evidence for amplifying this critique of the deskilling thesis, although they by no means obviate the need for continued focus on power and control. The famous Topeka system, for instance, designed by Richard Walton of the Harvard Business School for a dog food plant owned by General Foods and others like it, demonstrated the degree to which teams could integrate a variety of tasks, from basic processing and packaging to quality control, purchasing, maintenance, and the like. Team members rotated tasks among themselves and received pay increments for new tasks learned, thus encouraging members to continue learning and teaching each other. Workers would earn the team rate as they mastered all the tasks performed by the team, and eventually the plant rate for all tasks of the plant short of formal managerial ones. The experiment, initiated by management in 1970 in response to labor problems at other General Foods plants with the intent of keeping out the union, has been very successful in terms of productivity, lower absenteeism, and higher product quality, though it went through some difficult times in the mid-1970s. (It was not discontinued, as some commentators wrongly reported.) But one particularly interesting problem that Walton has noted in this and other similarly designed systems is what to do when workers, in response to the incentives of pay and the challenge of learning new tasks, become *too* smart. In the first few years there existed a "skill gap" as workers strove to master new tasks, and the experience of progressively closing this gap helped produce high levels of commitment. But their learning was so successful that a "skill surplus" soon developed. Since no new products or new process technologies were introduced after 1974, workers' skills began to outstrip the challenges posed by existing processes, and their high commitment and intrinsic motivation, though still greater than in comparable conventionally organized plants, began to slip. There in fact seems to be a general tendency in carefully designed systems such as these for worker skill and knowledge, and the problem-solving capacities of the teams as teams, to surpass, often considerably, the requirements of the technology, leading to what has been referred to as a "human resources surplus." This, in turn, produces an "equity gap," since workers come to feel that as they demonstrate their commitment and capacities for learning, and as the plant itself is economically successful, they neither have the opportunity to keep learning nor to keep earning pay increases at the rate they did in the earlier stages.[19]

Examples such as these raise many interesting issues. The most obvious, of course, is that they are living critiques of the Taylorist paradigm, combining participation and skill upgrading in a way that enhances productivity, and that, under certain circumstances, they can be the preferred strategy of management. But they also raise problems for management. The equity gap that Walton has noted seems to become more salient over time, and whether there will be strategies for its resolution on terms acceptable to management, such as profit or gain sharing, is uncertain. Changing products and technologies alleviate the problem to some extent by providing further opportunities for learning. But it does not seem reasonable to expect such continually changing products and technologies to provide the permanent basis for participatory systems in all or even most areas of production and service.[20] To the extent that participation becomes more generalized, I suspect that the open-ended learning model will itself have to be broadened beyond the boundaries of particular plants to include lifetime learning, career change, and opportunities for creative, high-commitment involvement outside the market as well as within it. Of course, whether this occurs, and whether the continued tensions surrounding equity and managerial control within participatory systems (which has led some experiments to be discontinued) will lead to challenges to the larger structure of power and ownership (e.g., worker participation in plant governance, worker ownership, control over investment) is uncertain. Participation and power at one level often lead to demands for the same at other levels. But this is not always the case, and often workers participating at the shopfloor level show little interest in firm governance or the election of management. And some argue that participation can be kept bounded.[21] In any case, there is certainly no *internal* dynamic leading to the generalization of worker participation, but rather numerous processes and elements of dynamic instability. How these develop is as much dependent on factors in the external environment, such as political and economic crises, trade union strength and mobilization, legislative intervention, and the like. But the open learning model, which is even clearer in the following case, nonetheless raises questions that transcend particular workplaces and challenge systemic obstacles to continual learning and open opportunity more broadly.

An even more ambitious sociotechnical design, developed with the participation of the Oil, Chemical and Atomic Workers union, is that of the Sarnia, Ontario, Shell Canada plant, which produces specialty chemicals.[22] The design was a response, on the one hand, to pressure from highly paid workers for more opportunity to develop their skills and to have greater control over the work process, and, on the other hand, to the suboptimal utilization of the technology under the deskilling assumptions that had guided the engineers who had originally designed the plant. Such suboptimal utilization, including costly errors and downtime, which often result from the neglect of the skills and commitment of the workers who operate complex technologies, has been noted not only by critics of the deskilling argument but by proponents and analysts of worker participation throughout the 1970s.[23] The organizational model chosen at Sarnia aimed to maximize learning and improve the response time to disturbances as they arose. The computer software was designed to respond to queries posed by the operators, but to leave decision making in their hands, and an offline computer served to facilitate learning. It was thus a "passive" information system without closed decisional loops whose purpose, to use Shoshanna Zuboff's terminology, was to informate rather than automate.[24] In order to make informed decisions and respond quickly, workers had to be supplied with technical and economic data conventionally only available to technical staff. The learning model treats the entire plant as the relevant unit for all workers, with no internal boundaries, so that plant-wide learning can take place. As a result of the agreement with the union to forego detailed job classifications and seniority-based promotion in return for the opportunity for meaningful work, continued learning, and participation (with no customary management rights clause in the contract), work could be organized without specific job descriptions, and teams made responsible for overall operations and the rotation of tasks among team members on a day-to-day basis. Each team of eighteen members and a coordinator operates the entire process, including the lab work, shipping, warehousing, janitorial work, conflict resolution, administration, and many aspects of maintenance, and each team rotates over the various shifts in an innovative way that will be discussed further below. The only nonrotating team is composed of maintenance "craftsmen-instructors," who not only do the basic maintenance work but teach such skills to all teams, as do the two lab specialists who also work the day shift. In this relatively flat organizational structure there are only the plant superintendant and operations managers in addition to the worker teams. And the fundamental premise of the design is that *organizational* learning requires unrestricted *individual* learning, and hence a system of open progression. Grade levels are based on skill, measured by exams and performance tests. Each member is expected to acquire all the knowledge and skill modules for process operations. Beyond this, there are different specialty areas, the combination of which define distinct career paths within the plant. Not only are there no quotas as to how many can progress through these career paths, but the expectation is that *everyone* will reach the top level, though there are no time limits placed on this, and workers are not forced to advance if they do not wish.

This example, and many of the sociotechnical designs that are similar to it, reveal how profound is the shift from the older forms of craft control and the informal or collectively bargained forms of job control based on narrowly defined skill classifications. Participatory sociotechnical systems, especially when combined with the informating potential of the new technologies, allow for multiskilling and permanent learning that cut across old demarcations, and often involve an understanding of the entire process of production. Workers' horizons become broader, and their skills more theoretical or intellective. Tacit, embodied, and often exclusive skills become more explicit, public, and shared. Technology itself becomes a tool for learning and exercising discretion, and information systems become more open and less blocked by hierarchical controls. And the theoretical skills learned to run one kind of informated process are often applicable to a variety of other areas of production, service, and administration as well. This is not only strikingly different from what deskilling theorists such as Braverman would have expected, but it gives the lie to the more radical version of the Marxist critique that sees capitalist principles to be embodied in the very essence of modern technological development.[25] Although such technologies, and the work systems that organize them, remain very much a contested terrain, they represent in many ways a sounder and more effective basis for organizational and workplace democracy than has ever before existed.

Unions and Participation

One way to ensure that the new technologies are not used to deskill work or to deprive workers of control and discretion, however, is for workers to participate in the very design and implementation of these technologies. Many unions, of course, bargain over the effects of new technologies, such as staffing plans, retraining and relocation, rating systems, or limiting their use for individual monitoring of performance. But the great majority of these bargain after the fact, i.e., after the new technologies have already been designed, and little can be done to alter their basic configuration.[26] Whether the deskilling effects of new technologies are unplanned, however,[27] or whether they reflect deeper managerial fantasies of complete control,[28] some unions have begun to demand participation—before the fact—in the design process itself.

Recent analyses indicate some of the innovative ways this is beginning to occur, particularly in the Scandinavian countries, and some of the difficult obstacles faced by workers and their unions in shaping the design process.[29] In the case of the UTOPIA project analyzed by Andrew Martin, graphic workers' unions in Sweden, Norway, Denmark, and Finland received public funding to develop new design specifications for a text and image processing system that would preserve the jobs, professional skills, and control exercised by graphics workers, while taking advantage of the flexible uses of the latest technology in printing. In other cases, agreements have been collectively bargained that have allowed worker and union representatives to participate in various stages of the design process. The methods for ensuring worker input have included the formation of local study circles and joint union-management technology committees to analyze the problems of existing technologies and to formulate alternative specifications, the election of data stewards, the hiring of outside consultants approved by the union (in some cases with employer funds), and the use of special laboratories for the development and testing of prototypes. In the case of the Norwegian savings banks analyzed by Howard and Schneider, for instance, working groups established in the different branches spent two-day sessions several times a month over the course of six months learning about system alternatives and making suggestions that they could discuss with the rest of their workmates. At the end of this period some of these people were chosen to go to the computer center for one month to work further with the system designers and to ensure that the workers' recommendations were followed. Not only were various systems developed that improved the quality of service and work, but the union agreement under which this occurred established a quota of training slots for women to counter the tendency of their becoming trapped in low-wage ghettoes within banking. Swedish metalworkers negotiated an agreement that resulted in the redesign of numerical control systems whereby machinists receive a machine tool design from the design department but utilize software that allows them to develop a program for its manufacture. And they can refine the control program through the successive use of modeling techniques, thus developing their own professional skill in the process.[30]

A number of very interesting alternative designs have been developed over the past decade that have involved rank-and-file workers and union representatives at various stages in the design process itself, and that have created new possibilities for learning, skill development, and initiative at work. And yet this form of participation presents more formidable challenges than many of the other forms of worker involvement, such as quality circles. To engage in a continual round of design, implementation, and evaluation, and to develop the in-house technical skills both at the rank-and-file level and among union staff to make this effective, requires a major commitment of resources, and the unions can often ill afford to divert such resources (time, training, money) away from the other tasks with which they are engaged. Nonetheless, if union representatives on labor-management technology committees are not to become hostages of managers' and system designers' points of view, if local study circles are to develop genuine competence in analyzing work organization and design alternatives, if demonstration projects are to receive funding to get off the ground, if permanent staff members are to develop the expertise to permit them to bargain effectively at subsequent stages, and if outside consultants are to be hired to represent labor's point of view, then a considerable commitment of resources is needed. Strong union organizations, such as those in Scandinavia, have been able to generate some of these resources internally and to bargain effectively for others, such as the funds from employers to hire outside consultants. But even here, especially as some unions find inadequate a strategy based solely on joint projects with management and seek to build up their own research capacities, the problem of resources remains a difficult one. Where the resources are available and the unions exercise a strong presence, however, they can be quite effective in providing the context for flexible and informal influence by workers on the shop floor—a crucial ingredient for the development of viable alternatives, as Howard and Schneider demonstrate. And strong unions are a key element in dynamizing the complex feedback loop that moves from local knowledge and participation on the shop floor, to the formulation of demands for alternatives and the fruitful collaboration with experts at various levels, to the development of actual prototypes and a new round of testing and local input.[31]

The political strength of unions is, of course, crucial if significant amounts of public funds are to be channeled into alternative technology projects with union participation in the design process. Martin's study of the UTOPIA project makes clear how critical public funds are, and how the unions cannot hope to compete against the resources of management without such funds. The effective democratization of knowledge and technology cannot occur without extensive public support and a reorientation of the research policy of the state. Even in Sweden, where the legislative context for participation developed quite favorably for the unions in the 1970s, where the Social Democrats have returned to power after a relatively brief interlude by the opposition parties, and where the unions have demanded a reorientation of research policy since 1981, public support for alternative technology projects that protect the skills and control of workers has been neither particularly strong nor coherent.

The other obstacles to a genuinely democratic technology policy with extensive worker participation are also quite formidable. Some of the new technologies, while dissolving old boundaries between professional and nonprofessional or between white- and blue-collar workers, also create the basis for intense occupational struggle over staffing and lines of demarcation. This is the case, for instance, between programmers and machinists on numerical control systems, and graphics workers and journalists working with computerized text and print technologies. And the problem is made more difficult when significant staff reductions are possible, when the general employment situation is not favorable, or when policies for retraining and placement are not well developed. Although some graphics workers and journalists in the UTOPIA project, for instance, were able to work these problems out on a local level, conflicts between their respective unions on the national level were so intense as to lead to a discontinuance of the formal project. As Martin notes, the project developed a rich fund of experience for developing new specifications, and these have served in local negotiations for various graphics workers' unions and for redesigning training requirements in the vocational colleges. But an effective general strategy for dealing with the shift in demarcations that many of the new technologies entail is contingent on innovative forms of cross-occupational cooperation and retraining. Fixed boundaries can no longer suffice as the basis for an industrial politics of opportunity that is equitable and democratic in an age of increasing technological flexibility. Participation provides some of the answers, but the problem itself is much larger.

In addition, international competition does not always act as a spur to flexible systems with increased participation, but often constrains firms operating within narrow profit margins from experimenting with alternative designs. A market-driven model of participatory work organization development, such as offered by Piore and Sabel, must thus be modified, and the factors in national and international markets favoring and hindering flexible participatory systems must be specified further. As Howard and Schneider point out, increasing participation may require that certain aspects of technology be taken out of competition through a broader framework of social regulation, in a way that health and safety or minimum wage levels have been. Needless to say, this is much easier to achieve on the national level than on an international scale, but the dilemmas are not fundamentally different from previous struggles to regulate health and safety, or working hours, where international competitiveness was also at issue. Of course, the international dominance of multinationals from countries with weak labor movements unable to shape the design process significantly (e.g., IBM), the increasing availability of "package systems," and the funding of technology and work organization development by the military place severe constraints on local participation in the design process.[32]

The challenges facing democratizers are thus quite formidable and complex, and require a multilevel strategy.[33] Unions must not only develop a perspective on the design of technologies at the earliest stage possible, they must generate significant resources so as to be able to present that perspective effectively and coherently at each stage of design, implementation, and evaluation. This is necessary both to facilitate and generate local knowledge and expertise among the rank and file, as well as among union staff. At each of the levels of worker involvement, communication and forms of alliance with technical staff must be developed in order to ensure good systems representing the concerns of workers. Strategies to deal with occupational demarcations and staffing issues must be worked out, and often this will require broader employment and training policies. State-sponsored research must itself be reoriented and sufficient funds provided to permit unions to shape technology policy according to the democratic principles of worker participation and skill enhancement.

The problem of resources, of course, is not confined to the technology bargaining process, but affects all participatory programs in which unions become involved. Even in those countries where the unions are quite strong, such as Sweden and Norway, there is competition for resources among various union activities, including various levels of participatory involvement (e.g., codetermination at the plant level or small-group activity). Where unions are generally weaker and under vigorous attack, as in the United States, the relative distribution of resources that management and labor can devote to participatory programs can determine whether these programs genuinely serve to enhance the quality of work and the input of workers, or whether they undermine the role of the union and the collective-bargaining process. Until now, management in the United States has generally had the upper hand in terms of relative resources. It has been able to commit more staff and spend more time. It has largely controlled the training of QWL facilitators, the writing of materials, and the selection of outside consultants. It has been able to do long-range planning, and it controls the daily resources (e.g., access to typewriters and photocopiers) as well as access to information that makes programs succeed or fail. It has provided channels of mobility for worker facilitators and thus poses a permanent threat of cooptation for even some of the more militant among the rank and file. Critics of QWL programs, such as Mike Parker, argue that such unequal resources fundamentally bias participatory programs against workers and their unions.[34] But even proponents of QWL concerned with strengthening labor and collective bargaining through the QWL process, such as Thomas Kochan and his associates, recognize that this requires unions to devote considerably more resources to the training of facilitators, the education of local leaders, and the development of national staff with specific expertise in QWL and its attendant problems. It entails providing opportunities for mobility within the unions for the many talented facilitators who come through QWL, and the cultivation of a broad range of activities (conferences and the like) that can help shape the network of QWL professionals and consultants according to labor's concerns. And it means that the national unions must be committed to supporting local activities, monitoring developments, and putting out fires when programs run into difficulties, as they inevitably do.[35]

But ambivalence toward QWL remains profound within American labor, despite the support of prominent unions such as the United Automobile Workers, the Steel Workers, and the Communication Workers—and even in these unions there is skepticism and opposition. The main reason for this is the larger context in which QWL exists. Not only have unions never been fully accepted by American employers, but the current wave of union-busting activity continues to sour labor-management cooperation. QWL is seen by some as part of a larger strategy to weaken or destroy unions. And there certainly has been a link in many cases. In some instances quality circles have been directly used to prevent unionization and to strongarm union supporters, and many union-busting consultants also peddle QWL programs.[36] In other instances the relationship has been more subtle and indirect—picking away at union power by using participatory programs to create alternative allegiances, or by making the union appear bureaucratic in its struggle for worker benefits, and management flexible and responsive by contrast. Or programs developed in union plants have been transplanted to nonunion ones, sometimes with attendant job losses in the former. The fact that the second generation of participatory programs developed in response to the external challenge of international competition and was accompanied by concessionary bargaining and layoffs in many instances makes unions considerably more ambivalent than they might have been to management initiatives. And perhaps no factor has been more disruptive of union participation in QWL programs than layoffs, which reduce the trust necessary for joint programs, or appear as an explicit violation of promises that no job losses will result from QWL. Although unions have in some instances been able to use QWL to limit job losses, or to develop more acceptable ways to handle what appears inevitable, the fact remains that it is hard to pinpoint whether efficiencies achieved through QWL are responsible for workforce reductions. Consequently, union leaders who support QWL as a means to prevent job loss are taking considerable political risks. Union leaders thus often feel compelled to respond to QWL initiatives, or to propose some

themselves, because of the threat of job loss but continue to feel ambivalent because they do not control the conditions under which reductions
are decided and because the larger context has been generally hostile to
unions. Both labor proponents and critics agree, however, that the environment within which QWL programs function makes it crucial to link
them to the collective-bargaining process and to institutionalize them
within contractual agreements, rather than to allow management to take
initiatives while the union looks on as a watchdog.[37] Both the micropolitics
of QWL within the firm and the larger political and economic context
outside make participatory programs very much a contested terrain. And
it is this macropolitical environment, as Cole argues, that has impeded the
development of a national infrastructure for participatory reform.[38]

In this context, innovative classification systems and sociotechnical
designs, pay for knowledge, and flexible team organization are not un-
equivocally empowering of workers. Many get increased access to training, greater variety of tasks, more control over the way work groups
organize their daily activities, and greater access to information on overall
plant operations and economic performance. But they trade off greater
flexibility to management in the way it can deploy human resources and
give up the protective functions that highly formalized and detailed work
rules and classifications perform. The tradition of job-control unionism
that had evolved in the United States over many decades has been an
important source of power for workers on the shop floor, protecting them
against arbitrariness, speedup, health and safety risks, and ensuring
negotiation over new requirements added to particular jobs. Less reliance
on common rule strategies and the increased variability and flexibility that
results from the reduction of detailed formal classifications make the
union's task of representing worker interests, limiting managerial arbitrariness, and containing competition among workers more complex.[39] The
skilled trades often feel most threatened and have least to gain from these
new systems. And in some cases the creation of broader categories and
"supercrafts" can perhaps function as a form of deskilling, with skilled
workers exercising a wider range of tasks but on a narrower set of
machines.[40] Whether workers and unions in the United States can turn
these more flexible systems to their own advantage and enhance their
power—perhaps extending joint participation in QWL programs and labor-
management committees into works councils at the plant level—or whether
flexibility and increased access to workers' knowledge will be used to
enhance managerial power and mobilize consent, is at this point quite
indeterminate.[41] But the extent to which participation is empowering or
cooptative does not depend so much on the formal design of the programs
themselves as it does on the mobilizing activity that the unions and
rank-and-file workers bring to them.[42]

Participation in Health and Safety

An area where there has been considerable movement toward increasing participation over the past decade and a half, especially in Europe, has been health and safety. The free-market philosophy that had viewed hazardous work as a matter of free choice, to be compensated by higher wages, had gradually come to be modified by the belief that the state should intervene to ensure protection, and that standards should be developed and administered by neutral bodies of technical experts. Rule-based strategies of state regulation entail the formulation of general rules, applied universally, stating exactly what conditions are to be allowed and disallowed. The process of regulation is one of matching facts to rules in the manner of judicial or quasi-judicial proceedings. More recently, however, the limitations of rule-based strategies have become more and more apparent, and the *rights* of workers themselves to participate in the process of making workplaces more healthful and safe, as well as their *competence* in establishing appropriate norms for the work environment, have been increasingly recognized. Workers' participation has come to be viewed as an effective way of monitoring and preventing hazards, of mobilizing workers to cooperate with safety regulations, and of ensuring collaboration of workers and managers in the process. At a more ambitious level, it has come to be increasingly recognized that workers can directly contribute to the very definition of what constitutes health and safety, and that their local knowledge can form the basis for effective short- and long-term solutions. Participation, however, came to be seen during the 1970s as not only a relevant and effective instrument but as a right—and for some workers and unions, an absolute and inalienable one at that.[43]

Perhaps the most thoroughgoing critique of rule-based strategies is that developed in Norway in the various work research institutes, and whose principles are now embodied in the Work Environment Act of 1977. This critique argues that rules cannot be developed for all relevant hazards, such as ergonomics or stress. Rule-based strategies permit activities unless there is a rule with a positive reason for disallowance, and hence they are not very effective where there is doubt and uncertainty—which is the case with many health and safety hazards, including carcinogens. Such strategies cannot keep up with technical change, and standards quickly become frozen and outdated. The discrete and unambiguous norms that rule-based strategies rely on make it difficult to treat the work environment *as a whole,* which is particularly important where threats are not the result of discrete hazards so much as the combined effect of interactive factors. In such cases a holistic approach that looks for synergistic effects of interactive factors is most appropriate. Rule-based strategies entail having a general rule for everything that defines exactly what is illegal and specifies what is to be done, and if such a rule cannot be formulated, the potentially hazardous activity is permissible. They focus generally on minimum requirements, for which it is easier to devise such norms, rather than long-term improvements, which cannot be formulated in similar terms. They tend to ignore problems that build up over time, that are not a threat immediately, and that cannot be perceived on short site visits by inspectors. Rule-based strategies also require too many experts, and critics have feared that the continuous expansion of the inspection and research capabilities of regulatory agencies would be required to make them effective. They also place too much emphasis on medical and technical research, rather than on social research into behavioral and social factors. The latter, of course, can seldom develop discrete rules in the way that technical research can, but medical research is limited to designating technical threats, rather than threats that may derive from the social organization of work.[44]

The extent of this critique of rule-based strategies for regulating health and safety has been uneven in the European Economic Community (EEC) countries, but a wide range of participatory reforms have been instituted to secure rights and develop competences at the local level. In Italy, where preeminence is given to workers' own experience, worker participation in health and safety matters has been established through contractual agreements (and thus unevenly) and has taken place through the *consigli di fabbrica* and special environmental committees. In other countries, such as France, Belgium, and Britain, statutory provisions exist for the establishment of safety committees, although in Britain it is up to the unions to decide whether or not to appoint representatives. In Germany, the Netherlands, and Luxembourg, safety committees are subordinate to the works councils that are established by statute in the larger firms—which, in fact, can lead to health and safety's not having high priority, given the councils' other concerns. The mechanisms, thus, are varied, as are the mandated rights and effective powers of worker representatives. In some cases workers can exercise veto power over managerial decisions affecting health and safety, and exercise codetermination over the choice of company health and safety staff. Information rights are widespread, as is consultation over yearly action programs to improve the workplace, and employers must keep detailed records that are open to inspection. Workers are entitled to be involved in workplace inspections and the investigations of accidents, and in Italy many agreements permit workers to hold their own inspection and accident investigation. Workers also have a variety of forms of access to health service experts, and physicians and safety advisers are generally required to cooperate with them. In some cases workers have the right to utilize experts of their own choice, often from local health services or universities, to ensure objectivity and independence of judgment. They also have various forms of access to the public authorities charged with regulating plants and offices, and can request inspections and action on specific hazards. In the Netherlands, for instance, an inspector who refuses to take action at the workers' request must justify this in writing, and workers can appeal the decision. And in a number of countries individual workers have the right to stop work in case of imminent or serious danger.[45]

Not all these rights, of course, are effectively exercised. In many cases managers refuse to set up safety committees, or unions and works councils do not place enough priority on these matters. White-collar workers generally do not take hazards as seriously as blue-collar ones, even when issues of ergonomics, stress, indoor air pollution, and the like might warrant concern and involvement. In some cases, such as France, institutional confusion and overlap impedes local involvement, and in others, such as Britain, the requirement that trade unions appoint safety representatives obstructs action where no union exists.

The Norwegian and Swedish systems seem considerably more coherent and effective because health and safety have been seen as part of a larger program of industrial democracy over the past two decades, and the "work environment" concept is meant to combine these concerns into a unified approach to upgrading work and enhancing participation. The Work Environment Act of 1977 in Norway was designed to shift the focus of activity to the local level. It provided for forty-hour training courses in health and safety issues and techniques, which a considerable portion of the workforce has begun to take—in the first three years alone 10 percent of all employees completed such courses. Although minimum standards are established and rule-based strategies are not totally abandoned, the goal of a "fully satisfactory work environment" is established in all workplaces. Each enterprise is under the obligation to develop a program for systematic improvement over a period of time, with employees, their committees, and safety stewards mapping out the problems and assigning priorities. Such developmental local activity, which legitimates the evaluations of those experiencing the problems, is meant to sidestep continued debates about the legality of particular norms and actions, and focuses holistically on the environment and its betterment. Most interestingly, lack of control itself is seen as a threat to health and safety, as is undiversified and repetitive work, and explicit recognition is given to the need for variation, initiative, and the use of judgment—and more broadly, to continued opportunity for personal and professional development. This stands on its head management's usual argument that human mistakes are the main cause of accidents by arguing that lack of power and control, and boring work itself, are the main causes of human mistakes. The validation of local insight, experience, and activity by workers themselves in the area of health and safety leads, in this case, to raising larger questions about control and the division of labor.[46]

The Swedish system has developed a similar emphasis on local activity, social and holistic perspectives, and worker rights to participate secured through national legislation. As a result of the perceived crisis in health and safety hazards and the worker protests of the 1960s, the Swedes moved to revive and expand labor-management safety committees and have progressively extended the power of safety stewards to monitor compliance, stop work temporarily if there exists an imminent danger, participate in follow-up work, and be actively involved in developing study circles with materials written by the union, instead of listening to lectures by company engineers and experts. And though national regulation is not neglected, worker participation and effective power at the local level have made the regulatory process itself flexible. The contrast with the United States, for instance, is striking. Under similar pressures, and for a variety of other political reasons, the United States moved from an essentially voluntaristic system (which amounted to industry's regulation of itself) to a highly bureaucratic, professionally administered, rule-based and punishment-centered system under the Occupational Safety and Health Administration (OSHA), established in 1970. The American system was shaped in this way primarily as a response to the fierce resistance by employers to any interference with their managerial prerogatives over workplace organization, and American inspectors have been from the start considerably more pessimistic than their Swedish counterparts have been about employers' willingness to comply with regulations without compulsion and penalties.[47]

This punishment-oriented system not only has many of the drawbacks noted above but in the United States it magnified the original managerial resentment and led rather quickly to organized attempts to limit if not dismantle OSHA. In addition, because of the adversarial quality of this rule-based and punishment-centered system, the transaction costs of regulation are considerably higher. These include more cumbersome documentation and inspection procedures designed to establish juridical proof rather than quick correction, and various levels of hearings and appeals, with lawyers, cross-examination, and the paraphernalia of judicial proceedings. The Swedish inspection process, by contrast, is considerably more informal, focused on sharing information, giving advice, reconciling differences, and making corrections as quickly as possible.[48]

The main reason that the Swedish system is so much more flexible than the American, with lower transaction costs and a more effective inspection process, is not, as Kelman argues, because of a different set of values of the regulatory personnel or the *overhet* tradition in Sweden that even now elicits deference to state authority among managers. Rather, there is opportunity for greater collaboration among inspectors, managers, and workers, and less emphasis on rules, fines, and adversarial procedures, because workers have been granted effective rights through national legislation to participate actively in regulation at the local level, and their power here, through the trade unions, and at the level of the state (where there has been long socialist incumbency) has made employer resistance and obstruction less likely to pay off than in the United States.[49] The statutory rights of workers to participate in health and safety matters are more feeble in the United States, the unions are weaker and have devoted few resources to health and safety at the national level, and the OSHA regulatory process has been subject to intense political and ideological conflict and White House budgetary oversight (through the Office of Management and Budget). The result has been inconsistent and ineffective policies, and ultimately immobility at OSHA. Employers campaigned hard throughout the 1970s to restrict OSHA's powers (though conceding basic statutory rights) and for the return to the voluntarist system. With Reagan's ascent to the White House, they have essentially achieved this, albeit invoking the rhetoric of the Swedish model and fostering limited forms of participation in order to exempt employers from inspections. By the late 1970s, however, the labor movement was itself beginning to appreciate that the answer to health and safety was not necessarily more inspectors, but knowledge and participation at the local level.[50] Future battles may yet be fought over the federal regulatory process. Meanwhile, the forms of participation in health and safety are being contested in the local workplace.

The Self-Management of Time

Working time is yet another area where the issue of participation has begun to emerge. Over the past decade and a half not only has flexitime become increasingly common but a whole range of alternative work-time options has been developed, and working at something different than the standard workweek has become increasingly legitimate. These developments have diverse sources: the increased participation of women in the labor market and concerns over balancing work and family life in a flexible and equitable fashion, changing work values among the baby-boom entrants into the labor force, greater longevity and better health of older people, and employers' various motives for wanting flexibility and part-time workers.[51] And the debate in Europe on shortening the workweek to spread employment opportunities has begun to raise the question of whether standardized reductions or individual options and voluntary time/income tradeoffs is the best means for achieving this.

Among recent work-time innovations are job sharing, permanent part time, voluntary reduced work time, flexitime and flexiyear schedules, compressed workweeks, innovative shift systems, and sabbaticals in non-academic settings. Job sharing entails two (or more) partners having joint responsibility for a job that is usually thought to require full-time commitment and that cannot be easily split into separate components. Partners may work a set number of hours, or they may vary this according to their own preferences and the needs of the organization. Permanent part-time options have many of the benefits and opportunities usually associated only with full-time jobs, and people choosing them often do so as entry, exit, or respite from full-time work and career commitment. (*Permanent* refers less to duration for the individual worker than to legitimation and availability of the option.) Voluntary reduced work time involves variable reductions in hours and pay, negotiated between individual and employer for a specified period of time, and can entail employees' moving back and forth between full- and part-time commitment. Flexitime can involve relatively minor adjustments in starting and quitting time, or can be expanded to include credit and debit hours over the course of the week or longer, although often with daily core hours to ensure coverage, common meeting times, and the like. Flexiyear schedules entail contracting for a specified number of hours over the course of an entire year, with a range of variations as to how these are distributed. Compressed workweeks and innovative shift systems do not involve a reduction of average weekly hours, but a compression into fewer days, longer shifts, the blocking of more extended periods of time off, and/or the rotation through different shifts. In many cases these various work-time options involve greater employee discretion beyond the initial choice not to work standard full-time hours, and some have developed with the joint participation of unions. Some union contracts, for instance, not only stipulate that job sharing and permanent part-time options be available to workers who want them, but specify a minimum quota of positions that are to be organized in this fashion. Others stipulate different levels of voluntary reduction, which can be negotiated between the individual and management periodically. Many state and local governments in the United States have mandated that part-time career options and job-shared positions be available to public employees, and the Federal Employees Part-Time Career Employment Act of 1978 does the same at the federal level.[52]

As in the case of health and safety, where division of labor and control issues emerge out of concerns with the work environment, so it is with time flexibility. The time autonomy achieved through flexible scheduling can stimulate other needs for autonomy and participation at work,[53] and participation increasingly leads workers to raise issues having to do with control of their schedules.[54] Flexibility in time commitments often requires flexibility in skill; and flexitime and other time options have in some cases contributed to greater job rotation, cross-training, and multiskilling among different categories of workers. For example, the innovative sociotechnical design at the Sarnia Shell Canada plant discussed above was partly motivated and then modified by an interest in equity and autonomy of working time. Dissatisfied with the burdens of shift work and the fact that the more senior workers tended to monopolize day shifts, workers helped design an innovative shift system to complement the other sociotechnical aspects of the plant. The $37\frac{1}{3}$ hour workweek was expanded to an average of 42 hours, with 12-hour shifts rotated on a regular basis, and the year was divided into eighteen-week cycles. During each cycle each worker received two nine-day blocks of time off (to compensate for the longer average work week), ten full weekends and four partial ones, i.e., in addition to regular vacation time. Workers in the self-managed teams could also decide to swap shifts with workers in other teams, thus providing increased flexibility. In order for such time flexibility to function effectively, however, job rotation, multiskilling, and cross-training within self-managed teams were essential.[55] Other compressed workweek innovations (4 days/40 hours, 3 days/38 hours) have for similar reasons also led, though often unintentionally, to job upgrading, greater autonomy, and participation in supervisory functions. Even clerical work seems to become more autonomous and varied under flexitime. And participation in the design of schedule changes enhances worker satisfaction with them.[56] Many participatory programs come to raise work-time issues. In one case discussed by Howard and Schneider, for instance, the QWL committee developed autonomous work groups that allowed workers to schedule and perform their jobs without first-line supervision, and the substantial savings went into a discretionary fund controlled by the committee to finance worker participation in company training programs.[57] In other cases workers receive the benefits of enhanced productivity from QWL programs in the form of "earned idle time" or "time incentives." In the joint union-management program launched at Harman's auto rearview mirrors plant in Bolivar, Tennessee, in the 1970s, for instance, workers who achieved their quota could go home for the rest of the day, or—as was quite common—could participate in one of the many in-plant educational and cultural programs that the workers themselves developed. The programs ranged from ones that were specifically job- or career-related, such as learning computer skills or studying for a high school diploma (also a mark of dignity for some), to car-care for women, theater groups, square dancing, Bible classes, art appreciation, and, of course, day care. The time aspects of the participation were developed in such a way as to spawn a "cultural renaissance" in the plant.[58] Training and education have been fostered both on and off the job as a result of flexible scheduling and increased time autonomy.[59] The synergistic and interactive effects of flexible time options and other forms of participatory and sociotechnical redesign thus seem to be diverse, and time autonomy is perhaps a more essential component of participatory reform than heretofore recognized.

Flexible work options provide a range of benefits both to individuals and to organizations, though they also present certain problems. These cannot be discussed here, though it is important to note one parallel in the unions' response to these and other forms of QWL and sociotechnical designs. To the extent that time options become diversified, the common-rule strategy becomes even less viable as a way of protecting worker interests, and unions must manage greater complexity and variety. Some unions, especially those with substantial numbers of women members (such as many Service Employees International Union and American Federation of State, County, and Municipal Employees locals in the United States), have welcomed part-timers as full members, and have bargained for seniority rights, benefits, and the general upgrading of alternative time options. But there remains deep suspicion among most unions toward workers who deviate from the standard workweek. Aside from male biases, which are profound among many union members and leaders, there exists the fear that flexible work-time options will make workers more vulnerable to managerial power both on the shop floor and in the labor market. Such options could erode labor standards, put pressure on workers for unpaid overtime, threaten benefits, and ratify even further the inferior status of women in the labor market. Unions fear that employers will use to their own advantage competition by part-timers willing to work for less pay and to accepi less job security. They also see part-timers as more difficult to organize and less committed to their jobs and to their union. And part-time options are seen by many as a distraction from other full employment policies and from the goal of a shortened workweek for all with no reduction in pay.[60] Many of these fears are indeed realistic, since it cannot be assumed that the interests of workers and employers in flexible options coincide—even though in some instances they are mutually beneficial—and since the standardization of hours performs a number of very important protective functions for workers.[61]

Flexible time options are thus no less a contested terrain for workers and unions than are other participatory and QWL programs. But as with these others, it is unlikely that labor can advance its interests by simply resisting the new flexibility. New technologies make diverse temporal (and spatial) relationships to work much more possible, and the time preferences of workers have themselves become increasingly diverse. Most part-time workers, for instance, including those who experience serious inequities in the labor market, do not prefer full-time jobs, and even full-time workers who are relatively content with the number of hours they work want greater control over the allocation of those hours. And most innovative work-time options, it is important to keep in mind, have been initiated by workers, not management. Recent attempts to formalize participation and autonomy in working time are not, in fact, altogether new. Not only have workers in the past often established quite flexible arrangements with their employers informally, but historical and sociological studies indicate that shopfloor struggles over the control of time have been persistent and pervasive, and have been very much a part of the broader struggles for control and dignity at work.[62]

These considerations have led to a number of recent attempts to outline the normative and empirical foundations for expanding worker participation to include the self-management of time. The French research group Échange et Projets, in its provocative *La révolution du temps choisi,* sees the "autogestion du temps" as a way of enriching self-management and argues for expanding citizen rights to include the right to work at freely "chosen time," with a variety of time/income tradeoff options that could alter the balance between time spent working in the market and outside.[63] Karl Hinrichs, Claus Offe, and Helmut Wiesenthal, in their analysis of the limits of trade union strategies for a general reduction of working time in Germany, have also posed the question of shorter hours in the broader framework of guaranteeing individual options and using welfare state mechanisms to encourage such choices and to support temporary and partial withdrawals from the labor market.[64] And Sirianni and Eayrs have indicated the centrality of work-time options for a feminist and participatory theory of equality, where the hegemony of the male career model and the structural segmentation of opportunities in the broader division of labor are open to question, along with the sociotech- nical and political relations of the workplace.[65]

Concluding Remarks

Work is being profoundly transformed in the late twentieth century, and participatory reforms of great diversity are an essential part of the changes that are occurring. The new technologies are less deterministic, more fluid and flexible, than perhaps ever before, and organizational paradigms of the past are in a state of crisis. Taylorist modes of work organization have been challenged in theory and practice. And yet there is little room for naïve optimism about the workplace of the future. In those sectors that are labor intensive, where workers are easily replaceable, high commitment not necessary, and/or the cost of error much lower than the cost of skill upgrading, many employers continue to pursue strategies of control and modes of work organization that limit skill requirements. Participatory reforms and skill enhancement have, for the most part, been limited to the primary sector of the labor market.[66] And despite some very successful examples of women's integration into participatory frameworks,[67] their disproportionate location in secondary labor markets limits the extent to which sociotechnical designs and the more advanced forms of participation immediately affect many of them. Outside the primary sector, unions themselves are weaker (or nonexistent), state legislation granting participatory rights often does not reach, and workers themselves have developed more negative and transitory attitudes to work, which do not serve as a promising basis for participation. But even in the more advanced sectors upgrading is far from automatic, and employers who may have an interest in better utilization of technologies often attempt to keep skills narrower and more firm-specific in order to enhance workers' dependence on the company and to limit mobility outside. And the extent to which participatory reform enhances the power of workers or becomes another technique of managerial control is part of the micro- and macropolitics that define participation as a contested terrain. Despite the fact that such reforms will undoubtedly continue to spread, the tasks facing democratizers within the labor movement are complex and formidable, and they warrant very broad, imaginative, and multilevel strategies. Such strategies involve legislative action to secure rights for participation, the shaping of technology research and development policies, the resources to effectively represent workers' interest in skill development and discretion, and creative alliances with the technical experts who design the new systems. They entail mobilization of resources at different levels of union organization to shape the everyday dynamics of participation on the shop floor, and efforts to manage difficult demarcation issues among production, office, and professional workers. Such strategies require imaginative policies for handling the increased flexibility and variety (of skill classifications as well as time options) in a way that protects collective interests and standards. And, finally, they entail a broad perspective on employment, lifetime learning and training policies, and methods for enhancing opportunity both within and outside the market in a way that begins to unravel and/or compensate for highly segmented opportunity structures. Participation is not in itself a solution to all these problems, but neither can it be cordoned off from them if its full democratic potential is to flourish. Workplace participation is very much embedded in larger structures of power and opportunity, and thus warrants an equally broad democratic and egalitarian perspective.

Notes

1. Steve Fraser, "The 'New Unionism' and the 'New Economic Policy'," in James Cronin and Carmen Sirianni, eds., *Work, Community and Power: The Experience of Labor in Europe and America, 1900–1925* (Philadelphia: Temple University Press, 1983), 174.

2. Carmen Sirianni, "Workers' Control in Europe: A Comparative Sociological Analysis," in Cronin and Sirianni, *Work, Community and Power*, 254–310.

3. See Henry Norr's essay in this volume.

4. See Robert Cole's essay in this volume. On the great diversity of meanings for worker participation, see also Peter Brannen, *Authority and Participation in Industry* (New York: St. Martin's, 1983), 13ff.; and Santiago Roca and Didier Retour, "Participation in Enterprise Management: Bogged Down Concepts," *Economic and Industrial Democracy* 2, no.1 (Feb. 1981): 1–25. The latter journal contains much useful analysis of participatory reform.

5. Michael Poole, "Theories of Industrial Democracy: The Emerging Synthesis," *Sociological Review* 30, no. 2 (May 1982): 181ff.; C. B. Macpherson, *The Life and Times of Liberal Democracy* (Oxford: Oxford University Press, 1977).

6. Paul Blumberg, *Industrial Democracy* (New York: Schocken, 1968).

7. Carole Pateman, *Participation and Democratic Theory* (Cambridge: Cambridge University Press, 1970); and Robert Dahl, *A Preface to Economic Democracy* (Berkeley: University of California Press, 1985).

8. Carmen Sirianni, "Production and Power in a Classless Society," *Socialist Review* 59 (Sept.–Oct. 1981): 33–82; "Participation, Opportunity and Equality," in Frank Fischer and Carmen Sirianni, eds., *Critical Studies in Organization and Bureaucracy* (Philadelphia: Temple University Press, 1984), 482–503; Carmen Sirianni and Michele Eayrs, "Tempo e Lavoro: Razionalizzazione, Flessibilità e Uguaglianza," *Rassegna Italiana di Sociologia* 26, no. 4 (Oct.–Dec. 1985): 523–67; and Philip Green, *Retrieving Democracy* (Totowa, N.J.: Rowman and Allenheld, 1985).

9. Sirianni, "Workers' Control in Europe"; Arndt Sorge, "The Evolution of Industrial Democracy in the Countries of the European Community," *British Journal of Industrial Relations* 14, no. 3 (1976): 282. And see, in particular, Poole's contrast of the cyclical and favorable conjunctures school with the evolutionary school in "Theories of Industrial Democracy."

10. Industrial Democracy in Europe (IDE) International Research Group, *Industrial Democracy in Europe* (Oxford: Clarendon Press, 1981); and *European Industrial Relations* (Oxford: Clarendon Press, 1981), 8. G. David Garson, ed., *Workers' Self-Management in Industry: The European Experience* (New York: Praeger, 1977), 222.

11. For example, see Rosabeth Moss Kanter, "Work in a New America," *Daedalus* 107 (Winter 1978): 47–78.

12. See the Cole and Ross essays in this volume.

13. Brannen, *Authority and Participation in Industry*, 47; also, Poole, "Theories of Industrial Democracy," 193–95.

14. Sirianni, "Workers' Control in Europe," 299ff.; and Gary Cross, "Redefin-

ing Workers' Control: Rationalization, Labor Time, and Union Politics in France, 1900–1928," in Cronin and Sirianni, *Work, Community, and Power,* 143–72.

15. Robert Cole, "Diffusion of Participatory Work Structures in Japan, Sweden and the United States," in Paul Goodman and Associates, eds., *Change in Organizations* (San Francisco: Jossey Bass, 1982), 184–85.

16. Michael Piore and Charles Sabel, *The Second Industrial Divide* (New York: Basic Books, 1984). The authors offer a refreshingly nondeterminist view of the history of technological and productive organization, conceived more as a series of branching points rather than as a narrow track. See also Horst Kern and Michael Schumann, *Das Ende der Arbeitsabteilung?* (Munich: Beck, 1984).

17. Harry Braverman, *Labor and Monopoly Capital* (New York: Monthly Review Press, 1974).

18. See David Stark, "Class Struggle and the Transformation of the Labor Process," *Theory and Society* 9, no. 1 (1980): 89–130; Richard Edwards, *Contested Terrain* (New York: Basic Books, 1979); Sirianni, "Production and Power," and "Workers' Control in Europe"; Larry Hirschhorn, *Beyond Mechanization* (Cambridge: MIT Press, 1984); Charles Sabel, *Work and Politics* (Cambridge: Cambridge University Press, 1982); Paul Adler, "Technology and Us," *Socialist Review* 85 (Jan.–Feb. 1986): 67–96; Kenneth Spenner, "Deciphering Prometheus: Temporal Change in the Skill Level of Work," *American Sociological Review* 48, no. 6 (Dec. 1983): 824–37.

19. Richard Walton, "The Topeka Work System: Optimistic Visions, Pessimistic Hypotheses, and Reality," in Robert Zager and Michael Rosow, eds., *The Innovative Organization* (New York: Pergamon Press, 1982), 260–87; and "Establishing and Maintaining High Commitment Work Systems," in John Kimberly, Robert Miles, and Associates, eds., *The Organizational Life Cycle* (San Francisco: Jossey Bass, 1981), 208–90.

20. Piore and Sabel's hopes for participatory work arrangements, for instance, seem too dependent on continually changing markets. Their analysis here is too market driven, both as an explanation for the rise of participatory systems, and as an anticipation of the methods for sustaining more participatory and egalitarian arrangements where markets are more stable.

21. Rosabeth Moss Kanter, *The Change Masters* (New York: Simon and Schuster, 1983), 274; and John Witte, *Democracy, Authority and Alienation at Work* (Chicago: Chicago University Press, 1980).

22. See Louis Davis and Charles Sullivan, "A Labour-Management Contract and the Quality of Working Life," *Journal of Occupational Behavior* 1 (1980): 29–41. On sociotechnical designs more generally, see, for example, Fred Emery and Einar Thorsrud, *Democracy at Work* (Leiden: Martinus Nijhoff, 1976). The work of Fred Emery and Eric Trist was particularly important as a practical critique of the Taylorist paradigm.

23. See not only Hirschhorn and Adler, but Peter Brannen et al., *The Worker Directors* (London: Hutchinson, 1975); the IDE volumes and the Bullock Report.

24. Shoshanna Zuboff, "Technologies that Informate: Implications for Human Resource Management in the Computerized Industrial Workplace," in Richard Walton and Paul Lawrence, eds., *HRM Trends and Challenges* (Boston: Harvard Business School Press, 1985), 103–39.

25. For example, Stanley Aronowitz, "Marx, Braverman, and the Logic of Capital," in *Work and Labor,* a special issue of *The Insurgent Sociologist* 7, nos. 2/3 (Fall 1978): 126–46.

26. See, for instance, Richard Walton, "Challenges in the Management of Technology and Labor Relations," in Walton and Lawrence, *HRM Trends and Challenges,* 199–216.

27. Ibid, 200.

28. Zuboff, "Technologies that Informate," 131.

29. Robert Howard and Leslie Schneider, in this volume; Leslie Schneider, "Technology Bargaining in Norway," in *Technology and the Need for New Labor Relations,* John F. Kennedy School of Government, Harvard University, Discussion Paper 129D (1984); Andrew Martin and Giuseppe Della Rocca, in this volume; Åke Sandberg, *Technological Change and Codetermination in Sweden* (Philadelphia: Temple University Press, forthcoming); and Giuseppe Berta, ed., *Inaustrial Relations in Information Society: A European Survey* (Rome: Adriano Olivetti Foundation, 1986).

30. See Sandberg, *Technological Change and Codetermination.* Compare this to the uses of numerical control to limit workers' skill and restrict their ability to modify programs, in Harley Shaiken, *Work Transformed* (New York: Holt, Rinehart and Winston, 1984); David Noble, *Forces of Production* (New York: Knopf, 1984). For an alternative view, see Sabel, *Work and Politics,* 63ff.

31. See Sandberg, *Technological Change and Codetermination,* in particular.

32. See esp. Howard and Schneider, and Robert Howard, *Brave New Workplace* (New York: Viking, 1985), 210ff., for a discussion of the U.S. Air Force's $100 million project for a factory of the future, which not only excludes participation by the machinists union, but aims to substantially diminish skill requirements.

33. The term has been used by various Scandinavian researchers, including Åke Sandberg, Bjorn Gustavsen, and Bertil Gardell.

34. Mike Parker, *Inside the Circle: A Union Guide to QWL* (Boston: South End Press, 1985); see also Donald Wells, *Soft Sell: Quality of Work Life Programs and the Productivity Race* (New York: Monthly Review Press, forthcoming).

35. Thomas Kochan, Harry Katz, and Nancy Mower, *Worker Participation and American Unions* (Kalamazoo: Upjohn Institute, 1984); and Thomas Kochan, ed., *Challenges and Choices Facing American Labor* (Cambridge: MIT Press, 1985).

36. Guillermo J. Grenier, *Inhuman Relations: Quality Circles and Anti-Unionism in American Industry* (Philadelphia: Temple University Press, 1987).

37. See Kochan et al, *Worker Participation and American Unions;* Parker, *Inside the Circle;* and Wells, *Soft Sell.*

38. Cole, in this volume.

39. Kochan et al., *Worker Participation and American Unions,* 189ff.; Harry Katz, *Shifting Gears: Changing Labor Relations in the U.S. Auto Industry* (Cambridge: MIT Press, 1985), especially 64–104.

40. Parker, *Inside the Circle,* 28ff., 83–84, 107ff.

41. Wells and Burawoy argue the latter, while Graham argues from his own case studies that this is not true, that workers' choice is not simply within narrower

limits, and that union solidarity is not broken down, even in cases where management violates joint power-sharing assumptions or no-job-loss provisions. Workers, according to Graham, have been quite capable of distinguishing which programs serve their interests, and have known when to withdraw from those that do not. See Michael Burawoy, "Between the Labor Process and the State: The Changing Face of Factory Regimes Under Advanced Capitalism," *American Sociological Review* 48 (1983): 587–605; Gregory Graham, "Who Will Control the Quality of Work Life?" (Ph.D. diss., University of Massachusetts, 1985). Kochan et al. cautiously entertain the empowering thesis, but their case study evidence on the extent to which participants in QWL programs feel they have greater influence over their jobs compared to nonparticipants is limited.

42. See also in this regard Evelyne Huber Stephens and John Stephens, "The Labor Movement, Political Power, and Workers' Participation in Western Europe," *Political Power and Social Theory* 3 (1982): 215–49.

43. J. K. M. Gevers, "Worker Participation in Health and Safety in the EEC: The Role of Representative Institutions," *International Labour Review* 122, no. 4 (July–Aug. 1983): 412ff.

44. Bjorn Gustavsen and Gerry Hunnius, *New Patterns of Work Reform: The Case of Norway* (Oslo: Universitetforlaget, 1981), 115ff.; Ragnvald Kalleberg, "Work Environment Reform as Participatory Democratization" (paper presented at the American Sociological Association annual meetings, Washington, D.C., Aug. 26–31, 1985).

45. See Gevers, "Worker Participation in Health and Safety," for an overview and country-by-country references.

46. Gustavesen and Hunnius, *New Patterns of Work Reform,* 139ff.; and Kalleberg, "Work Environment Reform," for a more recent evaluation of the areas of local activity where workers have been more—and less—successful.

47. Steven Kelman, *Regulating America, Regulating Sweden* (Cambridge: MIT Press, 1981); and Charles Noble, *Liberalism at Work: The Rise and Fall of OSHA* (Philadelphia: Temple University Press, 1986).

48. Kelman, *Regulating America,* ch. 6.

49. Vicente Navarro, "The Determinants of Social Policy, a Case Study: Regulating Health and Safety at the Workplace in Sweden," *International Journal of Health Services* 13, no. 4 (1983): 517–61; and Fischer and Sirianni, *Critical Studies,* editors' introduction to Kelman, 308.

50. Robert Kuttner, "Unions, Economic Power and the State," *Dissent* (Winter 1986): 41.

51. See particularly Fred Best, *Flexible Life Scheduling* (New York: Praeger, 1980); and Hilda Kahne, *Reconceiving Part-Time Work* (Totowa, N.J.: Rowman and Allenheld, 1985).

52. See Stanley Nollen, *New Work Schedules in Practice* (New York: Van Nostrand Reinhold, 1982); Maureen McCarthy and Gail Rosenberg, *Work Sharing: Case Studies* (Kalamazoo: Upjohn Institute, 1981); Gretl Meier, *Job Sharing* (Kalamazoo: Upjohn Institute, 1979); and Simcha Ronen, *Alternative Work Schedules* (Homewood, Ill.: Dow Jones-Irwin, 1984). For Germany, see Bernhard Teriet, *Neue Strukturen der Arbeitszeitverteilung* (Göttingen: Verlag Otto Schwartz, 1976);

and for France, *Échange et Projets* 27 (Sept. 1981) and 32 (Dec. 1982), special issues on *le temps choisi;* and Giovanni Gasparini, ed., *Tempo e Orario di Lavoro: Il Dibattito in Francia* (Rome: Edizioni Lavoro, 1985).

53. Jon Pierce and John Newstrom, "The Design of Flexible Work Schedules and Employee Responses: Relationships and Process," *Journal of Occupational Behavior* 4 (1983): 249.

54. Nollen, *New Work Schedules,* 51ff., 78, 87. On the prominence of worktime options among recent QWL innovations, see also Goodmeasure, Inc., *The Changing American Workplace: Work Alternatives in the 1980s* (New York: American Management Association, 1985).

55. Nollen, *New Work Schedules,* 81-101, 25-31, passim, for this and other examples; and Ronen, *Alternative Work Schedules,* passim.

56. Janina Latack and Lawrence Foster, "Implementation of Compressed Work Schedules: Participation and Job Redesign as Critical Factors for Employee Acceptance," *Personnel Psychology* 38 (1985): 75-92; Emily Stoper, "Alternative Work Patterns and the Double Life," in Ellen Boneparth, ed., *Women, Power and Policy* (New York: Pergamon, 1982), 93.

57. Howard and Schneider, in this volume.

58. Daniel Zwerdling, *Workplace Democracy* (New York: Harper, 1980), 48ff.; see also John Simmons and William Mares, *Working Together* (New York: Knopf, 1982), 70; and Parker, *Inside the Circle,* 44.

59. Gretl Meier, *Worker Learning and Worktime Flexibility* (Kalamazoo: Upjohn Institute, 1983); Ronen, *Alternative Work Schedules,* passim.

60. Nollen, *New Work Schedules,* ch. 4; Kahne, *Reconceiving Part-Time Work,* ch. 8. For Germany, see Claus Offe, Karl Hinrichs, and Helmut Wiesenthal, eds., *Arbeitszeitpolitik* (Frankfurt: Campus, 1982).

61. Karl Hinrichs lists four such protective functions: (1) limiting competition among workers on the basis of hours they are willing to work; (2) establishing a ratchet effect for further wage and hours progress; (3) establishing as socially valid the right to a full income; and (4) permitting workers predictable control over their own time. See "Flexible Working Hours: How to Match Employees' Preferences and Enterprises' Interests" (Conference on Critical Perspectives in Organizational Analysis, Baruch College-CUNY, Sept. 7, 1986).

62. See, for instance, Robert Blauner, *Alienation and Freedom* (Chicago: Chicago University Press, 1964), 21; Melvin Kohn, *Class and Conformity* (Homewood, Ill.: Dorsey, 1969), 174-76; and Pietro Marcenaro and Vittorio Foa, *Riprendere Tempo* (Turin: Einaudi, 1982), 48 ff.

63. Échange et Projets, *La révolution du temps choisi* (Paris: Albin Michel, 1980); and two issues of their journal devoted to the experiences and debates on *Le temps choisi: Échange et Projets* 27 (Sept. 1981) and 32 (Dec. 1982). Also see Giovanni Gasparini, *Il Tempo e Il Lavoro* (Milan: Franco Angeli, 1986).

64. Karl Hinrichs, Claus Offe, and Helmut Wiesenthal, "The Crisis of the Welfare State and Alternative Modes of Work Redistribution," in Alfred Kleinknecht and Tom van Veen, eds., *Working Time Distribution and the Crisis of the Welfare State* (Maastricht: Presses Interuniversitaires Européenes, 1986), 117-39; and Offe, *Disorganized Capitalism* (Cambridge: MIT Press, 1985), and *Arbeitsgesellschaft* (Frankfurt: Campus Verlag, 1984).

65. Carmen Sirianni and Michele Eayrs, "Tempo e Lavoro: Razionalizzazione, Flessibilità e Uguaglianza," 523–67; see also Carmen Sirianni, *Of Time, Work and Equality* (Cambridge: Polity Press, forthcoming); "Feminist Theory and Gendered Time," unpublished paper.

66. Sandberg, *Technological Change and Codetermination;* Brannen, *Authority and Participation in Industry,* 73; Charles Heckscher, "Democracy at Work: In Whose Interests? The Politics of Worker Participation" (Ph.D. diss., Harvard University, 1981).

67. The case of Scandinavia is especially hopeful, and work-time options hold particular promise for involving women in participation.

2

THE MACROPOLITICS OF ORGANIZATIONAL CHANGE: A COMPARATIVE ANALYSIS OF THE SPREAD OF SMALL-GROUP ACTIVITIES

Robert E. Cole

Beginning in the early 1960s a number of movements emerged in a wide variety of national settings for various kinds of worker "participation" in shopfloor activities. These movements seemed to promise to go beyond simply human relations and to reverse the historic process of deskilling that had characterized developments in the first half of the twentieth century (Bendix, 1974; Braverman, 1974; Nelson, 1975; Stone, 1975; Montgomery, 1976; Edwards, 1979). Usually initiated by management groups, these post–World War II movements involve efforts to change patterns of shopfloor organization from the specialization and compartmentalization that have characterized modern factory life. Often tagged as a form of "participative management" by their proponents, these new work structures tend to afford workers more participation in the execution of decisions than in their formulation. They usually include a stress on small-group activity, stimulating worker involvement in more facets of shopfloor operations and problem solving, and a more active mobilization of worker involvement and commitment than is common in most industrial regimes. To focus the research effort, I concentrated on small-group activities rather than on those that expand the range of tasks a worker performs or those that involve indirect forms of participation, such as membership on boards of directors.

Comparative analysts of participative organizational forms typically compare the structural characteristics and the value rationality underlying these altered forms of organization (e.g., Dachler and Wilpert, 1978; Rothschild-Whitt, 1979). Their agenda for research is to specify those matters over which employees are to exercise some control, compare the mechanisms through which workers are to participate in these decisions, measure the amounts of control these forms delegate to employees, compare the different value systems underlying different programs of participation, and evaluate the relative effectiveness of various strategies in terms of productivity and job satisfaction (see Tannenbaum et al., 1974; Katzell, Yankelovich et al., 1975; Bernstein, 1976; Cummings and Molloy, 1977).

The comparative agenda here is different. The purpose of this analysis is to explain why movements to popularize these new work structures have been sustained in some countries and not in others and why, when they spread, they are maintained to the degree they are. This involves exploring the processes through which diffusion occurs and the issue of whether these movements represent faddish episodes or have the capacity for more long-lasting impact. Most generally, the questions being asked are, Why and how do organizations change? The answers to these questions are important in their own right, because the phenomenon of work-reform movements has generated considerable interest across several social science disciplines and through much of the world. Moreover, many of the considerations grow out of the issues raised in the human relations school, traditionally constituting one of the largest if not the largest body of empirical literature in organizational analysis (Perrow, 1979: 109).

An explanation of the differing outcomes of these national work-reform efforts is of theoretical import as well. Because the level of analysis in this study is cross-national and because the units of analysis are industries and national environments, the findings are directly relevant to two concerns that have drawn a great deal of attention in recent literature. The first is the impact of power and politics on organizational form. Much recent theorizing has stressed these phenomena as explanations for the course of change in organizations (i.e., Harvey and Mills, 1970; Perrow, 1970; Zald, 1970; Pfeffer, 1978; Burawoy, 1983). The bulk of theory and research, however, has focused at the level of the organization as a setting for politics—the "micropolitics" of organization. The cross-national analysis presented here, by contrast, points to the importance of politics and loci of power at the level of industries or nations, as well—the "macropolitics" of organizational change. Here, I also join those recent efforts to delineate more specifically the nature and effects of organizational environments on organizational change. These objectives parallel recent efforts by Burawoy (1983), though our research strategy and conclusions are often strikingly different.

By focusing on macropolitics, one can distinguish the forest from the trees in a way that much contemporary theorizing and empirical research fail to do. Thus, in the case of research on small-group activities, researchers will often report factors within the organization that inhibit or enhance the probability of success, with success being measured in terms of survival of the innovation or contributions to improved quality, productivity, or increased participation or job satisfaction. These critical factors may include the mode of innovation, the amount of authority given to group sponsors and leaders, the makeup of the group, its leadership, the group's procedures and objectives, the nature of technology, how the small-group activities fit with wider organizational practices, the extent to which they threaten managerial prerogatives, and so forth. A pattern seen in other domains of organizational research is beginning to emerge in which we are left with a variety of often contradictory studies showing how under different conditions one or another variable contributes marginally to affecting outcomes.

Perrow (1979: 96–112) documented just such a pattern in his scathing critique of the human relations literature. He showed how the accumulated literature failed to demonstrate a clear link between leadership and morale, on the one hand, and productivity, on the other. The application of increasingly complex research methodologies and causal models only resulted in a loss of applicability and theoretical power. The variables became so numerous that we could hardly generalize to organizations or even to types of organizations.

By shifting from the microanalysis of a phenomenon to an examination of the macropolitics, we create the opportunity to get a grip on the broader environmental factors driving innovation. As Perrow (1979: 110) put it, "it may be, hopefully, that any theory that has the power to explain a good deal of organizational behavior will have to deal with more general variables than leadership and small-group behavior." Perrow further suggested that in treating these macrovariables, we may assume that the specific *micro*variables associated with small-group behavior are randomly distributed and thus have little effect when a large number of organizations are being studied.

In keeping with this vision, I will show in this study of small-group activities the importance of understanding the position of the national business leadership toward such innovations and how this interacts with national labor-market conditions and the positions of national union leaders. The overall hypothesis is that this will produce a far better and more generalizable predictor of success, as measured in the spread of small-group activities across and within firms, than an analysis of the micropolitics of small-group activities would allow.

The Study

The analysis is limited to three countries: Japan, Sweden, and the United States, and focuses on the period 1960–80. These are countries in which the author has linguistic competence and has carried out field and archival research based on primary source materials and interviews. In the case of Sweden, in addition to the voluminous scholarly literature in Swedish on the subject of small-group activities (semiautonomous work groups), the newspaper coverage was also extensive, and this allowed a different vantage point on developments. These data sources were supplemented with interviews of key informants and recognized experts in the unions, companies, universities, the employer federation, and research institutes. Volvo and Saab personnel were particularly receptive to discussions; because they were key innovators, their cooperation was especially useful.

For the United States, in addition to the scholarly literature on direct participation on the shop- and office-floor level, the author has been an active observer of the diffusion process of quality circles. My survey of some 176 early adopters of quality circles in the United States also yielded important background information (Cole and Tachiki, 1983).

In the case of Japan, a significant scholarly and management literature exists in Japanese on the subject of quality circles. Selected company visits and interviews supplemented this literature, as did interviews with employer federation officials and union leaders. The Japanese Union of Scientists and Engineers (JUSE), a key actor in the diffusion process, was particularly forthcoming in its cooperation and specifically in arranging for a variety of meetings with key informants. In addition, my U.S. counterpart survey of 302 early adopters of quality circles yielded important background data.

These three nations span a range of variation favorable to the comparative task. The United States is an example of limited change relative to the other two. Despite considerable advocacy of work reforms in academic and government circles, actual changes in the United States were rather limited through the 1970s. Of the other two nations, both of which have experienced significant although varying degrees of institutionalization of small-group activities, Sweden may be characterized as social democratic and Japan as liberal capitalist. These different political systems encapsulate considerable variation in the dimensions: group interest, labor-market conditions, managerial problems, political organization, and institutional mobilization.

Introduction of Small-Group Activities: Three National Experiences

The United States. In the early 1970s there were extensive discussions in the United States in academic, government, and foundation circles about the need to "humanize work" and raise the quality of worklife for employees. The proposed programs for change carried various labels, such as *job enrichment, job enlargement, job redesign,* and *job humanization.* By increasing employee participation in workplace decisions, increasing job variety, and making more effective use of worker potential, it was argued, not only would the quality of worklife be enhanced but organizational efficiency and worker productivity would be improved. The central argument made by advocates was that new work structures should be designed to allow employees to control aspects of their work that most directly affected their everyday lives. Small-group activities were central to that vision.

Efforts in the 1960s and 1970s to institutionalize these new work structures met with limited success. Generally speaking, most job redesign in the 1970s took place in new plants—often nonunion—with very little being accomplished in established ones (Davis and Cherns, 1975). Even in reputedly successful experiments, the innovation did not diffuse widely to other plants within the company (Walton, 1978). Widely publicized programs were often discontinued or scaled down a few years after their initiation, with little fanfare (e.g., quality control circles at Lockheed Air Missile). With few exceptions, American union leaders have been distinctly cool to proposed innovations affecting the boundaries and content of established jobs (e.g., Industrial Union Department, 1978). The movement received consistent support only from a scattered group of concerned academics.

Major institutional actors—management, unions, government—displayed little interest in introducing new work structures. The result through the 1970s was isolated, piecemeal experimentation. To be sure, not all such activities are widely reported nor easily counted. Some companies, particularly in newer industries such as electronics (e.g., Hewlett-Packard, DEC), prided themselves on developing a more participative management style than in the old-line manufacturing industries, without the adoption of specific programs. It must also be recognized that one's assessment of the degree of diffusion in the United States may reflect more one's initial value premises and expectations than it does any empirical evidence. Notwithstanding, as a general statement, it seems reasonable to conclude that *relative* to the changes taking place in the two other countries under consideration, movement toward adoption of small-group activities was slow in the United States.

The growing internationalization of the U.S. economy, and particularly the powerful competitive threat posed by the Japanese in recent years, has forced U.S. management and labor to reexamine small-group activities. Although data from a 1981 national survey of firms show high rates of adoption and trial on the part of individual companies, there is far less evidence of institutionalization (New York Stock Exchange, 1982). The same survey shows that quality circles had the highest rate of growth of human-resource innovations and had become synonymous for American managers with the quality-of-worklife movement. Yet, at the same time, there is ample evidence of strong management resistance to accepting quality circles at all levels of management (Cole and Tachiki, 1983).

Japan. The Japanese movement began in the early 1960s and accelerated after the middle of that decade. To be sure, there were prewar cultural models as manifested in the use of small work groups for solving productivity problems. But overall, strong authoritarianism and hierarchy were the central prewar legacies.

The key organizing principle for the postwar innovations is known as "small group-ism" (*shōshūdanshugi*). Management focused on the decentralization of decision making. Employees were to assume increasing responsibilities for a variety of everyday functions—most notably maintenance, safety, and quality control—that previously had been the province of management representatives. The vehicle for this increased responsibility was small-group organization. By the late 1970s various Japanese surveys estimate that some 50 percent of Japanese firms with more than thirty employees were practicing some form of decentralized decision making based on small-group activities (Cole, 1979: 135). Quality circles were among the most popular forms, with 1.7 million registered members accounted for by 200,000 registered circles; the number of unregistered circles is conservatively estimated to be four times that number.

Quality circles typically meet on the average of one hour a week and are relatively autonomous units composed of a small group of production or clerical workers from each workplace. The workers are taught elementary statistical techniques and modes of problem solving and are guided by their leaders in selecting and solving job-related quality problems and improving methods of production. Although workers participate in decision making through these kinds of small-group activities, it is clear that this approach does not threaten the hierarchical structure of management authority. First-line supervisors have not been significantly threatened by the reforms, in part because they typically serve as circle leaders.

Sweden. Swedish efforts to develop new work structures began in the late 1960s, with an emphasis on autonomous self-steering work groups (*självstyrande grupper*) as the basic unit of production organization. These ideas spread rapidly, accompanied by a long and intensive public debate on the need for democratized industrial organization in Swedish society. Though the diffusion of such practices has clearly been more limited than in Japan, the actual extent to which these practices have been institutionalized is difficult to specify. This is, in part, because there has not been an extensive system of formal registration and surveys as in Japan. The ideal of the autonomous work group, with workers making all their own decisions regarding work allocation, recruitment, planning, budgeting, and purchasing (Agervold, 1975: 46–65) is rare in actual practice. Yet, modified versions of this decentralized system of work organization appear in most large Swedish firms. One contrast with the Japanese case is that early Swedish efforts—in part because of the political setting of social democracy—explicitly challenged the hierarchy of managerial authority, particularly that of first-line supervisors. Consequently, middle managerial opposition was more common than in Japan, leading to a less complete diffusion of small-group activities.

General Observations on the Cases

The contrast of the experiences of the United States with those of Japan and Sweden is striking. In each of the latter countries over the past two decades small-group activities in one form or another have been adopted and sustained to a considerable degree. Despite wide differences in culture, economy, and politics, the Japanese and Swedish initiatives all have emphasized the small group as the core unit of workshop organization and participation in these small groups as a source of work motivation. In comparing the Swedish and Japanese experiences, one could say that the Swedes tried more and accomplished less while the Japanese tried less and accomplished more. By contrast, the Americans tried still less and accomplished very little.

The dependent variable—the spread and institutionalization of small-group activities in the three nations—makes it clear that reporting on the three national experiences is like comparing apples and oranges. In practice, the availability of data and the nature of the three national experiences led us to compare the evolution of quality circles in the United States and Japan and semiautonomous work groups in Sweden. Quality circles are "off-line" activities, that is, workers engage in these problem-solving teams separate from their "normal work" activities. Semi-autonomous groups, however, are designed to give teams of workers more control over the work process itself.

In Japan, the language used to describe the key innovations was *decentralization of responsibility,* and the term *participation* seldom appeared. In the United States the debate was dominated by the terms *participation in management, QWL* (Quality of Worklife), and *EI* (Employee Involvement). In Sweden the notions of joint influence and democratization of the workplace punctuated the early debate.

This different language is not a random phenomenon. It tells us a great deal about objectives and who were the central actors controlling the debate in each country. In the case of Japan, focusing the debate on decentralization of responsibility tells us that management was in charge; it could impose its own categories and labels on developments. In Sweden the focus on industrial democracy tells us, first, that management did not have full control of the agenda of solutions and definition of problems. Moreover, the Swedes had a highly centralized labor-management decision-making system. This meant that advocates of small-group activities within labor, management, and academic circles could argue forcefully and believably that there was something missing at the shop- and office-floor level in terms of democratic decision making and that semi-autonomous work groups could fill this vacuum. In the United States, unlike many western European countries, the labor movement had an active shopfloor presence. This preempted to a large extent the industrial democracy theme at the shop floor level; instead, there is a rather more modest focus on participation, leadership, and employee involvement.

It would be an artificial and sterile exercise to try to winnow down these different approaches to small-group activities to the lowest common denominator so as to assure an identical dependent variable across countries. Rather, the tack taken here is to acknowledge these differences and take them into account in explaining the extent to which small-group activities diffused in the three countries and how and why they took the different forms they did.

Although management has been the primary initiator of these new work structures, there is another driving force. Underlying the initiative in Sweden, and to a far lesser extent in the United States, is a focus on industrial democracy. Fuller participation in the decisions of the firm and over one's daily activities is seen as contributing to the democratization of the firm. Burawoy (1983: 602–603) ignored this theme, though many unions, most notably in Sweden, stressed industrial democracy as a basis for cooperating in the initiation and shaping of these new activities. Even in the United States union supporters have heavily stressed the theme of industrial democracy (Bluestone, 1978: 21–24). How this additional driving force interacts, complements, or opposes management initiatives is a matter for empirical examination in each nation, industry, and firm.

Managerial Interests and the Incentives to Innovate

Improving the quality of working life, reducing worker alienation, and enhancing self-actualization are the benefits of small-group activities most often stressed by academic proponents. Industrial administrators, however, are less motivated by these sorts of concerns, and it is they who must introduce and institutionalize these innovations. Management is concerned more with performance and economic payoff. To understand the diffusion of small-group activities, we must look more closely at the forces driving management to change existing practices; we must look for something other than a liberal reforming impulse.

Sweden and Japan. Extensive interviews with Japanese and Swedish managers and an examination of the relevant literature in these countries make clear that the driving force for innovation was quite similar in both cases. Both countries have faced severe labor-shortage problems over the last two decades.

In Japan, industrial employers confronted an increasingly tight labor market in the late 1960s and early 1970s. It became more difficult for the major manufacturing firms to recruit and retain those select employees they desired (Minami, 1973). Compared with the United States, labor turnover in Japanese industry was still quite low, but it occurred in the context of a serious shortage of recent male graduates entering the labor force, especially middle-school graduates. Replacing existing workers was thus both difficult and costly because there was no pool of workers willing to take the most disagreeable jobs in the manufacturing sector. Political and economic leaders considered and later rejected Southeast Asian immigration as a desirable option.

Rapidly rising educational levels in Japan, further, led to an increasing proportion of labor-force entrants who were unwilling to accept the least demanding jobs. The educational system was producing an increasing number of high school graduates who had come to expect white-collar jobs commensurate with their educational levels. Instead, an increasing number were being assigned to blue-collar jobs.

By the late 1960s and early 1970s the labor shortage was most serious for those manufacturing sectors that had the most standardized and routinized jobs and were characterized by hard physical labor under difficult conditions. Surveys reported extremely high turnover among new recruits to these industries (Ministry of Labour, 1974: 72). These circumstances constituted an important motivational force for Japanese managements to search for solutions to minimize their problems. Small-group activities appeared to be one possible strategy to make firms more attractive to well-educated potential recruits, thereby reducing turnover and labor unrest and contributing to productivity and quality goals. There was, however, little assurance of the outcome, and innovators operated under great ambiguity and uncertainty. Furthermore, other strategies were pursued simultaneously, such as locating labor-intensive production facilities offshore, in Southeast Asia. Firms in industries that suffered most from recruitment and retention problems—notably automobiles and steel—were some of the most active in early efforts at innovation. All this occurred in a context of growth in internationalization of the economy and resultant concerns that managers must make better use of their human resources if they were to survive in world competition.

The labor situation facing Swedish managers was similar but even more serious than in Japan. In Sweden a severe labor shortage had developed by the mid-1960s, educational levels had also risen rapidly, and labor-force entrants were increasingly unwilling to accept routine or arduous jobs. Swedish employers sought initially to alleviate these problems by acting to expand the labor force. They began more actively and quite successfully to recruit economically inactive women. A second strategy was to increase the employment of migrant aliens. The number of aliens taking jobs in Sweden increased steadily to 20 percent of total employment in the mining and manufacturing sectors (Statistiska Centralbyrån, 1978: 195).

By the late 1960s Swedish manufacturers became increasingly disenchanted with these strategies. It was still difficult for them to find enough workers to fill the least desirable jobs. Moreover, they were having to rely on what they considered to be labor of the lowest quality, and the large influx into Sweden of foreigners, concentrated in the least desirable jobs, came to be seen as a threatening social problem. Absenteeism and turnover, further, swelled to unprecedented proportions. Annual employee turnover reached 50 percent during 1970 in a number of metropolitan industries—notably auto manufacturing. Sweden's legislated unemployment and sick-pay benefits had made turnover and absenteeism relatively costless to employees.

All of these factors spurred management to consider strategies for restructuring work to bring native male Swedish workers back into the factories and cut turnover and absenteeism to manageable proportions. As in Japan, major innovations in work structures took place in precisely those industries suffering the most severe recruitment, turnover, and absenteeism problems.[1] Volvo Corporation, the largest Swedish private firm, experienced some of the most severe problems and later achieved fame as an innovator in creating new work structures. Multiskill training and teaching employees a fuller range of job tasks were part of the approach to small-group activities in Sweden. These practices facilitated a workfloor adjustment to high rates of absenteeism and turnover.

The United States. It is instructive to contrast the United States with Japan and Sweden. A large pool of unemployed labor exists in the United States to fill the most disagreeable jobs. Despite high rates, by world standards, of labor turnover, replacements have been readily available through this pool. This constituted a major barrier to the diffusion of small-group activities in the United States in the 1970s—there were no obvious economic incentives to interest managers in innovation. Until Japanese competition became impossible to ignore in the late 1970s, no pressing managerial problems triggered searches for new methods (Wool, 1973: 38–44).

The differences between the United States and Sweden and Japan are most striking in the auto industries during the early 1970s. Swedish auto officials found that some U.S. auto plants had turnover figures similar to those of Swedish auto firms—about 50 percent per year. Surprised that most American managers did not perceive this as a serious problem, they concluded that U.S. managers were accustomed to greater job mobility of workers and reasoned that they could train people for simple jobs so quickly that the turnover figures did not matter (Gyllenhammar, 1977: 7–9). Indeed, the assumption that large quantities of unskilled labor would circulate annually through the firm reinforced the strategy of using industrial engineers to increasingly simplify job content.

Although the original General Motors–United Automobile Workers (UAW) agreement on QWL was signed in 1973, little occurred until the late 1970s, despite selected "showcase" plants. Innovation that did occur was often piecemeal, rather than through the more systemic approach developed in Sweden (Tichy and Nisberg, 1976). Although Kanter (1983:221–347) documented high-level management concerns with participative management as a solution to problems of turnover and absenteeism within GM in the early 1970s, it is striking how long such discussions were confined to the corporate level.

It was not until the Japanese threat of the late 1970s and early 1980s that U.S. auto manufacturers began broadly to operationalize solutions addressing the costs of high rates of absenteeism and turnover. They came to the conclusion that they were suffering a competitive disadvantage because they failed to mobilize their human resources through a participative strategy. Data from our 1981 survey of the universe of early adopters of quality circles reveal that the greatest number of adopters were in automotive parts and manufacturing and the electronics industries (Cole and Tachiki, 1983). Early adopters tended to be in manufacturing sectors characterized by highly labor-intensive industries, industries in which quality has been a high priority in the past, and those in which quality and costs have received new emphasis as a result of Japanese competition. Auto and electronics both partially fit this characterization, although they differ in degrees of unionization, rate of growth, and the like.

Ideology and Organization: Mobilizing for Structural Change

If our preceding descriptions are accurate, we would expect the relative interests of major institutional actors to be reflected in the emergent national infrastructures for diffusing small-group activities. Specifically, one would predict that when at least one of the major parties to the labor market—especially management, given its leadership position in market economies—becomes strongly committed to small-group activities as a solution, a well-organized national infrastructure will be created. Through definition and publicizing of "best practices" and providing legitimacy, such organizations provide the national leadership critical to the emergent movement as it develops at the plant level.

In the cases of Japan and Sweden, the major incentive for management to develop this commitment to innovate was an evolving set of managerial problems relating to labor shortage that made earlier strategies ineffective. Motivation, however, is a necessary but insufficient condition for change. Managerial groups have to mobilize to implement these innovations. This has involved, in each case, the articulation of an ideology that justifies these changes and serves to persuade other members of the industrial community either to support or not to resist them.[2] It also involves the creation of an organized infractructure of communication and organization with which the resources of the innovating groups can be mobilized and changes introduced and institutionalized in firms. The emergence of a national infrastructure reflects the consensus of top management that it has identified the direction in which it would like to move; its leaders articulate the ideology that legitimates the new movement. It is this interplay of ideology and organization that is at the core of the rapid spread of new organizational practices. Without such an interplay, the emergent practices are more likely to assume the status of fad.

The United States: Late and Weak Managerial Mobilization

American managers had little incentive to reform existing work structures in the 1960s and 1970s. As a result, organization and mobilization for the diffusion of participative work structures was left to mavericks, who tried to convince managements that such innovations were in their interest.

Most of these advocates were from loose networks of academics, management experts, and, occasionally, business and union leaders. On this basis we would expect that the organized efforts to spread small-group activities would differ markedly from the same processes in Japan and Sweden.

Failing strong interest by the national business leadership, "outside" organizations like the Ford Foundation sought to stimulate institution building in the 1970s. However, achievements have been quite modest relative to what occurred in Sweden and Japan. Government-encouraged initiatives proved to be of modest value because of sharp fluctuations in the level of government support and because the government could not or would not provide management the long-term incentives that were necessary.

With the upsurge of experimentation in the United States in the 1980s, there has been a notable increase in the activities of various research and training organizations focusing on small-group activities, in particular, the American Society for Training and Development, the American Management Association, and the OD Network (Organizational Development Network). These kinds of organizations are not likely to create a national infrastructure, but they do supply much of the raw material for supporting its emergence.

Although there were a number of possible contenders for leadership of the small-group activity movement in the United States, none individually or collectively have come to play the same extensive role as key organizations did in Sweden and Japan. Existing national organizations reflecting top-management interests, like the National Association of Manufacturers, the Chamber of Commerce, and the Business Roundtable, saw the locus of their activities as Washington, with lobbying as the chosen method to achieve their ends.

Other organizations interested in the participation movement, such as the Work in America Institute, focused on improving labor-management relationships in the unionized sector, primarily through labor-management committees. This calls attention to a major problem in building an integrated national infrastructure in the United States. Those who focus on working with the unionized sector ignore 80 percent of the labor force. Those who include the nonunionized sector invite the suspicions of the unions that the real agenda is union busting. The failure of big business to accept unions as a legitimate force in the United States has worked against building a national infrastructure for small-group activities and has led, rather, to a splintering of efforts.

The American Society of Quality Control (ASQC) was a different kind of contender. It is a voluntary professional association composed primarily of middle-management specialists in quality. ASQC members did not, however, have a great deal of status in their firms. Just as important,

ASQC proved to be so tied up in knots by their bureaucratic structure of rules regulating organizational innovation and limited by their reliance on volunteer labor that they failed to provide leadership for the small-group activity movement.

The American Productivity Center, established in 1977 with top-management support from key business organizations, was a clear candidate for providing nationally recognized leadership for the small-group activity movement. For the most part, especially in its early years, however, its high-level corporate sponsors and board members saw the path to productivity improvement in terms of traditional approaches, like enhancing availability of capital at favorable terms, increasing technology investment, and improving taxation policy. Again, these individuals were more at home negotiating and lobbying for solutions in Washington than in the factories and offices of America. Union leaders on the board were just as comfortable focusing on the "big issues" associated with traditional labor-management concerns. Yet, support for small-group activities in terms of their productivity and quality payoffs requires the acceptance of a view that many small changes, in the aggregate, yield big changes.

The closest thing to a national organization designed to promote small-group activities is the International Association of Quality Circles (IAQC), begun in 1977 by two consultants; it served at least indirectly to promote their own business. That in itself is typically American. The organization officially reported some 7,000 members by the mid-1980s, and ninety chapters. It conducts a great deal of introductory training in circle activity and promotes national conferences.

While these are not insignificant achievements for a volunteer organization, IAQC continues to experience severe problems in carrying out its mission, moving from one crisis to another. The problems it has had illustrate well the differences between the U.S. experience and the Swedish and Japanese experiences. IAQC difficulties stem, above all, from an elected board of directors, composed now primarily of middle- and lower-ranking management officials (including quality-circle facilitators), most of whom have no experience running a complex national organization. Lacking national recognition, they were unable to bestow the mantle of legitimacy on the organization as the leader of the national small-group activity movement. Operationally, they have great difficulty tapping the coffers of major businesses and foundations, and financial instability has been a continuing problem. They have also had to rely heavily on volunteers, with all the problems of follow-through that this entails. Finally, consultant influence, though no longer dominant, has continued to create problems, as consultants have pushed to keep the organization out of activities where IAQC would be in competition with "their own members"—as the consultants like to phrase it. This has limited organizational initiatives. IAQC has yet to show that it will be able to legitimate and provide resources for the growth of the small-group activity movement in a way that occurred in Sweden and Japan.

Organized efforts in the United States to effect the implementation of small-group activities have emphasized careful research, measurement, and prior scientific demonstration of their effectiveness. By contrast, experience in Sweden and Japan shows that when management has a motivation to innovate, funding is forthcoming, organized infrastructures develop quickly, and efforts to institutionalize new work structures move ahead full speed with relative inattention, sometimes even self-conscious disinterest, in effectiveness research.

Japan: Early and Effective Managerial Mobilization

Japanese managers are far more likely than their American counterparts to think of solutions to managerial problems as coming from the area of human relations rather than technical relations. There are a number of historical and cultural precedents for this (Cole, 1979: 108–111). This view has been reinforced by the rapid translation and absorption of the American human relations literature in Japan. For these reasons, Japanese managers, when faced with the labor-supply problems of the late 1960s, readily turned to restructuring work arrangements and organizing workers in small-group activities designed to arouse in workers a sense of loyalty to the firm and an internalization of company goals. These activities have been carefully controlled, and involvement is not always voluntary for workers. These arrangements are premised on considerable sharing of information with workers on production schedules and plant objectives and performance (Cole, 1979: 224–50).

Not surprisingly, high-level management groups provided crucial leadership for the implementation of small-group activities. The Japan Federation of Employers' Associations (Nikkeiren) was especially important. Nikkeiren, though analogous in function to the National Association of Manufacturers in the United States, is more specialized in labor and personnel matters and more prestigious and powerful than its American counterpart. Many of Nikkeiren's early small-group activities can be dated from 1966. By 1970 the chairman of Nikkeiren, believing he perceived a trend toward "all-employee management," advocated support for this trend at a top-management seminar. Since that time Nikkeiren has engaged in a wide range of publicizing activities designed to explain and spread such approaches (Nakayama, 1972).

Specialized organizations such as the Japan Union of Scientists and Engineers (JUSE) also developed departments designed exclusively to propagate specific kinds of small-group activities. JUSE is a national nonprofit organization dedicated to providing services to participating Japanese companies in the areas of quality and reliability. It is composed of university professors in engineering and science, as well as engineers from leading firms, but is closely tied to business circles. Since 1948, shortly after its founding, the chairman of JUSE has either been the chairman of Keidanren (Japanese Federation of Economic Organizations), the most powerful business association in Japan, or a former chairman. Furthermore, the intellectual leadership of JUSE has been provided to a great extent by Ishikawa Kaoru, the secretary general. His father was the first chairman of Keidanren to sit simultaneously as chairman of JUSE. These linkages provided legitimation for JUSE initiatives; JUSE assumed the major leadership role in developing and diffusing the concept and practice of quality-control circles. Having corporate sponsors, JUSE could employ professional staff and not rely on volunteers for its core administrative functions. Central to its mission was gathering company experiences, defining "best practices," and feeding the information back to the field in its conferences and publications. Specific mechanisms included publishing a low-priced magazine for first-line supervisors and circle members, developing a plethora of training programs and publications, and establishing a quality-control-circle registration system. JUSE also created quality-control-circle conventions for companies to share circle experiences.

In summary, we see a firm linkage between the emergence of a national infrastructure designed to spread the innovation and top-management leadership and support in the private sector. It is this linkage that makes less likely the outcome of short-term faddish commitments and increases the probability that institutionalized firm-level structures will develop.

Sweden: Early Joint Management-Union Initiatives Followed by Weakened Commitment

In Sweden management was attracted by ideas that originated at the Tavistock Institute in England (Emery and Trist, 1969) and were propagated in Sweden by the Norwegian scholar Einar Thorsrud (Thorsrud and Emery, 1969). Tavistock ideas emphasized the development of the organization as a sociotechnical system, the interaction of social and technical factors in the organization of the workplace, and prescribed the development of small, cohesive work groups, which would maintain a high level of independence and autonomy. Jobs would be enriched, individual responsibility increased, learning possibilities enhanced, and, most importantly, from the standpoint of Swedish management, jobs would be more attractive to desirable recruits and labor turnover and absenteeism could be reduced.

The Swedish Employers' Confederation (Svenska Arbetsgivareföreningen—SAF) made a high-level decision in the mid-1960s to support small-group activities on the shop floor. The Tavistock ideas provided a coherent ideological framework and a practical direction for reform efforts. SAF, committed to Thorsrud's ideas, entrusted its program for research and popularization to its technical department, which began a large-scale training and publications program. Another organizational offshoot of SAF, the Personnel Administration Council (Personaladministrative Rådet), guided several important projects and played a key liaison role between academic research and the world of business (e.g., Björk, Hanson, and Hellberg, 1973).

In Sweden, unlike Japan and the United States, the strength and the orientation of organized labor were such that these management initiatives for the changes in the workplace had to be taken in cooperation with labor unions. In 1966 SAF, together with the white-collar (TCO) and blue-collar (LO) union federations, established the Development Council for Cooperative Questions (Utvecklingsrådet for Samarbetsfrågor) to facilitate labor-management cooperation.

The Development Council set up a special group for research, called URAF. Its general task was to make clear which factors stimulated workplace democratization and which factors hindered it. Its specific purpose was to initiate and supervise projects and conduct research. These efforts were anchored in development groups at the company level in which both management and labor were represented. URAF sponsored ten key pilot projects during 1969–1970. These pilot projects were well reported, usually in a favorable light, by both labor and management groups (e.g., Landsorganisation, 1976), and the reports served to stimulate further initiatives.

However important URAF was in the crucial early periods of the reform movement, this kind of cooperative union-management activity fell off markedly by the early 1970s, for two reasons. First, the unions began to articulate a competing ideology of worker control. LO wanted not only sociotechnical participation in an atmosphere of cooperation but more power for workers and the unions in the firm. Second, the employers' confederation, SAF, felt shackled by cooperative activity, especially with the increased militance of the unions, and preferred to proceed on its own with a freer hand (as its counterparts in Japan were able to do).

As LO turned increasingly toward legislation to further its aim of enhancing industrial democracy, SAF shifted its main initiatives to its own technical department and away from cooperative activity with the unions.

URAF was finally abolished in 1978. Similarly, SAF's interest in small-group activities weakened with the passage of the Co-Determination Law and the threat of the "wage earners fund";[3] this shift in focus came to be reflected in the spinning off of the technical department as a separate enterprise in the early 1980s. These developments, in effect, resulted in a weakening of the national infrastructure and thereby contributed to a loss of momentum in the movement itself.

Interests and Orientation of Organized Labor

The development of widespread managerial interest in innovation and the creation and use of organized infrastructures for national communication and mobilization do not uniformly assure successful diffusion. Other loci of interests, organization, and power must be entered into the political calculus. In this case, the strength, interests, and orientation of labor are crucial in determining the shape and outcome of the diffusion process. In each of the three nations labor has exhibited a different orientation toward shopfloor reforms, and this has served to shape the outcomes of the diffusion process in different ways.

The United States: Union Suspicion

With the notable exception of the UAW and later the Communications Workers of America, advocates of new work structures in the United States generally have failed to gain strong union-wide support for their programs. The major spur to across-the-board activity came in the early 1980s from the internationalization of the economy. In the auto industry there were some impressive achievements in the early 1980s with widespread establishment of employee-involvement groups and employee-participation groups, as the circles were known respectively at Ford and General Motors. Notwithstanding, in the eyes of many union officials and workers, many of these initiatives became negatively associated with concessions in bargaining. General UAW support for the QWL programs showed signs of evaporating by the mid-1980s (cf. Thomas, 1984). Deep division within the top leadership of the union as to the proper position toward QWL made forward movement difficult.

The leaders of most other major unions have generally been even more suspicious of management motives, seeing small-group activities as a management scheme to get more productivity from workers without sharing the increased economic rewards (Industrial Union Department, 1978). Another concern is that these approaches often break down established job boundaries, thereby resulting in "speedups" and reducing manpower requirements. They are also seen as a threat to existing collective-bargaining structures (Sorge, 1984). Finally, many union leaders, not incorrectly, see small-group activities as a device to avoid or weaken unionization by building loyalty to management. The result has been active union distrust of such reforms.

This union orientation arises from specific features of American industrialization and of the tradition of unionism that arose during the period, as a subsequent comparison with Japan will highlight. One of the most notable features of American unionism historically has been its orientation toward control of job opportunities (Perlman, 1968); unionization took place often under conditions of labor shortage, and American workers failed to assert themselves collectively as an organized force in national politics. It was decisively shaped, further, by the struggle between craft unions and management over control of the production process and the forms of remuneration involved, as management moved to reorganize the production process around the turn of the twentieth century (Stone, 1975; Montgomery, 1976). Behind the movement to reorganize production known as Taylorism (Braverman, 1974; Nelson, 1975) was a managerial strategy prompted by comparatively high wages in American industry, by contemporary world standards—wage levels that were the product of a labor shortage in industrializing America and relatively strong craft unions in older industries. To compete in international markets, U.S. managers adopted a high-wage, low-cost strategy. Since labor was relatively expensive, there were strong incentives for American managers to economize on its use and cut unit costs—thus the aggressive strategy of substituting machinery for labor and subdividing, analyzing, and reorganizing the labor process.

In the face of these managerial initiatives, unions were faced with two options. First, they could continue to struggle for the maintenance of craft control over the production process. Second, they could accept the shifting overall trend of power in industry and push for quantitative improvements in worker rewards within the emerging new patterns of labor relations—in effect, a rearguard action against scientific management and Taylorism. The first option was rejected in the face of management and government power arrayed against the unions. Instead, the unions generally adopted the more limited second strategy, where collective bargaining came to legitimate an increasingly extreme division of labor (Fox, 1974: 201, 204–205): In order for unions to control job opportunities, standardized rules of wage determination and job allocation had to be developed where none existed before. To negotiate and conclude labor contracts on this basis assumes the determination of pay rates on the basis of explicitly defined jobs. In pursuing this strategy, it became in the union's interest to set clear, precise job boundaries and negotiate pay rates for each job.

These practices became institutionalized in American work structures as industrialization proceeded, the scale of enterprises grew, and internal labor markets assumed increasing importance. There evolved a complex set of industrial relations rules in which the equity principle—predicated on the ability to identify and compare sets of clearly defined jobs—became a central basis for wage determination. In this context contemporary American unions are suspicious of small-group activities because they often threaten vested union interests in existing job structures, pay scales, and collective-bargaining arrangements.

Japan: Union Indifference and Uninvolvement

Japan's industrialization process gave rise to different forms of union-ism and to markedly different union strategies than those that arose in the United States. First, Japan experienced labor surplus rather than labor shortage throughout much of its industrialization, and wages were quite low by international standards. Second, union organizations were suppressed or severely restricted in their activities in the pre–World War II period and again in the 1950s (Ayusawa, 1966: 302–304; Cook, 1966: 97–98). Japan's history of industrial development was such that the Japanese skipped the craft stage of union organization (Dore, 1973), precisely the stage at which the model of precise job specification was most carefully worked out in the American experience. Under these conditions, Japanese industries could compete in foreign markets, because labor was cheap. Unions, relatively weak and facing a large pool of potential replacement workers, found job security a more viable goal than control of job opportunities. Given these conditions, when scientific management principles were adopted in Japan, time-and-motion studies were used not to determine jobs but simply to determine "correct" job procedures. Managers were interested in developing a disciplined workforce motivated to take on cost reduction and other management goals as a personal challenge. This desire, in interaction with union interests in job security, led to the institutionalization of "paternalism"—the emphasis on principles of permanent employment and promotion and pay according to a seniority system.

Japanese management's control of worker training under the seniority wage system, combined with the lack of a national labor movement in the course of industrialization, led to an acceptance of management's prerogative to decide unilaterally on work assignments, job demarcation, and the restructuring of job boundaries, along with changes in technology. Even today, management generally has a discretionary right to move its workforce about without union interference (Okamoto, 1975). In this context, neither management nor labor saw great benefit in tying wage determination to specific job performance. The interplay of union and management interests that led to sharp job demarcation and union commitment to these work structures in the United States led to the opposite outcome in Japan.

This different historical pattern led to Japanese labor's relative indifference to the introduction of small-group activities. Its agenda for participation focused instead on cooperation with management to set up an elaborate system of labor-management consultation committees at all levels of the firm. Because small-group activities are within the historically agreed-upon realm of managerial prerogatives and because they are consistent with union goals of creating greater economic prosperity, Japanese unions have maintained their relative uninvolvement in these changes.

Sweden: From Cooperation to Contention

Swedish trade unions, unlike those of Japan and the United States, took an active role in organized efforts to establish small-group activities in industry. The nature and effect of this involvement, however, have been quite complex and have had a mixed impact on the diffusion process. As an organized national force, Swedish unions are extremely potent, with organization rates of about 80 percent of the entire workforce (with almost similar rates of organization in blue- and white-collar sectors). These levels are far higher than the American and Japanese rates. Nationally, moreover, the organization of the Swedish trade-union movement is highly centralized, and through forty-four years of Social Democratic government that ended only in the 1976 elections, organized labor has been a much stronger force in national politics than its counterparts in the United States and Japan (Korpi, 1978: 74–75). The Social Democrats returned to power in 1982.

Historically the Swedish union movement has been hostile to the idea of direct workshop participation, not unlike most American unions. This orientation was not due to a vested union interest in existing job definitions, but rather to the unions' commitment to centralized national bargaining. The unions feared that increasing the decision rights of small groups in the shop would undermine this.

The union strategy for expanding workplace power in the mid-1960s focused on company-level works councils. A series of threats to the organizational integrity and discipline of the unions, beginning around 1970, changed the union leadership's orientations and moved them to support small-group activities as part of a strategy too democratize Swedish firms. In late 1969 a wildcat strike took place at the state-owned LKAB iron mine. The participants were well-paid miners who were protesting inept and unresponsive union and state officials as much as poor working conditions and lack of wage equity (Korpi, 1970; Dahlström et al., 1971; Hammarström, 1975). The LKAB strike, followed by a wave of wildcat strikes throughout Sweden during 1970 and 1971 (Berglind and Rundblad, 1975), set in motion a national debate on the meaning of work, the proper trade-union role, what employees had a right to expect from their work, and the possibility of restructuring work and authority relationships in the workplace. Media coverage of these issues was intense (Karlsson, 1969).

It was during this period that Thorsrud's ideas about autonomous work groups were being propagated among management circles. Direct workplace participation by workers through small-group activities appealed to top union officials as one way to accommodate the disaffected and rebellious rank and file while moving toward democratization of the firm.

This crucial early period of cooperation, however, was short-lived. The momentum of political events required changes that were beyond the scope of the initial experiments with small-group activities. LO in its 1971 convention endorsed a historic reversal of policies. Where previously the union had been indifferent or hostile to worker participation, it now committed itself fully to the worker-participation movement, demanding power for workers at all levels of the company. It demanded that this be guaranteed not merely through cooperation or bargaining with management to support small-group activities, but through national legislation. The LO policy, endorsed also by the white-collar federation, TCO, led to the passage of the Co-Determination Law.

The law represents a crucial shift in Swedish union strategy. Traditionally, Swedish trade unions were notable for their ability to agree with management on certain areas in which mutual interests could be served through cooperative action. Initially, this was the case for worker participation, as unions cooperated with management in the setting up of works councils and later through participation in URAF with experiments stressing small-group activities. They expected this activity to lead to greater worker and union input at all levels of decision making within the firm. When they found that management resisted efforts to extend worker participation beyond small-group activities at the shop and office floor, pressure grew for the shift in union policy that eventually took place in 1971. In this watershed year, the previously cooperative policy gave way to a new strategy of having the Social Democratic government enact legislation that would facilitate the democratization of the firm through union negotiation on the basis of these laws. The unions saw the Co-Determination Law as a collective-bargaining model for controlling participatory activities rather than bringing about direct participation of workers. This vision worked against the development of small-group activities, and the shift from cooperation to contention served to slow the initially rapid progress of their diffusion, since there now was a basic tension over the direction and scope of reform.

Implicitly, this shift in union position had another consequence that slowed the progress of shopfloor innovations. Small-group activities now became just one of several levels on which worker participation and union power were being pursued. In 1971 the LO congress also endorsed various representation schemes, including board of director membership for employees (passed into law in 1972) and expanded works councils, but there has been considerable union infighting over the priorities assigned these various forms of participation.

It remains to be seen whether the norms to be worked out to operationalize the Co-Determination Law will revitalize the small-group activity movement. The lack of a clear idea on how to concretize the legislation, combined with the shift to a non–Social Democratic government in 1976, led to a paralysis of the small-group activity movement. With the return of the Social Democratic government in 1982, new life seems to have been breathed into small-group activities (Mellbourn, 1984: 16). Slogans of the new movement are worker participation in "development" and "change" and "local solutions for local problems." In the private sector, this translates into a more flexible approach on the part of the unions. In early 1986 Volvo, Sweden's largest private employer, announced plans for rebuilding its largest plant as well as for a new plant. Both plans contained a strong emphasis on small-group activities.

The Macropolitical Dimensions of Work Reform

From the case-by-case comparison summarized in Figure 2-1, we can extract and highlight the macropolitical dimensions of work reform. To the extent that there is contention over the implementation of small-group practices—when groups have different interests with regard to change, articulate competing ideologies, and act on their respective interests—implementation becomes politicized. To the extent that different groups have congruent interests and cooperate in such efforts or to the extent that one group is indifferent to the change, the process is, in our terms, nonpoliticized. Whether the process of change becomes politicized or not has an important impact on the outcome, but this impact is not a simple one. A comparison of the three cases shows that the effect of degree of politicization is contingent on other variables at work in each national situation.

	Timing and Scope of Innovation	Management Incentives to Innovate	Characteristics of Mobilization	Political Dimensions
Japan	Began early 1960s. Now widely diffused. Limited initially to blue-collar workers at the shopfloor level.	Significant labor shortage and rapidly accelerated education levels with raised expectations.	Management organizations provide well-funded and organized infrastructure for diffusion.	Top management develops commitment to innovation. Unions in private sector passively accept.
Sweden	Began late 1960s. Now widely diffused. Spread rapidly to white-collar and public sector. Operative from shopfloor level to board of directors membership.	Severe labor shortage and rapidly accelerated education levels with raised expectations.	In early years joint union-management efforts develop effective infrastructure for diffusion. Later management organizations provide focus for shop- and office-floor efforts.	Top management, union leaders, and government all develop commitment to innovation. Union committed but sets its own agenda.
United States	Piecemeal experimentation in 1960s and 1970s. Limited primarily to blue-collar workers at the shopfloor level.	Few incentives perceived.	Many piecemeal efforts, absence of well-funded and centralized infrastructure for diffusion.	Neither government, union, nor management leadership committed to innovation. Unions often hostile.

FIGURE 2-1.

Work Reform in Three Nations: A Summary

NOTE: I am indebted to Linda Kaboolian for suggesting this summary format.

Nonpoliticized Patterns: The United States and Japan

In the United States neither unions, management, not politicians exhibited strong interest in small-group activities: unions because they would challenge vested interests in existing job structures and disturb long-standing strategies for the pursuit of their interests through collective bargaining, management because there were no acute problems with existing practices, and politicians because there was no manifest constituency. Unlike Sweden, there was no impact of the issue upon public opinion or national political discourse. With such a lack of commitment on the part of all major institutional actors, a strong national infrastructure failed to develop. The result was that no one contender or group of contenders effectively promoted the small-group activity movement in the United States.

In Japan, also, the process of change has been nonpoliticized. Unlike the United States, however, there has been a very widespread application of small-group activities. In Japan management became interested in such reforms because of difficult labor-market problems it faced in the mid-1960s and concern about utilizing an increasingly educated labor force. With the development of such a commitment, employers used existing organizations to create a national infrastructure for the diffusion of solutions such as small-group activities. Japanese unions, unlike their American counterparts, had no interest in opposing these changes in the workplace. Similarly, the ruling Conservative government had little incentive to take positions or action on this matter.[4] Therefore, in the absence of involvement by government, unions, and political parties, the implementation of these new work structures proceeded as a well-coordinated case of managerial innovation. There were no conflicts over reforms, as in Sweden, that threatened to push them in directions feared by managers, and there was no entrenched union opposition to such changes in traditional work structures, as in the United States. As a result, small-group activities diffused rapidly and thoroughly, management being able to control carefully the direction, scope, and content of reform in a way that Swedish management found impossible.

Politicized Pattern: Sweden

In Sweden, as in Japan, strong management interest in small-group activities resulted from serious turnover and recruitment problems due to changes in the domestic labor market. Union orientation toward such reforms, however, shifted from disinterest to cooperation and then to contention in a relatively short period of time. This rapid shift in union orientation coincided with the quick politicization of the issue. The issue of democratization of industrial life came to the center of public attention, with high media coverage, and spurred the Social Democratic government into action. More importantly, it resulted in a rapid shift in union orientation and strategy, as the centralized union hierarchy was threatened with challenges from below. Initially hostile to shopfloor participation and preferring centralized control, the Swedish union confederations quickly moved toward support of shopfloor reforms and eventually came to contend with management over the direction of reform by pursuing legislation to enforce changes. This meant that Swedish managers, unlike their Japanese counterparts, were unable to control carefully the direction, scope, and content of reform after the initial period of management-union cooperation. Later moves by the unions to extend democratization to worker involvement in decisions relating to capital investment and the like threatened traditional management prerogatives and authority. As a result of this basic tension, the initially rapid diffusion of small-group activities slowed as management became wary of changes that it could not completely control. The less complete diffusion of small-group activities in Sweden, despite the consensus of all major institutional actors that such reforms were desirable, is due to this basic management-labor contention over the direction of reform. This contention was heightened by the subsequent loss of power of the Social Democrats to the conservatives in the 1976 election.

The Macropolitics of Organizational Change

The explanation of why change took place in some countries and not in others has two essential components. The first is the motivation of management to introduce small-group activities, rooted in perceived managerial problems. In two of the cases examined in the period 1960–80 (Japan and Sweden), such motivation was present and arose from the characteristics of a changing national labor market; such motivation, however, also derives from more generalized concerns as well. The interaction of these generalized concerns with specific motivators poses enormous problems for social science as we ask what kinds of data will provide meaningful explanations of management behavior. We are dealing with an environment composed of numerous problems and solutions with various degrees of saliency at different times, acting and reacting upon each other in a variety of ways over time. Although I have identified labor-market factors as critical to precipitating out small-group activities, these factors are part of a broad constellation of factors in the total social system. How do managements' conceptions of problems and solutions actually crystallize in relation to competitive ideas? Certainly, longitudinal analysis is necessary. Questionnaire surveys alone are inadequate to the task. A variety of research tools prove useful, including participant observation, nondirective interviews that allow interviewees to explore the full social framework in which decisions are made, and surveys of management journals to see what managers are saying to each other. This suggests that a good social science answer is likely to be a work of art, as one sews together disparate pieces of information from various data sources. That is a disturbing answer from a positivistic perspective, but it has the potential to be a far better one, at least for the kinds of questions being asked here. This paper, still exploratory in many ways, is an attempt to do some of the initial stitching.

The second and determining factor in the spread of small-group activities is the political process that surrounded the change: the efforts of organized managerial or labor groups to enforce their preferences with regard to the change and their ability to call resources into play to do so. Crucial in this regard is the congruence or divergence of management and labor interests with regard to change, especially the orientation of labor unions, given their traditional strategies and their respective abilities to enforce their preferences. These fluid political processes are summarized in Figure 2-2.

This explanation of cross-national differences in the diffusion and survival rates of small-group activities does not rely on organizational level or group-level variables as much as it does on macropolitical processes. We can predict with some confidence that if a national business leadership is committed to small-group activities as a solution to perceived problems, and this is uncontested by labor, a national infrastructure to legitimate and promote small-group activities will come into place. This is independent of any small-group effects or organizational variables that might affect the process in a given company. It is this kind of analysis that allows us to see the forest for the trees. Similarly, if we take as our dependent variable cross-national differences in some of the most often-studied organizational variables—degree of task specialization and degree of differentiation of roles in the shopfloor—we find a similar situation. That is, our analysis suggests the importance of macropolitical variables in explaining these outcomes; such explanations are rarely seen in the literature.

These observations clearly go well beyond the study of small-group activities and provide support for Perrow's (1979) observations about moving away from microanalysis of many questions to broader explanatory factors in order to expand the generalizability and applicability of our theories.

It may indeed be that the most profitable route to studying the impact of macropolitical factors is to see these factors as a subset of a still broader set of environmental factors (cf. Freeman, 1978; Meyer, 1978). The dif-

	Traditional Union Orientation	Union Perception of Small-Group Activities	Union Action	Union Means to Enforce Preferences	Degree of Conflict/Consensus with Management	Outcome
Japan	Stress job security; allow management prerogative of organizing workplace.	Neutral: not a threat to vested interests.	Uninvolved, although consulted at plant level.	Industry-led agreements; factory-led negotiation.	Consensual process of change.	Thorough, rapid process of change.
Sweden	Centralized national collective bargaining and political action through Social Democratic party.	Initially suspicion; later seen as a means to satisfy rebellious rank and file; still later as one prong of strategy for work control.	Began own efforts, initially in cooperation with employers, later on own.	National-led labor agreements and passage of legislation through SDP.	Initial active cooperation, later contention over direction and extent of changes.	Initial rapid change, later halted because of conflict over course.
United States	Control of job opportunities; vested interest in existing job definitions and related pay scales.	Suspicion; as a threat to structure of bargaining at industry level; disinterest.	Little union action.	Industry-level agreements; factory-level negotiation.	Not an issue.	Very limited spread of new structures.

FIGURE 2-2.

Macropolitical Dimensions of the Process of Change

ferential survival and success rates of organizations and the creation of organizations are currently much studied from a population ecology perspective (Aldrich, 1979). It is apparent from this analysis of the variation in the type and form of national infrastructures for the diffusion of small-group activities that the explanations of such outcomes could benefit substantially from the introduction of macropolitical variables. Conditions affecting the ability of organizations to extract resources from the environment (as exemplified by the resource-dependence model) have long been a concern of those stressing the impact of environments on organizations. The analysis here suggests, however, that the role of macropolitical factors in resource acquisition has been underplayed in much previous research. Conversely, integrating the study of macropolitical factors into environmental research frees the study of macropolitical factors from the constraints of its primarily Marxist framework, which simply cannot do justice to the varied empirical outcomes.

The macropolitical perspective can also be useful in the study of innovation. Studies of factors affecting the adoption and diffusion of organizational innovation typically stress organization-level variables (Kimberly, as cited in Aldrich, 1979: 98), with at best some attention given to selected economic variables. Yet, it is apparent from this analysis that the adoption and diffusion of managerial innovations, e.g., small-group activities, depend in large part on the macropolitical factors outside the organization.

It might be asserted in response to this study that the changes described are not "normal" instances of organizational change, that they constitute special cases of well-defined national movements, and therefore the key explanations are necessarily macropolitical. The movements analyzed here, however, are the direct counterparts of previous movements that transformed industrial organization early in this century—the movements for the open shop, for scientific management, Taylorism, and Fordism. All these movements involved the same kind of interplay between management and labor, the same kind of managerial response to perceived problems, and the same kind of organization and mobilization for change through organized infrastructures. These are not abnormal instances of change. Social change usually takes place through these broader, macropolitical processes, and their effects on the micro-organization of factories can be quite profound.

Of course, macropolitics does not explain everything, or even most things, about the way factories and other enterprises are organized. We already have a rich literature telling us what these other variables at lower levels of social organization are. A great deal depends on the questions being asked. For the questions raised in this article, why small-group activities developed differently in the three countries, organization-level variables are not the most important ones. Comparative sociology makes a contribution here by highlighting factors that are always at work in any national setting and historical context. Because they exert relatively constant effects across a range of smaller units of organization, such factors are not clearly perceived without being studied in a comparative framework.

Notes

Acknowledgment: The data for Japan were collected during my tenure as Fulbright Research Scholar, 1977–78. I am indebted to the Fulbright Commission for its support and to the Japan Institute of Labour for providing research facilities. I also express my appreciation to the German Marshall Fund, which provided a research grant for collection of the Swedish data. Research facilities in Sweden were provided by the Department of Applied Psychology at Gothenberg University. Data collection for the U.S. was made possible by a grant from the Henry Luce Foundation, Inc. I am especially indebted to the many business organizations and associations in all three countries that gave freely of their time in an attempt to educate me in the intricacies of organizational change. While I am grateful to the institutional benefactors, they are not responsible for my findings.

My greatest intellectual debt is to Andrew Walder. Our joint working paper, "Structural Diffusion: The Politics of Participative Work Structures in China, Japan, Sweden, and the United States" (Cole and Walder, 1981), provided much of the framework and language that led to this article. Finally, reviewers and editors for the *Administrative Science Quarterly* were most generous with high-quality advice.

1. Burawoy (1983) did not include labor shortage as a motivating factor for workplace innovations. Although he referred to market forces and the labor process as factors in the emergence of "hegemonic despotism," a reputedly new stage of capitalism, he did not allow for differences in labor supply that affected the form of new work structures in the four nations he examined (U.S., England, Japan, and Sweden). His analysis, which compared one workshop in England with another in the U.S., was designed to hold labor process and market factors constant. This method highlights the macropolitical factors but entirely excludes the labor-market characteristics that are an important empirical link between the macropolitical factors and the organization of work.

2. This important concept cannot be treated adequately in the space available. Central to the analysis is Bendix's (1974) notion of "managerial ideology"; my use of the concept focuses on organized management efforts to promote change.

3. The Democracy of Work (or Co-Determination) Law (Medbestammandelagen), passed in 1976, provides Swedish workers and their unions with legal authority to bargain collectively over a wide range of management decisions that previously had been strictly managerial prerogatives.

4. There seems to be little basis, other than that it fits the Marxist perspective, for Burawoy's contention that state involvement in the Japanese industrial relations

system is quite low. Similarly, his description of Japan as closely approximating "the despotic order of early capitalism in which the state offers little or no social insurance and abstains from the regulation of factory apparatuses" (Burawoy, 1983: 599) is innocent of all facts (see Shirai, 1983; Gould, 1984).

References

Agervold, Mogens. 1975. "Swedish Experiments in Industrial Democracy." In Louis Davis and Albert Cherns, eds., *The Quality of Working Life*, 2: 46–65. New York: Free Press.

Aldrich, Howard. 1979. *Organizations and Environments*. Englewood Cliffs, N.J.: Prentice-Hall.

Ayusawa, Iwao. 1966. *A History of Labor in Modern Japan*. Honolulu: East-West Center Press.

Bendix, Reinhard. 1974. *Work and Authority in Industry*. Berkeley: University of California Press.

Berglind, Hans, and Bengt Rundblad. 1975. "The Swedish Labor Market in Transition." Unpublished paper. University of Gothenberg.

Bernstein, Paul. 1976. *Workplace Democratization: Its Internal Dynamics*. Kent, Ohio: Kent State University Press.

Björk, Lars, Reine Hanson, and Peter Hellberg. 1973. *Ökat inflytande i jobbet* (Increased Influence on the Job). Stockholm: Personaladministrativa Rådet.

Bluestone, Irving. 1978. "Human Dignity is What It's All About." *Viewpoint* 8(3): 21–24.

Braverman, Harry. 1974. *Labor and Monopoly Capital: The Degradation of Work in the Twentieth Century*. New York: Monthly Review.

Burawoy, Michael. 1983. "Between the Labor Process and the State: The Changing Face of Factory Regimes under Advanced Capitalism." *American Sociological Review* 48: 587–605.

Cole, Robert E. 1979. *Work, Mobility, and Participation: A Comparative Study of American and Japanese Industry*. Berkeley: University of California Press.

Cole, Robert E., and Dennis Tachiki. 1983. "A Look at U.S. and Japanese Quality Circles: Preliminary Comparisons." *Quality Circles Journal* 6(2): 10–16.

Cole, Robert E., and Andrew Walder. 1981. "Structural Diffusion: The Politics of Participative Work Structures in China, Japan, Sweden, and the United States." Working Paper Series no. 226, Center for Research on Social Organization, University of Michigan.

Cook, Alice. 1966. *An Introduction to Japanese Trade Unionism*. Ithaca, N.Y.: Cornell University Press.

Cummings, Thomas, and Edmond Molloy. 1977. *Improving Productivity and the Quality of Work Life*. New York: Praeger.

Dachler, H. Peter, and Bernhard Wilpert. 1978. "Conceptual Dimensions and Boundaries of Participation in Organizations: A Critical Evaluation." *Administrative Science Quarterly* 23: 1–39.

Dahlström, Edmund, et al. 1971. *LKAB och Demokrati*. Stockholm: Waldström and Wedstrand.

Davis, Louis, and Albert Cherns (eds.). 1975. *The Quality of Working Life*, 1. New York: Free Press.

Dore, Ronald. 1973. *British Factory—Japanese Factory*. Berkeley: University of California Press.

Edwards, Richard. 1979. *Contested Terrain*. New York: Basic Books.

Emery, Fred, and Eric Trist. 1969. "Sociotechnical Systems." In Fred Emery, ed., *Systems Thinking:* 281–96. London: Penguin.

Fox, Alan. 1974. *Beyond Contract: Work, Power and Trust Relations*. London: Faber and Faber.

Freeman, John. 1978. "The Unit of Analysis in Organizational Research." In Marshall Meyer and Associates, eds., *Environments and Organizations: Theoretical and Empirical Perspectives:* 335–51. San Francisco: Jossey-Bass.

Gould, William. 1984. *Japan's Reshaping of American Labor Law*. Cambridge, Mass.: MIT Press.

Gyllenhammar, Pehr. 1977. *People at Work*. Reading, Mass.: Addison-Wesley.

Hammarström, Olle. 1975. "Joint Worker-Management Consultation: The Case of LKAB, Sweden." In Louis Davis and Albert Cherns, eds., *The Quality of Working Life*, 2: 66–82. New York: Free Press.

Harvey, Edward, and Russell Mills. 1970. "Patterns of Organizational Adaptation: A Political Perspective." In Mayer N. Zald, ed., *Power in Organizations:* 181–213. Nashville, Tenn.: Vanderbilt University Press.

Industrial Union Department, AFL-CIO. 1978. "The Quality of Working Life." *Viewpoint* 8(3): 1–29.

Kanter, Rosabeth. 1983. *The Change Masters*. New York: Simon and Schuster.

Karlsson, Lars Erik. 1969. *Demokrati pa Arbetsplatsen* (Democracy at the Workplace). Stockholm: Prisma.

Katzell, Raymond, Daniel Yankelovich, et al. 1975. *Work, Productivity, and Job Satisfaction*. New York: Psychological Corporation.

Korpi, Walter. 1970. *Varför Strejkar-Arbetarna?* (Why Do Workers Strike?). Stockholm: Tidens Förlag.

———. 1978. *The Working Class in Welfare Capitalism*. London: Routledge & Kegan Paul.

Landsorganisation. 1976. *Arbetsorganisation* (Work Organization). Stockholm: Tidens Förlag.

Mellbourn, Anders. 1984. *"MBL Inte så Dålig som sitt Rykte"* (The Co-Determination Law Is Not as Bad as It's Rumored to Be). *Dagens Nyheter*, April 29: 16.

Meyer, John. 1978. "Strategies for Further Research: Varieties of Environmental Variation." In Marshall Meyer and Associates, eds., *Environments and Organizations: Theoretical and Empirical Perspectives:* 352–68. San Francisco: Jossey-Bass.

Minami, Ryoshin. 1973. *The Turning Point in Economic Development: Japan's Experience*. Tokyo: Kinokuniya Bookstore.

Ministry of Labour. 1974. *Koyō kanri shindan shiyō* (Indicators of the Conditions of Employment Administration). Tokyo: Employment Security Office.

Montgomery, David. 1976. "Workers' Control of Machine Production in the Nineteenth Century." *Labor History* 17: 485–509.

Nakayama, Saburo. 1972. *Zen'in sanka keiei no kangaekata to jissai* (All-Employee

Management Participation: Viewpoints and Practices). Tokyo: Japan Federation of Employers' Associations.

Nelson, Daniel. 1975. *Managers and Workers*. Madison, Wis.: University of Wisconsin Press.

New York Stock Exchange. 1982. *People and Productivity*. New York: New York Stock Exchange.

Okamoto, Hideaki. 1975. "*Jizen Kyōgisei no Ronri*" (The Logic of the Prior Consultation System). In Nihon Rōdō Kyōkai, ed., *Haichi Tenkan o Meguru Rōshi Kankei:* 43–93. Tokyo: Japan Institute of Labour.

Perlman, Selig. 1968. *A Theory of the Labor Movement*. Originally published in 1928. New York: Augustus Kelly.

Perrow, Charles. 1970. "Departmental Power and Perspectives in Industrial Firms." In Mayer Zald, ed., *Power in Organizations:* 59–79. Nashville, Tenn.: Vanderbilt University Press.

———. 1979. *Complex Organizations: A Critical Essay,* 2d ed. New York: Random House.

Pfeffer, Jeffrey. 1978. "The Micropolitics of Organizations." In Marshall Meyer and Associates, eds., *Environments and Organizations: Theoretical and Empirical Perspectives:* 29–50. San Francisco: Jossey-Bass.

Rothschild-Whitt, Joyce. 1979. "The Collectivist Organization: An Alternative to Rational-Bureaucratic Models." *American Sociological Review* 44: 509–27.

Shirai, Taishiro (ed.). 1983. *Contemporary Industrial Relations in Japan*. Madison, Wis.: University of Wisconsin Press.

Sorge, Marjorie. 1984. "UAW Lists Top Priorities for Talks in Canada." *Automotive News* (Detroit: Crain Automotive Group), April 23: 4, 8.

Statistiska Centralbyrån. 1978. *Arbetsmarknads-statistisk Arsbok 1977* (Yearbook of Labor Statistics 1977). Örebro: National Central Bureau of Statistics.

Stone, Katherine. 1975. "The Origins of Job Structures in the Steel Industry." In Richard Edwards, Michael Reich, and David Gordon, eds., *Labor Market Segmentation:* 27–84. Lexington, Mass.: Lexington Books.

Tannenbaum, Arnold S., Bogdan Kravčič, Manachem Rosner, Mino Vianello, and Georg Wieser. 1974. *Hierarchy in Organizations*. San Francisco: Jossey-Bass.

Thomas, Robert. 1984. "Participation and Control: New Trends in Labor Relations in the Auto Industry." CRSO Working Paper no. 315. Ann Arbor, Mich.: University of Michigan, Center for Research on Social Organizations.

Thorsrud, Einar, and Fred Emery. 1969. *Medinflytande och Engagemang in Arbetet* (Participation and Engagement in Work). Stockholm: Utvecklingsrådet for Samarbetsfrågor.

Tichy, Noel, and Jay N. Nisberg. 1976. "When Does Work Restructuring Work? Organizational Innovations at Volvo and GM." *Organizational Dynamics* 5: 1 (Summer): 63–80.

Walton, Richard. 1978. "Teaching an Old Dog Food New Tricks." *Wharton Magazine,* Winter: 38–47.

Wool, Harold. 1973. "What's Wrong with Work in America?" *Monthly Labor Review* 96(3): 38–44.

Zald, Mayer. 1970. *Power in Organizations,* Nashville, Tenn.: Vanderbilt University Press.

3

WORKER PARTICIPATION IN TECHNOLOGICAL CHANGE: INTERESTS, INFLUENCE, AND SCOPE

Robert Howard
Leslie Schneider

The concerns of this paper lie at the intersection of two highly visible trends in working life. The first is the technological transformation of work associated with the spread of computer-based systems throughout industry. The second is the proliferation of new organizational mechanisms for employee participation, designed to expand the scope of worker involvement in a variety of issues affecting the organization and performance of work.

During the past decade the idea of worker participation has attracted both increased attention and a multiplicity of meanings. In the early 1970s participation was championed as a way to counter what was perceived as a wave of increasing worker dissatisfaction in industrial societies and to improve the overall "quality of worklife." By the end of the 1970s, as industrial economies faced growing international competition and declining productivity, participation became a means to improve productivity and product quality along the lines of the "quality circles" first popularized in Japan (Hayashi, 1983). More recently, some observers have begun to redefine participation once again—as a response to the unique demands of the computerized workplace and a useful (indeed, necessary) mechanism for effectively managing rapid workplace technological change (Walton and Vittori, 1983).

Thus, what began as a concept to improve the quality of work-life and increase equity in the workplace has evolved into a technique to fulfill crucial business interests for efficiency—in particular, the effective exploitation of new workplace technology. A common assumption in much of the recent literature on worker participation in technological change is that participation offers managers and workers the best of both worlds: both a more equitable and a more efficient work environment.

The perspective of this paper is somewhat different. Although increased worker participation in technological change certainly has the potential to improve both job quality and efficiency, the precise path to these goals is rarely as simple or straightforward as some proponents of participation tend to suggest. Worker participation, like any innovation process, has its costs; the interests and goals that various social groups bring to the workplace can, and often do, conflict. Participation that is not only successful for the work organization but also meaningful for participants themselves may have to allow both for the possibility (indeed, the likelihood) of such conflicts and for the representation of conflicting interests in the participation process (Ciborra, 1985).

Put another way, worker participation in technological change may need to extend beyond the business interests of the individual firm to the myriad social interests at play in any technological change process: issues concerning technology and employment, technology and the organization of work, technology and the sexual division of labor—in short, the overall distribution of technology's social costs and benefits in the workplace and in society as a whole.

This paper describes a spectrum of approaches to managing workplace technological change and their implications for worker participation: The "technocentric" model conceives technological change as primarily a technical issue; participation is generally avoided as a potentially disruptive element. The "organization-centered" model conceives technological change, first and foremost, as an organizational issue; it sees participation as an effective mechanism for furthering business interests of increased efficiency and improved organizational effectiveness. Finally, the "negotiation" model conceives technological change as a social issue; and participation is the process by which the various social groups of the workplace negotiate tradeoffs, reconcile social interests and business goals, and equitably distribute the costs and benefits of technology in the work organization.

In the course of this discussion we shall also examine a few experiments at worker participation in technological change from the United States and Europe. Finally, we shall explore some of the most common obstacles to such participation and suggest a few ideas for overcoming them.

The Legacy of Traditional Industrial Organization: The Technocentric Model

British scientist Arnold Pacey (1983:4) has emphasized the importance of understanding technology "Not only as comprising machines, techniques, and crisply precise knowledge, but also as involving characteristic patterns of organization and imprecise values." What we think of as technological change is, in fact, a complex social process. And its impacts are the outcome of specific social choices and values.

Obviously, the capabilities of technology itself set the limits of the technically possible in any particular case. Within those limits, however, business firms can pursue a variety of organizational options that reflect everything from the markets in which they operate and the firms with which they compete to the prevailing ideas, traditions, and models of industrial organization that shape how business managers conceive of their responsibilities and their tasks.

The most important managerial model shaping the early stages of the computerization of work we call, following Peter Keen (1982), the "technocentric" approach. According to this model, the exploitation of new computer technology in the workplace is conceived primarily as a technical issue. The goal of workplace technological change is to increase efficiency by mechanizing production and reducing labor costs. And the design and implementation of new technical systems is the special responsibility of technical specialists, experts in "systems design" and often grouped in special electronic data processing (EDP) or information resources management (IRM) departments. (Mathaissen, 1981; Lanzara, 1983).

This description is something of a caricature, but anyone with experience in contemporary work organizations will recognize it, for the roots of the technocentric approach run deep in the traditions of scientific management, the dominant form of work organization in industrial societies throughout much of the twentieth century. Scientific management defines a set of principles for managing mass production industrial work: the functional separation of execution and design; the systematic standardization, fragmentation, and mechanization of work tasks; and the imperative of increased managerial control. The principles of scientific management, particularly as embodied in the discipline of industrial engineering, provided a handy model for the first attempts at the computerization of work (Strassmann, 1985).

The technocentric approach also closely corresponded to the early limitations of computer technology. As long as computer systems were relatively complicated to use and difficult to apply to work tasks, computerization reinforced the dominance of technical personnel. The technical problems associated with getting the system in and functioning smoothly became the predominant concern of most managers, not only the engineers who designed the new workplace computer systems but the line managers who had to use them.

Implicit to the technocentric approach is the traditional concept of the industrial work organization as a kind of military hierarchy with clear-cut lines of authority and a top-down decision-making structure. For this reason, the idea of worker participation in technological change is the antithesis of sound management, something to be avoided rather than encouraged. Participation threatens to dilute lines of authority and disrupt managerial control. To the degree that workers and their points of view are taken into account at all, it is usually as a problem of human engineering—how to minimize human intervention in new systems and thus avoid human error.

Recently, there has been extensive business literature criticizing this technocentric model. Nevertheless, the overly technical approach to workplace technological change is anything but a relic of our industrial past. Substantial recent literature has amply demonstrated the remarkable persistence of technocentric managerial attitudes about computer technology in American industry—even in the face of substantial costs to social equity and organizational efficiency alike (Noble, 1984; Shaiken, 1984; Howard, 1985b). Nor are such attitudes found solely among technical personnel. Line managers and workers themselves often share many of the assumptions of the technocentric approach. These assumptions constitute a kind of unrecognized and unexamined professional common sense about how to use computer technology in the workplace today.

Participation in the Service of Business Interests: The Organization-Centered Model

The recent managerial critique of the technocentric model is founded on a practical management problem: the tendency of early uses of computer technology in the workplace to create what Richard Walton and Wendy Vittori (1983) have called "unrealized gains" and "unanticipated costs." As computerization has spread to new industries and tasks (in particular, those of the rapidly expanding service sector), as computer technology itself has decreased in price and increased in versatility, managers have found that the assumptions of the technocentric model, far from ensuring the effective use of new technology, have become an obstacle to the successful implementation of the new technology itself.

For example, Paul Strassmann (1985:163) of the Xerox Corporation has recently estimated that, in the banking and insurance industry, where major investment in computerization has taken place, computerization has had "no discernible effect on labor productivity." Managers like Strassmann have located the source of this failure in the tendency of managers schooled in the technocentric approach to systematically underestimate the organizational dimensions of workplace technological change. This had led to a series of managerial misconceptions about work and technology that constitute a serious barrier to the efficient exploitation of workplace computer systems.

The words of one prominent management consultant capture the flavor of this, by now, quite common point of view: "The systems development Fiasco Hall of Fame," he writes, "is packed with examples of costly mistakes, costly in terms of disruption and morale, not just money, caused by the tenacious ignorance regarding users and their world. . . . The technocentric tradition has largely led to a naive view of the user, simplistic concepts of work, overmechanized and inflexible models of organizational and social processes, and, above all, a definition of 'productivity' in terms of the ethos of efficiency" (Keen, 1982).

Like the more general interest in employee participation during the past decade, the simplest versions of this critique of the technocentric approach have emphasized its human resources and labor relations costs—in particular, how ignoring the user can spark employee resistance to workplace technological change.

A more complex version emphasizes how industrial concepts of efficiency misunderstand both the nature of information work and the unique demands placed on workers by computer technology. On the one hand, much of the work done in offices is informal and unstructured, not amenable to conventional strategies of mechanization and standardization. Thus, the technocentric approach can end up creating rigid computer systems that violate the very logic of the work to be automated (Strassmann, 1985).

On the other hand, work with the new technology makes qualitatively new demands on workers. Work becomes more conceptual and abstract. Responsibilities are expanded and broadened. Workers become more interdependent, their individual tasks connected in a seamless web of integrated information systems (Zuboff, 1982; Adler, 1983; Hirschhorn, 1984). In such a work environment the fragmentation of work common to the technocentric approach tends to ensure that workers do not develop the requisite attitudes and skills for the effective use of the new technology.

Finally, some observers have argued that the transformation of world markets and the ongoing restructuring of the global economy have rendered increasingly obsolete the traditional model of efficiency on which the technocentric approach is based (Sabel, 1982; Piore and Sabel, 1984). In the new circumstances of the world economy market success is founded, not on mass production, but on "flexible specialization." And successful work organizations are those that dismantle rigid hierarchies and build flexible organizations based on a broad distribution of skill, decentralization of decision making, and increased worker initiative. In other words, sustained worker participation in work—including both the tasks at hand and the development of organization structures that are consistent with the demands of the new technology—becomes a key to efficiency in today's corporation.

For example, Japanese business school professor Masaki Hayashi (1983) has argued that Japanese quality circles, far from reflecting some intangible cultural predisposition toward collective decision making and consensus, are best understood as a managerial technique allowing Japanese manufacturers to meet the special challenges posed by work in a highly automated, computerized environment. The development of highly integrated computer-aided manufacturing systems, writes Hayashi, "has increased the necessity for cooperation between workers both in the plant and in the office as well as between engineers and management at their place of work and between the various departments of the firm." (1983:2). The idea of worker participation, embodied in quality circles and other forms of "small group activity" in the Japanese workplace, "has been introduced to cope with the demands coming from the [automation] of the production process." (1983:13).

All these arguments have contributed to the development of an emerging alternative model of technology management. Since it emphasizes the organizational dimensions of technological change, it can be called the "organization-centered" approach. If the model of industrial organization implicit in the technocentric approach is the military, the model of the information organization is, in Peter Drucker's apt metaphor, the orchestra, where each player has a different part to play, but where everyone plays the same score.

According to this perspective, technological change is one part of a much broader organizational change process. Its ultimate goal is not so much discrete gains in individual efficiency as the improvement of overall organizational effectiveness (Strassmann, 1985). And the role of the technology manager is not that of the technical specialist but of a "change agent" who knows how to address the complex organizational issues that new technology implementation can create and on which the successful use of the new technology depends (Keen, 1982).

Because the users of technology play such a central role in the organization-centered approach, both as a source of expertise and information about the work organization and as the ultimate arbiters of how best to use technology in order to better perform their jobs, participation is a key element of this approach to managing workplace technological change. Participation is the technique by which the effective use of the new technology is assured. At the same time it is a means to guarantee worker satisfaction and commitment to the technological change process itself. For this reason, user participation has become a standard element in vendor implementations.

One can think of the value of user participation in terms of three stages of the technology development process.[1] At the stage of design the people who actually do the work to be automated and who will operate the new technology once it is developed are a crucial source of information for systems designers. Without the involvement of these users, as informants or "local experts" during the design stage, designers run the risk of creating systems that do not accurately reflect the work tasks and work organization to be automated—what one designer has called "automating a fiction" (Suchman and Wynn, 1979; Suchman, 1980; Sheil, 1983).

Once a system is ready for implementation, user participation becomes especially important. If the views of users are not taken into account in the implementation process, technology managers run the risk of generating worker opposition to the new system and new work practices—what is known, in the parlance of the profession, as "resistance." Resistance can lead to the consistent underutilization of new technology or, worse, its outright rejection by users.

Finally, the absence of user involvement can have long-standing impacts even after systems are implemented. Effective use of new technology is intimately related to the quantity and quality of the training workers receive—a fact that the technocentric approach tends to overlook (Kelley, 1984; Schneider, 1984). Often, the best judges of how much and what kind of training workers need are the workers themselves. User participation can prove to be an effective way to organize worker training for new systems to ensure that users have the requisite skills for operating new technical systems.

One rather advanced model of user participation is a methodology, developed by Enid Mumford in conjunction with the Digital Equipment Corporation, known as ETHICS ("Effective Technical and Human Implementation of Computer-based Systems") (Bancroft, 1982; Bancroft et al., n.d.). From the moment an office or department is slated for automation, a "design group" consisting of workers from a broad cross-section of occupational categories is established. Advised by technical experts and in regular contact with a management steering committee that sets the boundaries of the design group's work, the members analyze their own workplace, propose alternative ways of organizing work tasks, and help select the technology best suited to the redesigned work organization.

The idea behind the ETHICS methodology is to include as many different perspectives as possible in the work redesign process. One ETHICS report (Bancroft et al., n.d.:4) even encourages companies to include a few "good 'devil's advocates'" in the design group in order to stimulate the consideration of alternative organizational plans. In this way, user participation is designed both to meet the efficiency goals of the organization and to win worker support for technological change. As the Digital report on ETHICS puts it, "Groups which are passive recipients of major innovation may be afraid and resistant; whereas those who are involved will learn how to cope, exert control and mold the change to fit

their own needs, and the needs of their departments and companies."
Participation in technology design and implementation, the report continues, allows employees to "mold their own futures" and to "acquire
confidence in their ability to contribute to the management of their own
change" (Bancroft et al., n.d.:11).

The Limitations of the Organization-Centered Model

The concept of participation common to the organization-centered
model seems to rest on a number of assumptions: That workers and
managers share a community of interests about the means and the ends
of workplace technological change, and that participation in the service of
business interests will also lead to better work quality and improved
worker satisfaction. At times these assumptions take on the quality of
"necessary conditions" without which participation becomes, at best,
problematic and, at worst, impossible.

However, what happens when the interests of various social groups
in the workplace conflict? When the claims of equity and of efficiency,
instead of reinforcing each other, prove contradictory? Because the concept
of participation implicit in the organization-centered approach to
workplace technological change is founded on the idea of consensus, such
conflicts tend to threaten the very idea of participation itself.

The possibility of such conflicts generally means that, in the organization-centered approach, managers are constantly trying to control
participation in order to make sure that it stays within predetermined
limits. Thus, while Walton and Vittori (1983:15) call for an organizational
approach to technological change and for active user participation in the
change process, they make clear that "the particular criteria and [organiza-
tional] preferences" on which participation is based "will depend upon
management's philosophy and values, the nature of the business and past
experience," in short, business concerns alone.

The recent history of user participation by technology vendors reflects
this same management-oriented conception of participation. Eleanor
Wynn (1983) has described how most technology vendors conceive of user
participation in a highly superficial way—more as a matter of marketing
(how to "sell" new systems to potential customers) than as a mechanism
for fundamental organizational transformation. According to Wynn, what
passes for user participation at many technology vendors does not involve
the ultimate users of the technology at all. Rather, it is a term to describe
vendors' efforts to communicate with and otherwise involve the line
managers who manage the implementation of new systems.

Even relatively advanced forms of user participation, such as

ETHICS, provide participants with little opportunity to actually influence the management decision-making process concerning technological change. Users are conceived exclusively as the performers of certain functions in the work organization, but not as bearers of social interests. And a management steering committee sets the parameters for the design group's activities and investigations. Crucial decisions about personnel requirements, layoffs, and other issues are often made beforehand, without worker influence or line-manager input.

Moreover, the organization-centered approach to participation tends to underestimate the considerable difficulties involved in moving an organization from one work system to another. The assumptions and attitudes of the technocentric model are deeply ingrained throughout most work organizations; these attitudes do not simply disappear when a change in policy is made at the top. It is one thing to create a participative, high-commitment work organization in a brand-new company in a brand-new industry (e.g., Silicon Valley). It is quite another to imagine radically changing an already existing work organization and a corporate culture that is based upon some version of scientific management.

Finally, the organization-centered model seems to imply that, to the degree that there are labor relations problems or conflicts of interest between stakeholders, they can be—and should be—resolved at the level of the individual firm. But this is not always possible and, again, the technology issue provides the best example. The impacts of technology are often of a scope extending far beyond the corporation itself. Companies buy ready-made technology from vendors; what are the mechanisms for its managers or workers to influence how those vendors design systems? And what about those workers who end up losing their jobs because of technological change? What are the mechanisms for addressing that impact? In short, this approach ignores the fact that addressing the social impacts of technology may require social regulation that transcends the individual work organization.

Such built-in limitations to the scope and content of worker participation in technological change may be relatively easy to ignore in a workplace where the degree of worker organization is weak. However, where workers are formally represented by a trade union, it is more difficult to contain participation within management-defined limits. In addition to the business interests and goals of management, unions bring their own collective and social interests and goals to the workplace. As independent user representatives, unions provide a mechanism where the very criteria of worker participation in technological change themselves become subject to participation and negotiation.

In recent years there have been a number of attempts at worker participation in technological change involving unionized workforces in the United States. Often, they have taken place in industries facing new competitive pressures, whether as a result of increased international competition, as in the case of the auto industry, or of the deregulation of quasi-monopoly markets, such as the airlines and telecommunications industries.

A common theme in many of these cases is the potential conflict between management and union over the scope of participatory programs. These conflicts suggest the limitations of participation conceived purely in terms of business interests. To the degree that the two parties have been able to define mutually acceptable goals, participation often works. But when both management and workers understand participation solely in terms of cooperation, they are generally ill-prepared to deal with the conflicts of power and interest that changes in technology inevitably stimulate.

Thus, on issues where goals or interests conflict, participation breaks down quickly and each side reverts back to traditional managerial principles. Though the new participatory mechanisms are certainly a necessary step for designing effective workplace systems, they are not sufficient for addressing the unequal distribution of the social costs of technology. And, often, they become an excuse to do nothing.

Perhaps the most revealing American example is that of the joint labor-management programs of AT&T, the Bell operating companies, and the three major unions of the telecommunications industry. Few industries have seen more technological change in the past decade than telecommunications, and few corporations have had more experience with viewing technology as an element in a far-ranging organizational change.[2]

Participation in the telecommunications industry was the product of both equity and efficiency concerns. Technological development in the Bell system had traditionally been a classic example of some of the worst features of the technocentric model, where system engineers and technicians from Bell labs set the technical standards and work organizations used throughout the entire Bell system. It had been highly centralized with engineers and systems designers at Bell Laboratories creating the systems used throughout the entire telecommunications network.

With the rapid computerization of telephone work in the 1970s, workers in the industry suffered the spectrum of social costs typically associated with the technocentric approach—including the erosion of job skills and autonomy, increased job pressures, and occupational stress (Howard, 1980, 1985b; Kohl, 1982). In addition to the negative impact of these changes on employee morale, Bell System managers were especially concerned that the workforce and work systems at the Bell operating companies were especially ill-suited to compete in the deregulated telecommunications environment that was rapidly taking shape. In response to these dual concerns of declining employee morale and growing worker protests, on the one hand, and managerial concerns about efficiency, on the other, the 1980 Bell System collective-bargaining negotiations established a network of joint labor-management committees designed to address some of the problems associated with rapid technological and organization change.

One was a National Committee on Joint Working Conditions and Service Quality Improvement, consisting of three company representatives and three union representatives. It was mandated to set up a system-wide QWL program consisting of shopfloor QWL committees. Although the letter of agreement establishing the program did not refer specifically to technology, for the unions this was clearly one of the many work-related issues that the Bell system QWL program would address.

The two sides also established joint Technology Change Committees where, according to the language of the formal letter of agreement, the unions could "discuss major technological changes with management before they are introduced" (AT&T-CWA, 1980). Unlike the shopfloor QWL committees, they exist on a much higher level of authority. Each AT&T division and Bell operating company has its own committee, usually consisting of three upper-level corporate managers and three full-time district union officials. As part of this provision, the corporation also agreed to provide the union with six months' advance notice of all major technological changes.[3]

Five years after the establishment of these joint labor-management participation programs, it seems clear that the Bell system QWL committees have been an important vehicle for building workers' informal participatory practice at the local level. According to a recent study sponsored by the U.S. Department of Labor (Communications Workers of America et al., 1984:1), the Bell system QWL effort is "one of the largest worker participation programs in the country." At the time of the Bell system divestiture in January 1984, there were more than 1,200 shopfloor QWL committees in operation throughout AT&T, involving nearly 15,000 unionized employees. And these QWL team members reported levels of job satisfaction 12 percent higher than those of the Bell system as a whole.

Though most of the committees have dealt primarily with environmental issues (improving the physical office environment, ameliorating local management practices and attitudes) in a few cases, they have gone further to touch upon issues of work organization and job redesign—for example, instituting flexitime programs or reorganizing office scheduling procedures in order to give workers some choice over their work hours. However, as the committees have moved closer to addressing issues that transcend the immediate workplace and involve company-wide policies about technology development, they have encountered some major obstacles. The choices and decisions about technology made by these technical personnel are largely beyond the capacity of local QWL groups to address (Howard, 1985b).

A case in point is what, for a time, was perhaps the most dramatic QWL success story, AT&T's new Hotel Office Business Information System (HOBIS) office in Tempe, Arizona. Under the guidance of a manager sympathetic to the QWL concept, the office was planned in close cooperation with a QWL team. The committee developed a new work organization consisting of autonomous work groups in which some 120 office workers scheduled and performed their jobs without any first-line supervision. The savings resulting from the group's reorganization plan (estimated at $250,000 in supervisors' salaries alone) were put aside in a discretionary fund controlled by the committee and used to finance workers' participation in company training programs.

However, in November 1985, executives at AT&T corporate headquarters decided for economic reasons to consolidate the Tempe facility with another HOBIS office in a different location. Despite the opposition of the local QWL committee and the Communications Workers of America (CWA) international, the Tempe office was closed and its promising experiment in worker autonomy cancelled. While some of the innovations developed in the Tempe HOBIS facility have been used in other AT&T offices, none has recreated the same degree of worker autonomy enjoyed by the Tempe workforce.

In theory, the Technology Change Committees, also established in the 1980 contract, are supposed to be the forum where these broader policy issues about technology can be addressed. Also, the six months' advance-notice provision, at least potentially, provides a way for workers' union representatives to be involved in company planning before systems reach the workplace. However, of the three joint committees established in 1980, the Technology Change Committees have been the least successful.

The formal union rights defined by the Technology Change Committees provision are extremely limited. The committees are primarily a vehicle for "notification" in which "the Company will advise the union of its plans with respect to the introduction of [technological] changes and will familiarize the union with the progress being made" (AT&T-CWA, 1980). The unions do not have the right to participate in the actual conception, design, or testing of new technical systems. Nor do the committees have any authority to make policy decisions or binding agreements about the technology development process. At best, the committees can only develop "facts and recommendations so that the company can make well-informed decisions regarding technological change" (AT&T-CWA, 1980).

The practice of the Technology Change Committees has reflected this narrow conception of participation. A Harvard Business School study[4] conducted in 1983 found that, in the first three years of the program, nearly two-thirds of the committees had yet to have a single meeting. Where they had, the management participants called the meetings, set the agenda, decided what issues would be discussed, and determined how much information about management plans would be provided to their union counterparts. In a survey of Technology Change Committee members, conducted as part of the Harvard study, over half of the union representatives who responded reported that management regularly failed to provide them with the mandatory six months' advance notice of major technological changes—a clear violation of the 1980 contract.

At times management involvement in the committees seems expressly designed to insulate management decision making about technology from effective influence on the part of the telecommunications unions. For example, the typical management representatives on the committees are labor relations personnel; their background and experience is in dealing with unions, not managing technological change. (In one case, management participants prepared their formal presentations beforehand with company lawyers, in order to avoid providing union officials with information that might prove useful in collective bargaining.) The engineers, systems designers, and other technical personnel who are responsible for determining how technology will be designed and used are rarely committee members. And those labor relations personnel who are on the committees often do not have basic information about new technical systems and their expected impacts—putting them in a position of ignorance not all that different from that of their union counterparts. (One point on which both management and union respondents to the Harvard Business School survey agree is that the prime obstacle to the effectiveness of the Technology Change Committees is their "lack of timely knowledge about the types of systems to be developed.") To the degree that line managers or engineers themselves try to make the innovation process more responsive to social concerns, they do so, not through the Technology Change Committee but independent of it. This means that the official participative structure is bypassed.

As for the idea that, through the committees, unionists might actually influence company planning and development of new technology, a full 75 percent of union participants said the discussion in their committee had never resulted in changes in the implementation of new technical systems or in their design.

Part of the problem is with the union representatives themselves. In general, they are full-time district officials who are usually quite removed from the new technological systems and their impacts on the shop floor. And their work on the committee is just one small part of their overall responsibilities. In general, the unions have barely begun to think through what it would take to make concrete their hopes for a substantial role in the development of new technology. They have not committed the necessary resources—in terms of personnel, training, time, or money—in order to effectively influence the technological change process.

Thus, despite considerable progress in developing informal practice through the shopfloor QWL committees, the lack of formal rights of participation in company decision making about technology has limited the impact of the telecommunications worker participation effort. A 1984 report from the CWA Development and Research Department (Straw and Hecksher, 1984) captured this ambiguous result: "Though the QWL process has led to improved relations and less burdensome supervision in many offices, it has not reached to the fundamental policies which shape the development of new technologies. It seems that for every improvement in individual locations, a dozen systems come from Bell Laboratories reinforcing the dehumanizing patterns we are battling." And the effectiveness of the Technology Change Committees, the report continued, "has been limited by the resistance of management . . . and by the lack of experience of union participants. As a result, membership attitude surveys over the past three years have shown, if anything, increasing levels of discontent with job pressures."

Participation in the Service of Social Interests

There is another concept of participation that transcends some of the limitations of the organization-centered approach. It is based on the premise that participation should include the possibility (indeed, the likelihood) of conflicting interests in the workplace. Such an approach might be termed the "negotiation" model.

According to this perspective, instead of depending on shared interests, participation would be the process by which interest groups balance their various concerns about efficiency and equity and negotiate tradeoffs between those concerns when they differ. In economic terms, participation becomes a mechanism for "internalizing" the social costs of technological change and bargaining their distribution in a particular work organization (Ciborra, 1983a, 1983b).

In order for this to happen, however, participation must also include sharing power or influence. As Pacey (1983: 157) writes, "to engage in a genuinely open dialogue is inevitably to share power over the final decision." Such influence can take two basic forms: "formal rights" giving workers an explicit role to play in company decision making concerning new technology; and "informal practice" or the constantly evolving activities, knowledge, and expertise that workers can bring to bear on company technology policies in the workplace itself.

The relationship between these two forms of influence is especially important. Without formal rights, informal participatory practice, however elaborate, runs the risk of becoming unstable, particularly when workers' interests do conflict with those of technology designers or management. However, in the absence of active (and informed) informal practice, even the most explicit formal rights usually remain unrealized. It is precisely the interplay of strong formal rights and robust informal practice that makes for effective worker participation.

Finally, a concept of participation as negotiation would also expand the scope of worker participation in technological change. A broad participatory scope would, first, extend worker influence beyond merely discussing the impacts of technology (such as takes place in the U.S. telecommunications industry Technology Change Committees) to the very choices that shape how technology is developed and designed. In other words, it would involve a concept and method of "participatory systems design" (Nygaard, 1983). Second, it would extend worker influence beyond both technical and organizational issues to include the social goals of the entire work organization.

The negotiation model of worker participation in technological change is far more common in Europe than in the United States. Participatory experiments in European countries often have an explicit social component, and efforts in specific workplaces occur within a broad social context of formal collective-bargaining agreements and national work environment legislation. Often, this serves to create a social framework that influences the form and the content of worker participation at particular firms.

Perhaps the most advanced version of the negotiation model can be found in the Scandinavian countries, particularly Norway. For more than twenty years there has been a strong tradition of worker participation in Norway. In the early 1960s the Norwegian Industrial Democracy project spread joint labor-management participation experiments throughout industrial enterprises. Many of these early efforts at participation were similar in form to current American QWL initiatives (in fact, some of the recent U.S. initiatives are modeled on these early Scandinavian experiences).

However, in the late 1960s Norwegian unions began to grow dissatisfied with the limits of these joint labor-management projects, particularly in the area of workplace technological change. They found that technology often was the source of conflicts of interest between labor and management that made cooperation nearly impossible. Thus, unions began to search for ways to develop their own independent strategy to address workplace technology issues.

An important contribution to this goal was a unique social dialogue between the unions and a small but influential group of Norwegian computer scientists and systems designers. Often working at government research centers, these technical experts were sympathetic to the unions' goals and joined with them in a series of action research projects aimed to build local union expertise on technology issues. These projects stimulated union activism and eventually led to the negotiations of the first labor-management collective-bargaining agreements on technological change, known as the Technology Agreements, in the mid-1970s.

The first national Framework Agreement was negotiated and signed by the Norwegian Employers Confederation (NAF) and the Trades Union Congress (LO) in 1975. Since then, similar agreements have also been negotiated in the public sector. And some of the provisions of the Technology Agreements have also been written into law in Norway's 1977 Work Environment Act (Hjort, 1983; Schneider, 1984).

Unlike initiatives in this country to encourage worker participation on technology issues, the Norwegian Technology Agreements establish a comprehensive array of formal worker and union rights. Unions not only have the right of access to company information about new technical systems, they also can participate in company decision making about technology and bargain over company plans. In other words, negotiation about technology has become a legitimate part of the collective-bargaining relationship between managements and unions.

Local unions can negotiate local technology agreements that elaborate on and occasionally expand the rights defined in the national agreements. They also have the right to elect a permanent local union representative responsible for technology issues—known as the "data shop steward"—and to hire outside "technology consultants" (at company expense) to help them research the impacts of technology and prepare their collective-bargaining demands (Nygaard and Fjalestad, 1979; Keul, 1983; Schneider, 1984).

But the Technology Agreements have not only articulated new worker rights. They have been designed to expressly encourage the development of informal participatory practice so that workers and their union representatives can successfully put these new rights into effect (Elden, 1981; Finne and Rasmussen, 1982). For example, according to the agreements, workers are guaranteed both job-related training on specific technical systems and general education about computer technology and its design. And, under the provisions of the Work Environment Act, some 150,000 Norwegian workers (nearly 10 percent of the entire workforce) have completed, on company time, a forty-hour basic training course in techniques for analyzing and improving their workplace (Gustavsen and Hunnius, 1981).

In the immediate aftermath of the Technology Agreements, there was a tendency on the part of many unions to assume that the very existence of their new rights was sufficient to increase worker influence over technological change. Union locals would pursue what might be termed an after-the-fact strategy. They would wait for new technical systems to be introduced in the workplace, then bargain with management over the details of work assignments, wage rates, and the like, much as they had in the past.

However, some unions soon realized that if they waited until new technology was appearing on the shop floor, it was already too late. They began to formulate a before-the-fact approach that extends union and worker participation into the planning stages of technology development and also into broader questions about the organization of work.

These two factors—an emphasis on both general formal rights and local informal practice, and the conviction that union involvement must take place before the fact and extend to broad issues of work organization—have allowed Norwegian workers to move beyond narrow function-based participation (such as management-directed participation programs that conceive users as performers of functions) and to experiment with participation based on social interests. It has also made possible the extension of worker participation from narrow technical issues and goals (which vendor to choose, how best to configure a specific system, and so forth) to the organizational and social criteria and choices that shape technology in the first place.

To grasp the extremely broad extent of participation in Norwegian industry, consider the example of the Norwegian post office.[5] In the late 1970s the Norwegian postal authorities inaugurated a large development project to automate the accounting functions in about 450 local post offices across the country. As is typical throughout Norwegian industry, the postal workers union negotiated representation on the formal project steering committee to oversee the development of this new system. Two experienced union members participated in three project subgroups—one developing system specifications, one analyzing training and work environment issues, and a third devoted to ergonomics.

The presence of these union workers on the steering committee proved very important in the early stages of the project, but not in the way that the union had hoped. The workers found that their role was primarily that of "end user informants" rather than as representatives of the union's interests. In other words, the technical team wanted their advice on various technical aspects of the system. This role was not unimportant. The workers' knowledge about work processes and organizational problems helped the systems designers to develop reasonably accurate specifications for the counter transactions to be automated. However, the unionists involved found that they were becoming preoccupied with planning the technical details of the new system—what they called becoming "hostage" to the technology—rather than examining what the impacts of the new system might be and whether they were desirable or not.

Convinced that it needed to broaden the scope of worker participation and union involvement in the project, the union requested that management commission a study of the work environment consequences of the new technology. An outside consultant from the Norwegian Computing Center, a public research institute, assembled two informal worker research teams consisting of sixteen postal employees drawn from a variety of occupational categories and from post offices all over the country.[6] These teams set out, not merely to analyze the prospective impacts of the new system, but to actually develop a set of social, organizational, and technical criteria which would guide the development of the system itself.

Instead of starting with the proposed system specifications already developed by the design team, the worker participation groups began by analyzing their own work organization. From this analysis, they developed criteria for the kind of work organization most desirable from a social point of view. Then they evaluated the systems specifications developed by the design team against these criteria, suggesting numerous changes.

For example, the specifications had originally foreseen the establishment of data-entry centers where data would be read into the new automated system. To avoid the creation of what they considered to be narrow and monotonous data-entry jobs, the groups recommended that optical character readers be installed in each local office.

The original specifications had also called for worker access to information by means of video display terminals (VDTs) placed to the side of each post office window. However, because the space at each window was so limited and because they worried that VDT operation could potentially disrupt contact with customers and become an obstacle to quality service, the groups recommended that the VDTs be replaced with a small movable "text window" adequate for the information that workers would need.

It should be emphasized that worker research teams had no formal status in the technology design process. However, they came to have a great deal of influence. Although the changes they recommended were controversial and, at times, expensive, they were able to influence major aspects of the system specifications. One reason is that they had union support. There were strong ties between the formal union representatives on the design team and the union members involved in the informal worker research effort. Another reason is that, in the course of their fifteen-month research effort, they made themselves into the resident experts on the relationship between technology and work organization at the post office. This new expertise was something to which the design team and management had to respond.

The effort at the Norwegian post office concerned the development of a specific technical system. Other Norwegian unions have tried to institutionalize broad participation across the spectrum of workplace technology issues. In the process, they have systematically included union social goals and one criteria in the technological change process.

An appropriate example is the work of the Norwegian Bank Employees Union (NBF).[7] One important aspect that has shaped this situation is that women make up approximately half of the union's 26,000 members. They hold the lowest level jobs (usually those to be automated first), and nearly 70 percent work part time. According to a union-sponsored survey, 68 percent of these women have had no formal professional training.

These factors have shaped the union's technology policy. The NBF is especially concerned that, as new technology transforms jobs in the banking industry, requiring new kinds of skills and more formal work knowledge, many of the union's women members will become trapped in a progressively smaller low-wage ghetto and will be passed over for promotion to the skilled jobs that technology may create.

Therefore, the union has tried to design its technology policy so that it furthers social goals of equal opportunity in the banking industry. For example, as new technologies reorganize work, access to training becomes a determining factor of opportunity in the workplace. In the Norwegian banking industry, union and management have set aside a minimum of 40 percent of the places in their joint industry training center for women. This is an extremely important step because promotions and salary increases depend upon completing institute courses.

The union has also negotiated special access to training for worker mothers—including five hours per week of education study on company time for all women with children ten years old or younger.

Union technology policy also states that technology should be used not only to rationalize work but also to improve the quality of both workers' jobs and customer service. It sees participation in technology development as only one part of a broad participatory process. Union officials like to talk about the "three legs of the stool"—three areas of participation necessary in any effective work organization: technology development, organizational development, and personnel development. This way, technology does not become isolated from other factors, in particular, the organizational and social needs of the workforce.

The NBF has developed elaborate structures to guarantee its participation in technology development. The union has its own internal technology policy committee, which develops and implements the union action program for new technology (revised and updated every two years); the members of the committee are also the union representatives on the steering committees of major industry technology development projects.

Union representatives also participate actively in the design of new computer-based systems both nationally and locally. For example, in November 1982 Norway's twenty-one savings banks announced a joint project to design and implement a $70 million state-of-the-art computer system in 300 branch banks over a four-year period. Over eighty bank employees from a variety of jobs (expedition clerks, back office clerks, tellers, and others) were involved in developing the preliminary system specifications for the applications software. Ten working groups (each consisting of eight users and one technical specialist) met for three two-day sessions every month for a five-month period. Between meetings, the user participants returned to their workplaces to discuss and evaluate proposed recommendations with their coworkers. Once the recommendations were finalized, someone from the group was chosen to write up the findings as formal system specifications.

When systems designers at the banking industry's research and development center proposed the acquisition of an automated loan-processing system, a union-management team at the largest savings bank chain in eastern Norway evaluated it to determine whether the proposed system was consistent with organizational goals. The team, made up of managers and workers from local branches, suggested a number of changes. For example, whereas the systems designers had planned to build loan criteria directly into the system (this was also true for the loan limits of individual loan officers), the union wanted the individual bank worker to retain the decision-making power to grant or not to grant loans. They also suggested that the dialogue between user and the computer be flexible so that data could be entered in any order rather than in one specific way. The group argued that these recommendations would improve both the quality of workers' jobs and the services provided to customers.

It should be pointed out that, although the NBF counts on the formal rights of union participation as the foundation of this elaborate participatory process, the union realizes that these formal rights are not sufficient. For example, unlike other Norwegian unions, the NBF does not use the data shop steward system, in the belief that setting up worker technical experts can become an obstacle to broad worker participation on technology issues. Thus, the worker representatives in systems design projects are usually normal shop stewards or rank-and-file workers.

The union also emphasizes the importance of developing informal relationships or alliances with bank technical personnel, in an ongoing effort to educate them about the union's social goals for technology. This relationship has developed to the point where some designers at the bank industry's research and development center see union and worker participation as the preferred approach to creating new technical systems.[8]

One should emphasize that this kind of worker participation in technological change is always a balancing act. There is an ongoing effort, not always successful, both to use the formal rights provided by collective-bargaining agreements and legislation and, at the same time, to develop the informal practices which make those rights effective. From this perspective, participation is a kind of learning process, alternating between moments of cooperation and moments of negotiation over conflicting interests and goals. Workers are able to ask questions about changing fundamental aspects of their organizations (Argyris, 1983a; 1983b). What is more, informal cooperation becomes possible precisely because management recognizes the union's formal rights. And, where interests of union and management conflict, the existence of these formal rights can become especially important.[9]

The work of Norwegian unions with the Technology Agreements does not eliminate all obstacles to worker participation in technological change. Nor are the specific mechanisms of participation, part of the unique social, political, and labor relations climate of the Scandinavian countries, easily translated to other contexts. However, the Norwegian experience does constitute an intriguing example of participation as a true negotiating process, one that, far from being limited to discrete projects or experiments, represents a new model for the overall organization of working life.

Barriers to Worker Participation

The extensive worker participation in technological change reflected in Norwegian union work with the Technology Agreements does not take place in a vacuum. Any participatory project faces a number of obstacles or barriers that threaten to constrain either the interests subject to participation, the degree of influence that workers actually have, or the scope of issues open to participation. What follows is a brief list of the most common of these obstacles.

Obviously, firms with a disadvantageous market position can find participation based on social interests especially difficult to maintain. When near-term competitive pressures are overwhelming, the short-term costs that participation can entail become too expensive. Often, worker participation is relegated to the back burner of both managerial and union priorities.

For example, workers at the Norwegian conglomerate Viking Askim (a manufacturer of automobile tires and rubber boots) were among the first in the Norwegian labor movement to develop a local technology agreement, dating back to the late 1960s. However, during the past decade the firm has faced increased international competition, which has forced the closing of some of its Norwegian operations and the shifting of production abroad, primarily to Southeast Asia. Faced with economic crisis and declining jobs, both management and union at Viking Askim have tended to see participation in technological change as a secondary concern, far less important than the more immediate priorities of economic restructuring and saving jobs.

At the same time, other firms see participation as an important means to becoming more responsive to competitive markets. This is certainly the case both at AT&T and the Norwegian banks. In both cases, work organizations that previously enjoyed a quasi-monopoly position are now confronted with new kinds of competition. In both situations technology plays a crucial role in determining ultimate competitiveness. Participation has become a mechanism to improve the organization's ability to adapt to both changing technology and changing markets.

A second potential barrier to broad worker participation in technological change is the state of technology itself. Indeed, one can think of the opportunity for participation throughout the period of development of any particular technology as a kind of bell-shaped curve. Early applications of the technology often take place when both the technology and the uses to which it can be put are poorly understood. Technology experts dominate the situation and narrow technical concerns loom large. Broad participation in such a situation can prove extremely difficult if not impossible. As particular applications of the technology become better understood, however, organizational flexibility and, along with it, the possibility for participation expand. Finally, when the particular application becomes mature, the possibility for participation may decline once again as clearly defined package systems become the sensible option from an economic point of view.

Certainly, the development of computer-based technical systems reflect this trend. In the early phases the technocentric approach predominated. In the second phase, as the technology itself has increased in flexibility, the organization-centered approach and user participation has become more popular. But already-packaged systems are making any but the most superficial function-based participation difficult to put into effect. For example, in Norway, many unions have found that the increasing tendency of companies to rely on system packages (often designed in the United States, where the social concerns of the Norwegian unions are often less successfully articulated) has become an obstacle to their ability to influence how workplace technology is designed.

However, there is another argument that suggests that computer-based systems, unlike previous technologies, presents unique opportunities for participation. As the automation of discrete functions is increasingly replaced by the integration of entire computerized work systems, effective work will increasingly depend upon broad worker knowledge of both technology and the work organization itself. Participation may prove to be the most effective means for ensuring that that knowledge is widespread throughout the firm. In this respect, the evolution of workplace computer technology may actually require more worker participation, not less.

Another potential barrier is not so much technological as organizational—the ingrained practices and habits of thinking and working that influence (and, often, inhibit) what can be described as the organizational learning process. Using new technology effectively seems to require thinking about it in a new way. Instead of seeing technology management as merely a technical process (whether for the techniques of Taylorism or user participation), it conceives the design and development of new workplace technical systems as fundamentally social (or even political)—that is, as central to the realization of the goals and values of the organization as a social institution. From this perspective technology management is simply one facet of a much broader task—the overall organizational development of the firm. And precisely because technology is so important, it cannot be left to managers alone. Rather, it becomes the responsibility of both managers and workers, with company and union as equal partners.

But this still will not ensure that participation will extend to the social interests that various social groups bring to the workplace. One final barrier to the broad worker participation that we have described is the absence of formal institutions to represent worker interests in the workplace. When participation is managed entirely by management, there is a tendency in situations of conflict to revert to narrow business interests or to do away with participation altogether. This tendency to view participation as taking place entirely at the level of the individual firm ensures that participation will almost always remain hostage to the imperatives of efficiency and competitiveness. The idea of negotiating social tradeoffs between equity and efficiency will be weighted to the latter.

Part of the solution is similar to that developed in other areas of working life, such as occupational health and safety: to create a regulatory environment extending beyond the individual firm that, in effect, takes technology out of competition and sets certain standards or criteria for working life across the entire economy. This has been the impact, for example, of the Work Environment Act in Norway. This same mechanism is at work in occupational health and safety, equal opportunity, and minimum wage legislation in this and other industrial countries.

Of course, this is no simple task, especially when long-term social interests come into conflict with the immediate demands of international competition. However, it may be that this broader conception of worker participation in technological change is one part of a long-term evolution of labor relations in industrial societies. And one step in the creation of new institutions more suitable to an economic world founded on innovation and change.

Notes

1. Of course, these three stages of the technology development process are abstractions. This is not to imply that the process has a discrete beginning, middle, and end. In fact, systems design is an ongoing, iterative process. Once particular systems are in place, they are constantly being updated, maintained, and adapted to new uses. This makes user participation all the more necessary.

2. There are three unions representing workers at AT&T and the Bell operating companies—the Communications Workers of America (CWA), the Telecommunications International Union (TIU), and the International Brotherhood of Electrical Workers (IBEW). In 1980, AT&T established Quality of Worklife (QWL) committees with each of the three unions. The examples used in these pages are drawn from the experience of the CWA and TIU.

3. When more than one union represented workers in a particular AT&T division or Bell operating company, a separate Technology Change Committee was established with each union. The 1980 Bell system collective-bargaining agreement also established a joint Occupational Job Evaluation committee. The work of this group is not considered here.

4. Dr. Schneider conducted this study in conjunction with Professor Richard E. Walton. The following information is based upon as yet unpublished personal interviews and survey data from that research project.

5. The description of worker participation at the Norwegian post office is based, in large part, on internal reports from the Norwegian Computing Center to the Norwegian Postal Directorate and on personal interviews conducted by the authors.

6. The worker participants were jointly chosen by management and the union. Although involvement in the union was not a formal criteria for selection, most of the participants were in fact union activitists.

7. This example is based on personal interviews conducted by the authors.

8. According to the NBF official responsible for technology issues: "It used to be that there was always a big discussion about precisely when the union should be informed. The question was, 'When does a pre-project actually become a formal project?' Now, our attitude is, 'The moment an idea strikes you, that's the time to call the union and begin discussing it.'"

9. As the NBF official says, "You can cooperate on these issues, because management, by and large, has come to recognize the union as an equal partner. They have also recognized that technology has social costs. They may not consider

it as much of a problem as we do, but at least they recognize that, when you implement technology, you have to deal with the social and organizational consequences. When they stop listening, the union can always bang our little green collective bargaining contract and data policy on the table. Usually, that is enough to begin the dialogue again."

References

Adler, Paul. 1983. "Rethinking the Skill Requirements of New Technologies." Working paper HBS 84-27, Harvard Business School, Harvard University.

Argyris, Chris. 1983a. *Reasoning, Learning and Action.* San Francisco: Jossey-Bass.

———. 1983b. *Strategy, Change and Defensive Routines.* Boston: Pitman.

AT&T-CWA. 1980. *National Bargaining Report.* Washington, D.C.: Communications Workers of America.

Bancroft, Nancy H. 1982. "Productivity in the Office." Prepared for the Manufacturing Distribution and Control Business Group, Digital Equipment Corporation. Westminster,Mass.: Office Systems Consulting.

Bancroft, Nancy H., Enid Mumford, and Bonnie Sontag. n.d. "Participative Design—Successes and Problems." Unpublished paper, Digital Equipment Corporation.

Bermann, Tamar. 1984. "Not Only Windmills: Female Service Workers and New Technologies." Published in the proceedings from the IFIP (International Federation for Information Processing, Work Group 9.1) Conference on "Women, Work and Computerization" held at Riva del Sole, Italy, Sept. 17-21, 1984.

Brooks, Harvey et al. 1984. *Technology and the Need for New Labor Relations.* Discussion Paper 129D, John Fitzgerald Kennedy School of Government, Harvard University.

Ciborra, Claudio. 1983a. "The Social Costs of Information Technology and Participation in System Design." In U. Briefs, C. Ciborra, and L. Schneider, eds., *Systems Design for, with, and by the User,* 41-50. Amsterdam, New York, Oxford: North Holland.

———. 1983b. "Bargaining Over the Social Costs of Information Technology." In Daniel Marschall and Judith Gregory, eds., *Office Automation: Jekyll or Hyde?,* 22-29. Cleveland, Ohio: Working Women Education Fund.

———. 1985. "Reframing the Role of Computers in Organization: The Transaction Costs Approach." In Lynn Gallegos et al., eds., *Proceedings of the Sixth International Conference on Information Systems,* 57-69. Indianapolis: Society for Information Management and Association for Computing Machinery.

Communications Workers of America. 1984. "The Quality of Work Life Process of AT&T and the Communications Workers of America: A Research Study After Three Years." Condensed version of the report on the Quality of Work Life research project submitted to the U.S. Department of Labor. Washington, D.C.: Communication Workers of America.

Elden, Max. 1981. "Varieties of Workplace Participatory Research." Unpublished paper, Center for Effective Organizations, Graduate School of Business Administration, University of Southern California, Los Angeles.

Fellesdata, A.S. 1983. "Sammendrag Av Bankrettet Kravspesifikasjon for Ny Terminal." Unpublished paper. Prepared for the Bankrettet gruppe i NTG.

Finne, Hakon, and Bente Rasmussen. 1982. *Strategic Competence and Learning from Experience: A Course Model for Improving Local Trade Union Action.* Norway: Institute for Social Research in Industry (IFIM).

Fjalestad, Jostein. 1980. "Teknologi og Deltaking." Prepared for Norsk Regnesentral/Norwegian Computing Center, Oslo, Norway.

Fossum, E., ed. 1983. *Computerization of Working Life.* New York, Brisbane, Chichester, Toronto: Halsted Press (a division of John Wiley & Son).

Gustavsen, Bjorn, and Gerry Hunnius. 1981. *New Patterns of Work Reform: The Case of Norway.* Oslo, Bergen, Tromso: Universitetsforlaget.

Hayashi, Masaki. 1983. "The Japanese Style of Small Group QC-Circle Activity." Tokyo: The Institute of Business Research, Chuo University.

Hirschhorn, Larry. 1984. *Beyond Mechanization: Work and Technology in a Postindustrial Age.* Cambridge, Mass. and London, England: The MIT Press.

Hjort, Lisbet. 1983. "Labor Legislation in Norway: Its Applications to the Introduction of New Technology." In Daniel Marschall and Judith Gregory, eds., *Office Automation: Jekyll or Hyde?,* 143–49. Cleveland, Ohio: Working Women Education Fund.

Howard, Robert. 1980. "Brave New Workplace." *Working Papers for a New Society* 7(6):21–31.

———. 1985a. "Utopia: Where Workers Craft New Technology." *Technology Review* 88(3):43–49.

———. 1985b. *Brave New Workplace.* New York: Elisabeth Sifton Books, Viking Press.

Keen, Peter G. W. 1982. Editor's preface. *Office: Technology and People* 1(1):1–11.

Kelley, Maryellen R. 1984. "Computer-oriented Machines and the Disruption of Workplace Productivity: Establishing a New Labor-Management Relationship." In *Technology and the Need for New Labor Relations,* discussion paper 129D, John F. Kennedy School of Government, Harvard University.

Keul, Vidar. 1983. "Trade Union Planning and Control of New Technology." In U. Briefs, C. Ciborra, and L. Schneider, eds., *Systems Design for, with, and by the User,* 207–18. Amsterdam, New York, Oxford: North Holland.

Kohl, George. 1982. "Changing Competitive and Technology Environments in Telecommunications." In Donald Kennedy, Charles Craypo, and Mary Lehman, eds., *Labor and Technology: Union Response to Changing Environments,* 53–76. University Park: Pennsylvania State University, Department of Labor Studies.

Lanzara, Giovan Francesco. 1983. "The Design Process: Frames,Metaphors, and Games." In U. Briefs, C. Ciborra, and L. Schneider, eds., *Systems Design for, with, and by the User,* 29–40. Amsterdam, New York, Oxford: North Holland.

Mathiassen, Lars. 1981. *Systemudvikling og systemudviklingsmetode* (Systems development and systems development method). Department of Computer Science, University of Arhus, Denmark.

Noble, David F. 1984. *Forces of Production: A Social History of Industrial Automation.* New York: Alfred A. Knopf.

Norske Bankfunksjonaerers Forbund. 1983. *Malsettings-og handlingsprogram.* Oslo, Norway.

Nygaard, Kristen. 1983. "Participation in System Development: The Tasks Ahead." In U. Briefs, C. Ciborra, and L. Schneider, eds., *Systems Design for, with, and by the User,* 19–25. Amsterdam, New York, Oxford: North Holland.

Nygaard, Kristen, and Jostein Fjalestad. 1979. "Group Interests and Participation in Information System Development." Paper presented to the Special Session on Microelectronics, Productivity, and Employment. Working party on Information, Computer and Communications Policy, OECD, Paris, Nov. 27–29, 1979.

Pacey, Arnold. 1983. *The Culture of Technology.* Cambridge, Mass.: The MIT Press.

Piore, Michael J., and Charles F. Sabel. 1984. *The Second Industrial Divide: Possibilities for Prosperity.* New York: Basic Books Inc.

Sabel, Charles. 1982. *Work and Politics: The Division of Labor in Industry.* Cambridge: Cambridge University Press.

Schneider, Leslie. 1984. "Technology Bargaining in Norway." In *Technology and the Need for New Labor Relations,* Discussion paper 129D, John F. Kennedy School of Government, Harvard University.

Shaiken, Harley. 1984. *Work Transformed: Automation and Labor in the Computer Age.* New York: Holt, Rinehart and Winston.

Sheil, B. A. 1983. "Coping with Complexity." *Office: Technology and People* 1:295–320.

Strassmann, Paul A. 1985. *Information Payoff: The Transformation of Work in the Electronic Age.* New York: The Free Press.

Straw, Ronnie J., and Charles Hecksher. 1984. U.S. Report. *QWL Focus: The News Journal of the Ontario Quality of Work Life Center* 4(1).

Suchman, Lucy A., and Eleanor Wynn. 1979. "Procedures and Problems in the Office Environment." Unpublished paper, Xerox, Advanced Systems Department, Palo Alto, Cal.

Suchman, Lucy A. 1980. "Office Procedures as Practical Action: Theories of Work and Software Design." Presented at the Workshop of Research in Office Semantics, June 15–18, 1980; Chatham, Mass.

Thoresen, Kari. 1980. *Skrankemaskiner og Arbeidsmiljø.* Oslo: Norsk Regnesentral.

Tranøy, Espen. 1983. *Sannsynlige Utviklingstrinn I Framtidens Bank.* Prepared for the Norske Bankfunksjonaerers Forbund.

van Beinum, Hans. 1981. "Organisational Choice and Micro-electronics." *QWL Focus: The News Journal of the Ontario Quality of Work Life Center* 1(3):1–6.

Walton, Richard E. 1982. "Social Choice in the Development of Advanced Information Technology." *Technology in Society* 4:41–49.

———. 1984. "From Control to Commitment: Transforming Work Force Management in the United States." Prepared for the Harvard Business School's 75th Anniversary Colloquium on Technology and Productivity, March 27–29, 1984.

Walton, Richard E., and Wendy Vittori. 1983. "New Information Technology: Organizational Problem or Opportunity?" *Office: Technology and People,* May 1983, 249–73.

Wynn, Eleanor H. 1983. "The User as a Representation Issue in the U.S." In U. Briefs, C. Ciborra, and L. Schneider, eds., *Systems Design for, with, and by the User,* 349–58. Amsterdam, New York, Oxford: North Holland.

Zuboff, Shoshanna. 1982. "New Worlds of Computer-mediated Work." *Harvard Business Review* 60(5):142–52.

4

UNIONS, THE QUALITY OF WORK, AND TECHNOLOGICAL CHANGE IN SWEDEN

Andrew Martin

In recent years the Swedish trade union movement has been trying to work out a strategy for influencing technological development.[1] The ability to do so has come to be seen as essential to the achievement of work-quality objectives on which the unions have been putting increasing emphasis. In Sweden, as elsewhere, this emphasis has many sources. Among them is the growing dissatisfaction with Tayloristic modes of work organization, not only by new generations of workers but also by managers seeking ways to meet intensified competition by harnessing those workers' commitment to changing production strategies, particularly those facilitated by new computer-based technologies. The degree to which unions can articulate worker dissatisfaction and mobilize it to influence the character and extent of the shift toward new forms of work organization is bound to affect the viability of the unions' roles in the workplace and hence in the society beyond it.[2] Some union response to the challenge posed by pressures for change in work organization is thus an imperative of organizational viability.

The flux in work organization presents unions with opportunities as well as threats, opening up the possibility of reasserting demands for autonomy and satisfaction in work that are deeply rooted in the labor movement's ideological heritage but that had been subordinated in the instrumentalist bargain struck with "Fordist" mass production.[3] Of course, the strength of this strand in the labor movement's ideological heritage and the extent to which unions tap it in their response to the challenge of changing work organization vary considerably from country to country.[4] In Sweden this strand, couched in such familiar terms as *industrial democracy,* has emerged as a salient feature of the unions' current stance, after having been almost entirely obscured in the earlier postwar period.

As work-quality issues assumed growing importance for the Swedish labor movement, it found itself increasingly confronted by technological constraints on change in the content and organization of work. The scope for improving the quality of work was perceived as being significantly limited by technologies already in place. The unions were accordingly driven to seek a voice in the selection of technologies in order to bring work-quality considerations, specified from a worker perspective, to bear on those choices. But they found that even a strengthened voice in those choices could not affect the quality of work significantly insofar as the scope for doing so was limited by all the available alternatives. Thus, unions were driven to seek ways of assuring that work-quality considerations were already incorporated in the very design of the technologies that became available. The urgency attached to this imperative was intensified by the fundamental technological change being precipitated by the computer revolution. Computerization was recognized as having widely diverse potentials for enhancing or diminishing the quality of work, depending on the values that were incorporated in the design of computerized systems. To press their work-quality objectives effectively, then, the unions thought it had become particularly important to find ways to influence the design of computerization.

The tasks to which the unions were thereby drawn are difficult ones for them, for the tasks are very different from those which unions have historically carried out. Unions have been geared primarily to bargaining over wages and hours and providing some protection against arbitrary exercise of managerial authority—maintaining a modicum of due process or "constitutionalism" in the workplace. As a device for organizing joint action by workers, they have served as a means by which workers could in some measure offset and limit the power conferred on managers by the command over productive resources institutionalized in the organization of the firm. Their effectiveness has depended on their ability to turn numbers into power; the essential skills have been those of mobilization and negotiation, including expertise in the substance of negotiation over such matters as the details of wage scales and contractual rights. Their members could be the source of the requisite skills as well as the solidarity on which bargaining power rested, even as the skills came to be embodied in full-time union staffs.

Swedish unions have amassed an exceptional amount of power in terms of such resources. Their members comprised about 85 percent of the labor force as of 1983. Their capacity to mobilize this membership is facilitated by a high degree of internal centralization. It is also enhanced by the concentration of the membership in relatively few unions organized primarily along industrial and sectoral lines, although within these categories the unions are divided on broad occupational lines. Thus, there are three sets of unions, affiliated to three separate confederations. The largest and oldest is the Swedish Confederation of Labor (Landsorganisationen i Sverige, or LO), consisting of twenty-four unions organizing largely blue-collar workers and accounting for 52 percent of the labor force. The second largest is the Central Organization of Salaried Employees (Tjänstemännens Centralorganisation, or TCO), consisting of most of the unions organizing white-collar employees and accounting for 26 percent of the labor force. The smallest of the three is an organization of unions organizing upper-level white-collar employees with university degrees in their professions (SACO/SR) and accounting for 6 percent of the labor force.[5]

The confederations are also divided along political lines. Throughout its history, the LO has been politically identified and organizationally linked with the Social Democratic party, while the other two confederations are formally nonpartisan, embracing memberships with political loyalties spread across the whole political spectrum. Although the very high proportion of the labor force in unions consequently does not translate into a corresponding degree of electoral support for the Social Democrats, it goes a long way toward explaining why they have been able to control the government from 1932 to 1976 and again since 1982.

Extended Social Democratic rule has provided Swedish unions and particularly the LO with a political alternative to bargaining as a way of advancing their objectives. Although the unions have avoided resort to that alternative with respect to wages in the interest of preserving their autonomy in this central function, they have turned to it in connection with other objectives, including pensions and, more importantly for our purpose, union power to press workplace issues. Those issues had been kept beyond the reach of collective bargaining by the correspondingly encompassing and centralized private sector employers' organization, the Swedish Employers Confederation (Svenska Arbetsgivareforeningen, or SAF), which had long insisted that all issues concerning the organization and content of work fell within the exclusive domain of managerial prerogatives. Unable to overcome this barrier through negotiation, LO and TCO jointly succeeded in getting it removed by legislation in 1976. That was the culmination of a series of laws enacted over the preceding years that strengthened union and worker rights with respect to health and safety, job security, and position of local union officials.

Reflecting the unions' power in the Swedish political arena, then, the legislation of the 1970s opened up the way for unions to utilize their bargaining power in the market arena to press their work-quality objectives. It proved difficult for the unions to convert their newly won right to bargain over workplace issues into agreements regulating them in new ways, however, for in the changed political context defined by the shift in control of government from the Social Democrats to the three so-called bourgeois parties from 1976 to 1982, SAF felt able to resist the demands for a central agreement by which the general principles embodied in the legislation were translated into more detailed guidelines for industry and company level practice and for which LO and the negotiating organization of private sector white-collar unions Privattjänstemannakartellen (PTK) jointly pressed. But even if this source of difficulty could be overcome, as it was to some extent when a central agreement was finally reached in 1982, there remained and continues to remain another, in some respects more fundamental, source of difficulty.

The resources on which the unions' power in both the political and market arenas has been based, and the organizational forms for deploying those resources, do not equip them adequately to carry out the tasks involved in pursuing their work-quality objectives, particularly insofar as they are contingent on being able to influence technological development. To do so, it is essential to draw upon scientific and technical expertise, which is not the kind of expertise that has primarily been built into union staffs, whose size is in any case limited. Nor can the membership be a source of such expertise except in the case of unions organizing scientific and technical workers—even if workers' skills and experience remain a relevant source of knowledge about how specific kinds of work can be done.

On the other hand, the scientific or technical component of the relevant expertise, whose importance is growing as technologies such as those involving computers become increasingly science based, is precisely the kind of productive resource over which management is given virtually exclusive command by the organization of the firm. This gives management an overwhelming advantage over unions in defining the requirements that technological development is compelled to meet. That advantage can be offset only insofar as unions gain independent access to such resources and, in addition, insofar as both unions and those possessing the scientific and technical expertise learn how to utilize it for the unions' distinctive objectives. At a minimum, this requires the addition of such expertise to union staffs simply to enable them to tap external sources of expertise effectively. But the latter can never occur on a sufficient scale unless the way in which access to scientific and technical resources is institutionalized is changed—that is, unless the financing of research and development is changed in ways that permit unions to autonomously define the requirements to be met by technological development.

Having come up against this fundamental source of difficulty, the efforts of the Swedish labor movement to work out a strategy for influencing technological development have been focused on overcoming it by change both in their own organizational practice and in public policy concerning the social distribution of access to scientific and technical resources. This essay describes some aspects of these efforts.

The first of the two parts of the essay is an account of the evolution of the policies of the Swedish labor movement concerning technological change. The forces underlying the evolution are referred to only briefly. Instead, the discussion concentrates on the rationale provided for the policies in the documents in which they are set forth. Because the rationale is typically presented in some depth, it is possible to see how the relationship between technological change and union objectives has been understood as the objectives themselves have changed, culminating in the importance now attached to work-quality objectives.

To illustrate the challenge posed by the pursuit of those objectives, the second part of the essay is a case study of a technology development project that constitutes an especially promising approach to meeting the challenge. At the same time, the project, evocatively referred to as the UTOPIA project, also points clearly to difficulties that have their source not only in the social distribution of access to scientific and technical resources but also in conflict over changing work roles among different occupational groups built into the structure of the trade union movement.

The Evolution of Trade Union Technology Policy

The position of the Swedish labor movement on technological change has been shaped largely by the interaction of two concerns. One is the role of technological change in maintaining the economic basis of full employment and the welfare state. The other is the impact of technological change on the character of work.

The first has been an essentially constant factor throughout the history of the labor movement, particularly in the postwar half-century. The labor movement has relied heavily on the growth of the economy as a whole and on government action to stabilize that growth and allocate a large part of its fruits to advance its members' economic interests. This national, macroeconomic political orientation reflects the large portion of the labor force that the unions organize and the close links of the largest union confederation to the normally ruling party, along with a strong awareness of the vulnerability of Sweden's small, open economy to international competition. From this perspective, technological change has been viewed as an indispensable ingredient in the international viability of the economy, so that it is to be not only accepted but also encouraged.

The second factor is one that has been changing as the labor movement has given increasing attention to the quality of work. This is illustrated by the successive widening of the movement's conception of its occupational health and safety objectives. Initially confined to protection against physical injury in the narrow sense, the conception has gradually expanded to embrace psychological health in very broad terms, including not only protection against hazards such as stress and isolation but also provision of conditions for personal growth through participation and skill development. Stemming from a variety of sources, as suggested above, the increasing concern with the quality of work has evoked an increasingly critical attitude toward technological change and particularly toward the basis of management decisions determining the specific directions it takes. This has not led the Swedish labor movement to abandon its support of technological change, which is more than ever viewed as an imperative of the economy's viability. Instead, unions have sought to reconcile the requirements of that imperative with the requirements of the other objectives that have become increasingly salient. In the process, the terms on which technological change is acceptable have been redefined, becoming successively more stringent.

The resulting evolution of the position of the labor movement can be schematically broken down into four phases, each characterized by the assertion of a new condition for supporting technological change that is added to those set in preceding phases. The conditions marking each phase can be summarized as follows:

- manpower policy so designed and on such a scale as to enable all workers displaced by structural and technological change to get alternative jobs;
- industrial policy capable of channeling financial and technical resources into industrial expansion sufficient to assure new jobs to replace those eliminated by structural and technological change;
- extension of collective bargaining to workplace and enterprise decisions that affect workers' interests concerning the pace and composition of structural and technological change and the quality of jobs that result;
- union influence on the development of new technology that determines the scope for choice concerning the characteristics of jobs resulting from structural and technological change.

The evolution of trade union policy has thus been marked by an expansion in the scope of the conditions on which acceptance of technological change has been predicated. The successive conditions have also involved an increasing role in the process of structural and technological change for the state and, more recently, for the unions themselves.

In describing this evolution in trade union technology policy, the following discussion will draw primarily on the positions taken by the LO. The focus on LO policy rests on its dominance in terms of ideas as well as power over the postwar period as a whole. Thus, TCO's policy has generally developed along the same lines as LO's, although the multipartisan composition of its membership has compelled it to avoid positions identified closely with Social Democratic party policy. It is also only in more recent years that TCO has made technology policy a major focus of attention. It has now become equally active in this area, cooperating extensively with LO at the peak organization level, although the erosion of old demarcations between blue- and white-collar jobs by technological change has generated some jurisdictional conflict between LO and TCO unions.[6] With respect to union participation in technological development, TCO has to some extent taken the lead, particularly where its membership gives it access to the relevant technical resources that have become crucial for union participation. There is, of course, an even higher concentration of technical expertise in SACO, which has also developed a position on technology policy. However, the technical expertise of SACO's membership comprises the resources for research and development (R&D) addressed to problems defined from business and academic rather than trade union perspectives. How such resources can be mobilized in the service of the latter is primarily a problem with which LO and TCO are concerned.[7]

Phase 1: Facilitating Displaced Workers' Transition to Alternative Jobs

Manpower policy, or labor market policy as the Swedes prefer to call it, was specified as a condition for accepting structural and technological change within the framework of an overall strategy for managing the economy in which such change was viewed as a central feature. This strategy was worked out in the late 1940s and early 1950s by two LO economists, Gösta Rehn and Rudolf Meidner, and is referred to as the Rehn-Meidner model, or simply the Rehn model. LO adopted the strategy as it was set forth in a document presented to its 1951 Congress, *The Trade Union Movement and Full Employment.*[8]

The Rehn model was designed as a means for attaining noninflationary full employment without state intervention in the wage bargaining process, and thus as an alternative to state-run incomes policy. In addition to labor market policy, it had two other main ingredients. One was a moderately restrictive fiscal policy, aimed at what subsequently came to be called a full employment surplus, so that fiscal and international competitive pressures would be combined to make it hard for employers to pass on increased costs in increased prices. The other was a standard rate, or "solidaristic," union wage policy aimed at enforcing equal pay for equal work, regardless of employers' profitability. The combination of such fiscal and union wage policies was expected to subject firms to a differential profit squeeze, depending on how efficient and profitable they were. By favoring firms that could expand out of profits while forcing firms that could not do so to improve efficiency or else contract or go out of business, continuous change in the structure of industry would be stimulated. The proportion of low-cost, competitive firms able to pay standard rates would consequently increase relative to high-cost, uncompetitive firms that are not able to.

The third ingredient in the strategy, labor market policy, was intended to help workers who lost jobs in firms forced to contract or go out of business move to jobs in firms able to expand. Differential wage rates to induce workers to move from the former to the latter were ruled out by both the equity and efficiency objectives of solidaristic wage policy. Moreover, reliance on differentials would impose on workers subject to job loss in declining firms additional costs and put them at a disadvantage in competing for jobs in expanding firms insofar as the skill requirements and location of the jobs were different. It was accordingly held necessary to provide information both about new jobs and about various forms of support to assist workers in making the transition from old to new jobs—for example, providing retraining and relocation assistance. The associated costs of the structural change was supposed to be thereby shifted from the individual workers affected to the society as a whole, which benefited from the change. An "active" labor market policy of sufficient scope and scale to accomplish these objectives was accordingly viewed as an essential condition for acceptance of the structural change involved in the strategy.

What distinguishes this condition from those in the subsequent phases in the evolution of trade union technology policy is that it involved no direct intervention by either the state or unions in the process of structural and technological change itself. It was assumed that the process could be left to itself or, more precisely, to management at the enterprise and workplace levels and to the R&D performers who developed the new technology on which the growth of productivity depended. In other words, as far as the process itself was concerned, all that the combination of state and union policies was designed to do was keep up the pressure on management to be efficient. Under these conditions management was assumed to be willing and able to adopt rationalization measures, including new technology, on a scale that was sufficient from the overall economic perspective from which the strategy was devised. The impact of the measures on the quality or volume of jobs was not in question, nor was the capacity of the R&D system to come up with new technology at a sufficient rate. This confidence that the process could be left to itself, which prevailed in the 1950s, was eroded during the 1960s, leading to the crystallization of the second phase in trade union technology policy.

Phase 2: Assuring Employment for Displaced Workers

Industrial policy came to be viewed as essential to effective implementation of the structural change strategy by the later 1980s. An important early expression of this position was a report presented to LO's 1961

Congress, *Economic Expansion and Structural Change.*[9] It analyzed the policy problem as one of increasing the economy's "adaptability," emphasizing the need for mobility of capital as well as labor. To improve capital mobility, the report prescribed a variety of measures to reduce obstacles and establish new channels for it, along with new planning institutions and procedures to coordinate these measures with macroeconomic policy over a longer time horizon more commensurate with the structural change process than the short-term perspective typical of stabilization policy.

The analysis was predicated on the disappearance of the "very favorable external conditions for the Swedish economy prevailing in the preceding postwar period." As a result, "Sweden with its limited domestic market and significant export dependence . . . will in all certainty require greater exertion, more intensive investment activity, and a more rational utilization of our resources" in order to continue to be a "welfare society."[10]

The 1961 report was not a policy document, however, and LO did not adopt the position it set forth until after the middle of the decade. It was only then that the difficulties of implementing the structural change strategy effectively in the face of increasing international competition became palpable, precipitating political reactions that compelled some response. In particular, there was a growing reaction against the costs imposed by the high geographical labor mobility associated with the strategy. Among those costs were some that were not compensated despite massive expansion of labor market policy, and others that had not been anticipated or recognized as costs. Such costs received much greater attention in a report to LO's 1966 Congress, *Trade Unions and Technological Change.*

The report observes that "the costs associated with the fraction of labor turnover that was not 'voluntary' on the part of the individual worker" includes

> not only the actual costs of removal but also the losses sustained in the process of disposing of old and acquiring new housing, the interruptions in the children's school attendance, foregone non-wage benefits, reductions in income or additional periods of training. To these must be added the social and psychological sacrifices often involved in a change of environment and adjustment to a new social setting. At the same time, there are costs incurred by society, both by the depopulated local authorities in the form of lost economic and population bases for their social services, and for recipient local authorities which . . . must create new services.[11]

Nevertheless, the report rejects the conclusion that "the structural transformation of industry should be halted or slowed down. We urge instead that our national labor market policy program, which is at present ineffective in dealing with this problem, be expanded to the point where it can have a significant impact."[12]

Thus far, the argument was not that labor market policy was inadequate but only the scale on which it was implemented. But the report went on to argue that even a much expanded labor market policy would not suffice, and reiterated the contention of the 1961 report that an "active industrial policy" was necessary as well. LO made this its official policy at its 1966 Congress. The shift in LO's policy was paralleled in the Social Democratic party, in which it was given a powerful impetus by a sharp setback in local government elections a few months after the LO Congress. This was widely attributed to a reaction against the rapid and unstable economic growth that the structural change strategy fostered but could not control. To establish such control, new instruments for implementing an industrial or, more precisely, economic development policy were believed necessary. Joint LO and party committees were set up to formulate the policy. With a national election due in 1968, however, the Social Democratic government felt compelled to set up a cluster of industrial policy institutions without waiting for the committees to report.

The first of the institutions was a State Investment Bank to provide long-term capital for investment projects, preferably in areas of advanced technology. To plan the policy and coordinate the institutions being created for it, a new division of the Ministry of Finance was set up and then turned into a separate Ministry of Industry. A holding company, State Enterprise, Inc., was established to take over a miscellany of state-owned firms and gear them to policy goals. In addition, various forms of government support for technological R&D were brought together in a new Board for Technical Development.

The rationale provided for these measures by the LO-party committees displayed a shift in emphasis when compared with LO's 1961 document, although most of the measures were foreshadowed by the latter, which had in fact proposed to go further. Though the earlier document stressed the removal of hindrances to factor mobility, the later ones stressed the importance of establishing conditions necessary to make structural and technological change compatible with security and justice, as well as environmental protection and other values in which social costs and returns diverge from the private costs and returns of individual enterprise. More explicitly than before, "technical and economic development . . . formed in large part . . . in other countries that we are dependent on" were recognized as posing threats to these values as well as being a source of increased material living standards.

> Economic development presents us with the possibilities but also the demands of a new era. . . . But the promise they give of better living conditions for people in the future can only be realized if we have the

political will to exploit the possibilities and overcome the difficulties that development creates.

Full employment and a secure income are not given when industrial life changes. If economic forces are given free play, restructuring will be accompanied by new economic and social injustices. Therefore we must in our policies constantly work to unite economic progress with security and justice for individuals.

Although resistance to change is declared to be self-defeating, as in the earlier document, the necessity of controlling change is stressed.

If we should try to create security by resisting the development . . . by clinging tenaciously to what there is today, the world around us will nonetheless change. . . . The longer we allow us to be lulled by the illusion that we can achieve durable security that way, the harder the awakening will be. . . . Our security lies in development, in change. But the development must be steered so that it is of benefit to all. Therefore we a need a conscious and active industrial policy, inspired by our fundamental outlook and our demands for equality and security.[13]

As suggested by the measures adopted, the industrial policy program relied primarily on expanding the role of the state. There is no more than an allusion to expanding the role of the unions. This is in connection with a brief discussion of "industrial democracy" as a means for enabling workers to influence decisions affecting work environment and conditions at an earlier stage and at all levels of the enterprise. The need for this had also been pointed to in *Trade Unions and Technological Change*. As emphasized there, however, a major obstacle to movement in that direction was posed by the SAF's insistence on defining all decisions about who does what with what technology as managerial prerogatives beyond the scope of collective bargaining. This position was formally enshrined in the well-known paragraph 32 of SAF's constitution, which required a clause to that effect in all collective agreements. In the words of the 1966 LO report, "Any consultation on an even footing can hardly take place as long as the clause concerning management's exclusive right to manage and allocate labor as well as freely hire and dismiss workers remains in the collective agreement."[14]

By the time its next Congress met in 1971, LO had decided that it was imperative to eliminate the obstacle posed by paragraph 32.

Phase 3: Extending Collective Bargaining to Workplace Decisions

In a policy statement entitled *Industrial Democracy,* adopted by LO at its 1971 Congress, extension of collective bargaining to issues concerning the organization of work was declared to be essential to assure forms of organization "which can take advantage of modern technical effectiveness without being burdened by its [social] disadvantages." This marked a major shift in LO's position. It now demanded a direct union as well as state role in the process of structural and technological change, which had earlier been left up to managerial decision making.

Various pressures for this shift were building up in LO over a long time, but they intensified in the later 1960s. There was a growing conviction that the rationalization of production by technological and structural change was imposing greater costs on workers than had been anticipated or than could be compensated by labor market policy, no matter how "active." By intensifying the pace of work, creating new and often unperceived physical dangers, increasing stress and social isolation, and in other ways, the rationalization process was now seen as hurting workers who retained their jobs in firms keeping up with technological change as well as workers who lost jobs in firms that failed to keep up. Increasing labor turnover as well as absenteeism and recruitment difficulties were interpreted as reactions to the process, while complaints filtering up through the unions and repeatedly expressed in motions at union congresses pinpointed many specific sources of dissatisfaction. In addition, surveys by LO and some national unions recorded its content and widespread prevalence.

One consequence of all this was a changed conception of occupational health and safety policy, as reflected in a joint LO–Social Democratic party "action program," *A Better Work Environment,* in 1969 and a policy statement, *The Trade Union Movement and the Work Environment,* adopted at the 1971 LO Congress.

Policy in this area had traditionally been confined to regulations aimed at reducing industrial accidents and well-known occupational diseases, but the 1969 and 1971 policy statements describe responsibility for the work environment in much broader terms. Besides extending the scope of policy to a wider range of physical risks, including new ones created by technological change, it extended the scope to psychological risks as well, so that occupational health was viewed as including satisfaction from work. Moreover, the limitation of policy to measures designed to avert risks associated with production equipment and organization once they were in place was rejected. Instead, it was declared essential to introduce work environment considerations at a much earlier stage, when the equipment and organization were planned. Nor could work environment policy be treated in isolation from other kinds of policy. Its requirements had to enter into the "formation of industrial policy, labor market policy, and structural change within industry." But it was "not enough" to assure "better attention and integration of work environment questions" in business and government policy formation. It was also necessary to "analyze the basis of technical development and the rationalization process in order to determine the conditions that have to be satisfied in future development from a trade union point of view." Thus, it was "urgent to utilize known technology and develop new technology" to improve the work environment. Moreover, the division of responsibility for providing resources for developing that new technology had to be more clearly defined, including the "degree and manner in which STU [the government R&D support agency referred to above] should be assigned a more active role in the effort."

Steps in this and a variety of other directions were cited as necessary. Particular emphasis was placed on legislation to strengthen the position of local union officials to press work environment demands. Union power in the workplace was viewed as an indispensable condition for achieving the expanded goals defined for work environment policy. Thus, LO's 1971 work environment statement concludes by saying that

> the decisive question is to what extent the trade union movement can create the possibilities for influence by employees in the planning and decision-making process. It is a vital task to work for increased union influence through a successive advance of our positions in bargaining with our counterpart. There is no doubt that precisely the work environment area is especially appropriate for deepened industrial democracy.[15]

The adoption of more ambitious work environment goals was thus an important factor contributing to LO's determination to overcome the obstacle to collective bargaining over workplace issues posed by the official employer stand on managerial prerogatives. This factor was powerfully reinforced by the unions' response to the unprecedented wave of wildcat strikes in the winter of 1969–70. The strikes demonstrated a loss of authority by the unions that they felt compelled to repair. To do so, it was believed essential to strengthen the unions' capacity to protect the interests of their members at the workplace, where most of them had their only direct contact with the unions. At the same time, abandonment of centralized wage negotiations (which was one source of discontent) in order to give unions more to bargain about at the local level was ruled out by LO's long-standing organizational and economic strategy. Accordingly, it was all the more necessary to make it possible for unions at the local level to negotiate over nonwage workplace issues.[16]

Since that objective was believed unattainable by negotiation, LO called for legislation, which was eventually enacted in the form of the Law on Joint Determination (Medbestämmandelagen—MBL) in 1976. This was the culmination of a whole series of labor laws enacted during the preceding half-decade. Together, they enlarged union power at the workplace, especially with regard to the work environment, imposing stringent restrictions on the right of management to dismiss workers and obligations on management to negotiate over changes in the production process, thereby nullifying SAF's paragraph 32.

Although the legislation was not regarded as satisfactory in all respects, it was seen as removing a major obstacle to more effective pursuit of the more ambitious work-quality goals to which unions had become committed. As pointed out in the report *The Work Environment,* presented to LO's 1976 Congress, however, reconstruction of the legal framework was "only a first step." To realize the possibilities thereby opened up would take much "difficult and laborious" effort. The focus of attention was accordingly shifted to specifying what had to be done and building up the requisite capability. Out of this has crystallized the growing demand for greater union involvement in the process of technological R&D, which characterizes the fourth, current phase in the evolution of union policy on technological development.

Phase 4: Extending Union Influence to Technological Development

Union influence on technological development has come to be regarded as essential to the achievement of union goals concerning the quality of work—its environment, organization, and content. This position is predicated on the conviction that there are severe limits on what can be accomplished to achieve those goals at the stage when negotiations take place over the introduction of new technology that has already been developed and adopted. By then, the scope for choice has been sharply narrowed. Therefore, those goals have to be pursued at much earlier stages. Unions must be able to influence not only the whole process of planning changes in production within the enterprise from the very beginning, but also the preceding R&D process by which the technological options that become available are themselves shaped. At the same time the exercise of such influence is recognized as a largely new function for unions, and one they are as yet poorly equipped to perform. Building the capability for doing so is consequently given high priority.

This position has been elaborated on in increasing detail since the mid-1970s. As the challenge of realizing the possibilities opened up by the legislation in the preceding half-decade was confronted, LO's understanding of the tasks involved, including their formidable scope and magnitude, was enlarged, and the tasks were spelled out with increasing concreteness. The main directions in which LO's position has developed were set at its 1976 Congress, soon after the enactment of MBL. Several reports to that Congress took stock of what had been accomplished and what remained to be done.

The report on the work environment cited earlier emphasized the need for local union action to assure compliance with existing regulations and agreements, not least with respect to known risks and known safeguards against them. As far as unknown risks were concerned, local union action was said to be hampered by serious shortcomings in the responsible authorities' effectiveness in identifying the risks and prescribing safeguards. This was all the more serious in the face of new risks generated by rapid technological change, as in the case of chemicals and computers. The regulatory process, with its traditional approaches and inadequate resources, was declared unable to keep pace with the effects of technological change.

Even keeping pace would not be enough, however, for averting risks before they are built into the production process was a much more effective way of creating a good work environment than trying to remedy them afterward. "It is in connection with the construction of machinery and equipment, planning and forming work processes and places, that the work environment's conditions are created." Therefore, it is "already in the investment and planning stage" that the requirements of a good work environment have to be incorporated. To assure that they are, workers must be in a position to see that they are incorporated from that stage on. For workers to do so, they must participate right from the beginning in project groups set up within or by the health and safety committees prescribed by law, assisted by experts of their own choice, paid for as part of the firms' planning and investment.

Even this would not suffice, however. The solutions that can be arrived at within firms, including the availability of substitutes for dangerous products or processes, depend on the extent to which R&D outside as well as within the firms is addressed to the problems for which workers seek solutions. "As consciousness of work-environment questions has grown and the possibilities for influence strengthened, so too has the workers' need to be able to steer research toward the work environment problems experienced as most central." While "the trade union movement . . . has certain possibilities for directing and influencing research in the work environment area," research is still in "too high a degree steered and initiated by employer interests." Therefore, the trade union movement's "influence must be significantly built up and strengthened." It must "provide itself with better resources to articulate and specify its needs and desires" and be "able to attach researchers to itself to a greater extent" than it has been able to.[17]

The conviction that greater trade union influence was needed across the whole spectrum of R&D, expressed as well in a report entitled *Education for Work and Democracy,* led to a decision to work out a detailed research policy program. A committee, referred to as LOFO (the initials of the Swedish words for LO's research policy), was set up to prepare such a program for presentation to LO's 1981 Congress. A special effort in the area of computerization was also initiated. Stressing the importance of computerization for the possibilities of improving the work environment and democratizing work, another report, *Solidaristic Joint Determination,* recommended that an LO computer council be established to focus union efforts in this area. Such a council was set up and called upon to report to the 1981 Congress as well. The documents prepared by LOFO and the computer council are major statements of LO's fourth phase position. Each of them will accordingly be discussed in turn.

LO Research Policy

In its 1981 Congress report, *The Trade Union Movement and Research,* LOFO proposed a research policy addressed to the tension it perceived between the promise and threat of technological change. It grounded the policy in the trade union movement's basic goals of "full employment, a good work environment, and a democratic working life." These goals, the report warned, are threatened by the economic crisis and the fundamental structural changes in the international economy that underlie it. The possibilities of defending the progress toward the goals already attained and of realizing them more fully depend more than ever on research (the term being used to cover the whole R&D spectrum from basic science to industrial product and process development) through the technological development it permits and the economic and social policy solutions it yields.

> It is therefore more important than ever that the trade union move-
> ment engage itself in research . . . by increased union influence on the
> planning and direction of research and by widened dialogue with re-
> searchers. Union organizations must have the possibility of defining the
> questions and problems that have to be the object of research in order to
> be solved.[18]

The report recalled the labor movement's traditional view of "research and technical development as essential and necessary means for raising society's material and cultural level" and its stress on freedom for research as a condition for assuring its quality. At the same time, the labor movement has understood that the directions of research and the questions it addresses are "strongly influenced by power relations and values in society." In particular, power is exercised over research by those who decide which research is to be financed. In industry, this power is concentrated in the management of a relatively few large firms. Management's power determines not only what research is done in firms but influences what research is done in technical universities as well, through the research for which it contracts, by being "well represented in state organs that allocate funds and decide on research staffing" and through effective pressure on the government and parliament. Business influence extends to the social sciences, particularly economics, as well as technical and pharmaceutical faculties. "It is business questions that stand at the center and it is business that forms the future labor market for students and researchers."

Cooperation between industry and the universities was nevertheless acknowledged as essential. Indeed, LOFO argued, it should be increased, for university resources must be utilized for the industrial renewal that is crucial. However, cooperation between industry and the universities "should not take place solely on industry's terms." "We need development, but not at any price, not at the cost of the environment and people's health and well-being." Development must be "meaningful" and be "distributed justly." For the trade union movement, therefore, research on questions of how to make development meet those conditions is urgent. Yet research addresses those questions "far too little." One reason is that the trade union movement has far too little influence in the country's research organization; hence, it has to secure greater influence.[19]

To do so, the report stressed, the trade union movement had to acquire the capacity to act independently in defining research problems and bringing research resources to bear on them. What the unions seek is not simply or primarily greater participation with others on research addressing problems they have in common. Much of union experience of research has been with efforts carried out jointly with their employer counterparts, as provided for in laws and collective agreements such as those concerning the work environment. But such "two-party common interest" research limits the scope for questions the unions are concerned with, for it precludes research employers do not regard as in their interest. "It is research on our terms, from our perspective, and with union problems and goals that the trade union movement wants to get done."

> Within the framework of the research organization we have and the researchers who work at the universities, different research institutes and out in firms, the main aim is to bring about changes in the directions of research and to influence the questions one chooses to work with. It is, so to speak, to bring about [union] interest-oriented research within a research system that is in large part already steered by other interests, not least from the employer side. What is new and unusual is that it must be to a greater degree the worker side that impels research.[20]

This, the report insisted, was not a call for research that was itself biased. "Research does not become inferior, viewed as research, when it proceeds from clear values or is conducted to solve specific problems." For the research to be useful, however, its integrity and quality must be upheld. "No one has any use for deficiently performed research. Bad research is worse than none at all, because it is misleading and lays claim to valuable resources." The unions' interest in the utility and quality of research is best served by clearly formulating the problems they want studied and taking responsibility for applying the findings, while placing their confidence in researchers to freely carry out their distinctive task of developing knowledge to the best of their ability.

Informed by these general considerations, the LOFO report discussed a broad range of research policy issues and presented a number of specific proposals. It called for a change in the whole way in which government conducts research policy, proposing the appointment of a new cabinet minister in whom responsibility for a "coordinated research policy" would be vested. This was proposed to remedy serious deficiencies seen in the way research policy was conducted. Many of the deficiencies were attributed to the growth of a "sectoral" approach, by which support for research was divided up among various ministries and agencies responsible for specific policy areas, such as defense, industry, education, medical care, housing, and so forth. Though this has resulted in resources for research on important policy problems, it leaves no place in the research policy structure for attention to the relationships among the different efforts or to problems that cut across them.

Thus, there has been little coordination of policy for university research with industrial policy despite the critical interdependence of the two. And of special concern to the unions, there has been little research on how to integrate work-quality considerations into technological development, since it requires the combination of engineering and social science resources divided between different governmental bodies with different missions—e.g., STU, which finances engineering R&D on new technology, and the Work Environment Fund (Arbetarskyddsfonden, or ASF), which finances medical and social science research on the effects of existing technology on the work environment.

Such multidisciplinary research was among a variety of areas identified as requiring the initiation of immediate efforts, adding up to an overall increase in funds allocated to research. These would flow largely through existing agencies, but some changes in the organization of the research structure as well as in the funding agencies' operations were urged. For example, establishment of state development companies to run major projects in selected areas and greater reliance on research institutes independent of both the higher education bureaucracy and industry was recommended. At the same time, the report called for not only greater union participation in research planning and decision making but also the resources required to build up union capacity to exert real influence through such participation as well as to take responsibility for projects addressed to questions unions define.

The new emphasis on union capacity for autonomous research initiatives reflected the limitations ascribed to participation in contexts dominated by other actors and their purposes. In principle, union representation was sought in all the bodies that plan and administer research, including the governing bodies of national funding agencies, universities, industry institutes for cooperative research, and companies, as well as reference groups for particular projects. Such representation was seen as a means of access to information about research that is and is not taking place, an opportunity to exert some influence on decisions about the allocation of research resources, and some possibility for initiating research on problems of concern to unions. But there are drawbacks and risks as well. Representation takes time from the many other functions unions have to perform, further stretching resources already strained. And since there can therefore rarely be more than one union representative in any of the bodies, the lone union representative can easily be put into a hostage situation. Without much influence on the decisions made, his or her presence may nevertheless confer a claim of legitimacy on the decisions, placing on unions a share of responsibility for decisions that may not advance union members' interests much if at all. While necessary, then, representation can at best be only a "complement to other forms of influence."

Among the most important of these is "direct cooperation and dialogue with researchers," even though it is "demanding, requires time, and can also bring with it conflicts." A broad network of contacts with researchers is required to give the unions their own access to expertise needed to exert any independent influence on research through representation and negotiation. And unions must have direct contact with researchers to initiate research on questions that concern the unions, to be carried out under contract with the unions, in addition to whatever research on these questions can be carried out within the framework of ongoing programs in which others are involved.

The main limitation on such an autonomous union research policy was seen in the scarcity of resources, particularly of staff with competence and experience relevant to implementing the policy. This imposes on unions the need to be selective with respect to both the bodies on which they seek representation and the research they seek to get done on their own. Finally, it underscores the need for public funding, which means that research addressed to problems defined by the unions as well as the development of union capacity to define the problems and administer the research must become part of national research policy.[21]

The LO Computer Council

The general position elaborated in the LOFO report was applied specifically to computer technology in the computer council's report to the 1981 LO Congress, *Union Computer Policy*. In it, " computer technology's special possibilities and threats" were viewed from the perspective of the broad aims of the labor movement, reiterated as "work for all, democracy in working life, good work environment, higher standards, and continued expansion of collective services." The long-standing belief that technical development is "one of the prerequisites for achieving better and more human conditions" was reaffirmed yet again, along with its insistence on "a more just distribution of the increased material resources that could be created with the help of the technology." The economic crisis facing Sweden now made "the need for technical development" greater than ever. "A stagnant industrial development—attributable in part to technology that is obsolete compared with that in firms in other countries and to declining investment—constitutes today the greatest threat to the possibilities of achieving these aims."[22]

On the other hand, the report emphasized, the trade union movement is no longer willing to confine itself to the distribution of the economic surplus resulting from the "technical development that took place largely on private industry's terms." The role now claimed by the movement was set in the context of the evolution of trade union policy reviewed earlier. Referring to the reaction against the social costs of structural change during the 1960s and 1970s, the report cited the growing "demand for economic democracy . . . and for a direct influence over decisions on investment and the shaping of new factories," and to the legislation enacted in response to those demands. Now,

> the whole labor movement . . . confronts a new and still greater challenge. [It] must take the initiative for an industrial development such that Sweden's possibilities as an industrial nation are not destroyed. But it is as important to create the possibilities and instruments [needed] to determine which technology shall be developed and how it shall be utilized in practice, which thereby decides also the possibilities for achieving our demands for content-rich and meaningful work, solidarity, community, justice and a good work environment.[23]

The challenge is posed most sharply by computer technology because of its fundamental, all-pervasive character. Moreover, since the essence of the technology is the command over information it provides, and since "those who have knowledge and manage information possess power," the technology is an instrument of power with great potential for those who can control its development and use. It therefore has a "dimension and significance for the future development of society different" from earlier technological change, affecting "the conditions for political democracy as well as economic democracy and the democratization of working life." Thus, the development of computer technology opens up both enormous possibilities for and grave threats to the realization of labor movement aims. Which of these directions its development will take will depend on who controls it. Because it is now to "such a high degree controlled by private owner interests," as preceding technological development has been, computer technology is being "developed in the wrong directions in decisive areas."

This pessimistic outlook was elaborated primarily with respect to worklife, contrasting the way the technology is being developed with the way it could be. Because computers have been harnessed primarily to management's efforts to "centrally direct and control" the work process,

> the dominating experience of computerization today is that it brings to most of those affected an impoverishment of work content and tasks while new risks and health problems arise in place of those that are eliminated. Separation between people in production grows. Work contacts are replaced by conversations over computers. Central planning becomes more detailed. Isolation in work life is thereby increased. Control becomes all the more effective. Instead of democratized management, increasingly effective systems for giving orders . . . are built up. This is a development that seriously threatens the trade union movement's and democracy's fundamental values.[24]

Computer technology offers entirely different possibilities, however. It can give workers "an improved overview of the work process and thereby continuously increase and develop their knowledge." The information it can make available can facilitate the organization of production by autonomous work groups, in which the content of work is enriched by responsibility for planning, rotation among tasks, and the combination of new computer knowledge with "traditional occupational skills." Computer technology can thereby serve as "the workers' tool" rather than a "control system dominating the workers." For business strategic decisions as well as detailed production planning, moreover, the speed with which computers permit information to flow enlarges the possibilities for democratic participation.

While development of computer technology in this alternative direction is a "more effective way of exploiting its possibilities" for production as well as the quality of work, it is likely to occur only if "wage earners' influence increases." But achieving such influence is extremely difficult in the face of the powerful forces dominating the development of computer technology and "contemporary power relations in industry."

Very few companies, those in which computer R&D and production is highly concentrated, above all IBM, dominate the direction of development. Powerful influence is also exerted by major purchasers, whose demands the suppliers strive to meet. Among the most important purchasers are governments engaged in the arms race. Also important are "the few large multinational enterprises that dominate each branch [of industry] and shape the technical development and forms of computer applications . . . according to their needs and specifications," providing models for computer application by other firms. Since these multinationals also operate in countries where labor movements are politically weak or entirely suppressed, the models are likely to reinforce the development of computer technology in the wrong direction.

While the basic directions of computer technology development are therefore largely beyond the reach of Swedish unions, even the adaptation of systems to Swedish firms is difficult for the unions to influence, for the instruments placed at their disposal by legislation and collective agreements are insufficient. Thus, MBL does not provide for influence on development that takes place in a large conglomerate's subsidiaries separate from those in which the systems are to be introduced. Even when development takes place in the latter, workers and their representatives enter into the development process "too late to influence the development to a decisive extent." Given the formidable obstacles to increasing worker influence on the development of computer technology, "the circumstances can seem to be extraordinarily difficult. But this makes it all the more urgent to immediately take on the problem, giving priority to concentrating political as well as union resources on it."[25]

The report went on to suggest how to proceed. To begin with, legislation and collective agreements must be changed to enable unions to enter the design process at the stage at which a firm first considers the introduction or modification of computer systems. This also "requires a significant strengthening of unions' resources, including the availability of their own experts to develop their own alternatives and provide an informed basis for evaluating and negotiating over management proposals."

Such "trade union methods do not suffice," however. To provide the economic and industrial policies on which the effectiveness of trade union methods depends, as well as to create the conditions under which they can be applied in the first place, requires action at the national policy level. This is so with respect to many additional dimensions of the challenge of computerization, such as its effects on employment.

Two sharply contrasting beliefs about those effects were cited. One, resting on the long-run growth of employment despite repeated technological transformations in the past, is that "computer technology will—more or less automatically—create full employment." The other is that computer technology "will lead to mass unemployment." While stressing the impossibility of determining with certainty which is correct, the report rejected both. The first fails to recognize that the far-reaching structural transformation that computerization precipitates cannot take place on socially acceptable terms without "strong action of an organizational kind, to assure that the social costs are borne equitably and that profits resulting from productivity gains are reinvested in new jobs." The second fails to recognize the possibilities for coping with the problems posed by computerization or the potential it offers for enlarging the resources with which to fill social needs. Moreover, it overlooks the even greater threat to employment if the technology needed to survive in international competition is not adopted. Accordingly, there is no alternative to adopting the new technology, but there are alternative policies that can make a great deal of difference to its employment effects. "The total level of employment and unemployment in the country is determined not by technology but ultimately by how society is organized, the distribution of available resources through collective bargaining and political decisions."[26]

The report accordingly concluded by reiterating LO's fourth phase position.

> If the development [of computer technology] is allowed to continue along present lines, the divisions in society would increase. Sweden's traditionally greatest asset, a broad and deep knowledge among the workers and internationally competent firms, threatens to be weakened. Wage earners would justifiably resist changes that entail worsened conditions. The new technology would not be utilized and Sweden's leading position as an industrial nation would be seriously threatened.[27]
>
> The new technology can be used to secure employment and welfare and provide the conditions for meaningful work and a good environment. Cohesion and solidarity can be strengthened. To achieve these requires that we use the possibilities for influence we have better than we do today. But it in addition requires means of control that neither society nor the union organizations have at their disposal. Time is short. Programs and measures have to be put in place quickly.
>
>   [Thus] the growth of investment in new technology is in everyone's interest but wage earners cannot accept it if the conditions are increased gaps in wealth and the exclusion of employee influence over how the new technology is introduced and used. Forms must [therefore] be created to enable Swedish industry and the labor market to be renewed and developed in a democratic way in which changes take place with the participation of the wage earners.[28]

It is on developing forms for more effectively influencing the development and utilization of new technology generally as well as computerization in particular that the efforts of LO and its affiliated unions have concentrated since its 1981 Congress. These efforts have proceeded in the context of an essentially unchanged public policy framework, with respect to both collective bargaining rights accorded to unions by MBL and funding for union technology development initiatives by state R&D support agencies. What happened within that framework will be just briefly sketched.

Recent Developments

The main event in connection with collective bargaining over technological change was the conclusion of an agreement on implementing the MBL provisions between the private-sector employers belonging to SAF and their two principal union counterparts, LO and the negotiating body for private-sector white-collar workers, PTK, in 1982. Like much Swedish legislation, MBL laid down a set of general principles and guidelines, leaving the details to be spelled out subsequently. In this case, the details were to be spelled out in collective agreements between the employer and union organizations, adapting the principles to the distinctive situations in each of the sectors covered by the respective peak organizations and, with successively greater specificity, from the peak organization to the industry and finally workplace levels. Such joint determination agreements (MBA) were reached in the separate central government, local government, state enterprise, and cooperative sectors in the years immediately following the enactment of MBL. In the private sector, however, negotiations for such an agreement between SAF and LO and PTK were repeatedly deadlocked, broken off, and resumed.

While LO and PTK adopted a common bargaining position calling for provisions designed to reinforce the rights accorded by MBL, SAF rejected the union demands and took positions implying a dilution of those rights. It seemed as if SAF was bent on resisting implementation, confident that the nonsocialist or "bourgeois" parties that were governing since 1976 would not provide the unions with a legislative alternative to negotiations, as the Social Democrats had done. If this was the expectation, it was confirmed, although disarray among the bourgeois parties made them ineffective state arena allies for any employer offensive against the unions in the market arena, as demonstrated in 1980 when SAF failed to win its objectives in the largest lockout since 1909.

Whether it was the possibility of the Social Democrats' return to office in September 1982 (which is what happened) or satisfaction with the extent to which the union demands had been worn down, SAF finally settled with the unions in April 1982, nearly six years after MBL's enactment. Without summarizing the terms of the so-called development agreement (rather freely translated into English by SAF as "agreement on efficiency and participation"), it can be said that it did not appreciably strengthen or weaken the unions' ability to influence workplace decision making. SAF won a lot of language about the importance of "developing" firms' "effectiveness" for the maintenance of employment. The design of change in technology and work organization so as to utilize and develop workers' skills was in turn treated as instrumental to effectiveness. The unions won language that reserved their rights under MBL and nailed down their right to bring in outside consultants and researchers to assist in evaluating the information about enterprise performance and plans and to participate as observers and analysts (but not actors) in technological and work organization change projects.

The evidence on how MBL and MBA have worked out in practice is mixed. A recent survey of employers showed them to be generally satisfied with the operation of the law, with very little indication that it had introduced the inflexibility SAF had warned against when MBL was proposed. The survey evidence of the employers' contentment might be interpreted as showing that joint determination as prescribed by MBL and the negotiated agreements has not made much difference after all. Complaints to that effect have indeed been voiced by some unionists. Such complaints were the basis for motions at the most recent Metalworkers Congress calling for the negotiation of technology agreements that would guarantee more timely information and influence over technological change. But the motions failed in favor of the union leadership's position that the law and agreements were working reasonably satisfactorily and should be given more time to prove themselves. This presumably reflected the atmosphere of compromise that had been renewed with the conclusion of the private-sector joint determination agreement, which the leadership was probably not inclined to disturb.

A parallel expression of this atmosphere of compromise was a large program of joint union-management computer application projects financed by the government and administered by ASF, the work environment research funding body. The projects, like ASF itself, are quintessentially corporatist—that is, they are two-party common-interest exercises of the kind whose limitations the LOFO report had pointed out. To some extent, the new program appears to be a restoration of the kind of union participation in management-initiated applications of new technology that was fostered by SAF's technical department in the early 1970s. Dissatisfaction with this had contributed to the unions' demand for an extension of collective bargaining to workplace issues and subsequently for autonomous union development of technological alternatives. In any case, the joint projects in the ASF program concern the introduction of technology that is available or on the verge of being available rather than the development of new technology.

No substantial change in national research policy in the direction of supporting such development under autonomous union auspices has occurred either. In response to continuing pressure from LO and TCO, the government's technological R&D support agency, STU, did provide some funding for the formulation of suggestions for R&D projects aimed at questions of concern to the unions, as well as funding to the graphics workers union to engage in an actual technology development project. In addition, the importance of a union role in bringing R&D to bear on technological issues was for the first time cited explicitly by STU in a major program document in 1983. But this did not really entail a change of policy in principle and did so even less in practice.

Meanwhile, a great deal of experience about worker participation in the application of new technology is being accumulated, testifying to the wide scope for variation in the applications, in union roles in designing them, and in perceptions of what is at stake in alternative applications. Some illustrations are provided by flexible manufacturing system (FMS) installations being tracked by the Metalworkers' union. These range from a case in which an autonomous group has achieved an extremely high utilization rate to one subjected to very tight managerial control, set up when an attempt to run a system with inexperienced workers resulted in too much downtime. Although these cases suggest that autonomous groups of workers with high, multiple skills may be most effective in achieving managerial goals of high utilization, management is evidently threatened by dependence on the workers' knowledge, including the risk that they will leave and apply that knowledge elsewhere and the consequent weakening of managements' wage-bargaining position. Managerial counterstrategies of cultivating workers' identification with the companies they work for, including incentive schemes and applications that inhibit the buildup of skills that are not company specific are, in turn, seen by unions as a threat to their ability to retain membership identification while securing applications that further work-quality goals.[29]

These and other cases, along with the lack of significant change in the policy framework, suggest that the problems and possibilities of union influence on technological development remain pretty much as they were described in the reports to LO's 1981 Congress. There is neither sufficient space nor data to provide a comprehensive review of the evidence for this judgment. We shall instead take one case, the graphics union project partially funded by STU cited earlier, and describe it in some detail. The project is referred to by the evocative name "UTOPIA," an acronym formed by the Swedish words for its full title, undoubtedly chosen for that reason, "training, technology, and products from a quality of work perspective" ("Utbildning, Teknik Och Produkt I Arbetskvalitetsperspektiv"). The UTOPIA project is probably the most promising demonstration of how unions might bring technical expertise to bear on the development of alternative technologies; at the same time it illustrates especially clearly some of the most serious difficulties in doing so.

The UTOPIA Project

Broadly stated, the aim of the UTOPIA project was to reverse the tendency of computerization to impoverish or even eliminate the work of graphics workers—skilled craftsmen in the printing trades.[30] It sought to achieve this aim principally by developing alternative computer technology that graphics workers could use as a tool for producing high-quality products, and by developing the work organization and training required to utilize the alternative technology. Initiated jointly by the Nordic Graphics Union (Nordisk Grafisk Union, or NGU) and the Swedish Center for Working Life (Arbetslivcentrum, or ALC) in 1980, the project focused on computerized text and image processing for page makeup in newspapers. It was carried out by a fifteen-member team consisting of social scientists at ALC, one of which was the project leader, graphics workers employed in several Nordic newspapers, and computer scientists at a Danish and a Swedish university. Representatives of graphics unions in Denmark, Finland, Norway, and Sweden also constituted a reference group to which the project team reported. After its inception UTOPIA entered into cooperation with a large Nordic commercial project aimed at developing technology of the kind with which UTOPIA was concerned. Referred to as TIPS, for Text and Image Processing System, the development project was led by a subsidiary of a large, Swedish state-owned publishing company, Liber AB. Cooperation with TIPS proved crucial for carrying out the UTOPIA project.

Forging a Development Coalition

The UTOPIA project had two sources. One was the concern of the graphics unions over the revolutionary changes being brought about in the printing industry by computerization during the 1970s. The other was a set of studies done at ALC on the implications of technological change in general and computerization in particular for the quality of work. The connection between the Swedish graphics workers and the researchers went back to 1973, when the union sought the support of researchers at Lund University. Some of those researchers went on to ALC, where the union contacts continued. The local branch of the graphics union at one of Sweden's major dailies, *Svenska Dagbladet,* participated in one of four studies that were part of an ALC project, DEMOS, begun in 1975 and aimed at developing "knowledge about planning, control and computer use" needed by trade unions to engage in negotiations and training in connection with the introduction of computer technology.

The graphics union needed the researchers' support in order to take advantage of the opportunities opened up to it by a "technology agreement" it had concluded with employers in the industry in 1974. This was the first such agreement in Sweden, preceding MBL's enactment by some two years. The agreement provided for some employment guarantees in connection with the introduction of new technology, rights to retraining for changed work tasks, and rules concerning the manning of new equipment. Further provisions concerning the introduction of integrated text processing were added to the agreement in 1980.

The Swedish printing industry technology agreement illustrated a widespread trend in the Nordic countries. A General Agreement on Computer-Based Systems was concluded between the Norwegian Federation of Trade Unions (LO) and the Norwegian Employers Confederation (NAF) in 1975. A general technology agreement was concluded between the peak organizations of unions and employers in Denmark in 1981, which the Danish graphics union sought to supplement with employment guarantees like those won by its Swedish counterpart, though so far without success. In Sweden, as we saw, no general agreement in the private sector was struck until 1982. Throughout the Nordic countries, there are many agreements between individual newspapers and local unions concerning worker rights in connection with the transition to new technology. Of course, there have been and continue to be conflicts between graphics workers and other occupational groups, particularly the journalists, over how the radically changed tasks are to be distributed among them. Particularly in the Swedish case, conflict between the graphics workers and journalists has proven to be a serious obstacle to the realization of UTOPIA's potential—a point to which we shall return.

The technology agreements reflected not only the problems with which the new technology was confronting the graphics unions but also the possibility of influencing the development of the new technology in ways that permitted the problems to be solved on terms acceptable to both the graphics unions and the employers. Creating a framework for cooperation in developing the technology, the agreements also offered a potentially significant market advantage for suppliers that could develop technology satisfying union as well as employer requirements. Formulating those requirements in such a way that they could be incorporated into technical development was a new and difficult task for the unions, however. Initial efforts underscored as well as concretized the difficulties involved. The lessons drawn from those efforts, including the DEMOS project, shaped the rationale and design of UTOPIA.

As stated in its prospectus, UTOPIA was specifically addressed to the difficulties encountered in previous trade union efforts to advance their members' interests in the quality of work—skill content, democratic organization, and a good work environment. The difficulties were ascribed to two main factors: (1) disparities of knowledge and power between management and unions, and (2) limitations imposed by available technology. With respect to the first, management was described as having "relatively unambiguous and well-defined targets for technological development (e.g., productivity and efficiency measures) which can conflict with trade union demands, and . . . extensive experience of technological development from the traditional company-oriented viewpoint which dominates over trade union demands." With respect to the second, it was pointed out:

It is often difficult to make basic changes in the content and organization of work if production technology is not altered at the same time. This difficulty is worsened by the growing tendency to purchase technology in the form of "turn-key" packages. Another difficulty is that the accompanying training only comprises general servicing of equipment; it does not allow for changes to be made nor does it provide a view of the process as a whole.[31]

These factors tended to confine trade union work-quality demands to resistance to deskilling and displacement. But this was characterized as a "defensive strategy" that was ultimately bound to be futile as "production is increasingly based on scientific and technological expertise" and as demand for "practical experience of trade skills" declines. Technology thus comes to be perceived "as adverse or just plain evil," eroding the positive attitude to technology "traditionally held by the trade union movement." Trade unions had to instead pursue an "offensive strategy" aimed at developing technological and training alternatives more consistent with work-quality demands.

Instead of defending the status quo an offensive strategy can be developed for another type of technology that improves the quality of work and products, [and] that is not inflexible but can be dynamically changed at individual workplaces as the workers develop their skills. . . . Training [therefore has] to be developed to provide workers . . . with the means to adapt and use the system so that it meets their demands for the work and the product.[32]

To pursue such a strategy, it was necessary not only for the unions to have access to relevant technological and work-organization expertise but also to develop methods for bringing the expertise to bear on the unions' concerns. UTOPIA was conceived as an effort to develop such methods in the course of developing specific alternative technologies and associated work organization and training. Thus, it was both "a technology development project and a social-scientific experiment to understand the conditions for technology development" responsive to union goals.

In its design UTOPIA sought to cope with the fundamental constraint on unions' capacity for an offensive strategy posed by the costs of developing production technology, generally entailing investments so large as to make it impossible for unions to undertake such development on their own. Yet this was not equally true for all aspects of technology, such as the software crucial to computer technology. "The development costs of programs," the prospectus pointed out, "are considerably less, generally speaking, than of hardware." Accordingly, focusing on software offered a possibility for overcoming the cost obstacle. It was seen as offering additional strategic advantages as well. "Developing alternative software also enables a dynamic technology to be created [which] can be further developed at local level if alternative training programs are simultaneously developed." Unaltered hardware would still impose limits to the trade union goals that could be realized, but those limits would be more precisely identified in the process of software development, making it possible to specify demands for subsequent hardware development. Thus, software was viewed "as a foot in the door for trade union technological development."

Finally, software for text and image processing in newspapers seemed an especially promising application on which to work. This was clearly a next stage in the technological change that was rapidly transforming the printing industry. The change that had already occurred gave workers in the industry strong stakes in gaining some leverage on the process of change—their numbers were declining, many of their traditional skills were no longer needed, and "knowledge of typography and layout, the basic trade skill" threatened to disappear, along with the "quality of graphical products." At the same time, conditions for developing trade union alternatives were especially favorable in several respects. The technology agreements established a favorable climate, and the graphics workers' technical sophistication put them in a good position to participate. Moreover, the several thousand companies in the Nordic countries formed a significant potential market for alternative text and image processing technologies that might be developed under the joint auspices of the Nordic graphics unions.

This market potential is what prompted Liber's entry into the picture. Liber had set out to capitalize on its comprehensive knowledge as a user of printing equipment to enter the field of producing it. To that end, it organized the TIPS project, which if cofinanced with the Nordic Industrial Fund, an R&D support agency formed by the Nordic governments. A subsidiary, Liber System AB, was set up to run the development project.

Various aspects of the work were carried out by Imtec, a spin-off company from Linkoping Technical University that became a Liber subsidiary; Typlan, a subsidiary of Nokia, a large Finnish conglomerate; and the Graphics Laboratory at Helsinki University. Liber's strategy was to establish itself as a major supplier of the next generation of newspaper production technology in the Nordic market, which would give it a basis for entering the international market. Acceptability of the new technology by the Nordic graphics unions would clearly be an advantage, if not a necessary condition, for achieving its Nordic market goal. The prospects of acceptability would certainly be enhanced if the new technology met the unions' work-quality demands. Union as well as newspaper concerns were incorporated into the TIPS project through a reference group, but UTOPIA offered TIPS the opportunity of integrating union concerns into the development project more directly and organically. Liber accordingly had a strong interest in establishing a link between the two projects.

UTOPIA obviously had much to gain from cooperation with TIPS as well. Such cooperation promised an opportunity to formulate, test, and revise the system specifications that UTOPIA was designed to produce in the context of a concrete production technology development project of the kind it could never expect to carry out on its own. Given these mutual interests, an agreement on the terms of cooperation was readily reached. UTOPIA committed specified resources to continuously develop, test, and revise its specifications of requirements and suggest ways of meeting them in the technical development process, and to develop training materials and organization for the system being developed. TIPS likewise committed specified resources to try out alternative solutions aimed at meeting UTOPIA's specifications and evaluate the system in terms of them. UTOPIA was not bound to endorse the particular technical solutions adopted by TIPS, which the latter remained free to choose in the light of the commercial, economic, and time constraints under which it operated. The agreement also provided for the use of early prototypes and purchase of early series installations on favorable terms by the various institutes involved in UTOPIA and other Nordic printing trades training institutions.

Implementation of the agreement was contingent on additional funding of UTOPIA's participation. At the same time, the agreement improved the prospects for financing UTOPIA. Financing had turned out to be an intractable problem, even on the smaller scale required for software development. The difficulties encountered by the project in this connection underscore the fundamental issue of government support for development of technological alternatives that the unions had been stressing.

NGU and ALC provided the initial funding for UTOPIA. This sufficed for the planning stage of the project, but additional funding was needed to go on with the actual development work. The computer scientists required for that had been identified at the Institute for Numerical Analysis and Computer Science Group (Numerisk analys och datologi, or NADA) at the Royal College of Technology (Kungliga Tekniska Hogskolan, or KTH) in Stockholm, and the Computer Science Department (Datalogisk Afdelning, DAIMI) at Aarhus University in Denmark. One possible source of funding for their participation was the ASF, mentioned earlier. Run by a tripartite board including employer and union representatives, ASF was established by the government to support research on the work environment and was ALC's principal source of support. Typically, as noted already, ASF supported research on the effects of existing technology on the work environment, in the broader sense of work quality as well as health and safety, rather than on the development of new technology with work-environment implications. Although ASF was at the time planning the new program of research on work-organization issues associated with the introduction of computer technology, it was not clear that it would support development of new technology. Even if it did, the support would not be available for some time. Moreover, as LO argued, the fact that there already existed an agency for funding technical research and development, STU, made it seem the appropriate source for funding of the technical as opposed to work-organization aspects. So funding was sought for NADA's participation from STU and for DAIMI's from the Danish counterpart of STU.

Although STU had put a high priority on research in computer technology, repeated efforts to secure funding from the section of STU responsible for such research were unavailing. UTOPIA was evidently a new kind of project for STU that did not fit precisely into the categories of projects it was accustomed to handling. These typically were conventional R&D projects undertaken by business firms or technical universities, from which STU staff members usually came. To them, R&D projects for which unions were responsible could apparently not be regarded as serious or even legitimate, particularly if conducted by researchers tainted by the reputation for radicalism acquired by ALC. In any case, rather than responding imaginatively to this new kind of project, STU's computer technology staff seemed almost to go out of its way to find in the existing project category definitions reasons for rejecting UTOPIA's proposals.

The prospects for a favorable response from STU were much improved by UTOPIA's association with a vendor having a commercial stake in the successful outcome of the development project, for the absence of such an association had been one of the grounds for rejecting earlier proposals (although the computer science aspect of the project for which support had been sought could readily have been interpreted as falling into a "knowledge development" category for which such a requirement was not set). With the backing of LO, which had been pressing STU to accept responsibility for supporting union projects, a new proposal was submitted, but this time to STU's technology procurement section rather than its computer section. Although UTOPIA did not fit into the procurement category any more precisely than into the other ones, the proposal was approved. Whether this was because the staff now involved was more imaginative or less biased against unions, or because the top administration felt that a positive response to LO's persistent pressure was desirable (or all of these reasons) is not clear. Whatever the reasons for it, the decision provided UTOPIA with the funds it needed to go on. But the terms on which it was made did not resolve the underlying policy issue of public support for autonomous trade union development of alternative technologies. Thus, having been defined as a technology procurement project, UTOPIA was unable to get further STU funding to continue its association with TIPS once it reached the first pilot installation phase at the end of 1984.

Operationalizing Work-Quality Goals: The Tool Perspective

As a technology procurement project, UTOPIA's main task was to specify the requirements to be met by the system being developed. The method for formulating the specifications that was worked out is one of UTOPIA's most important results. As defined in the project, the problem was whether "the new technology could be designed as a tool for skilled printing workers." From this "tool perspective," it was necessary first to identify the functions the new technology had to perform in order to enable the workers to implement judgments based on their knowledge of what constitutes good quality in the product and then to specify the characteristics and capabilities required to perform the functions. The tool perspective can best be described by illustrating its application.[33]

In the case of newspaper page makeup, the essence of the skilled workers' competence was conceived as lying in their understanding of the visual ingredients of readability. This is what enables them to give "typographical form" to the "journalistic model" of a page produced by the editorial work of choosing content, producing text, distributing it among pages, and so forth. To give the journalistic model typographical form requires judgments concerning the positioning of different kinds of material on a page—main text, pictures, headlines, rules, white space,—based on the skilled workers' distinctive training and experience, including the resulting "tacit knowledge" that enables them to achieve high quality with the infinitely varied material with which they work.

The tools with which to implement those judgments are provided by the technology of page makeup. For centuries the tools were those of lead (hot metal) technology. Only in the late 1960s were they replaced by the tools of paper pasteup technology. This resulted from the introduction of photo typesetters and computer word processing, producing the material to be made up into pages in the form of paper or film rather than lead. Now, paper technology is already being replaced by technology that produces the material entirely in the form of digitalized data, enabling the material to be positioned on pages with computers and then serving as instructions for the machines that make the plates with which the printing is done.

The problem for UTOPIA, then, was how computer technology could be made to serve as a tool as did lead and paper technology, enabling workers to carry out at least the same operations on the material as they could with conventional technology. To propose the capabilities and characteristics that the computer technology therefore had to have, the computer specialists had to learn from the graphics workers what the operations were. To evaluate the adequacy of proposed capabilities and characteristics for carrying out the operations, in turn, the graphics workers had to learn from the computer specialists what the possibilities and limits of computer technology were, at its current or near-future state of development.

Such a mutual learning process between workers with particular occupational skills and scientists with the relevant technological and work-organization skills is itself essential to the conduct of trade union technology development projects. Developing the capacity for engaging in such a process has frequently proven difficult, however. By trial and error UTOPIA achieved it to a considerable extent. "More or less formalized description methods ranging from scenarios to data flow" were attempted initially but "did not function very well as a vehicle of communication" for the workers. A mock-up to simulate computerized page makeup proved to work much better. With it, the workers could go through the page makeup process step by step. At each step corresponding images were drawn on simulated display screens, and the operations and interactive devices required to implement them identified and recorded by the computer specialists. Crude at first, the mock-up was later made more realistic in appearance, paper simulation of display screens was replaced by back-screen projection, and a "real computer workstation with a high-resolution screen and a tablet with a puck" was used "to experiment with and illustrate aspects which were difficult to simulate with the mock-up such as coordination between puck movements and screen image changes."

With these and other components UTOPIA built up an experimental and research milieu or "technology laboratory." This proved to be an effective instrument not only for collaboration between workers and technical specialists within UTOPIA but also for other purposes. One was for training in vocational colleges and retraining programs. This presupposes that the graphics workers' occupation (if not the number of jobs) would be preserved through the development of computer technology that called for typographical and layout skills and that there would also be scope for further development in the workplace by the workers themselves, for whom programming and related understanding therefore became part of their essential job skills. Another use to which the instrument was put was the formulation and evaluation of proposals in negotiations over local union-management contracts and over purchase contracts with suppliers of equipment and software.

In the process of translating page makeup operations into specifications for computerized systems, both the limitations and potential of available computer technology were underscored. Display screen technology was revealed to fall far short of requirements. To be able to see what a page looks like when materials are positioned in a particular way, workers need to have the whole page before them "in a resolution good enough to facilitate effortless reading of the body text." The capabilities and characteristics that the display screen accordingly had to have were:

- it is large enough to hold the whole page or spread in natural size plus a little extra room for a work area;
- it has a resolution of a quality that makes the body text easy to read in its true size and in all details;
- it is non-light emitting, which means that the display should have a variable degree of density, just like the printed page.

However, "not even . . . the most advanced available display technology" could meet these requirements for a "satisfactory representation of the page and its material as a basis for the makeup person's professional evaluation and processing." There were no screens large enough to display a whole page at full size, but there were none with sufficient resolution to permit the body text to be readable when a page was reduced sufficiently for it all to fit on the screen. Text had to be black on light background to approximate the appearance of the printed product, but the resulting amount of light emission strained eyes so much as to impair evaluation. Light emission could be avoided with liquid crystal display technology, but this was not yet developed to the point where it offered sufficient size, resolution, and speed. The magnitude of the gaps between the requirements and available technology, at least when the project was carried out, was indeed large, with processors estimated as being some one hundred times too slow and screen resolution ten times too low.

Nevertheless, other features of computer technology offered many advantages over the earlier technologies. The greatest was freedom in making changes of any kind. They could be made more easily, more rapidly, and at any time, right up to the last minute. Multiple alternatives could be tried without consuming much time, and pages could be made up without having to wait for all material to be in. In these respects computer technology promised to provide more powerful tools than either lead or paper. In addition, it could recapture an advantage of lead that had been lost by the shift to paper: precision in positioning so that all material can be exactly rectilinear, spacing uniform where desired, and so on. For the potential of computer technology to be realized, however, it was necessary to find some way to deal with the display screen limitations as well as to provide the programs and interaction tools to select and implement the needed operations, so designed as to permit modification by the workers as they learned of new needs and possibilities.

To work out ways of meeting these requirements, a "user model" for conceptualizing the process of making up a page on a display screen was devised. The model postulated a "table" on which a page ground, menus, material lists, status information, and a work area were placed. Given the limited screen size, a capability for viewing the whole page and any portions of it at various levels of reduction or magnification, along with the other items on the table, was conceived as a set of "lenses" at the worker's disposal. To look at the same portion with different magnifications at the same time, different lenses could be used simultaneously (e.g., to look at one portion in its position within the whole page through one lens and to look at it in higher magnification in the work space through another, which apparently might be on an adjacent screen). All operations could be implemented on the material, regardless of the lenses through which it was viewed.

Working with this user model, the project team specified the additional capabilities required to make operations on the material easy and natural. These included fixed scales rather than continuously variable reduction and enlargement to facilitate rapid and precise shifts among lenses, the availability of gravitational field pointing for automatic precision positioning, and the like. They also included the various interaction tools required to select and implement all the operations. In contrast with display screen technology, available interaction tools such as those for pointing to material like an electronic pen directed at the screen or a puck ("mouse") moved on a tablet, a keyboard, and function keys were evidently deemed adequate, if the software permitting them to be used in required ways could be provided. Thus, the software had to permit the simultaneous use of several tools, continuous feedback via cursors and status information, and retrieval of preceding statuses, whether immediate or remote.

Pending developments that overcame the limitations in available and prospective technology and leaving aside the idea that page makeup should not be computerized until the limitations are overcome, UTOPIA thus concentrated on designing a system that was as good as possible from the standpoint of work and product quality, given the limitations. That meant formulating specifications designed to satisfy work-environment and work-organization requirements as well as those concerned with the page makeup process itself. Of course, the latter inescapably involved work-environment considerations, as in connection with the eyestrain associated with display technology deficiencies. Using the technology laboratory to simulate the computerized work process, UTOPIA compiled a substantial list of other requirements for ergonomically satisfactory equipment and procedures embracing the entire work station as well as the computer technology itself.

But the work environment in the broader sense shades into work organization. To facilitate thinking about work organization, the simulation technique was supplemented by a "construction box" of functions or tasks involved in page makeup with which to visualize alternative ways of relating the functions to each other. In the graphics workers' case, as in others, a fundamental union goal was to diminish the social division of labor by widening the range of tasks within any production process on which each worker works and to provide the conditions for "a more democratic work organization where a collective of autonomous workers can be responsible for and distribute multiple work tasks." In addition to the workers involved in page makeup on which we have focused, those involved in image processing are also engaged in the page preparation process. A choice can be made between a division of labor in that process that assigns these two sets of tasks to two separate, specialized groups of workers or one that allows the same group of workers to alternate between them. To be able to opt for the latter, it was necessary for the technology to facilitate rotation among tasks. This led to a variety of specifications for computerized page preparation technology. One of them was a sufficient degree of standardization between the page makeup and image processing hardware and software to minimize the need to learn different operational skills to do both kinds of work, while allowing sufficient flexibility to allow adaptation of operations to individual work styles, capabilities, and handicaps. Another was administrative software permitting easy retrieval of work in progress at the stage at which it was interrupted. Along a different dimension of job enlargement were requirements concerning user maintenance and repair.

Work-organization issues bearing on system design became controversial and difficult to deal with when they impinged on the tasks of separate occupations organized in separate unions, however, particularly when they concerned the consequences of computerization for the graphics workers and journalists. As in other industries where technological change is reducing the demand for labor while changing the labor process, workers in the affected occupations are pitted against each other in competition for the remaining jobs, and unions are plunged into conflict with each other as jurisdictional demarcations based on previous technologies are eroded. As elsewhere (but not everywhere), the newspaper industry in Sweden has been beset by disputes between graphic workers and journalists over who will do what in the chain of processes from "manuscript to plate" which computerization makes increasingly possible to integrate. Journalists feared loss of influence over layout if computerized page makeup workstations were staffed by graphics workers, while also anticipating new employment opportunities if journalists got the right to staff them. But if journalists did so, then the graphics workers, in turn, feared the loss of a key function of their occupation and with it the loss of the associated jobs.

UTOPIA's premise was that these processes could be designed in such a way as to permit both "graphic workers' and journalists' occupational skills, identity and pride to live on." One way to do it would be to simply duplicate traditional work organization with new technology. But this approach, it was pointed out, made it difficult to exploit the possibilities for flexibility—e.g., eliminating restrictions on alteration or introduction of new text imposed by traditional page makeup technology—opened up by the new technology. So a model work organization that would permit journalists and graphics workers to cooperate on material accessible to both through an integrated computerized system was suggested. This model was largely based on experience in a small Norwegian newspaper at which graphics workers and journalists worked side by side and communicated directly with each other about the journalists' intentions and the graphics workers' efforts to give them typographical expression. The possibility of realizing UTOPIA's premise in practice was thereby given some confirmation. Yet, the tensions between the Swedish graphics workers' and journalists' unions precluded the joint development of that model from becoming a part of the UTOPIA project.

Thus, journalists did not participate in the formulation of specifications constituting the core of UTOPIA's first stage, neither in the project itself nor in the reference group to which it reported, although there were journalist representatives in the TIPS reference group. Opposition by the journalists was also a major factor preventing implementation of what had been intended as UTOPIA's second stage. This was to occur in connection with the first pilot installation of the TIPS system. The UTOPIA project group was to evaluate the system in the light of the specifications that had been formulated, leading in turn to further revision of the specifications, and to develop an experimental work organization for utilizing the system in which graphics workers and journalists would both participate.

Although the site chosen for the first pilot installation was a Stockholm afternoon daily owned by the LO, *Aftonbladet,* it proved impossible to undertake the work-organization experiment. The unions of graphics workers and journalists (the latter is a TCO union) could not agree on staffing rights or on how to carry out the experiment. In the absence of agreement by the unions, *Aftonbladet*'s management could proceed without such an experiment, which it preferred not to have. And in the absence of a desire for it by the purchaser of the first pilot installation, STU was unwilling to press for such an experiment, which it evidently did not see as part of the technology procurement project it was supporting. As a result, the second and final stage of UTOPIA was scaled down drastically. It was confined to observation and documentation of what happened when TIPS was tried out at the newspaper, without any systematic effort to realize the potential for work and product quality that UTOPIA's participation in its development had incorporated into it. With this to be carried out in 1986, UTOPIA will have come to an end.

The UTOPIA Project's Implications

All of UTOPIA's results are accordingly not in—and the full story of what it has done so far has not been secured at the time of writing—but enough is known to permit some tentative conclusions, not only about the UTOPIA project itself but also about the issues of trade union technology policy on which it sheds light.

To begin with, the project has had some immediate, practical results. The set of specifications it developed, preliminary as they are, are serving several purposes. They have entered into the design of the TIPS system, although precisely how is not indicated by the available information. They are also serving as the basis for negotiations between local unions and management at several newspapers concerning the purchase and utilization of computer technology and, in turn, for negotiations with suppliers (including suppliers other than Liber). The technology laboratory and construction box developed for the purpose of formulating the specifications are themselves important results, providing techniques that are being used in adapting the specifications for local negotiations and for training in the vocational college.

More broadly, UTOPIA serves as a valuable demonstration project, providing a rich fund of experience bearing on the problems and possibilities of developing a trade union strategy for influencing technological development. On the positive side, its most important contribution has been its demonstration of how workers can participate actively in technological development, incorporating their skills, including tacit knowledge built up through long experience, directly into the design process. This provides a credible countermodel to the conventional approach to technological development that dispenses with workers by relying on experts alone to incorporate operations equivalent or alternative to those carried out by workers into the design process on the basis of theoretical knowledge and formal description.

The lessons drawn from this experience have been articulated by contrasting the "tool perspective" from which UTOPIA worked and the "systems perspective" that prevails in the design and construction of computer technology. Although such technology is readily conceived in systems terms, those terms are seen as fostering a conceptualization of applications in ways that have negative work-quality consequences. Thus, in systems terms applications are viewed "from the top of the organization," the organization is viewed as a "structure, whose important aspects may—and should—be formally described," and workers' jobs are reduced to "algorithmic procedures" so that workers and computers are viewed "as information processing systems on which the described data processing has to be distributed. This conceptualization is said to facilitate, even if it does not cause, a tendency for applications to reduce the "need for experience and skill," allow "less control over and understanding of the production process," increase the division of labor, and diminish "planning as part of the job." By instead taking the skills that workers display in practice as the point of departure, and by conceptualizing computer applications as tools for exercising and enlarging those skills, the tool perspective is aimed at designing applications that more adequately meet union work-quality objectives. UTOPIA thus demonstrated the feasibility of using the tool perspective in developing a specific computer application.

The claim is not that the tool perspective provides a model for achieving union work-quality objectives in all applications, but that it is one alternative to a systems perspective, most relevant in situations where "some kind of material is refined by skilled workers." The range of such situations is wide, including many kinds of office work as well as industrial work, such as that of machinists. However, in other situations, such as those in which there is "more formalized (or formalizable) data processing with long sequences of predeterminable operations," the need to develop other alternatives is called for. In that connection, UTOPIA offers an example only at the most general level of combining workers with technical and work-organization specialists in developing alternative technologies.

Major obstacles to doing so are also illustrated by UTOPIA's experience. One concerns the resources required. As the LO documents cited earlier point out, R&D resources are heavily concentrated in large private firms, particularly multinationals based outside of Sweden, with additional resources scattered among other firms, universities, and governments so that the resources are directed toward the objectives of those institutions. Unions, on the other hand, do not have the revenues from sales or taxes enabling them to direct R&D toward the distinctive work-quality objectives for which they are the most significant voice. They must therefore rely primarily on their ability to influence the other institutions' definitions of the problems on which they bring R&D to bear. This influence can take various forms, including direct participation in problem definition in the other institutions, shaping the demand for technology by setting standards through collective bargaining, and by collaboration with suppliers (as in the UTOPIA project.) But all of these forms on influence are contingent on at least sufficient command of technical resources to be able to autonomously operationalize union objectives as specific technical problems and to evaluate the solutions that result from R&D efforts.

In the last analysis, as LO argued, unions cannot have that minimal command over R&D resources without public funding, and this will not be available except insofar as the unions' work-quality objectives become incorporated into public policy, as have the other kinds of objectives that have been incorporated into policy guiding public funding of R&D, such as industrial competitiveness, defense, health, and education. Since the extent to which this happens ultimately depends on the political strength of the unions, this might at least have been expected to happen in Sweden, where that strength is probably greater than in any other country. Work quality has indeed become an objective of public policy in Sweden, as the legislation of the 1970s on the work environment and extension of collective bargaining to workplace issues indicates. But the limits of the policy commitment are clearly demonstrated by the difficulties UTOPIA encountered in securing funding from STU, the government's principal agency for supporting technological R&D.

Although STU finally did provide the funds needed for UTOPIA's first stage, it did so by treating it as a type of project with which it dealt all along, technology procurement, rather than recognizing union capacity to bring R&D to bear on work-quality problems they define as a new type of technological development project entitled to support. A redefinition of STU's mission in this way is unlikely to occur unless the government does so explicitly, and this does not seem to have happened. To be sure, STU has financed some union participation in development projects, such as one concerned with computerized medical information systems, and also some work by central LO and TCO staffs on the kinds of projects for which unions seek support. But the significant shift in research policy needed to enable unions to play an autonomous role in technological development, which LO called for in 1981, has not yet occurred.[34] Until it does, UTOPIA is likely to remain an isolated demonstration of what could be a "new Scandinavian model" of technological development rather than an important step in the realization of that potential.

The unions' effectiveness in bringing about such a shift in national research policy has certainly not been enhanced by divisions among them created by conflicting stakes in technological change. This is another major obstacle to achieving union influence over technological change that is underscored by UTOPIA's experience. Its inability to secure collaboration between graphics workers and journalists reflected the fact that in the newspaper industry, as in other industries where technological change is reducing the demand for labor while changing the labor process, workers in the affected occupations are pitted against each other in competition for the remaining jobs, and unions are plunged into conflict with each other as jurisdictional demarcations based on previous technologies are eroded. The specific consequence in UTOPIA's case, as we saw, was that the conflict blocked implementation of the project's second stage as it was originally conceived. If the two unions had been able to agree that a work-organization experiment in the pilot installation should be conducted, it is doubtful that the newspaper management could have refused to agree to it. Under those circumstances, it is in turn doubtful that STU would have cut off funding for UTOPIA's participation.

Similar conflicts arise between other occupational groups and the unions that represent them, such as machinists represented by the metal-workers' union and technicians such as designers and programmers represented by the private-sector industrial salaried workers' union. The blurring of occupational lines distinguishing the latter two unions that results from technological change has led some union officials and some employers to propose a merger between them. But the obstacles to that are formidable, not least the political obstacles posed by the fact that the metalworkers are linked to the Social Democratic party and the salaried workers' union is not. Short of merger, there may be some scope for collaboration between them, for there is broad similarity in the work-quality objectives espoused by the two unions, and there are individual work sites where they are engaged in joint efforts to influence the introduction of new technology. Yet, the conflicts over staffing of new technology that requires fewer workers are likely to be too great to permit the unions to develop a common strategy for influencing the development of the new technology.

What prevents a common strategy at the local and industry levels makes it very difficult to pursue a common strategy at the national policy level. The necessity of pursuing a "multilevel strategy," in which union efforts at these different levels reinforce each other, is in fact one of the main lessons drawn from the UTOPIA project by its members. But the need for it to be pursued in common by all the affected unions is evidently as important a lesson. For, as a UTOPIA document concludes, the "lack of union cooperation—not the technology, the newspaper proprietors, nor the suppliers—can tragically enough be the decisive factor preventing the utopia from becoming a reality."[35]

Notes

1. This essay is derived in part from a report prepared for the Swedish National Board for Technical Development (Styrelsen for Teknisk Utveckling, STU), under a contract to the Massachusetts Institute for Technology Center for Policy Alternatives. The author is grateful to the many STU and union staff members and others who generously gave their time for interviews.

2. Harry C. Katz and Charles F. Sabel, "Industrial Relations and Industrial Adjustment: The World Car Industry," *Industrial Relations* 24 (3) (Fall 1985); 295–315.

3. Michael J. Piore and Charles F. Sabel, *The Second Industrial Divide* (New York: Basic Books, 1984).

4. See Robert E. Cole, "The Macropolitics of Organizational Change," ch. 2 in this volume.

5. *Statistiska årsbok 1985* (Statistical Yearbook) (Stockholm: Statistiska centralbyrån, 1985), 203.

6. Conflict has been especially marked between printers and journalists, as noted later in this essay. Less intense but perhaps more important for the future of the labor movement are the rival stakes of the LO metalworkers union and TCO private-sector clerical and technical workers union (Svenska Industrit-jänstemannaförbundet, SIF).

7. The following account, particularly of phases 1 through 3, is based on Andrew Martin, "Trade Unions in Sweden: Strategic Responses to Change and Crisis," in Peter Gourevitch, Andrew Martin, and George Ross, eds., *Unions and Economic Crisis: Britain, West Germany, and Sweden,* 191–359 (London: George Allen & Unwin, 1984).

8. LO, *The Trade Union Movement and Full Employment* (Stockholm: LO, 1953), English translation of LO, *Fackföreningsrorelsen och den fulla sysselsät-tningen* (Stockholm: LO, 1951).

9. T. L. Johnston, ed. and transl., *Economic Expansion and Structural Change* (London: George Allen & Unwin, 1963). This is a translation of LO, *Samordnad näringspolitik* (Stockholm: LO, 1961).

10. Rudolf Meidner, addressing the 1961 LO Congress. LO, *Kongressprotokoll* (Stockholm: LO, n.d.), 336. All translations from Swedish, including document titles, are by the author unless otherwise indicated.

11. S. D. Anderman, ed. and transl., *Trade Unions and Technological Change* (London: George Allen & Unwin, 1967), 122. This is an English translation of LO, *Fackforeningsrörelsen och den tekniska utvecklingen* (Stockholm: LO, 1966).

12. Ibid., 134–35.

13. *Program for aktiv näringspolitik. Näringspolitiska kommittens slutrapport* (Program for an Active Industrial Policy. The Industrial Policy Committee's Final Report) (Stockholm: Socialdemokraterna, 1968), 5–6, 13–14.

14. Anderman, *Trade Unions and Technological Change*, 258.

15. This and the quotations in the preceding paragraph are from LO, *Fackföreningsrörelsen och arbetsmiljon* (The Trade Union Movement and the Work Environment) (Stockholm: Prisma, 1971), 29–35.

16. For further discussion of the employers' position, including SAF's encouragement of change in work organization on management terms, see Cole's chapter 2 in this volume, as well as Martin, "Trade Unions in Sweden," 254–58.

17. LO, *Arbetsmiljon* (The Work Environment) (Stockholm: Prisma, 1976), 85–94, 126–28, 148–49.

18. LO, *Fackföreningsrörelsen och forskningen* (The Trade Union Movement and Research) (Stockholm: Tidens Förlag, 1981), 9.

19. Ibid., 18–19, 72–74.

20. Ibid., 21–22.

21. Ibid., 19–20, 56–72, 74–98.

22. LO, *Facklig datapolitik* (Union Computer Policy) (Stockholm: Tidens Förlag, 1981), 9–13. The decline in Sweden's advantageous position in the international economy, which had been under way for some time, was sharply aggravated by the impact of the first oil price increase and subsequent international recession. The impact was delayed by policies designed to "bridge over" the recession but that may well have intensified the impact when it could no longer be averted, which was after the Social Democrats were replaced in office by the bourgeois parties. The structural crisis that emerged then put a greater premium than ever on structural and technological change to restore the Swedish economy's competitiveness. For a fuller discussion, see Martin, "Trade Unions in Sweden," 288–310.

23. LO, *Facklig datapolitik*, 105–106.

24. Ibid., 106–108, 50–51.

25. Ibid., 51–56, 92–101, 108–109.

26. Ibid., 56–61, 101–104.

27. Ibid., 12.

28. Ibid., 117–19.

29. The text of the private sector agreement is available in English as *Agreement on Efficiency and Participation: SAF-LO-PTK* (Stockholm: Swedish Employers Confederation, 1982). Additional sources for the discussion of recent developments include press accounts, interviews, and materials generously supplied in response to mail and telephone requests.

30. The following account of the UTOPIA project is based on interviews with the project leader and others at the Center for Working Life (ALC), union participants, and STU staff members, as well as extensive documentation issued during the course of the project, including the project's information bulletin, *Graffiti,* and more detailed reports on specific aspects of the project.

31. *The UTOPIA Project;* English translation of the UTOPIA research program (Stockholm: Center for Working Life, 1981), 12–13, 7.

32. Ibid., 13, 27–28.

33. An English language discussion of the tool perspective and its application to newspaper makeup work is provided in Pelle Ehn and Morten Kyng, "A Tool Perspective on Design of Interactive Computer Support for Skilled Workers," Computer Science Department, Aarhus University, Aarhus, Denmark, DAIMI PB-190, January 1985.

34. Since this was written, STU has taken a further step by agreeing to LO's proposal to establish a standing committee of STU and union representatives dealing with the whole range of projects in a large new program on computer R&D recently authorized by the government. In addition to providing information on the projects, the committee is supposed to facilitate collaboration between the unions and the researchers involved and to initiate new projects.

35. *Graffiti* 7 (Dec. 1984): 9. The UTOPIA experience is set within the perspective of a multilevel trade union strategy for technological change in a book by one of the participating researchers, Åke Sandberg, *Technological Change and Codetermination in Sweden* (Philadelphia: Temple University Press, forthcoming).

5

IMPROVING PARTICIPATION:
THE NEGOTIATION OF NEW TECHNOLOGY
IN ITALY AND EUROPE

Giuseppe Della Rocca

This essay will seek to examine a contention circulating among employers, the media, and industrial relations researchers that we are witnessing an inevitable decline in industrial relations as a central regulating system of society. This decline, it is held, is due above all to a decrease in the effectiveness of union action, and the general social and institutional consequences of this.

The reasons for this situation, so different from the one that characterized the 1960s and 1970s in Europe, are well known: they range from the results of a prolonged phase of crisis and economic depression, to the restructuring and contraction of the industrial sector, to the crisis of welfare policies and the joint regulation strategies pursued by many European governments.

However, in addition to these factors, a further element has arisen, one to which an increasingly greater importance has been accorded: technological innovation, considered the greatest threat to collective union action. Although other social and economic factors are represented as being cyclical and/or only partially able to modify the nature of industrial relations, technological innovation is experienced as a *structural change* and as a factor capable not only of weakening union action but also of changing the very nature of collective bargaining itself. According to such a thesis, the transformation of work lies at the root of a weakening of the union as a form of worker representation; the potentialities of the new technologies, especially of electronics-informatics, constitute a challenge more fundamental than the economic crisis itself to the consolidated practices regulating collective-bargaining relationships.

This essay will attempt to understand how unions intend to control innovation and which social and economic criteria can be adopted to protect and promote workers' interests.

My hypothesis is that changes in technical-productive structures and the industrial relations system are interactive and interdependent. If technological innovation contributes to defining the nature of work and occupation and this in turn helps to define both the type and method of representation of individual and collective interests, industrial relations traditions are in turn a factor in selecting the type, timing, and characteristics involved in introducing technical-organizational innovations. The relationship between technical innovation and industrial relations is circular rather than unidirectional: the behavior of one helps to explain that of the other; technical-organizational changes, from the industrial revolution to today, demonstrate not only that technological changes influence union behavior but also that the way in which the latter interact influences the work process within which such technology is utilized and implemented. An analysis of the relationship between technological innovation and industrial relations necessitates going beyond the interpretive limits imposed by an exclusively institutional point of view in the study of industrial relations. This latter approach has laid emphasis on a detailed description of the legal structure of collective bargaining, of the history and development of the current themes in the political strategy of each organization. But it has not adequately taken into account employers' strategies, partly because their political and operational strategies have not been consolidated within any form of employers' association. The "institution" for the employer is not the employers' association (as opposed to the workers' unions) but the enterprise itself. At this level management feels itself to be fully represented, and it is principally here that it is possible to perceive the practices and strategies employed.

The Italian case will be extensively illustrated in this essay. Work transformation will not be examined directly, however. The analysis will focus rather on those union agreements that refer to technical-organizational modifications, the new elements introduced by them into the industrial relations tradition, and those aspects of the introduction of technological innovation that such agreements are to regulate. Changes introduced by these agreements into industrial relations structures and into the procedures and contents of work protection receive special attention. This analysis will be undertaken in sections 1–4. Sections 5 and 6 will compare the Italian case with other European countries. A general convergence between the various countries does not exist. Rather, significant differences persist as a result of traditional industrial relations factors, in contrast to technological ones. However, a persistence of differences does not indicate traditional models that are substantially static but, on the one hand, different ways of adapting union action in each country with respect to technological innovation and, on the other, some convergent phenomena.

For this analysis it is important to consider distinct types of industrial relations traditions, insofar as these imply substantial differences in structure, procedures, and collective-bargaining contents. The first is the type of industrial relations tradition in which a confrontation with technical-organizational innovation takes place, primarily through the control and protection of occupational and craft traditions. This is the case in Great Britain, where the principal characteristics are the decentralization of bargaining (the most important level of industrial relations activity being the workplace at a company level rather than at a national level), voluntarism, and occupational segmentation (union and collective-bargaining organization is, for the most part, divided up on the basis of occupation), and a tradition of conflict. Traditionally, there is a high level of informality surrounding rights and procedures. This informality is part of a system recognized both by unions and by employers, and its origins lie in customs and practices of bargaining that have been more or less consolidated within the various sectors, industries, companies, and occupations. This system functions not only between workers and company but also among various occupational groups in defining demarcations and rights that are continually revised and adapted according to their relative needs and power.

The second type is represented by an industrial relations system heavily influenced by an institutional and normative tradition existing outside the workplace. This is the case of Scandinavia and West Germany, in which work rights are guaranteed by institutions external to the workplace. The characteristics of such systems are a centralization of industrial relations structures; general representation by the unions; and a high level of legislative ruling regarding procedures that regulate the relationship between workers, union, and employers. The control of working conditions takes place, for the most part, by means of external regulations. Such regulations tend to allow unions and workers' representatives the right of consultation and codetermination on all decisions influencing the workforce. Important differences exist between these countries, to be sure. Certain of them, such as Sweden, tend not to impose specific regulations on working conditions; others, such as West Germany, seek more detailed regulations. Thus, in Sweden, the centralization is accompanied by high union density, and the workplace representation is union based; in Germany, instead, the union density is much lower and formal structures of workplace representation tend not to be union based. The general, and partly generic, nature of such regulations and the insistence that they place on consultation and codetermination procedures give rise to informal negotiations at workplaces and to agreements that are not always consistent with national negotiations.

The third type comprises an industrial relations tradition in which the control of technical-organizational innovation takes place primarily through the protection of unskilled work. Such is the case in Italy, where control over working conditions is carried out in the workplace, but, in contrast to the English case, is both detailed and formal. This system is characterized by a bipolar industrial relations structure, with both centralized and decentralized bargaining; general union representation at the national level and in the workplace; a high degree of politicization of industrial relations, which has led to a plurality of unions organized on this basis rather than that of occupation; and a high level of conflict. The formalization of rights gives importance to the union's role, to the detriment of the informal power of organized groups. However, such rights, though formalized, are of a grassroots character, being in most cases formulated by means of heavy bargaining, with frequent recourse to collective action due to the employers' resistance to conceding negotiation rights in the workplace. These and other characteristics of the Italian case will be more fully illustrated in sections 2 and 3.

1. The Characteristics of Industrial Relations in Italy

The foundations of the collective action of Italian unions lie in the primacy of politics. Economic and social difficulties, backward conditions, and the limited industrial development in most of Italy up to the end of World War II have, as far as the unions are concerned, given primary importance to the recognition of their own rights of representation and recourse to political resources. This phenomenon has been explained by Alessandro Pizzorno in the same way in which Gerschenkon defined the birth and process of industrialization in Italy in the last century: starting from a position of backwardness always necessitates an investment of a political nature. In the case of the unions, strong resistance on the part of Italian society to a complete and widespread recognition of bargaining has resulted in explicitly confrontational politics through an elaboration of often highly ideological principles of action. This, in turn, has effected the orientation and the criteria of choice of demand, as well as the modality and forms of aggregation and social solidarity.[1]

This form of representation has contributed above all to the development of a centralized type of union organization and industrial relations system. It has consolidated a type of organization that has not been determined spontaneously, as in the case of English and American unions.

The primacy of political action has had the effect of making this very pluralism of Italian union organizations one that is political-ideological by nature rather than occupational, such as is typical of English or other European unions. The centralization is based upon an adherence to three union confederations, divided by differing political traditions, which organize white- and blue-collar workers belonging to all industrial sectors, including agriculture and public service.

The winning of bargaining rights in the workplace (1969) has in part modified this centralized model of organization. The birth of shop or office representatives, organized into factory committees, elected by the workers without reference to a confederation list, has given a more grassroots character to these organizations. The shop steward committees (*consigli di fabbrica*) represent all three confederations in workplaces, with bargaining rights and the power to sign formal agreements at the factory level. A single line of worker representation at the shopfloor level has meant that since 1969–70 the organization of Italian unions has also been called a divided one, split into two contrasting models: on the one hand, a centralized structure outside the workplace, based upon three confederations, each comprising several industrial unions, which draw up national agreements; on the other hand, the shop steward committees in workplaces, elected by all the workers regardless of the union to which they belong, with the right to sign formal agreements at company, shop, or office level.

Industrial relations are characterized by nearly exclusive emphasis on collective bargaining, with little recourse to the application of legislative rulings. Collective bargaining has been the principal instrument for asserting the unions' negotiating power over working conditions and the right of disclosure of company information.

The orientation of union and management is conflictual. Collective negotiations function above all to defend the established interests of each party and are directed toward obtaining increasingly greater advantages with respect to those already consolidated. The realization of its aims by one of the parties presupposes, if not "defeat," in any case a reduction of the economic, normative, and representational powers of the other.

Unlike other countries, the conflictual orientation in Italy has no basic legislation, no arbitration, and/or formalized bargaining *procedures.* However, bargaining is highly formalized in large and medium-sized businesses with respect to the *content* of agreements.

The bargaining structure, for the reasons stated, presents itself as bipolar. Decentralized bargaining activity, however, is not consistent with centralized activity with respect to contractual content, such as the amount and type of wage increases. Since 1970 there has been a tendency toward an overlapping of, and interplay between, bargaining levels rather than the creation of a functional division between the various levels, with well-defined procedures and instances with respect to the tasks and contents to be negotiated.[2]

2. Work Tradition and Bargaining Attitudes in the Workplace

Work tradition in large production units in Italy is based on written rules. Forms of solidarity are not constituted by the skill-based pattern of work but by the characteristics of the work organization in which the worker operates. An increase in workers' rights is a response to the working conditions of each job, which themselves reflect the operational status of particular technological-organizational conditions. This tradition of formal rights tends to give priority more to job stability than to skill, to the rigidity of rules than to technical-productive innovation and flexibility. Work is mainly understood as the condition required to obtain an income and maintain it rather than as a possibility for individual and group development, open to qualitative improvements (Della Rocca, 1982).

This pattern of work tradition can be explained by considering the various elements that have contributed to its formation: the more recent characteristics of industrial development and management attitudes, the collective and spontaneous response of industrial workers to radical rationalization processes, and the role played by unions in representing the industrial workers' protests.

This pattern of work tradition is the result of the creation during the 1950s and 1960s of a "new work-force system" within large industrial firms. Various factors had a role in determining its main features:

1. a growing level of fragmentation and rationalization of work in large and medium-sized companies, which was more intense than in other European countries, and gave rise to a steady impoverishment of the quality of work.
2. the low degree of upgrading and labor mobility. An enquiry carried out on a cross-section of workers during the second half of the 1960s brought to light the crisis in careers and the low importance that they have for industrial workers. The results of this study underline the fact that promotion from the shop floor to the office is not appreciable, that such upgrading is insignificant, and that in certain cases there is even a downgrading and a dequalifying process in the internal labor market of the enterprise (Paci, 1972:150–51).
3. lastly, the attempts by employers to create new identities and job profiles based upon job analysis and evaluation, which were intended to replace criteria of worker evaluation that had become obsolete as a result of ongoing technical-organizational change; and the introduction and diffusion of company benefits, linked to company activities but destroying working-class traditions where they existed (Berta, 1983:153).

This tradition of formal rights is the industrial workers' response to the manufacturing system and the result of a widespread refusal of work in large, rationalized units. The cycle of conflict in the period 1969–72 has provided evidence of this negative attitude. Collective action was oriented toward challenging work organization and caused a crisis, particularly within incentive systems and worker involvement in production. The more important forms of struggle during this period were those based upon a slowdown of the work pace (called, for example, in the slogans of striking workers, the self-limiting of production) in a department or factory (Regini and Reyneri, 1971:74).

The demand for more or less equal wages is the most widespread claim, even though it has varying meanings. Above all, for those workers who most frequently strike spontaneously, it assumes a meaning of solidarity. Across-the-board, or flat, increases tend to underline common interests compared to the practice of percentage increases. The latter, which differ according to worker skill, undermine unity by creating division between groups of workers. The motivation here is one of solidarity, since any reference to job differences is ignored. The voluntarism inherent in the demand for flat increases for everyone lies in the fact that the workers will have to put themselves into identical wage conditions, leaving out of consideration a priori what they are and do within the organization of production. Furthermore, this demand, which has been put forth by hundreds of thousands of workers, rejects the hierarchical significance of worker qualifications and bonus scales as a system of job incentive and motivation (Regini and Reyneri, 1971).

Challenging the organization in factory conflict has led the union to produce a system of formal guarantees, directed toward limiting management power. On the one hand, union strategy has oriented itself toward formal and detailed regulation, modeled on the Tayloristic organization of work, so as to protect workers from more negative effects. On the other hand, it has asked for the abolition and/or complete modification of any kind of job incentive and motivation program.[3]

Union proposals during spontaneous struggle aim at the abolition of the piece-rate system and at equality in pay. The proposal to abolish or freeze payment by piecework is a strategy that manifests itself to some degree everywhere in large units in the industrial sector.[4] Even more widespread are active attempts to make the labor factor more rigid: from controls on work rates (including the abolition of time studies in certain production units), workforce size, and breaks, to the limiting of shifts and the abolition of overtime.

For the unions, equal pay, more than the abolition of the piece-rate system, is a choice that favors unskilled workers over those who are skilled. Since 1969 this has meant the abolition of the principle of percentage pay increases, which supported an incentive policy for skilled workers in the national contract. The policy of equality has led to the reduction of the differences of pay classification, the elimination of the lower categories, and the introduction of automatic promotion on the basis of seniority rather than on the skill and performance of the individual white- or blue-collar worker.[5]

Subsequent consideration has highlighted the main limits of this bargaining activity. First and foremost is the limit implicit in the very term *challenge* of work organization, which presupposes a negative attitude toward a change in the quality of work. Union negotiating strategy is oriented toward a regulation of work at the shopfloor level, based upon the existing work organization. This regulation is put forward as a constraint and not as an innovative factor, and neither does it foresee the possibility either of development or of change in production organization. Such rules, if applied rigidly and without a positive attitude toward the organization, can lead to only one possible result: the decrease of productivity without creating either premises or alternatives for the future (Butera, 1972:9).

No less important is the unions' failure to appreciate the need for a long-term strategy. The lack of such a strategy has led to much ideological talk of challenging the capitalist organization of work (*contestazione dell'organizzazione capitalistica del lavoro*) and the power of workers and unions at shopfloor level, without, however, achieving institutionalized rights for union control over the labor market and managerial prerogatives.

Such limits can be seen in the Italian unions' refusal to find more coherent solutions to the problem of long-term control. The reason for this refusal, or tendency toward short-sightedness, lies in the negative attitude toward any form whatsoever of participation or coresponsibility in the management of either businesses or public institutions, even when dealing with important matters, such as state employment agencies and vocational training. This policy has limited the Italian unions to bargaining over changes in the balance of power in the market and at the workplace, and has confined them to the defense of rules bargained at the shopfloor level.

3. Technological Innovation in Industrial Relations

In Italian collective bargaining there are no specific clauses concerning the regulation and protection of workers facing technological innovation, apart from article 15 of the national contract of the employees of newspaper publishing and printing companies and press agencies.

The absence of such regulations may be due to the fact that information technology is not as widespread as in other countries.[6] Despite this delay in technological innovation, the principal cause that may explain the absence of any contractual and legislative regulation regarding technological innovation is the tradition of collective bargaining itself in Italy.

Technological innovation is only one element of rationalization as a response to crisis. Such matters as management requests for layoffs and labor mobility inside and outside the company—common phenomena during an economic crisis—have been dealt with generally, but technological innovation as such has not been directly brought up as a subject of negotiations.

Consequently, the effects of technological innovation have been handled within the framework of traditional regulations. Numerous agreements have been made regarding unemployment benefits for temporary layoffs (Cassa Integrazione Guadagni, CIG), early retirement, job mobility, personnel retraining, pay guarantees, and shorter work hours and shifts (the shortening of working hours, for instance, from forty hours per week to thirty-six hours by increasing the number of shifts and making them shorter, from eight to six hours per day. This, however, means working six days per week, that is, on Saturdays). However, it is impossible to identify which agreements make reference to technological innovation as such. Problems related to the handling of technical-organizational innovation are, from the perspective of this tradition, *management problems* for which union initiative is unnecessary and, if possible,to be excluded. For this reason, the bargaining institutions formed in the 1960s suffice to protect jobs; and consultation and verification procedures have always, at least until 1975, been viewed with suspicion.

At least until 1975-76 company agreements in Italy in nearly every case were not structured contracts with guidelines and timing of the application and consultation phases related to a single or limited number of objectives. Rather, the agreements have been a series of definitions of rules on numerous issues, often very different as far as content is concerned and from which any possibility of experimentation or verification has been excluded.

There are two exceptions to this general picture of company bargaining in Italy: the agreements on work organization and the utilization of the right to the disclosure of information.

The agreements on the organization of work (Organizzazione del Lavoro, OdL) represent the first contractual innovations, promoted by the unions and certain sectors of management, that modify the more rigid and static aspects of the industrial relations system at the workplace. They constitute a model of bargaining, though never explicitly formalized, and represent one of the means by which Italian unions have carried out negotiations with respect to technological innovation as well. Though not making direct reference to such technology, these agreements constitute a way of dealing with it. In particular, with the introduction of automated information systems, organization becomes more and more a part of operative planning (implementation). This is especially true with respect to the increase in automation: the more automation increases, the more organization influences the ways in which the machinery is employed (De Maio et al., 1982). For this reason, processes of organizational development may well be part of the processes of information-systems implementation.

Since the mid-1970s the number of agreements on work organization has grown. What characterizes them is that they entail a global and unified organization model, which, introduced in various phases, is to be managed from within the sphere of industrial relations. The principles, aims, and technical and organizational methods of such plans, as well as the phases, procedures, and content of working conditions, are to be defined in a contract. The nature of this contract is unity of objective and plurality of contents and procedures. It is, moreover, experimental and entails the need for subsequent verifications and possible agreements that would modify and correct the process of experimentation and application.

The Olivetti agreement of April 5, 1971, was the first and became a pattern for further agreements. This agreement granted the union thousands of upgradings and formally committed the company to substantial changes in work and organization. It established an initial industrial relations model that responded to the workers' and unions' criticisms of certain elements of the system, particularly piecework and qualification scales—criticisms that represented an ideological and political commitment to eliminate alienating work and to restructure the labor process. The company agreed to this and proposed a new organizational model, namely, "the assembly island." In addition, the company and the union were to bargain over the aspects that traditionally fall within the competence of the unions and that arise from the model (incentives, work rates, breaks, qualifications) (Butera, 1984:67).

The emphasis of planning is not placed on technology as such but rather on the micro-organization of departments. However, this is understood in terms of a global plan of production as a whole (including process and product technology), and it has thus been called by the unions "collective workmanship." Both work mobility and learning are defined in terms of multiple skills, which result in a greater technical capacity, a fuller knowledge of the production cycle, and an enhanced capacity to intervene and check production—though such qualities refer more to the group than to the individual workers (Chiaromonte, 1978).

Because the union views this as an experience of new skill capacity and of workers' judgment and autonomy in the exercise of their own work, the team concept justifies certain aspects such as mobility, which otherwise would have been considered negative. Furthermore, both unions and management have finally acknowledged, to a greater extent than in any other agreements, that certain basic managerial requirements, such as the improvement of productivity, are not necessarily incompatible with others, such as the improvement of the quality of work.

In Italian industrial relations this type of bargaining has had a limited diffusion, and the hypothesis maintained by some that the contents, procedure, and form of this type of contract might be the object of general agreement among the social parties, as has happened in other countries, has never become a reality.[7] In any case, at company level this experience has provided a model for the rules of the game in dealing with organizational change, particularly in regard to all disclosure of information.

Introducing the right to the disclosure of information has been more straightforward. It has been defined by the regulation of details introduced into the national contracts in 1976 and is hardly anomalous in the European context. This right constitutes a second way in which Italian unions have succeeded in bringing about negotiations on technology.

During the economic crisis of 1975 the unions had requested and obtained rights to the disclosure of information, with the specific intent of urging and demanding union control over prerogatives that are more precisely part of a managerial role. These did not relate directly to production organization but to company policies and, particularly, the capacity for decision and innovation.

By 1977 the right to the disclosure of information was an established fact of industrial reality, at least as far as large businesses were concerned. Though differing from sector to sector, in substance such rights give access to information on investment programs, innovation and technological modifications, subcontracting, the location of new sites, horizontal mobility, and the expected consequences with respect to employment and work organization. With the right to verify and examine information on these, the unions intend to assert the possibility of control.

In many cases it has been used only to inform the union of decisions already made. This denies the union any option in such matters or simply elicits union participation while keeping it in a subordinate role. Information rights represent a turning point in bargaining only in those cases in which a bargaining practice is established that has its own instruments for handling information and the various processes of innovation and/or rationalization to which such information refers.

These are cases in which the right of information disclosure is used with respect to technical and organizational change (Della Rocca and Negrelli, 1983). The agreements on technical innovation cannot be separated from an effective utilization of the right of the disclosure of information. And in these cases it is not so much a form of pressure to force the company to invest in new sites or a control of the company's financial activities and economic policies as it is an instrument for handling the social effects of technical-productive innovation.

In the latter cases there were important innovative aspects in the field of collective-bargaining. The first, and most important, innovation is that the right of information disclosure allows both management and union to forecast each other's behavior in the short- and medium-term. Change is therefore created by the movement from a situation in which unpredictability is the rule to one in which the behavior of all parties is known. In this case the diffusion of such information plays an essentially strategic role. The second innovation, introduced by the right of information disclosure, lies in prior discussion of many of the changes brought about by employer strategy. And the third consists of the development of informal relations between union and management. In fact, the lengthening of procedures by means of advance information establishes a period of consultation that precedes negotiations, properly speaking. In a situation of conflict, in which every element is rigorously signed and formalized, the right to the disclosure of information represents the introduction of a consultative phase that does not necessarily end in negotiations and that in any case, precedes them. Consultation does not formally commit the parties or oblige them to take explicit stances as in negotiations, and it may allow for a phase of examination and specific planning on issues that pertain more to the area of company management. This informal activity does not, in its turn, impede a fuller and better informed development of the actual bargaining.

4. Technological Innovation in Industrial Relations: A Summary of Empirical Findings

In this section agreements on work organization and on the use of the right to the disclosure of information with respect to controls over the introduction of information technology will be examined.

Under examination were seventy-six agreements on work organization drawn up in forty-two companies and signed, for the most part, between 1980 and 1984. For some it was necessary to go back to the late 1970s and, in the case of two companies, the early 1970s. The majority concern the iron and steel and engineering sectors, although there are also a significant number from the chemical, textile, and clothing sectors, and a few covering the public services. This confirms a characteristic already pointed out in the European Trade Union Institute's report on bargaining over information technology, namely, that with respect to other European countries, Italy seems to be the only country whose agreements primarily cover mass production and blue-collar workers instead of public services, public employment, and white-collar workers (Evans, 1982).

Further confirming this are the production areas directly affected by the agreements examined, i.e., those of engineering, assembly, paint shops, and fitting. Office work has become part of bargaining contents only since 1979–80, but usually without going beyond a general reference to the necessity of reorganizing office work and with no indication of the specific characteristics of such change or of the procedures to be used.

The sample is enlarged by another thirteen plans for technological restructuring presented by the employers in the newspaper printing sector since August 1982. The presentation of such plans to local unions is a right signed for in the national newspaper contract. Article 15 of the contract is dedicated to technological innovation and appeared for the first time in 1968. This was quite novel for the period, since the right to the disclosure of information *prior* to the operative introduction of new technology was maintained for the first time. There are no specifications regarding technology, but it is recognized that information is necessary to lessen the negative effects on employment levels, and very brief mention is made of the necessity to work toward employee upgrading.

During 1979–82 it was partially changed and reinforced because of the possibility of companies' introducing new integrated systems and the elimination of repeated typing, which gave rise to the problem of "demarcation rules" between the work of typographers and journalists. To protect both unions and printing workers, a detailed phase of experimentation was recognized, as well as the presentation of plans for technological restructuring and the creation of a national joint committee to examine these plans. In addition to the means already existing and those established by the law for dealing with possible redundancies, seven days of additional reductions in work time annually (with respect to the contractual thirty-five-hour week) have been established but are to be used only to avoid redundancies.

A further group of agreements was examined from the 1984–85 period, when such agreements and others directly connected to information technology (with or without using the right to the disclosure of information) became widespread. There are fifty-one agreements, and one can see an increase in union bargaining among white-collar employees, especially in banking and insurance.

The main innovative elements introduced into the practice of industrial relations in large businesses are, in the first place, circumscribed by information procedures. The degree of complexity of such agreements differs greatly from one to another. In the agreements it is unclear whether the information is to be supplied during the phase of analysis, planning, or implementation of the new technology. Broadly speaking, *prior* means the development of information and consultation activities before or during the operative implementation of systems and machinery.

Our study reveals various procedural types: those concerning the right of information disclosure exclusively and others that foresee consultation, bargaining, verification, and the existence of work groups and mixed committees.

The right to the disclosure of information. This is a right agreed upon in the national contract. Besides confirming what has already been determined at a national level, company agreements apply such clauses and contain either general information on the overall volume of investments or, more often, data concerning levels of technological developments and market strategies, of which the unions take note. The introduction of new technology is, in certain cases, accompanied by specific information giving technical data on the new machinery.

The right of consultation. Within this category fall all types of prior activity that do not limit themselves to the straightforward acquisition of information but allow for the possibility of "joint examinations," and for the union to express an opinion on specific aspects of technical-organizational innovation, without any obligation on the part of company management.

The most frequent content of such examinations is job design, the way in which experimentation should be launched, the technical criteria and parameters of reference, the content and the scheduling of vocational training, and the effects of technological innovation on working conditions.

The right of bargaining. With respect to all the matters mentioned, some agreements provide for prior activity that is not only of consultation but, more precisely, of negotiation. That is to say, the union has won the right to intervene in implementing organizational change that is generally the prerogative of management. In particular, the most important aspects upon which the union may intervene are decisions with regard to the choice of area in which experimentation is to begin, the technical criteria and parameters of new work organization, the procedures for the formation of work groups, the way in which they should function, and the definition of aspects related to working conditions.

Verification procedures. This right, which is very widespread, differs from those examined up to now in that it is not a prior activity. It nearly always results from the right of consultation, though it takes effect during the implementation stages. In by far the majority of cases the subjects of such verification are the results of experimentation in organizational change (carried out on the basis of previously agreed parameters of productivity), in improvement of product quality, or the rationalization of productive flows.

Steering and consultation committees. In certain companies the definition of procedures is accompanied by the formation of joint committees or planning groups entrusted with specific analysis and planning duties or, very often, those of checking and assessing conditions prior to the enactment of organizational innovation. This is the situation in which an attempt at change in the very model of industrial relations is most evident, moving from traditions of a conflictual nature to institutionalized forms of worker participation.

All the clauses relating to employment security are very important, even if traditional. With respect to employment levels there is a prevalence of clauses that protect against negative effects, with agreements on the recourse to the Cassa Integrazione Guadagni (Unemployment Benefit Fund), early retirement, rules regarding the discipline of intercompany mobility, or a commitment to maintain employment levels. The Cassa Integrazione Guadagni is among the principal public instruments that may give support to technical-productive innovation, since it guarantees the wage and employment of workers who are laid off and allows the company a greater flexibility in utilizing the work force. The use of the Cassa Integrazione Guadagni helps to reinforce the procedural aspect of the agreements. Prior to utilization, this must be approved by the public authorities, following the request of the company and unions. The handling of the Cassa Integrazione Guadagni necessitates meetings and joint analyses by the social parties regarding the reasons for its use and solutions to be adopted.

With regard to employment, another new element to be considered separately is the role assumed by training as a subject of bargaining. In the event of technological change, retraining becomes part of bargaining in the area of workers' rights. Some types of technological innovation, however, have demonstrated that the role of training in industrial relations cannot be viewed solely as a simple retraining activity but also as an instrument used by companies to develop a new, more general knowledge of a technical-organizational and managerial character.

Training, as has been demonstrated in other studies of collective bargaining, is also important since it represents an intervention by public authorities in workplace industrial relations for the first time in Italy.[8] In this case the role of public authorities does not lie only in distributing aid for whomever has been temporarily laid off (as is the case with the use of the Unemployment Fund), but also in financing training activities related to technical and organizational projects. In this way state institutions enter into company negotiations, or intervene at least, as a third party in finalizing change and in supervising effects not only on the quantity but also the quality of employment.

Another important element is represented by the number of agreements related to job design and workforce allocation.

The number of clauses in agreements related to job design is fairly homogeneous and allows for the following subdivision: (1) redefinition of jobs; (2) formation of semiautonomous groups; and (3) responsibility sharing in objectives, and the partial elimination of supervisory hierarchies.

Rules regarding *job description* are the most numerous. Two-thirds of the agreements, in fact, contain general mention of, or specific references to, the redefinition of duties. Often it is a question of job enlargement, or even enrichment. Such duties are normally expanded to include quality and maintenance functions.

The rules relating to *semiautonomous work groups,* with a redefinition of duties, have been instituted in well over 20 percent of the sample. These cases provide for the formation of semiautonomous groups to replace individual job assignment.

The rules relating to *responsibility sharing on objectives, integration between functions, and the elimination of hierarchical roles* may be regarded as the most important. A significant number of agreements associate the creation of semiautonomous groups with their responsibility sharing in work objectives, defined generally in terms of quantity and/or with other parameters such as quality, scheduling, consignment dates.

A part of the content of the agreements relates to working conditions, but no important changes have been achieved. Significantly, different elaborations of skill classification and pay policies do not emerge in these agreements, even though new job profiles have been introduced. The sole exception in this context is the introduction of incentive wages in certain agreements, which constitute a new element with respect to traditional industrial relations policy in Italy. There are also few cases concerning the ergonomic aspects of work, such as standards in video display units (VDUs), which contrasts with bargaining in other European countries.

One agreement related to the use of video terminals, however, has the function of protecting workers from having their work computer-monitored at a distance. This IBM agreement, of February 23, 1982, establishes that the "checks on access to all programs, transactions and data will be effected by means of group codes that do not permit the identification of the individual operator," and guarantees the union representatives in the company the opportunity to check "the state of procedures and programs" so as to be able to verify that they conform to what was agreed upon. It is interesting to note that this agreement came about following a statement made to the Magistrature by a local union, claiming violation of article 4 of the Statute of Workers' Rights (Statuto dei Lavoratori, 1970).

To sum up, it may be argued on the basis of these data that the orientation of industrial relations in formal and written job rights is changing. This orientation was the product of the large factory system, characterized by a lack of mobility and a poverty of work content. In the agreements previously analysed, the *partial* abandoning of a written and detailed regulation of jobs, with respect to contents, may be noted.

More than the individual job content, *the type of union and worker participation in organizational change becomes the object of dispute and bargaining.* Only with participation in organizational change is it possible to discuss the organizational choice to be implemented in the long term, which will then influence working conditions. This explains why, in an age of change and union recognition, more attention is paid to the rules that define *procedure* rather than results, with discussion of procedures, structures, timing, and the phases of verification and participation between the parties rather than discussion of medium- to long-term effects on working conditions. Participation therefore becomes the *bargaining issue* in a local context (from which it had been excluded and in which rules regarding it do not exist at an institutional level). Participation, as with technological innovation, has therefore an operational diffusion, linked to chance decisions that are not justified by the negotiating strategy itself.

5. Negotiations on the Introduction of New Technology in Europe

This section will undertake a comparative summary of the impact of information technology on industrial relations in Great Britain, Scandinavia, and West Germany. The results of a recently concluded study[9] will be utilized, seeking to determine the main characteristics of collective bargaining on this theme; the main problems experienced by unions in negotiating technological innovation; and, where they exist, the most important changes in industrial relations traditions brought about by this type of bargaining in each country. Comparisons between the Italian case and these other cases are also considered.

In Great Britain the most important mechanism for union control of technological innovation continues to be collective bargaining. Where this coexists with other forms of participation, however, such as the "works councils," or the "joint technology working parties," it has the potential of prohibiting as well as incorporating such types of activity. The control of technological innovation in Great Britain has been carried out, above all, by means of the *technology agreements,* a term that indicates a specific contractual model negotiated at the level of the production unit and/or the company. These technology agreements do not modify the English industrial relations structure, which remains decentralized. This itself creates substantial problems in coordinating and learning the extent of their diffusion. The information contained here is drawn from the analysis conducted by Robin Williams (Berta, 1986), who examined about 240 agreements of this type.

The matters dealt with in these agreements are various, ranging from employment guarantees to training, changes in the job evaluation system, and the quality of working life. In the first place, what is most evident in these agreements is the union's attempt to develop and put into effect *rights of consultation and information,* beginning with the initial phases of the introduction of new technologies. However, very few of these agreements have resulted in union involvement in the initial decisions. A large proportion of the agreements establish bargaining rights mainly during the implementation phases of the technology, after the principal technological choices have been made but before the final choices regarding instruments and working methods.

With regard to contents, *job security* is by far the most frequently cited point. Demands for job guarantees are there to eliminate the risk of collective dismissals and to protect the workforce already employed. The reduction of working hours as a formula for avoiding a reduction in the numbers employed, following the introduction of new technology, has been applied in very few agreements, however, despite the emphasis that such demands have been given in official union documents.

The protection of the physical and psychological conditions of workers at video terminals is yet another demand that is very widespread in technological agreements. In contrast, however, to bargaining on clauses regarding ergonomic improvements, agreements concerning job design and the quality of work are very few and rather vague. This aspect has been touched upon in various agreements from the point of view of the protection of specific interests through the definition of *demarcation rules.* Here the intention is to outline the various areas of skill.

As can be seen, there are many aspects common also to the Italian case. In general, however, what characterizes Great Britain is the emphasis placed upon the protection of occupational interests by the various unions and the competition, not only between management and workers but also between the unions themselves with regard to the enactment of this type of protection. Technological innovation changes the structure of tasks, skills, and occupations, and creates conflict between the various occupational groups with respect to the distribution of costs and benefits brought about by such changes. In the case of Italy and other European countries this phenomenon is not particularly noticeable. In Great Britain, though, because of union fragmentation, this phenomenon is easily discernible in the competition between unions within the workplace itself.

On the basis of this approach it is possible to single out the other new elements, beginning with the *introduction of consultation* within an industrial relations tradition by nature hostile to the formulation of participatory procedures. As in all cases involving the introduction of the disclosure of information, negotiations are modified by a more participatory attitude as a result of the consultatory phase that precedes them.

However, the way in which information disclosure rights are defined is very often influenced by the way unions have traditionally dealt with the theme of job control. This distinction is particularly important in comparing craft unions with the others. With regard to the craft unions, the disclosure of information relates to specific changes and to immediate objectives in negotiating wages, occupational guarantees, and qualifications. With regard to the other unions, however, the technology agreements have a greater procedural importance, remaining equally valid for any kind of technological innovation, including those to be introduced in the future, giving greater attention and detail to consultative aspects, covering a much larger area of contents and problems and seeking the protection of the largest possible number of workers.

In the second place a greater formalization of bargaining by means of the development of consultation may be witnessed. Consultation on technological innovation is above all related to practice. Most agreements, in effect, contain an assurance by unions that their members would cooperate with changes in equipment and methods in exchange for commitments by management—whether to provide certain safeguards and inducements or to follow certain procedures. However, some of the technology agreements also contain specific provisions that would affect the impact of technology on the regulation of working practices, the bargaining power of labor, and other instruments of union organization. Thus, the agreements include provisions regarding the use of subcontracting, limits on the use of technology, labor demarcation, and the allocation of "new tasks."

The provisions in the technology agreements regarding task allocation reflect the differing objectives of management and unions in this matter. For the former the aim is to *increase* labor flexibility; for the latter it is to *regulate* such flexibility. The establishment of spheres of demarcation in the workplace between different groups of workers (often represented by different unions) has been a major feature of industrial relations in many British companies, especially in manufacturing sectors where multi-unionism, particularly occupational craft union organization, predominates.

In all these cases, regardless of how they have been concluded, there is a formalization of rules, tasks, and demarcation lines that previously were either indefinite or subject to informal bargaining.

In the third place, 75 percent of all technology agreements have had one signatory on the union side; this figure underlines the fact that new production and administration systems frequently cross traditional demarcation lines, with a gradual tendency toward a centralization of bargaining at the company level. This phenomenon is the result of a number of factors, beginning with the nature of technological change and the formalization of bargaining itself—both giving rise to the development of union roles of coordination (senior shop stewards) at the company level. The most important aspect is the weakening of the multi-union phenomenon, with the crisis for some of the craft unions and the growth and development of certain occupational unions, particularly those regarding office workers.

In a pure sense the craft tradition of controling entry to, and the monopoly of, certain skills has been eliminated to a great extent, and technological changes have led to the erosion of other skills and to the formation of unions representing all specialized workers in a particular sector (e.g., the typographers' union, NGA). Certain craft unions have thus been strengthened, but in a way that has altered their nature to some extent, through a modification and widening of the types of skill to be protected.

Besides the change in craft unionism, there has been an increase of influence and membership of the white-collar trade union. In fact, the contractual procedures of the technology agreements to a large extent have originated with, and are used by, the white-collar unions (Association of Professional, Executive, Clerical and Computer Staff, APEX; Association of Scientific, Technical and Managerial Staff, ASTMS; Banking, Insurance and Finance Union, BIFU; National and Local Government Officers Association, NALGO). They sign local agreements that are, in certain cases, within the framework of a consultative activity and a bargaining tradition that is centralized and formalized at the company level. This aspect is particularly true among civil servants and state employees. Furthermore, these unions tend to represent the entire workforce, although their number is never as high as among manual workers in the industrial sector.

In Scandinavia the union organization's most important instrument in controling innovation remains the participatory procedures at company level, regulated and strengthened either by legislation put into effect by a prolabor government or through national agreements that are valid for all workers. Here one is dealing with regulations, therefore, that are external to workplaces and tend to minimize all forms of conflict (considered counterproductive for the country's economic development), especially at a local level, and to promote a high degree of participation within companies.

There are, however, certain important new elements. In Sweden the *Co-Determination Act* (1976), though a "frame law" with no specific reference to technology, contains important indications regarding the possibility of negotiations and the working out of common rules. Two aspects of the law increase union power with respect to the employer: *negotiation rights are extended* to include issues pertaining to the organization and innovation of the productive process; and in many cases the employer must negotiate *before* making a decision concerning working conditions. Furthermore, in the event of nonagreement over codetermination matters the union interpretation remains in force while awaiting a further deliberation, not, as in the past, the interpretation of the company.

The Co-Determination Act presupposes its supplementation by collective agreements covering the various fields of the act. Central agreements have been concluded in all sectors of the Swedish economy. The first agreement was reached in the civil service sector (1978) and designated several areas for local collective agreements: rationalization and administrative development, planning mobility of employees, personnel development, work supervision, and staff and union information. This agreement includes a more extensive obligation for the provision of company information than the law does. In 1979 an agreement was concluded covering the state-owned and consumer cooperative enterprises. Then, in 1982, after six years of negotiation, an agreement was reached for the private sector.

Following a preamble that calls for a mutual understanding so as to promote company efficiency and profitability, the agreement goes on to specify the areas and themes of codetermination: work organization, technological development, the economic and financial position of the company. In a second section it details how codetermination should be conducted. In the third section the possibility of the union's introducing its own experts, paid by the employer, is dealt with in detail. The *introduction of experts,* in particular, represents an important element in employer opposition. The paragraph sanctioning it recognizes that jobs should be open to studies on the quality of working life (another possible area of intervention by such experts relates to the company's economic and financial problems). The final part of the agreement establishes rules for *central negotiations in the event of nonagreement at a local level.*

In most branches the codetermination agreements do not differ essentially from the central agreements. There is only one agreement in existence that deals exclusively with the introduction of new technology, the one for the printing industry. This agreement was signed in May 1980 and will terminate in April 1986. It guarantees that the introduction of new technology will not lead to dismissals; instead, journalists, printing workers, and clerical employees will be retrained during working time, retraining plans being worked out by a joint branch council. Under this agreement these three categories of workers will continue to carry out their respective jobs as at present but it will be possible for the jobs to be transferred from one category to another after local negotiations. Local agreements must be approved by the national trade unions.

As far as we are informed, local technology agreements have been concluded between the union of civil servants and, respectively, the Postgiro Service, the National Telecommunications Administration, and the National Government Pay and Pensions Board. The one with the Postgiro is very interesting, being a project agreement concerning the development of a new production system. All these agreements contain statements about the general purposes of new technology, general criteria about work and work organization, and procedures to be followed when introducing new technology (Christis, van Klaveren, and Pot, 1984: 21).

In Norway, by contrast, regulations explicitly concern technological innovation as such and have been fully formulated by means of an initial *central agreement* between the social parties, which was negotiated and signed in 1975. This agreement contains the same concepts as those described in the Swedish case: a commitment to cooperation by both parties so as to increase productivity; the requirement that employers should keep workers informed, with such information being compiled comprehensibly; and the right of consultation for external experts. There are two main differences with respect to Sweden: first, the workers have the right to elect *data shop stewards* within the existing system of union representation to supervise and negotiate technological development projects; and second, *the employer is forbidden to use the personal data* of the workers without their permission.

In both Sweden and Norway, *work environment laws* establish certain general principles with respect to checking and modifying environmental conditions and set up control committees with a notable power of veto over the utilization of particularly dangerous and harmful machinery. This centralized activity seeks to *strengthen areas of participation and negotiation at a local level.* The attempt to develop such activity takes place exclusively by means of procedures, with no specific reference to contents. In contrast to other European unions, the unions of these two countries do not recognize the validity of contents such as the reductions of working hours, determined by centrally negotiated regulations. The Scandinavian unions are not convinced that the development of information technology will lead to negative consequences with respect to employment. In their opinion, levels of employment are, in the final analysis, determined by the way society is organized and by the capacity to distribute resources by means of political and institutional decisions, external to the individual company, regarding the management of the labor market—political decisions that the unions must know how to influence and manage.

However, the principal problem is still that of the efficacy of this procedural apparatus within the local context, and a question mark remains regarding the main results at a local level and how they have been achieved. A partial answer, though itself constituting a new ingredient in Scandinavian industrial relations, lies in what have been called *local-level knowledge-development programs,* carried out by the unions themselves by means of systems development projects. The first project of this type was the Iron and Metal project, conducted by the Norwegian unions in this sector in 1971–73 (Nygaard, 1979). The project, led by a group of experts set up at a national level, had the task of studying the development of information technology in certain companies and of discussing possible changes in these information systems. Such initiatives, with more or less similar characteristics, have since become widespread in Sweden. The main projects of this type in Sweden have been the Demos project (Democratic Planning and Control in Working Life), 1975–79; the PAAS project (Perspectives on Administrative Development), 1974–80; the UTOPIA project, 1981 (a project for technological training and development in the newspaper production industry). The most important results of this project have been the diffusion of knowledge of new technology and the establishing of possible alternative utilization, especially with regard to the instruments to be used and the job design.

The general impression, given a lack of detailed research into local industrial relations in Sweden, is that this development of decentralized activity is principally aimed at influencing employers and giving unions the opportunity of becoming *equal partners in projects of organizational change already undertaken by the management* on the basis of new philosophies regarding company management and control. Such philosophies are above all based upon a decentralization of company decision-making structures, a greater autonomy and a lesser rigidity of work, and more informal consultations with the workers.

In this way greater union participation and involvement in company changes have been brought about, without a particular expansion of bargaining in the real sense. Despite the unions' having sought to strengthen negotiations, the local level is still constrained by nationally imposed limits regarding union action (in the event of nonagreement at a local level, recourse to strikes is impossible) and by the tradition of concentration, which leads, at a company level, to many informal negotiations over themes concerning wages and working conditions.

In West Germany the union response to technological innovation has been the demand to strengthen the rights of codetermination in controling the introduction of new technologies; negotiations over the reduction of working hours so as to prevent a further increase in unemployment; and an increase in company negotiations to protect workers from the negative effects on working conditions. A document by the Deutsche Gewerkschaftsbund, dated 1984, gives a full idea of strategy and a detailed description of the main union objectives.

The most important problem for the unions is employment. They have asked the government to put into practice an unemployment program and have demanded (and obtained) in the metalworkers' sector a reduction in working hours. The other two objectives given prominence by West German unions, however, are less precise, namely, the proposal to extend codetermination rights and the improvement in the quality of work (or work humanization).

In West Germany technology agreements can be divided into two types, a division that is linked with the twofold system of labor relations in that country.

The first type consists of paragraphs on new technology, being part of collective contracts between trade unions and employers' organizations at national or regional levels (Tarifverträge). At the national level, only the printing industry has an agreement (the "RTS Tarifverträge") in which the introduction of new technologies (in this case, computer-controlled typesetting and word processing) is the main content. This national agreement was concluded in 1978, after a long and (by German standards) harsh period of industrial action. Its main clauses contain an individual protection against dismissal and lowering of income, a demarcation schedule between journalists and printers, and a guarantee that qualified printers have the exclusive right to do the computerized typesetting work for eight years to come. Moreover, the agreement specifies rest periods (every hour), ergonomic standards, and eye tests for VDU operators. Although the IG Druck und Papier had to fall in with the employers on a number of issues, the union leadership considers this agreement an important step toward a greater say by the workers in the introduction and use of new technology.

The second type of technology agreement has been concluded at the company level, with company or plant management and works councils (Betriebsräte) as signatories. Legal clauses on codetermination at company level (the Betriebsverfassungsgesetz of 1972) opened the possibilities for this practice. By this act, the works council has been granted advisory and information rights in planning changes in plant layout and premises, technical installations, and the labor process. The works council represents all the employees in the company, and although its representation is not wholly union based in the workplace, it has the right of codetermination concerning (1) the introduction of technical installations designed to control the behavior and performance of employees; (2) the making of rules to prevent health and safety hazards; and (3) whether the composition of labor tasks and workplaces is obviously opposed to the state of the art of scientific knowledge concerning the humanization of labor. Many company agreements about the introduction of new technologies start with concerns about health hazards (clauses about VDU work) and management control of the employees (clauses about personnel information systems, PIS). The introduction of these PIS has been an especially vivid issue in West Germany since 1981, and an issue of great worry for several trade unions. The scope of these agreements remains an issue of public debate, as the employers' organizations deny that the codetermination rights of the work councils extend to decisions concerning technical innovation and labor organization (Christis et al., 1984: 16).

Approximately 400 agreements on technological innovation have been discovered so far. What renders these agreements different from other national European cases is their being constituted mainly of contents rather than procedures. A large part of these contents concerns problems of an ergonomic type and working conditions at VDUs, or they relate to the application of working-hour reductions obtained in the national contracts, qualification guarantees, or job design.

The absence of specific procedures concerning the decision-making process related to technological and organizational changes may generally be explained by the fact that codetermination rights already exist. The limits of these rights, from the unions' perspective, is that they are very vague with regard to technological innovation. This is the reason for the proposal made in 1977 by IG Metall, the metalworkers' union, to try to overcome these limits by singling out forms of control related to technological innovation. The IG Metall proposal included a requirement on the part of employers to supply the unions with detailed information regarding technological innovation; the possibility of *making joint studies of the feasibility* of the new systems, the social effects of their introduction also being taken into consideration; the setting up of *joint committees,* with the specific task of technical consultation regarding the introduction of technological innovations; general guidelines regarding job security and pay, with the *obligation on the employer to negotiate additional agreements* at company level with respect to all aspects of working conditions affected by technological innovation. This last aspect is confirmation of a general tendency of unions in West Germany to seek a decentralization of negotiations and a formalization of the results. The IG Metall proposal has had only limited application, because of employer resistance and the limits of the workers' representatives in the works council in extending codetermination rights.

6. Concluding Remarks

Technological innovation is one of the most important aspects of restructuring processes, since changes may well modify the composition of the labor market and workers' attitudes about collective bargaining over the long run. This could foreshadow reductions in union membership, because of a growth in the number of the occupational groups in which the unions have little influence and a reduction of the groups that are highly unionized. However, this vision of the future of industrial relations and the possible effects on union organization is still premature. The figures for declines in union membership in Europe are worrying for the unions but not dramatic, and up to now there is little evidence that any decline in union activity is structural rather than the outcome of a reversal of more favorable economic and political trends.

What emerges from an analysis of negotiations on technical-organizational changes is that these industrial relations structures, though still maintaining a strong link with their traditions, are not static and are themselves subject to innovation. The unions particularly seek out new instruments and new levels in order to control and guide technological innovation as far as possible. These changes cannot be generalized as fundamental shifts in collective bargaining and industrial relations but indicate only the possible tendencies of union action in the 1980s, tendencies that maintain a substantial continuity with past traditions.

As may be noted, changes in collective bargaining exist that are common to all the countries under consideration. The foremost, certainly the most widespread, relates to the introduction or strengthening of *means and procedures of discussion between the parties.* As a result of the demand for, and application of, the disclosure of information, technological innovation becomes a matter for consultation between union and company. There is thus a decentralized activity, at a local level, in which the unions request a preventive check and information both on the technical and on the organizational characteristics of the investment and on the effects this will have on working conditions.

Generally, the formalization of procedural rights creates permanent relationships, and for this reason it is difficult to put into practice the *traditionl concept that separates negotiations from participation* (in which the anticipated result is not necessarily a union agreement). This method is partly in contrast to normative negotiation models (specifically utilized within the antagonistic and conflictual traditions of industrial relations), the contents of which are also subject to previously determined obligations and rules. Independently of the success or method with which this phase is carried out (and it often prolongs the negotiating process), it would seem that the new procedures and methods bring about an inductive, rather than deductive, approach.

A second aspect common to all such experiences is the diffusion of *regulations concerning working conditions of an ergonomic type, particularly at video terminals.* The ergonomic factors concerning hardware planning involve scientific knowledge, the possibility of access to information, legal rulings, and rights of control that are reasonably precise and universally applicable. But such a possibility does not exist with respect to job design itself. The latter requires knowledge and standards that are less precise and more discretionary. It is largely dependent on the success of implementation and on managerial, company, social, and industrial relations traditions.

In most of the countries examined the normative success in ergonomic bargaining, particularly with reference to video terminals, may be explained by the possibility it allows of establishing rules regarding the protection of working conditions, both at a national and a local level, prior to the development of implementation. However, in the case of job design, participation and process-control rights are much more effective, since it is not possible to determine beforehand the results of the process, the organizational contents and standards, and the choices that must be made during the implementation period.

The third common aspect is the interest in regulations regarding the objectives of the organizational model, or the principles that lie behind work distribution. Insistence on this theme is not, as union documents often claim, due to a rise in the quality of collective bargaining but rather to the nature of new technology itself, which not only radically changes the work processes in many cases but also modifies the boundaries that used to distinguish the various occupational groups. The possibility that new technology can bring about more integrated organization and modify the functional relationships between roles and areas of activity gives rise to a need for regulations on boundaries; these regulations often represent a confrontation between the various occupational groups with respect to the distribution of the costs and benefits of technical-organizational innovation itself.

This last aspect is not always grasped by the structure, procedures, and contents of bargaining. Competition between groups and the way in which it is resolved is probably identifiable only through an analysis of *informal* negotiations. The impression is that the sphere of informality has grown considerably, not only because of consultation but also because of problems concerning work allocation, and competition and conflict between occupational groups.

To sum up, the main bargaining innovations involve a broadening of procedures, organizational changes, and knowledge development as an activity necessary for the realization of the objectives for which the parties have signed the contract. All these aspects are interdependent and have the common characteristic that they refer to *processes* rather than to specific contents circumscribed by tradition. As in all processes, the handling of the *context,* more than the definition of a precise mandate, assumes strategic importance. Consequently, steering structures, more than forms of representation, may also become particularly important. Very often such structures, comprising both company representatives and unions, may be seen as *participatory structures in company management* in the real sense.

The handling of these processes alters the relationship between union representatives and workers. Whoever represents the workers cannot, as in the past, have a worker's mandate rigidly defined beforehand, restricting union negotiators to carry out their task within highly circumscribed objectives and parameters understood precisely by everyone.

Such common phenomena, however, should be considered in the context of differing tendencies that owe their origins to the specificity of industrial relations traditions. In the first place, because of its nature, the control of technical-organizational innovations gives rise to local initiatives, but the results of such local initiatives with respect to industrial relations do not produce convergent effects in the context of differing national cases. Countries with previous procedural participation and control structures determined at a central level seek, by means of a *reinforcement of procedures, greater liberty of action at a local level,* thus enlarging negotiation rights. This tendency toward decentralization is a response to inadequacies in national negotiations. National rulings and the institutional power of the unions in these countries do not seem adequate in controling labor market dynamics and in allowing the regulation of working conditions and direct effects of technological innovation.

Countries in which there is no previous procedural structure at a national level *seek to build one up at a local level,* with a *tendency toward central negotiations.* There is no similarity between Great Britain and Italy with respect to the way in which this latter aspect takes place. Centralization in Great Britain takes place slowly and through voluntary channels, above all through the reduction of multiple unions; in Italy, which already possesses centralized collective bargaining, it takes place through institutional channels. In Italy it is a question of the state and the employers recognizing a framework covering rights and instruments of participation and control both at the company level and on the labor market. For the unions it is a question of moving from a centralization that has its origins in ideological-political collective action to one that is more institutional and better able to achieve control over labor market mobility, training, and participation structures. Italian unions maintain that only through institutional channels, not exclusively by means of company bargaining, can such control become generalized and consolidated for all workers.

The second aspect in which these countries differ relates to formal and informal traditions of control and the instruments by means of which unions handle conflicts between occupational groups and job rights at workplaces. In countries such as Great Britain, in which the control of change takes place above all through informal rights that are fragmented according to occupational groups, there occurs a new form of bargaining accompanied not only by a recognition of procedures but also by the formalization of contents, which was traditionally left to informal customs and practices. The distribution of costs and benefits, however, is left to competition among unions, and between unions and employers. The system adapts itself *spontaneously* to new conditions, with the development of white-collar unions and changes in the representational logic of craft unions. How far this tendency will prevail over tradition, however, is a question that will be settled only in the long run. The development of white-collar unions with a tradition of more formalized and centralized company negotiations, however, points in this direction.

In countries in which work control is guaranteed by means of external institutional channels that regulate participation, the tendency is toward enlarging such rights. The extension of these rights involves the timing, introduction methods, and organizational effects of the new information technology, with the consequent strengthening of local bargaining. The available data, however, do not allow for the complete evaluation of the diffusion and efficacy of such rulings at a local level. In particular, it is unknown whether there has been a diffusion of company negotiations equal in intensity and efficacy to those other countries in which this activity has already been consolidated. In West Germany company bargaining has had evident results regarding the *contents* of working conditions (factors relating to ergonomic protection and working hours), although the demand for enlarged codetermination rights over technological changes has met with less success. In Scandinavia attention is for the most part concentrated on *processes* and on union control by means of participation instruments. In fact, as far as Scandinavia is concerned, the most significant new elements in local-level initiatives relate to *projects of technical and organizational development managed directly by the unions.* The task of these projects is to supply union representatives with possible alternatives and solutions to be proposed for adoption during discussions with employers on themes concerning the introduction of new technology. Rather than contributing to negotiations in the real sense, these projects have for now helped to reinforce local union autonomy in committees and in informal participation.

This difference of approach between West Germany and Scandinavia with respect to the extension of local-level bargaining rights is made explicit by the different way, in each country, the reduction of working hours has been interpreted as a union response to rationalization processes. The reduction of working hours is connected with the degree of institutional power of the union in each country. In West Germany the reduction of working hours represents an important normative gain, to be negotiated later at a local level; in Scandinavia the redistribution of occupational resources is entrusted to institutional instruments of national and local labor market management, under the joint control of the social parties.

Another important factor, besides the degree of institutional power of the union, that explains the difference between West Germany and the Scandinavian countries is union density. While centralization of the regulation of working conditions and participation is a common policy of the two systems of labor relations, the union density in this centralized context has an important effect on the degree of integration of different levels of worker representation. Where union density is high, as for example in the Scandinavian countries (the membership is 85 percent to 90 percent of the working population), the integration of workplace representation and central union structure is very high. Where union density is lower, as in Germany (the membership is about the 35 percent to 40 percent of the working population), the structure of the works council provides relatively fragile linkage between the company and establishment levels, and weak relationships between works councilors and the membership. This encourages the works council to adopt a parochial approach to many matters related to job security and the reduction of working hours, as well as plant rationalization.

In countries such as Italy, in which the control of changes in productive processes is undertaken by unions in ways that are both formalized and detailed, there is a partial inversion of this tendency. Rigid and specific rulings are maintained only with respect to certain aspects considered important in job protection, particularly the aspects that concern employment guarantees. But this rigidity is not maintained with respect to job mobility and flexibility in internal labor markets (workforce allocation, skills, systems of payment). The unions have developed *new forms of guarantee:* enlarging the utilization of the Cassa Integrazione Guadagni (Unemployment Benefit), trying to control training and skill requalification, determining procedures and joint structures for the control and reconversion of production at a local level. Either these latter activities have not been considered in the past, or recourse to them has been seen as negative. However, the absence of a national agreement and of a general recognition of procedures and instruments of control in rationalization processes, by employers and government, renders the behavior of the social parties uncertain and unstable. This instability may be seen in the continual oscillation in collective bargaining between participatory issues and issues of a more distributive type.

Notes

1. The theory of the primacy of politics has been fully dealt with by A. Pizzorno (1971). The reference to A. Gerschenkron (1965) relates to studies he carried out on industrial development in Europe and Italy. The political attitude of Italian unions, accompanied by a heterogeneity of models and union-party relationships, is also emphasised by Cella and Treu (1982). According to these authors, such attitudes were noticeably reduced during the seventies but tended to reemerge when the three confederations (CGIL, CISL, and UIL), "being weakened in the bargaining market, sought a voice and influence in the political market."

2. This kind of centralized activity and structure has given rise to a model of industrial unionism founded upon the identity and stability of working conditions within the workplace. Today this system is in crisis, since stability and predictability are clearly being replaced by change and discontinuity. The new strategic needs and a different interpretive framework have been put before the unions and, in general, the various figures involved in industrial relations (Treu, 1984: 81-90).

3. According to observers, social conflict in factories has not been so much a problem of workers' *rights* over working conditions as a problem of *power*, with demands tending toward the removal of social control instruments from the "hands of the bosses." Union initiatives have followed up such spontaneous demands, codifying and regulating them and hence obtaining important agreements in all industries.

Within this frame, regarding the theme of work usage, the unions have substantially taken up a position with four types of demand:

1. egalitarian demands on the theme of qualifications, strongly challenging, in certain cases rejecting, the various forms of economic incentive (such contents having rendered the traditional forms of work force integration less practicable for the employer);

2. demands tending to make the work factor less flexible: from the control and limiting of overtime, to the reduction of working hours, the limiting of shifts, the control of work-rates, etc. (all of which have pushed companies towards seeking other forms of flexibility);

3. demands on all themes relating to the harmfulness of work environments, accompanied by the diffusion of a new policy with respect to health;

4. demands aimed at effecting changes in the structuring of jobs and in work organization, with interventions of control or contesting management solutions and, also, in certain large companies, of autonomous proposals.

Today it is difficult to say, without research material on the overall structure of Italian industry, which of these demands have had most effect in launching the more important organizational changes. However, the hypothesis that I continue to maintain as being most valid relates to the greater overall influence of the first two types of demand (Cella, 1978).

4. In this way the unions abandon what has been their traditional strategy, with respect to piecework, on three points: (1) the acceptance in principle of piecework and, at a more general level, the linking of pay to productivity as an objective necessity of work organization and as an advantage for the worker; (2) the accusation, directed at the company, of not using the piecework system correctly and tending to constantly increase productivity at the cost of the workers, by means of deadlines that are too strict, the institution of inadequate breaks and manpower, the continual cutting of rates, and so on; (3) the need for the recognition of the union's function in bargaining over certain aspects of work organization, in order to eliminate these from the unilateral settlement of piecework by the employers.

5. Pay equality in Italy can only be partially compared to the system implemented by unions in other countries, such as Sweden. Although in Italy the union's pay policy has, in this case, favored the lower pay levels by means of equal increases for everyone, in Sweden the equal-pay policy is more articulated and, at the same time, more generalized. In fact, in Sweden the egalitarian policy foresees a reduction in pay differences between territorial areas, adjusting and unifying the various parameters of the cost of living; pay in the weakest sectors of industry has been increased; pay equality between men and women has been achieved by means of recourse, in the last two cases, to annual percentage increases that are higher for ordinary workers.

6. The different cycles of industrialization in various countries are calculated on the basis of the highest employment levels achieved in the industrial sector. For Italy this indicator was established in 1970, for France in 1965, for West Germany and the United Kingdom in 1955, and for the U.S.A. in 1950. The number of computers in Italian industry rose from 34,000 in 1974 to 101,000 in 1982. Throughout the 1970s the utilization of VDUs spread with extreme rapidity, and in 1982 there were an estimated 900 robots in use (Colombo and Lanzavecchia, 1983).

7. What has been lacking in the Italian case, unlike those of Sweden and West Germany, is a general agreement by the social parties, supported by public powers, on how to further economic development and the quality of working life on the societal scale. Nevertheless, the Italian case is today influenced by "rules of the game" at a company level, which have modified the classic sphere of bargaining in the direction of some instances of joint regulations in certain companies and large industrial groups (Butera, 1984; Della Rocca, 1982).

8. With respect to the financing of such training activities, recourse to public structures is common practice, particularly in the regional boards, which have specific funds for job training, or the European Social Fund, which is the European Economic Community (EEC) organ for the financing of personnel retraining processes in the event of technological innovation.

9. The study, *Industrial Relations in Information Society* (Berta, 1986) was conducted and financed by the Fondazione Olivetti. It is a descriptive work,

dealing with national cases, and is by various authors: Robin Williams analyzes the case of Great Britain; Herbert Kubicek, that of West Germany; Bengt Abrahamsson, that of Sweden and Norway; François Sellier, that of France; and Giuseppe Della Rocca, that of Italy.

References

Abrahamsson, B. 1986. *Computer Technology and Industrial Relations: The Case of Sweden and Norway.* Roma: Fondazione Adriano Olivetti.

Batstone, E., and S. Gourlay. In press. *Unions, Unemployment and Innovation.* London: Basil Blackwell.

Bartezzaghi, E., and G. Della Rocca. 1983. "Impresa, gruppi professionali e sindacato nella progettazione delle tecnologie informatiche." *Quaderni della Fondazione Adriano Olivetti* 1.

Berta, G. 1983. *Lavoro, solidarietà, conflitti.* Roma: Officina Edizioni.

Berta, G., ed. 1986. *Industrial Relations in Information Society: A European Survey.* Roma: Fondazione Olivetti.

Butera, F. 1972. *I frantumi ricomposti.* Padova: Marsilio.

———. 1984. *L'orologio e l'organismo.* Milano: Franco Angeli.

Cella, G. P. 1978. *Uguaglianza e rivendicazione.* Roma: Edizioni Lavoro.

Cella, G. P., and T. Treu, eds. 1982. *Relazioni Industriali: Manuale per l'analisi dell'esperienza italiana.* Bologna: Il Mulino.

Chiaromonte, F. 1973. "L'organizzazione del lavoro: i problemi del movimento sindacale italiano." *Economia e lavoro* 2/3.

———. 1978. *Sindacato, ristrutturazione, organizzazione.* Roma: ESI.

Christis, J., M. van Klaveren, and F. Pot. 1984. "Technology agreements: possibilities and limitations." Paper presented to the EGOS Colloquium, Trade Unions in Europe: The Organizational Perspective, Oct. 11–13, at Amersfoort, The Netherlands.

Colombo, U., and G. Lanzavecchia. 1983. "La posizione relativa alla technologia italiana." Paper presented at the Nomisma Conference on Technological Innovation and Production Structures: The Italian Position, at Milano.

De Maio, A., et al. 1982. *Informatica e processi decisionali.* Milano: Franco Angeli.

Della Rocca, G. 1982. *Sindacato e organizzazione del lavoro: analisi comparata del sistema di Relazioni Industriali in cinque paesi.* Milano: Franco Angeli.

Della Rocca, G., and S. Negrelli. 1983. "Diritti di informazione ed evoluzione della contrattazione aziendale (1969–1971)." *Giornale di Dirirtto del Lavoro e di Relazioni Industriali* 19.

Evans, J. 1982. *The Negotiation of Technological Change: A Discussion Paper on Development in Western Europe, 1975–82.* Bruxelles: ETUI Publication.

Gerschenkon, A. 1965. *Il problema dell'arretratezza economica.* Torino: Einuadi.

Kochan, T. A. 1980. *Collective Bargaining and Industrial Relations.* Homewood, Ill.: Irwin Inc.

Kubicek, H. 1986. "Information Technology and Industrial Relations in the Federal Republic of Germany." In G. Berta, ed.

Momigliano, F. 1983. "Problemi di analisi delle determinanti ed effetti dell'innovazione nei paesi industriali avanzati e in Italia." Paper presented at the Nomisma Conference on Technological Innovation and Production Structures: The Italian Position, at Milan.

Nygaard, K. 1979. "The Iron and Metal Project: Trade Union Participation." In A. Sandberg, *Computer Dividing Man and Work*. Stockholm: Arbetslivscentrum.

Paci, M. 1972. *Mercato del lavoro e classi sociali in Italia*. Bologna: Il Mulino.

Pizzorno, A. 1971. "I sindacati nel sistema politico italiano." *Rivista trimestrale di diritto pubblico* 4:1510-59.

Regini, M., and E. Reyneri. 1971. *Lotte operaie e organizzazione del lavoro*. Padova: Marsilio.

Reynaud, J. D. 1979. *Problemi e prospettive della contrattazione collettiva nei paesi della Comunità*. Brussels: Commissione della Comunità Europea.

Treu, T. 1984. "Relazioni Industriali: declino inevitabile?" *Il Progetto* 19/20: 81-90.

Williams, R. 1986. "Information Technology and Industrial Relations in Britain." In G. Berta, ed.

6

WORKER PARTICIPATION AND THE GERMAN TRADE UNIONS: AN UNFULFILLED DREAM?

Christopher S. Allen

Rapid industrialization in the latter half of the nineteenth century fundamentally transformed Germany. As a growing industrial society displaced the remnants of a largely feudal one, wage laborers particularly were affected. Many of them had to make the transition from agrarian peasants to factory workers within the space of a generation. During this period workers suffered great hardship, and large numbers responded with militant collective action. A wave of unionization soon followed as these peasant workers tried to withstand the changes that expanding capitalism had imposed on them.[1]

One factor that aided workers' collective response was the penetration of Marxism (and other socialist theories) into the working class. The nascent organized working class drew on these theories and—building on German craft skill traditions that had their roots in the feudal guilds—soon made demands for worker participation, if not control.[2] Yet cutting across this participatory trajectory was the strong reliance by German labor on the benefits derived from the state. Chancellor Otto von Bismarck initiated a social insurance system in the 1880s to coopt the militant edge of the left. He also simultaneously banned the social Democratic party (SPD) from 1878 to 1890. This kind of state paternalism became deeply embedded in German political institutions and left its mark on the organized working class.[3] By the early twentieth century, however, the reemergence of the SPD and the growing strength of unions as industrialization continued resulted in increased benefits for the working class from the state. Yet a tension developed within organized labor around the issue of participation. Should the labor movement primarily emphasize strategies of worker control at the point of production, or should it use its increasing access to the state to create participatory institutions that would help enhance their power in the workplace?

This article will examine this long-standing tension around worker participation in Germany. It will argue that the simplistic "choice" between workplace or statist strategies has shaped patterns of response within the labor movement that have led it down blind alleys. The limitations of this either/or false choice have sometimes even let unions slide even further away from participation only to emphasize American-style wage bargaining. In essence, German unions have been frustrated in their goal of attaining worker control via participation because they have been unable to synthesize both approaches. On one side are those who are concerned primarily with worker participation and control within firms but who do not develop strategies to spread it throughout the labor movement. On the other side are those who rely on the state in hopes that it will then give greater institutional and legal support for worker participation and influence but who neglect the workplace.

The conclusion will suggest that strategies to increase participation and influence over working life in West German society depend on finding an approach that avoids this false either/or choice. Such an approach would have to link the microstrategies of the workplace to the macrostrategies of pressuring the state. In so doing, it would not only increase participatory power within the West German labor movement, it might also generate a labor movement better able to address the increasingly adverse structural and political conditions in the West German economy of the 1980s.

Rapid Industrialization, Reliance on the State, and the Erosion of Participatory Workplace Traditions

As the first wave of heavy German industrial expansion shot forward in the 1850s and 1860s, German firms in the Ruhr (by then under Prussian control) faced a desperate labor shortage. Both through their own initiative and under the aegis of the state, the region's employers soon recruited thousands of workers from rural eastern Prussia for employment in the coal mines and the iron foundries. But the initial response by German workers proved to be a radical one.[4] Rapid industrialization produced a general economic and social dislocation. Combined with the taking root of the ideas of Marx and other German socialists and the fact that these peasant workers collectively faced the same kind of subordinate relationship with their new industrial employers as they did with their old feudal ones, a large labor movement soon grew in Germany.

But though the nature of the rapid industrialization created a militant labor movement, the type of militance did not emphasize the earlier tradition of participatory skill of German workers. Prior to this period of rapid industrialization the numerous German states had been characterized by small-scale artisanal production. The guildlike structure of this still feudal society accorded skilled workers with an important position. Yet during the third quarter of the nineteenth century German industry stressed large-scale capital investment and export-led growth. A major change had occurred in the structure of German industry. Investment goods were emphasized, which meant that domestic demand took second place. Thus, the early trade union and socialist leaders had first to mobilize around issues that addressed the low pay and very adverse working conditions, and only secondarily those that played on workers' skills. For despite the genuine radical impulses among early trade unionists, demands for a fundamental alteration of the economic and political order were forced to take second place to more immediate material needs.[5] By emphasizing consumption, however, the unions had found an issue that spoke directly to workers' concrete needs. The movement then grew rapidly during the 1870s and intensified its attacks on the employers' harsh methods of industrialization as the late nineteenth-century depression took hold.[6]

This radicalization in the late 1870s and the early 1880s caused Chancellor Otto von Bismarck to undertake the two-pronged action of banning the SPD via his "anti-socialist" legislation, yet simultaneously stealing some of the movement's thunder by initiating numerous welfare state measures.[7] Bismarck took this action both because of the "fragility" of the country's political economy and because he doubted whether individual industrialists would be able to see beyond their own specific interests to those of the economy as a whole:

> The evolving conflicts between state and social democracy convinced the state bureaucracy, that the political question must be solved by state policy and not by private contracts. Therefore the state took away some . . . rights over the worker from the entrepreneur. But this was not done to give the worker more codetermination, but to give the state more security over its citizens.[8]

Although the "outlawed" SPD was made legal again in the 1890s (after growing still stronger as an underground movement in the 1880s), the intervention of the state had an important impact on the SPD and the trade unions. Although Bismarck's action was ostensibly a maneuver to "coopt" the nascent German left, this action left a legacy often described as a *Staatsfixierung* (state fixation) within both the "political arm" and the "labor arm" of the organized working class.[9]

Although such state action in the 1880s imposed heavy restrictions on the working class, considerable benefit was provided, a fact not lost on the leaders of the German left. This contributed to the SPD's changing its political perspective following the death of Friedrich Engels in 1893, as Eduard Bernstein emerged as the party's leader and began to stress "evolutionary" as opposed to "revolutionary" socialism.[10] Trade union leaders also came to believe that, were they to fail to attain the goals that they considered most important via their struggles in the labor market, they then could turn to the SPD and the state and try to fulfill them in the political arena. Significantly, this reliance of the union movement on the state for important needs served to reinforce the powerful thrust of legalization that had long pervaded other aspects of social and economic relations. In fact, this development placed the German union movement on a trajectory in which it would devote substantial effort to achieving and maintaining institutional legitimacy. In many cases unions would look to the state to sanction forms of participation between workers and employers, rather than first pressing for participation themselves via militant action. They were encouraged in this belief by the 1910 Imperial Court (Reichsgericht) decision that trade unions and wage-bargaining contracts had to be accepted by industry, thereby giving the unions a degree of institutional legitimacy that had been denied them even during the Bismarck years.

Although some analysts considered such change in direction as a necessary adaptation to a changed landscape,[11] critics on the left argued that the German unions and the SPD lost much of the participatory and transformative vision that had been present (though not prominent) since the 1860s and 1870s.[12] The latter group did not necessarily argue that the "parliamentary road to socialism" was an inappropriate avenue. They did, however, assert strongly that primary emphasis on electoral action and reliance on the state tended to turn the movement away from the equally important task of transforming capitalism in the industrial arena.

More important for this article, however, the German labor movement devoted most of its labor market activities to "quantitative" change in the size of pay envelopes, and to attaining access to political power that had been denied them by the inequities of the Wilhelmian Reich's political system. Consequently, they tended to downplay the participatory thrust that also earlier underpinned the German labor movement. Furthermore, by identifying their fate with immediate material interests, the needs of their respective firms (as defined by business leaders), and an increasingly militaristic German state, the trade unions surrendered the opportunity to challenge the direction of the German economy as World War I loomed.[13] Thus, by 1914 major portions of both the trade unions and the SPD—lacking a vision to transform German capitalism—supported the declaration of war, a decision that caused a deeply rooted split on the left both within Germany and internationally.[14]

The Rise and Decline of the Workers' Council Movement During the Weimar Republic

In many respects the split that World War I actualized within the German trade union movement (and, more broadly, within the German left) was part of the same debate that had originated in the nineteenth century. Namely, was the trade union to be a vehicle for the securing of material and social rewards for its membership by relying on the state in capitalist society, or was it to be a vehicle for transforming society via a socialist program for worker participation and control? The debate over goals and strategy resumed even more sharply at the outset of the Weimar Republic. The loss of the war, the destruction of the Second Reich, and the economic chaos that followed caused the left wing of the unions and the socialist movement to question again whether they could attain their goals by relying only on fragile and uncertain parliamentary institutions.

The most visible manifestation of this response was the Council Movement (Rätebewegung) during 1918–19, when German labor experienced its most militant push toward worker participation and control. But the councils did not spring from thin air. This renewed surge of militance by some German workers was not just the result of the war and the breakdown of the Second Reich's political institutions. It had earlier roots. Although demands for worker participation declined in some industries during the course of rapid industrialization from the 1870s to the 1910s, important participatory patterns survived in others, particularly those that were more labor intensive.[15]

Moore noted that participatory traditions eroded in the more capital-intensive iron and steel industries (i.e., the most reactionary prior to World War I as well as in the 1920s and 1930s). Although highly paid throughout the war years, iron and steel workers had lost interest in participation within the workplace due to the increased capital intensity and the reduced control over the changes that management imposed from above. Yet when the later war years and the turmoil of 1918–19 sharply constrained the iron and steel employers' maneuverability, the union leaders representing these industries had no experience bargaining for (or winning) more qualitative workplace demands. They preferred to embark on a pattern that offered them integration into the institutional hierarchy of Weimar, and not an opportunity for greater power.

The more-labor-intensive coal industry, on the other hand, generated a different response. Although nonmilitant with respect to wages before the war (as compared with workers in iron and steel), workers in this sector had bargained for and won a considerable number of rights concerning the structure of the workplace. Yet, when the employers in this sector tried to impose some of the same retrenchment-oriented demands as did employers in iron and steel, they were met by a very militant union response. Moore argued that the miners' capacity for rebellion against the mine owners owed much to the miners' having a positive standard from the past (i.e.,before the employers' concession demands) to compare against the present. Perhaps the miners even continued to push for workplace control because they already had a degree of control before the war and viewed as an injustice the employers' taking away this bargained-for right.[16]

It was this residual issue from the nineteenth century—worker control—that animated much of the debate within the German unions and working class in 1918-19. The old regime had collapsed with the Kaiser's abdication after Germany's loss of World War I. And the long-suppressed German left believed the political vacuum was an opportunity to achieve social, political, and economic justice. The revolutionary upsurge of late 1918 and early 1919 soon followed. A major force behind the short-lived revolution at the outset of the Weimar years was the movement within the factories for workers' councils (*Arbeiterräte*). The councils were envisioned as mechanisms that could address sectoral and workplace issues that their adherents felt the trade union leadership had long since neglected. The movement drew strength during this brief period—organizing workers and soldiers councils during 1918-19—in which questions of what to produce (as well as direct self-government) were major considerations. Not surprisingly, many union leaders saw this movement as a threat to their authority in the workplace.[17]

Opposition to the councils came from the employers, of course. But it also came from the leadership of the unions. For the first few years of the Weimar Republic there were two forces within the socialist trade union confederation (ADGB), namely, the "council democrats" and the "social partners."[18] The former tendency was represented primarily by the mine workers and by elements of those Metalworkers Union members not in iron and steel. The movement reached its apex during 1918 as it argued for worker control via councils that were to be instituted at the region, firm, and plant levels and would oversee both production and investment. The latter tendency, which arose in 1918 with the formation of the Central Labor Community (Zentrale Arbeitsgemeinschaft), argued for a "cooperative" posture among the unions, employers, and the state. The community proposed that the employers' associations and the unions acknowledge each other as "agents of order" (*Ordnungsfaktoren*) responsible for disciplining those of its members who became unruly, in order that the performance of affected sectors not be impeded. The community hoped to avoid the more strident forms of conflict among the parties, thus paving the way for an environment that would be mutually beneficial.

In making their demands on the state, the "social partners" criticized the "council democrats" for engaging in a form of struggle that could undermine the institutional legitimacy that the unions had long since fought for and finally won. The latter, on the other hand, felt that this particular form of union integration served only to officially confirm the same kind of "junior partner" status that labor had held during the late nineteenth and early twentieth centuries. This case was fraught with danger in the eyes of the "council democrats" because the unions would then bear responsibility for events over which they had no real control. This split between the two organizations that represented the working class on the shop floor obviously proved disastrous for the ability of either tendency to fashion an appropriate response. The "council democrats" felt betrayed because they felt that the official union movement was willing to dispatch shopfloor democracy in exchange for recognition by the employers, but without gaining any real power in return. The "social partners," on the other hand, felt that these rank-and-file workers failed to appreciate the gains that had been made when compared with the unions' position prior to the war. Consequently, an opportunity was lost for a reciprocal relationship in which the leadership and the rank and file could rely on each other for an even greater measure of strength than each possessed individually.

The split between the rank and file and the leadership was further solidified when the ADGB leader Carl Legien joined forces with the increasingly conservative SPD government leadership and the employers' association to pass legislation that established works councils (*Betriebsräte*) as opposed to workers' councils (*Arbeiterräte*).[19] The "social partners'" victory over the "council democrats" was thus complete. Although one of the main reasons for the union leadership's preference for works councils over workers' councils was that the employers believed that the latter threatened to undermine its authority at the workplace, the works councils in practice tended to do just that, but from a different direction. Each of the works councils was firm- or plant-specific, existed in all workplaces with twenty or more employees, and was officially independent of the unions. Consequently, in practice many eventually came to be dominated by the firms and thus "competed" with the unions in a way the leadership had never envisioned.

With the beating back of this radical impulse from the rank and file by the leadership during the early 1920s, the dominant "social partners" among the leading unions still felt that they could achieve their goals via cooperation with the employers and the SPD-led government. However, the prolonged recession in the early 1920s, followed by the hyperinflationary wave in 1923, caused these union leaders to initially question some of their post–World War I assumptions. Yet after 1924 there was some change in the mainstream union position on new approaches. Some felt that they had greater latitude to combine elements of the "social partnership" approach with more radical attempts to democratize the economy.[20]

Several left-wing economists within the labor movement saw this opening as an opportunity to move beyond this "foot-in-the-door" status and begin to direct the German economy in a much more democratic direction.[21] Napthali argued in 1925 that such a transformation of the economy was possible for several reasons: (1) the highly organized and cartelized condition of the economy facilitated a greater degree of social control, (2) the large monopolies were highly visible and thus generated many opportunities for their monitoring, (3) one of the major advantages of democracy was that popular forces could be elected and thus use the state in a way that satisfied needs of working people, and (4) the general inability of private capital to successfully self-regulate would force it to turn to the state for aid, to which the left would then attach numerous conditions. Among the ways in which Napthali felt that these goals could be effected were by: state control of the monopoly sectors, the establishment of *Gemeinwirtschaft* firms such as a workers' bank, the institution of industrial democracy in the large enterprises in which the unions would have increased influence at both the firm-wide and plant levels (cf. the works councils), and a general democratization of labor relations in which workers would be formally recognized as persons and not as a commodity or factor of production.[22]

The movement for economic democracy during the Weimar period however, proved comparatively short-lived since it had not made deep enough inroads into union bargaining. In fact, with the more shell-like works councils having supplanted the more rank-and-file-based workers' councils as the dominant plant-level institutions, it was much more difficult to mobilize workers after organs that would have been ideal for this purpose had themselves been demobilized.[23] The left-wing economists' attempts to use the state to democratize the labor movement from above did not work, as the split between the rank and file and the union leadership was not to be easily overcome. In fact, the opportunity to develop participatory skills during the immediate post–World War I years and then use them to create supportive national-level institutions had been lost. With the deepening splits on the German left, the onset of the Depression in 1929, and the rise of the Nazis, the possibilities looked even bleaker.

Thus, when the Depression arrived, the union leaders and the SPD discarded attempts at participation—if only in this "top down" fashion—in favor of defending their respective interests. The radical push for worker control, as symbolized by the workers' council movement, had been pushed back. And because the debate over participatory strategies had been framed in such workplace-vs.-statist terms, another opportunity had been lost to cast this issue in more positive-sum terms. This weakened position of German organized labor with respect to strategies of participation proved illustrative of the left's larger failure to shape the agenda of the German political economy in a different direction as the Weimar Republic was overcome by the Nazis. Consequently, under the "labor front" of the Third Reich, workers suffered extensively as all of the Weimar labor organizations, and all of the left and centrist political parties were abolished by the mid-1930s.[24]

"Half a Loaf": Institutionalization of Worker Participation

With the near-complete destruction of German economy and society during World War II, the organized German working class faced formidable problems in 1945. But because the large firms were discredited for their complicity with the Nazis, the labor movement also had opportunities. The unions—having been smashed by the Nazis—had widespread political legitimacy after the war. Hans Böckler, the leader of the (West) German Confederation of Labor (Deutsche Gewerkschaftsbund, DGB), articulated a two-pronged union strategy that—not surprisingly—drew on German labor's statist and workplace-based ideals of participation. The first goal called on the state to guarantee the influence of organized labor by allowing it, via specific legislation, to play a much more democratic and egalitarian role in the strategies of firms, thereby influencing the macroeconomy. The second goal called for organized labor to act simultaneously as a greater "counterpower" (*Gegenmacht*) to the employers via increased participation in the workplace.

To attain these goals of societal and workplace participation, the unions returned during the immediate postwar years to a key theme that they hoped would bring both goals to fruition, namely, economic democracy.

> Democratization in this framework, by necessity, always implied the active participation of workers in the production process. Only through the complete democratization of economic life could capitalism's *Profitlogik* (profit logic) be defeated by a more equitable and more socially oriented system. This democratizing process, never fully implemented during Weimar, was to involve the institutionalization of an all-encompassing framework of *Mitbestimmung* (codetermination). . . . Moreover, *Mitbestimmung* was important in the unions' eyes . . . because it was seen as the

chosen strategic vehicle for implementing the other parts of the unions' package of postwar (objectives)—full employment, production for social needs, socialization of key industries and social justice.[25]

Yet, as the Cold War developed, as economic growth based on a free-enterprise capitalist model took hold, and as the conservative Christlich-Demokratische Union/Christlich-Soziale Union (CDU/CSU) became the dominant political actor, the unions found each of their two goals increasingly less attainable. The rapid economic growth—combined with the changed postwar political climate—quickly accorded to the employers a rehabilitated stature that resulted in much less successful union attempts at worker participation than they had hoped for in the late 1940s. Specifically, the unions got less institutionalized participation through the state and less participatory influence in the workplace than they had hoped. More importantly, rather than being mutually compatible, these two weakened forms of participation created a new institutional division among German workers.

First, the economic takeoff during the 1950s worked directly against the unions' (and the SPD's) macroeconomic goal, namely, that the state take a more active role in economic affairs. Specifically, for the unions, this can be seen by the outcome of the 1951 Codetermination Law in Coal and Steel (Montanmitbestimmungsgesetz), which was much more limited than the unions had originally envisioned, although there were clearly some benefits for the unions in this law. First, since labor and capital were granted parity on the supervisory board of directors (*Aufsichtsrat*) and since unions were allowed to place union leaders from outside the company on this board, union members occupied over 90 percent of the labor board seats. Second, the unions won the right to name the "labor director" to the day-to-day management board (*Vorstand*) of each firm. Third, the law provided for a neutral member of the board of directors—appointed by both labor and capital—to cast the tie-breaking vote on deadlocked issues.[26]

Yet this law proved ultimately limited in that it was confined to only coal and steel and, to this day, has never been extended to other sectors of the economy. What was to serve as the grand foundation to link influence and control of firms and sectors to the macroeconomy was institutionally limited from the outset. It became a "special" provision for coal and steel. Furthermore, under Montanmitbestimmung the unions were restricted to only *near* parity at the supervisory board, which met infrequently. Last, most important plant decisions were made at the management-board level, and the labor director was always only one member of this management-dominated board.

The 1952 Works Constitution Law proved even more restrictive for the unions, but in a way that restricted their ability to gain participatory rights within the workplace.

> This law severely restricted the unions' scope of action within the plant and made the works councils the only legal representative of the workers on the shopfloor. At the same time, this law also limited significantly the *Betriebsräte's* (works councils') range of activities in the plant. For example, works councils could not participate in the mobilization of strikes, were prohibited from divulging company secrets, including to the unions, and were asked to help maintain a harmonious relationship between employer and employees. Their tasks, according to this law, remained largely confined to the supervision of grievance procedures and certain forms of workplace security. Thus, the unions' original model of an ideal-type *Betriebsrat*—an activist on the shopfloor involved in economic, political and social matters—became merely a mediator of personnel problems.[27]

This meant that day-to-day union politics was stripped of many of its qualitative dimensions and replaced with the more quantitative concerns of attaining higher wages. Thus, at a theoretical level, the structure of the West German industrial relations system—both codetermination and the works councils—served to channel organized labor's response within distinctly manageable directions. The net result was that the structure sharply constrained the unions' ability to have real influence either in the macroeconomy (via the boards of directors) or in the workplace.

Despite the absence of genuine participation, the period from the early 1950s through the mid-1960s for the West German unions was viewed as a mixed blessing. If the unions were unable to achieve their original goals, they at least had the satisfaction of attaining codetermination in limited form. If there was no official union influence in the councils, at least many union members were active in the councils. The works councils may not have been the organs of control originally envisioned, but they did provide a number of tangible benefits for workers. Moreover, as German economic performance improved, wages increased and unemployment decreased. And, as a further measure of the supposed cooperativeness of the German trade unions, several authors have pointed to the relatively low strike levels in the Federal Republic as compared to other industrialized countries.[28]

Yet, in a way, this period represented a somewhat false paradise. The easy acceptance by the unions of a regime of increasing wages, generous fringe benefits, and decreasing unemployment took them that much further away from their goal of genuine participation, either in the workplace or via statist institutions. The unions seemed lulled into a false sense of security that depended on the employers' "delivering the goods." And as long as this was the case, then the unions' quantitative emphases were quite appropriate. More fundamentally however, the unions' position signified something else: Once the unions established this quantitative posture, it became that much more difficult to mobilize the membership around such qualitative issues as participation when the years of economic growth ended. Plus, with the full circumscription of the power of the works councils to shape fundamental change, any attempt to use these institutions to deal with issues of new technologies and changed workplace relations would be most difficult indeed.

Participation, Institutions, and Political Mobilization

The 1960s and early 1970s saw increased structural changes in the West German economy. Among these were greater capital intensity, the beginnings of disparities among groups of sectors, and the influx of *Gastarbeiter* (guestworkers) to overcome the labor shortage that began in the 1960s.[29] The unions saw an opportunity to increase their power and did so by again stressing statist and workplace forms of participation.

A key factor that enabled the unions to push both forms of participation from the mid-1960s to the onset of the crisis in the mid-1970s was the SPD's attaining political power. When the SPD participated with the CDU/CSU in the Grand Coalition from 1966 to 1969 and became the major political actor in the social-liberal coalition after 1969, the unions believed that "their" party had finally attained power. The unions felt that the weakened participatory arenas of the 1950s would be augmented by stronger ones during the 1970s.[30] Although Willey may have overrated the post-1969 left-wing influence, the period did witness a growing union emphasis on political institutions as an arena for struggle after the primary emphasis on collective bargaining from the early 1950s to the mid 1960s. The unions' initial hopes for the SPD-led coalition lay in the area of improving the two laws governing worker participation, namely the workplace-oriented Works Constitution Act (Betriebsverfassungsgesetz) and the more macroeconomically important extension of full codetermination (*Mitbestimmung*) from the coal and steel industries to all sectors of the economy.[31]

The unions proved successful in attaining increased power at the shop floor (at the expense of the works councils) when the Works Constitution Act was revised in 1972. Their hopes for the extension of full-parity *Mitbestimmung,* on the other hand, were less well realized.[32] Although a watered-down version was finally passed in 1976, it was not finally approved by the Constitutional Court (Bundesgericht) until 1979.[33] These two pieces of legislation indicated very clearly the limitations of what the unions could expect from "their" party as the economy worsened during the years following the first oil crisis in 1973–74.

In essence, the SPD-led government was much less "theirs" than they had hoped. A number of constraints still continued to face the unions. The employers put great pressure on the government to prevent the extension of full-parity codetermination. The "junior" member of the government coalition, the Freie Demokratische Partei (FDP), became increasingly anxious as the unions pushed for increased power and influence. Some of their members began to complain of a "trade union state." Last, the complicated legal structure of the industrial relations system had a degree of institutional permanence that was very difficult to alter.

Although the unions derived greater benefits from statist and workplace-oriented forms of participation in the early 1970s than they did in either the 1920s or 1950s, the two forms of participation never were adequately synthesized. Two examples are most illustrative.

First, in the euphoria of the high-growth, low-unemployment years of the Willy Brandt–led SPD/FDP coalition, concern began to be raised—initially by left-wing unionists and the youth wing (Jusos) of the SPD—that the state should deal more directly with the question of investment. This school of thought argued that the new government move beyond the Keynesian "global guidance"[34] and allocate capital in areas that would combine social utility and the maintenance of high employment levels. In other words, this would be a direct form of statist participation. Called *Investitionslenkung* (investment direction), it would make up for some of the "antisocial" deficiencies of investment decisions based on market-oriented criteria, its advocates argued. Similar in intent to French-style planning, *Investitionslenkung* proved far less influential in Germany. Its adherents were unsuccessful in gaining much support among either the mainstream of the SPD or a majority of the trade union movement.

Meeting with considerable opposition by the more probusiness FDP, the government was able only to pass legislation establishing *Investitionsmeldestellen* (investment registries), which required firms to "advise" the state where they planned to make future investments. As the boom years faded with the onset of the OPEC oil shock in late 1973, so too did demands for *Investitionslenkung,* which (in this particular incarnation) seemed to be as dependent on a growing economy as was the mid-1920s model of economic democracy. This 1970s vision of *Investitionslenkung* seemed to remain only at the level of economic theory, as its supporters were unable to apply it successfully to the real problems of structural change, which grew more severe by the mid 1970s. It remained unconnected to the workplace.

The second upsurge of participatory sentiment to arise in the early 1970s was the beginning of union demands (in this case by IG Metall) for the "humanization of work" via "qualitative" changes in the workplace.

First surfacing in 1972 at a conference (and then in a wage framework contract during the following year), these demands went beyond the unions' traditional goals of higher wages and fringe benefits.[35] Among the issues raised were a growing dissatisfaction with the repetitive nature of mass-production work, concern over workplace health and safety issues, and a growing concern with the possible adverse impact of technological change. Unlike *Investitionslenkung,* however, these demands later found their way into union bargaining rounds during the late 1970s and early 1980s.

The problem for the unions during the 1970s (as much as it was during the 1920s) was that the demands for economic democracy at the macro level and the demands for participation and worker control at the micro level remained out of sync. The humanization-of-work demand remained confined to the workplace level and the macroeconomic demands such as *Investitionslenkung* remained only a "top down" concept. Consequently, this led some analysts to view the unions' primary reliance on the SPD-led coalition government during the late 1960s and early 1970s (and not using their own strength to develop new departures such as a radical form of humanization of work) as an avenue that would not prove fruitful in the long run.[36]

Members of this latter group viewed the unions' position in the German political economy as one of weakness rather than one of strength. In the unions' two-pronged emphasis on higher wages in the labor market, on the one hand, and reliance on "their" SPD on the other, these observers claimed that unions were merely solidifying their "junior partner" status by playing too passive a role with respect to those forces who wielded real power in the West German political economy. Pointing to such German union response as a prime example of "corporatism," analysts such as Schmitter and Panitch found it unlikely that the German unions could improve their position, especially in an economy that began to deteriorate by the mid-1970s. Jacobi and Mueller-Jentsch, however, did see the possibility for more effective union response if militant shop stewards (in part helped by the 1972 Works Constitution Act, which gave the unions slightly more workplace power at the expense of the works councils) could serve as a better link between the rank and file and the leadership.[37] Yet they argued that the unions, given this entrenched corporatist trajectory, would likely be unwilling to push rank-and-file demands far enough for any real gains.

In one sense this latter group of critics was right in that the unions were confronted with an ever more unsympathetic SPD-led government as the 1970s progressed. And when combined with the employers' more aggressive tactics in the labor market, their theories seemed that much more well reinforced. The employers undertook such measures as forcing the unions to accept considerable wage restraint after 1975, turning to the lockout as a collective-bargaining tool, and attempting to have the 1976 *Mitbestimmung* law ruled unconstitutional. Consequently, these critics' characterization of the unions' posture as one of comparative timidity appeared not that far from the mark. However, lacking from this left-wing criticism was any concrete alternative to synthesize the two participatory traditions. However, new attempts to do so would take place in the 1980s, with only limited success.

The Unions, Structural Change, and Worker Participation

As a much more perilous economic era arrived by the mid-1970s, the unions were generally ill placed to deal with the crisis they faced. They had little understanding of how these structural changes would fundamentally alter the institutional framework within which they had worked since the early 1950s. In short, the majority of union leadership felt that the best remedy to their troubles was simply more of the kind of aggressive wage bargaining and demands on the SPD-led state rather than innovative forms of participation. The mainstream union leaders rarely acknowledged those critics inside the labor movement who wanted to mobilize the membership around both qualitative (i.e., participative) and quantitative goals, and not just an exclusive concentration on the latter. Whether this pattern will continue through the 1980s remains uncertain.

In fact, both the chemical workers' union (IG Chemie) and the metalworkers' union (IG Metall) missed opportunities to mobilize their respective memberships. At its convention in 1980, IG Chemie dramatically put down a rank-and-file challenge that emphasized just these issues. In IG Metall the innovative demands of regional leader Franz Steinkühler in Baden Wurttemburg in 1978 were not picked up by the IG Metall leadership in Frankfurt. As a result, both unions seemed to have lost a golden opportunity to challenge (and possibly shape via widespread worker participation) the scope and pattern of German industry's transformation.

In one respect, the unions' continued emphasis on wages and fringe benefits—while neglecting to make full use of those participatory institutions they had—played right into the hands of their most severe critics. This right-wing view called for increased employer latitude because it was argued that the strength of the unions (i.e., with respect to their retaining comparatively high wage standards) had begun to result in the "overload" of the system.[38] Ranging from such prescriptions as continued union wage restraint, increased freedom by employers to invest outside of the Federal Republic, more rapid introduction of labor-saving technology, and, in general, more "room to maneuver" by German business, these conservative suggestions were largely rejected out of hand by both union leadership and the rank and file. Yet despite the verbal opposition to the employers' bold new overtures, the unions generally missed the opportunity to use the works councils and Mitbestimmung to place conditions on the kinds of aggressive demands that the employers had begun to make.

Because militant forms of participation—both statist and workplace oriented—had long been neglected, the leaders of the DGB and many major unions faced a serious dilemma in explaining the difficulties the union movement faced. More importantly, they were uncertain how to chart a course that would extricate them from their precarious situation. As a movement that had retained a postwar adherence to increasing consumer demand via aggressive bargaining for wages and fringe benefits (not surprising, given German industry's historic preoccupation with investment-led economic growth), the leadership of the German trade unions continued to emphasize Keynesian solutions—and not power-enhancing participation—throughout the 1970s. Not only did they adhere closely to their "wage consumption model" as the basis of their economic philosophy,[39] they failed to appreciate the full structural dimensions of the crisis, and the possibilities that existing—if shell-like—organs of participation offered.

One reason why they retained this faith in the capacity of increased demand was that they thought that a similar application of Keynesianism on a large scale would help the German economy "export its way out of the recession," as these measures did during the recession of 1966–67. Yet when this policy failed to produce economic recovery because of the resistance of the employers to increased wages, the German union leadership became uncertain as to how to proceed. And, given their having put most of their political emphasis on the legal attainment of full-parity *Mitbestimmung*—without attempting to mobilize and empower the rank and file—the unions faced tighter constraints.[40]

The push for the 1976 *Mitbestimmung* law is an excellent example of how the concern for attaining a more legally "legitimate" participatory mechanism was unaccompanied by the more fundamental need to mobilize workers at the point of production. The unions reasoned that the broadening of the codetermination mechanism would help them immensely. Yet, in doing so, they placed far more emphasis on the form than they did on the content.[41] The unions seemed to think that if the law were only passed, then they would have more influence and control at the workplace. What the unions apparently did not fully realize was that effective influence and control depended not on the passage of a law but on the active mobilization and participation of their membership.

After 1977, however, union analysts finally began to stress solutions that were more structural as the increased levels of unemployment (to 4 and 5 percent by the late 1970s and to 8 and 9 percent by the early 1980s) called into question the efficacy of a primary reliance on Keynesian solutions. However, most of the "Strukturpolitik" that the unions demanded was defensive and revolved around demands for subsidies that would protect jobs in the most disadvantaged sectors (i.e., steel). But the union leadership rarely was able to make an effort to go beyond these limited strategies and mobilize workers around more offensive policies. An example of the failure to apply offensive structural policies was seen in the DGB's failure to resuscitate the concept of "investment direction" (*Investitionslenkung*) at the 1981 congress when it was raised on the convention floor.[42]

Some individuals during the post-1975 period, both inside and outside the union movement, went beyond the limitations of the mainstream DGB approaches. They tried to address the structural dimensions of the crisis that the German unions faced by linking potential solutions to structural problems with innovative forms of participation. In particular, they looked at the impact of new technologies, structural adjustment, and investment patterns as the German economy was rapidly being transformed.[43] Naschold's contribution was especially valuable because he argued that the most appropriate method to get at these issues was for the unions to unite the micro issue of humanization of work (*Humanisierung der Arbeit*) with the macro issue of investment direction (*Investitionslenkung*). He argued that a successful resolution of the problem of technological change depended on each of these two programs' reinforcing the other. And the glue that could do so would be a type of genuine worker participation that could mobilize workers for workplace change that would also lead to progressive, job-creating economic growth. He concluded that humanization of work (without longer term goals) and investment direction (without the support of the union rank and file) as separate programs would be far too easily circumvented by the employers and their political allies.

More specifically, if the unions were interested in a safe and humanized workplace, then they would have to be interested in qualitative issues of technology. If the unions were interested in technology, then they would have to address issues of how it was introduced into the workplace. And if they were interested in how it was introduced into the workplace, then they would have to concern themselves with patterns of investment. And despite all the discussions that had taken place in the German labor movement over at least a decade on these general themes, very few individuals had been able to understand how they might all fit together.

The union that took the most innovative approach to using forms of participation to address structural problems was IG Metall. But even this union was blocked from the late 1970s to the mid-1980s by more traditional forces within the union from implementing these approaches. A good contrast can be seen in the conduct of two major strikes by IG Metall in 1978 and 1979. The first was in the metalworking and auto sectors in the Stuttgart area. The second was in the steel industry in the Ruhr. The different conditions of the respective industries meant that the union had to stress different themes in each sector. For machine tools and autos—sectors that were still very strong but needed some transformation—the major issues involved union attempts to shape this process of technological change. Yet for steel—an industry in profound decline—the major issues involved union attempts to share a decreasing number of jobs in a declining sector. For one union to devise different policies for the different conditions in various sectors proved a most difficult task.

In an attempt that began to deal with these changes, the metalworkers' union (IG Metall) introduced a series of qualitative issues into the collective-bargaining process during the 1978 wage-bargaining round. Concerned very much with the structural and technological change that had disastrous impact on its workers (particularly in the auto and metalworking sectors in the Stuttgart area), the regional IG Metall leadership in the person of Franz Steinkühler brought to the collective-bargaining table issues that had been discussed in his portion of the union since the early 1970s. Namely, he argued that the union in these sectors should demand both quantitative and qualitative outcomes. He reasoned that the pre-1973–74 pattern of waiting for the employers to grant ever-increasing wage packets had gone and that if the union wanted to reattain secure employment, high wages, and fringe benefits, then it would have to take the concept of worker participation seriously and bargain for the reshaping of industry in ways that would benefit German workers. Steinkuehler and IG Metall were successful in integrating these qualitative, or worker control, issues into the collective-bargaining framework during the spring of 1978. IG Metall won concessions on deskilling and dequalifying workers and also gained access to new areas of information regarding job classifications, which previously had resided only with the employers. The union was also able to institutionalize regularized consultation between works councils and employers about all new developments regarding changes in the production process, an especially significant development since the employers, at that time, still had held up passage of the 1976 *Mitbestimmung* law.[44]

Despite these successes in adding participation and control dimensions to union strategies in these sectors, the experience in other industries retained a more traditional West German postwar pattern. In late 1978 and early 1979 IG Metall struck the Ruhr-based steel industry. Just as the economic position of steel differed from autos and machine tools, so too did IG Metall's strategy in the Ruhr differ from the Stuttgart-area experience. Instead of qualitative collective bargaining over the most appropriate way to introduce new technology, IG Metall bargained in the steel industry for a workweek of less than 40 hours. The union originally saw this as an innovative demand because it argued that reducing the workweek would force the employers to add more workers and thereby alleviate the region's above-average unemployment rate.

The union failed to attain its goal of a substantial reduction of the workweek, settling for an "approach toward" (*Einstieg in*) its goal. In practice, this meant that the average workweek was reduced to approximately 39 hours. But more seriously, the gradual introduction of work-time reduction allowed the employers to manage this change in their production schedules without any increase in jobs at all. Thus, rather than being an innovative strategy of challenging the employers on work scheduling, this action was economically not very different from the more traditional Keynesian measures the unions had practiced for years. Specifically, because the union never explicitly challenged the employers' ability to control the work process, this "innovative" shorter workweek served only to increase industry costs; the union never devised a strategy to restructure the production process. In short, because the unions were not able to combine the issue of shortened working time with qualitative demands to control the outcome of this process, they have been unable to create the new jobs Germany badly needs.

Unfortunately for those in the union movement who wanted to follow through on the Stuttgart area's qualitative, participatory collective bargaining of 1978, the outcome of the steel strike left a difficult legacy. The union leaders believed that the strike failed because they had not bargained hard enough or long enough for a reduced workweek. Most of the leaders did not consider that perhaps the strike failed because of their unwillingness (or inability) to more directly challenge the employers over control of the process of restructuring.

This development had adverse effects during the first few years of the 1980s because the failure of the 1979 strike simply increased the union's resolve to push the reduced work-time issue even more strongly the next time (1984) they could bargain with the employers over nonwage, or general framework, issues. Ironically, it was Steinkühler himself who led the fight for the 35-hour week during the metal industry strikes in the spring of 1984. As much as those in the unions who shared Steinkühler's perception realized the need to move toward qualitative collective bargaining, the overwhelming sentiment among the union leadership was to push the 35-hour issue.

And push the 35-hour workweek demand was precisely what the IG Metall leadership did in a bitter seven-week strike during the spring of 1984. Suffering a similar fate as in the steel strike in 1979, IG Metall was able to win only a gradual introduction of a workweek reduction to 38.5 hours, and only for some workers. Like the steel strike, the 1984 metalworkers' strike was also unable to move beyond the simple demand for an immediate introduction of a 35-hour week. Gone were the innovative participatory demands of 1978 that involved workers on the shop floor in the introduction of new technology and the general restructuring of the industry. During the 1984 strike there were virtually no attempts to bargain over such qualitative issues as the introduction of technology, the restructuring of the workplace, or the response of the employers to demands for more workplace "flexibility." And IG Metall was not alone in this pattern of backsliding from qualitative to quantitative issues. The printing union (IG Druck und Papier) also conducted a strike in 1984 over the same issue and with essentially the same result.

On a theoretical level, the problem with the issue of the 35-hour week (and perhaps work-time reduction in general)—at least in their current incarnation—is that they assume that there is a static number of jobs. Once one buys this explanation, the only path available is to find a way to share this finite number of workplaces among all workers.[45] The problem is that this conception cedes a crucially important portion of the industrial terrain to the employers without a struggle. It never challenges them about what work is and who defines how it is to take place. It takes too literally the German terms for *employer* and *employee,* namely, *Arbeitgeber* (work giver) and *Arbeitnehmer* (work taker). By focusing only on shortening existing work time and not on the creation of productive and socially valuable work that needs to be done in all industrialized societies, this movement will likely prove far less successful than its adherents hope. Without innovative forms of participation as a foundation, proposals to reduce work time are too easily circumvented by the employers.

Conclusion

Why the departure from the more innovative participatory patterns of the 1970s to the more traditional quantitative bargaining (despite the supposed innovativeness of the 35-hour demand)? Or more fundamentally, why have German unions during four distinct historical periods—the Second Reich, Weimar, the immediate postwar period, and the post-oil-crisis years—been unable to generate more impressive forms of worker control out of these participative institutions? Despite the elaborate participatory traditions—at both the state and workplace levels—the unions still remain unconvinced as to the transformatory possibilities of genuine participation and the actualization of their own potential power. The primary lesson that the German unions should take from alternative movements like the Green party is not the 35-hour demand, but rather the new concern for qualitative improvements in working life.

Unlike those in most other industrialized countries, workers in West Germany already have structures in place that could be used to challenge the employers and propose solutions to economic crisis themselves. Unions in West Germany, as in all industrialized countries, should realize that the post–World War II age of receiving ever higher wages and fringe benefits is gone. Employers are no longer able to "deliver the goods" to workers as they did during the 1960s and early 1970s. In fact, employers in most sectors have no monopoly of wisdom on how to perform in an increasingly competitive world economy. In short, if German unions are to take up issues that management can no longer solve, then they—like all unions in these difficult times—must begin to see themselves as producers of value in society and not just as consumers. In so doing, they will come to see themselves as also having the right to direct such previously sacrosanct management functions as work scheduling and the scope and pace of technological innovation. Ultimately, they will have to be prepared to use measures that challenge management's unilateral control of the production process.

But they also have to find ways of taking their participatory successes in the workplace and linking them to broader movements for economic and political control. This mobilization from the bottom is particularly important because—as the corporatist literature has shown—there is real danger for any labor movement in believing that participation can be generated from the top. Higher level participatory institutions are crucial, but only as vehicles to diffuse participation that has already been generated within the workplace.

Notes

1. See the "peasant worker" argument of Charles Sabel in his *Work and Politics* (Cambridge: Cambridge University Press, 1982).

2. See Wolfgang Abendroth, *A Short History of the European Working Class* (New York: Monthly Review Press, 1972).

3. See Edward Crankshaw, *Bismarck* (New York: Viking, 1981).

4. Lawrence Schofer, "Patterns of Labor Protest: Upper Silesia, 1865–1914," *Journal of Labor History* 5, no. 4 (1972): 21–38; and Peter Stearns, "Adaptation to Industrialization: German Workers as a Test Case," *Central European History* 3, nos. 3–4 (Dec. 1970): 303–331.

5. Dieter Schuster, *Die Deutsche Gewerkschaftsbewegung* (Bad Godesburg: Vorwärts-Druck, 1976); Helga Grebing, *Geschichte der deutschen Arbeiterbewegung: Ein Überblick,* 2d ed. (Munich: Nymphenburger Verlagshandlung,

1966); and Bernd Otto, *Gewerkschaftsbewegung in Deutschland* (Cologne: Bund Verlag, 1975).

6. Hans Rosenberg, "The Political and Social Consequences of the Great Depression in Central Europe, 1873–1896," *Economic History Review* 8 (1943): 58–73.

7. Vernon L. Lidtke, *The Outlawed Party: Social Democracy in Germany, 1878–1890* (Princeton: Princeton University Press, 1966).

8. Eckhard J. Häberle, "Worker Participation and Entrepreneurial Power in Industrial Organization: An Hypothesis on the German Historical Development" (unpublished, Institute of Political Science, University of Heidelberg, March 1977).

9. For a more thorough discussion of this theme, see Andrei S. Markovits and Christopher S. Allen, "Trade Unions and the Economic Crisis: The West German Case," in Peter Gourevitch et al., *Unions and Economic Crisis: Britain, West Germany and Sweden* (London: George Allen and Unwin, 1984).

10. Guenther Roth, *The Social Democrats in Imperial Germany* (Totowa, N.J.: Bedminster Press, 1963).

11. Gerhard Ritter, *Arbeiterbewegung im Wilhelmischen Reich* (Berlin: Colloquium Verlag, 1963).

12. D. Groh, *Negative Integration und revolutionäre Attentismus* (Frankfurt am Main: Propyläen, 1973); and Hans Joseph Steinberg, *Sozialismus und deutsche Sozialdemokratie* (Bonn: Dietz Verlag, 1979).

13. Ritter, *Staatskunst und Kriegshandwerk,* 4 vols. (Munich: R. Oldenbourg, 1954).

14. A. Mendelssohn-Bartholdy, *War and German Society* (New York: H. Fertig, 1971); and Jürgen Kocka, *Klassengessellschaft im Kriege* (Göttingen: Vandenhoek und Ruprecht, 1973).

15. Barrington Moore, *Injustice: The Social Bases of Obedience and Revolt* (White Plains, N.Y.: M. E. Sharpe, 1978).

16. Robert Giebish, "Miners and Workers Control in 1918–19" (paper presented at the Center for European Studies, Harvard University, Oct. 1980).

17. Eberhard Kolb, *Arbeiterrate in der deutschen Innenpolitik, 1918–1919* (Düsseldorf: Droste Verlag, 1962). For an excellent analysis of workers' council movements throughout Europe during this period, see Carmen Sirianni, "Workers' Control in the Era of WWI," *Theory and Society* 9, no. 1 (Jan. 1980): 29–88; and for a more elaborate analysis, see Carmen Sirianni and James Cronin, eds., *Work, Community, and Power: The Experience of Labor in Europe and America, 1900–1925* (Philadelphia: Temple University Press, 1983).

18. Hans Limmer, *Die deutsche Gewerkschaftsbewegung* (Munich: Olzog Verlag), 50–54; and Gerard Braunthal, *Socialist Labor and Politics in Weimar Germany* (Hamden: Archon Books, 1978).

19. The SPD became the dominant party of government during the early Weimar years, but its policies grew increasingly conservative as party right-wingers gained the upper hand and as it entered into coalitions with nonsocialist parties.

20. David Abraham, "Economic Democracy in Germany" (paper presented at the Center for European Studies, Harvard University, Oct. 29, 1982).

21. Hilferding, *Finance Capital* (London: Routledge and Kegan Paul, 1981); and Fritz Nephali, *Wirtschaftsdemokratie: ihr Wesen, Weg und Ziel* (Berlin: Verlagsgesellschaft des Allgemeinem Deutschen Gewerkschaftsbundes, 1928).

22. Napthali, *Wirtschaftsdemokratie.*

23. Peter von Oertzen, *Betriebsräte in der Novemberrevolution* (Dusseldorf: Droste Verlag, 1963).

24. Timothy W. Mason, *Arbeiterklasse und Volksgemeinschaft* (Wiesbaden: Westdeutscher Verlag, 1975); "Labour in the Third Reich," *Past and Present* 33 (April 1966): 112–31; Max H. Kele, *Nazis and Workers: National Socialist Appeals to German Workers, 1918–1933* (Chapel Hill, N.C.: University of North Carolina Press, 1972); and Juergen Kuczynski, *Germany Under Fascism* (London: Frederick Muller, 1944).

25. Markovits and Allen, "Trade Unions and the Economic Crisis," 96.

26. Ibid., 97.

27. Ibid., 98.

28. Walter Korpi and Michael Shalev, "Strikes, Power and Politics in Western Nations, 1900–1976" (paper presented at the Conference of Europeanists, Washington, D.C., March 28–30, 1979).

29. Andrei S. Markovits and Samantha Kazarinov, "Class Conflict, Capitalism, and Social Democracy: The Case of Migrant Workers in the Federal Republic of Germany," *Comparative Politics* 10, no. 3 (April 1978): 373–91; and Stephen Castles and Godula Kosack, "Immigrant Workers and Trade Unions in the German Federal Republic," *Radical America* 8, no. 6 (Nov.–Dec. 1974): 55–77.

30. Richard J. Willey, "Trade Unions and Political Parties in the Federal Republic of Germany," *Industrial and Labor Relations Review* 28, no. 1 (Oct. 1974): 38–59. For a critical view of the first few years of the Brandt government, see Emil Bandholz, *Zwischen Godesberg und Grossindustrie oder Wo Steht die SPD?* (Reinbek bei Hamburg: Rowohlt Verlag, 1971).

31. Gerhard Leminsky and Berndt Otto, *Politik und Programmatik des deutschen Gewerkschaftsbundes* (Cologne: Bund Verlag, 1974).

32. Alfred Diamant, "Democratizing the Workplace: The Myth and Reality of Mitbestimmung in the Federal Republic of Germany," in G. David Garson, *Worker Self-Management in Industry: The Western European Experience* (New York: Praeger, 1977); and Hans G. Nutzinger, "Mitbestimmung in der Bundesrepublik Deutschland: Stellung und Perspektiven" (unpublished, University of Heidelberg, Alfred Weber Institut, Feb. 1977).

33. "Das Mitbestimmungsgesetz ist verfassungsgemass," *Frankfurter Allgemeine Zeitung*, March 2, 1979.

34. Jeremiah M. Riemer, "Crisis and Intervention in the West German Economy: A Political Analysis of Changes in the Policy Making Machinery During the 1960s and 1970s" (Ph.D. diss. Cornell University, 1983).

35. IG Metall, *Werktage werden besser* (Frankfurt am Main: IG Metall, 1973).

36. Joachim Bergmann and Walther Mueller-Jentsch, "The Federal Republic of Germany: Cooperative Unionism and Dual Bargaining System Challenged," in Solomon Barkin, ed., *Worker Militancy and its Consequences*, 2d ed. (New York: Praeger, 1983); Guenter Minnerup, "The Bundesrepublik Today," *New Left*

Review 99 (Sept.–Oct. 1976): 3–44; and Jörg Goldberg and Heinz Jung, *Die Wirtschaftskrise 1974–1976 in der Bundesrepublik Deutschland* (Frankfurt am Main: VMB, 1976).

37. The unions had always viewed the "dual" nature of the union and council systems as a real impediment to union influence on the shop floor. They were, however, able to use their influence with the SPD-led coalition to pass in 1972 a revision of the Works Constitution Law in their favor.

38. Michael Crozier et al., *The Crisis of Democracy* (New York: New York University Press, 1975); and OECD, *Working Paper on Industrial Relations, Collective Bargaining and Government Policies—National Report: Federal Republic of Germany* (Paris, May 16, 1978).

39. Andrei S. Markovits and Christopher S. Allen, "Trade Union Response to the Centemporary Economic Problems in Western Europe: The Context of Current Debates and Policies in the Federal Republic of Germany," *Economic and Industrial Democracy* 2, no. 1 (1981): 49–85.

40. Gerhard Leminsky, "The German Trade Unions" (paper presented at the Center for European Studies, Harvard University, Nov. 15, 1980).

41. See Jutta Helm, "Codetermination in West Germany: What Difference Has It Made?" (paper presented at the 1984 APSA Meetings, Washington, D.C.).

42. DGB, *Geschäftsbericht, 1977–1981,* passim.

43. See the numerous articles on these themes in Andrei S. Markovits, ed., *The Political Economy of West Germany* (New York: Praeger, 1982). See also Frieder Naschold, *Probleme einer "sozialorientierten Forschungs und Entwicklungspolitik"—Das Program "Humanisierung des Arbeitslebens" am Scheideweg* (Berlin: IIVG, 1979); Eckart Hildebrand, "Im Betrieb überleben mit der neuen Technik: Arbeitserfahrungen eines Drehers," in Otto Jacobi, Eberhard Schmidt, and Walther Mueller-Jentsch, eds., *Moderne Zeiten—Alte Rezepte,* Kritische Gewerkschaftsjarbücher, 1980–81 (Berlin: Rotbuch Verlag, 1980); Joseph Huber and Jiri Kosta, eds., *Wirtschaftsdemokratie in der Diskussion* (Cologne: Europäische Verlaganstalt, 1978); Guenter Brandt et al., *Computer und Arbeitsprozess* (Frankfurt am Main: Campus Verlag, 1975); Otto Ulrich, "Technicher Fortschritt und die Gesellschaft des Arbeitslosen," *Technologie und Politik* 10 (April 1978): 28–47; and see also *Gewerkschaftliche Monatshefte* (April 1980), the entire issue of which was devoted to the impact technological change was having on German workers.

44. Markovits and Allen, "Trade Unions and the Economic Crisis," 168. The printers' union, IG Druck und Papier, also waged a strike in 1978 over qualitative issues and was successful in winning concessions from the employers on input into job redesign. See Projektgruppe Gewerkschaftsforschung, *Tarifpolitik 1978: Lohnpolitische Kooperation und Arbeitssicherungskämpfe* (Frankfurt: Campus Verlag, 1979).

45. Claus Offe, "Worktime Reform Politics" (paper presented at the Harvard University Center for European Studies, March 27, 1985). To paraphrase Offe, "if there is no more work, then let's distribute it more evenly." This theme is treated more broadly in Claus Offe, *Disorganized Capitalism: Contemporary Transformations of Work and Politics* (Cambridge: MIT Press, 1985), particularly in chapter 5.

7

AUTOGESTION COMING AND GOING: THE STRANGE SAGA OF WORKERS' CONTROL MOVEMENTS IN MODERN FRANCE

George Ross

France has been an exception to the trend toward statist definitions of working-class liberation in capitalist democracies. Anarcho-syndicalism was a lively current in early French labor politics, as in many other places. The fact that similar themes persisted well into the twentieth century made France unusual, however. *Autogestion,* a modern reformulation of anarcho-syndicalism, has been central in the most recent French discussions. Yet despite the unusual openness of French leftist political debate on nonstatist definitions of workers' control, concrete results in policies and programs have been meager. On the rare occasions when reform from the left has been possible in France, statist definitions have predominated. An explanation of the liveliness of nonstatist leftist ideas in recent French life and the paucity of their concrete political outcomes is the goal of this essay.

Themes in History

As French labor moved toward the twentieth century, the precise meaning to be attached to general themes of workers' control was still in dispute. Anarchism or anarcho-syndicalism provided one pole of this dispute—Proudhon, after all, was a French thinker.[1] To revolutionary syndicalists, capitalists and capitalism disempowered workers in the workplace in the first instance, distorting workplace-community ties in the process. The most pertinent and radical forms of anticapitalist struggle, therefore, were those in which workers took back power at such levels, removing capitalists and establishing democratic and cooperative local control. Explicit in this was not only a rejection of capitalist exploitation in an economic sense but, perhaps more important, the coordinating and organizing role of capitalists in production (i.e., as managers in a modern division of labor). French anarcho-syndicalism therefore refused to accept the inevitability of what many others regarded as the defining aspect of modernity—an elaborate division of labor based on rationality and involving delegation of power to experts and complex organizations.[2]

In France, as elsewhere, more statist definitions of workers' control developed as well. In these visions liberation from capitalism would come only after labor amassed political strength, which ultimately would be deployed through the state to work change. For those who held this general position, accumulating political power was the essential prerequisite for serious movement toward workers' control. There was considerable disagreement within this statist camp about how to proceed, however. Reformists were willing to use political power to strike deals with capital for piecemeal limitations of capital's freedom to maneuver. Revolutionaries wanted to amass political power in order to destroy capital in one fell swoop. The statist tradition was more modern than anarcho-syndicalism in its acceptance of social evolution and of the inevitability of the division of labor. Here Marx himself was most eloquent. Capitalism was not simply to be abolished but transcended, once it had performed its historically liberating mission—from localism, ignorance, and scarcity—and had become a fetter on the emergence of the true modernity of socialism and communism.

Statism and Leftist Pluralism

France did not escape the overwhelming drift of labor in capitalism toward statist definitions of workers' control and management in the twentieth century. In 1920–21 two major ideological and political actors, sworn enemies of one another but both statist, occupied most of the available space on the left. French social democracy became ever more reformist over time, focusing on the need for nationalization, economic planning, increasing working-class power over economic decisions, and stimulating economic activity through state macroeconomic policies and social programs. French Communists were revolutionaries, closely tied to the Soviet experiment, who sought to "seize state power" and abolish private property and "bourgeois democracy" in the interests of "proletarian dictatorship." Following the Soviet model, the Communists foresaw access to workers' control through the substitution of centralized political levers and public enterprise for the market and private capital. Although the differences between these two political families on issues of political process and liberties were huge, from a sufficient distance it was clear that both were branches of the same general nineteenth-century tree.

200 Autogestion Coming and Going

The fact of labor movement division meant, however, that France resisted powerful trends elsewhere toward the unification and reformist homogenization of working-class politics. Disunity and conflict between Socialists and Communists created space for the expression, if often only weakly, of other and different definitions of the meaning of working-class liberation. Thus anarcho-syndicalism and other minority visions of social change survived ideologically throughout the first half of the twentieth century. Anti-statist attitudes associated with working-class Catholicism also survived.

During those rare moments when the left had sufficient social and political power to change France, the statism of the "big two" was what counted. In the Popular Front of the 1930s and the resistance-liberation period, the left in power produced classically statist reforms, initiating a package of nationalizations and welfare state programs (health care, pensions, schooling, family allocations).[3] The French left was unusual in its willingness to establish a system of national economic planning, even if this was a joint product of the right and left and was pointed toward economic modernization more than workers' control.[4] True, after liberation in 1944 steps were taken to achieve a degree of workers' control over the health insurance system (whose administration was elected by the insured from lists presented by the unions until 1967, when this system was abolished). There were also trade union administrators on the boards of nationalized industries, but they had little access to key information and decisions. Both departures from strict statism were efforts to plug token workers (more often, union officials) into the top of organizational hierarchies alongside controlling elites, more than anything else. The one measure aimed more directly at a more decentralized type of workers' control was the creation after liberation of works committees (*comités d'entreprise*), which owed much to Vichy corporatism and Communist desires to create new levels of enterprise power.[5] These committees were granted access to a limited amount of economic information about the firm, but they were generally shunted off with small budgetary allocations to animate social activities—sports, culture, and tourism. They became important financial and agitational levers for trade unionism but only the thinnest of perches for workers' control.[6]

Left statism fell on harder times during the Cold War in ways that eventually fertilized the soil for the renaissance of anarcho-syndicalist views—*autogestion*. Left reformist optimism ended in May 1947 with the eviction of Communists from the French government by a Socialist prime minister. Subsequently both major families of the French left found themselves in difficult situations. The Socialists, who were on the American side of the Cold War internationally and were consequently unable to ally with the pro-Soviet Communists, were obliged to ally to their right to have any influence in the multiparty Fourth Republic. The political consequences of this were that Socialist reformism virtually disappeared as Socialist ministers accepted increasingly more conservative economic and social policies at home and involvement in colonial warfare abroad. The credibility of French social democracy as an agent for progressive change of any kind was thereby severely tarnished, while Socialist electoral support began to decline (from a postwar high of nearly 25 percent to the mid-to-lower teens).[7]

The trajectory of the Communists was very different. Aligned on the Soviet side of the Cold War, the Parti Communiste Francais (PCF) retreated from the adaptive subtlety of its earlier alliance politics into a reaffirmed neo-Bolshevik identity. During its worst Cold War moments (1947–53) the PCF adopted an absurd personality cult of Stalin, and its own leadership carried out campaigns in favor of socialist realism and "proletarian science," got deeply implicated in eastern European purges, and enthusiastically bought the worst Stalinist hallucinations.[8] Perhaps the most caricatural and damaging event of all occurred in 1956 when the party refused to acknowledge the existence of Kruschev's report on the crimes of Stalin (calling it a concoction of the bourgeois press, the "report attributed to Kruschev") and then wholeheartedly supported the Soviet invasion of Hungary.

Openings to Change

In the context of the Cold War the particular situation of a pluralistic left thus worked to discredit both forms of French statist leftism. Social democracy still talked Marxism and radical utopias, yet it practiced coalition-mongering centrism. The Communists, isolated in a purist, Marxist-Leninist, pro-Soviet ghetto through the 1950s, acentuated their commitment to the illiberal, undemocratic, and repressive "existing" utopia of the Stalinist and post-Stalinist USSR. If statism dominated the field of French leftist discourse, then its specific forms presented by the two major leftist families left a great deal to be desired.

First reactions to this, beyond the small world of anarcho-syndicalist sects with ties to nineteenth-century ideas, came from groups of intellectuals. In many other contexts such reactions would have been barely noticeable. With Parisian centralization, exaggerated reverence for words, and the consequent strategic importance of the intelligentsia, the clubs and bands of intellectuals striking out in new directions have often had considerable importance in France. Attempts prior to the mid-1950s to break away from the Socialist-Communist duopoly failed, as the existentialists' history and Sartre's ultimate grudging support for the PCF showed.[9] After the events of 1956 much more was possible. *Arguments,* a review put together by dissident and ex-Communist writers who insisted upon the problem of bureaucracy and the centrality of democracy for the left, was one of the more important early breakthroughs.[10] An even more mixed group composed of ex-Trotskyists, trade unionists, and former Communists joined to edit *Socialisme ou Barbarie.*[11] *Socialisme ou Barbarie,* which may well have been the single most important source of the renewal of decentralized workers' control notions in France, emphasized the importance of anti-Stalinist, antibureaucratic *basiste* shopfloor organizing and placed great stock in the creativity and energy of ordinary workers. Other contributors to the ground swell of reflection on face-to-face democracy at the base were left-wing Catholicism, which had begun to percolate through the JOC and JAC youth movements (Jeunesse Ouvrière Chrétienne and Jeunesse Agricole Chrétienne); scouting, which (incredible as it may seem to North Americans) became a hotbed of young radicalism in the later 1950s; and the Confédération Française des Travailleurs Chrétiens (CFTC), which was the Catholic trade union. Interest in workers' control in Yugoslavia also spread at this point among intellectuals and trade unionists looking for a "third way" between communism and social democracy.

The Algerian War (1954–62), France's last paroxysm of colonialism, provided added impetus to the development of an independent left with an anarcho-dencentralized tinge. For various reasons both major leftist parties restrained their opposition to this very nasty war. The Socialists had presided over the war's beginning and were thereby deeply implicated in its pursuit. The Communists were more concerned in this period with getting out of their Cold War ghetto, which they thought involved wooing allies to their right, such as the Socialists. Given the positions of the Socialists, the PCF came to advocate a rather careful peace movement. Quite as important, the PCF's own working-class base, whose sons were being drafted to fight in Algeria, was mildly infected by colonialist nationalism. With neither of the major forces on the left willing to promote strongly militant antiwar activities, there was thus room for a semiautonomous antiwar movement animated by students, intellectuals, and leftist Catholics. This movement, partly for its own reasons and partly because it spent much of its time responding to the chilling anathemas cast upon it by the PCF, developed its own strongly decentralizing antibureaucratic radicalism. The personnel and ideas of the student and intellectual antiwar movement were to be of great importance to the rise of *autogestion* in the 1960s.[12]

Thus by the early 1960s there were numerous movements in France pointing toward a renaissance of decentralized workers' control, directed as much against the unsatisfactory alternatives presented by the left's "big two" as toward anything concrete. Social change brought by France's postwar economic boom intensified such trends. France was transformed practically overnight from an insular, protected, agrarian, and underindustrialized country to a modern, urbanized, consumerized, open society. Demography, urbanization, changes in the structure of industry, the rise of a modern service sector, the electronic media, the universalization of the automobile, and a host of other things began to decompose the working class, which had provided the underpinnings of traditional leftist politics and trade unionism. New middle strata expanded rapidly, as did higher education. Old-fashioned habits and attitudes of all kinds fell under siege.[13]

This social upheaval created new political space. New people with new outlooks and goals, working at new things in new ways, sought new eyes with which to view the social world. Changes in France's constitutional organization in 1958, plus consequent changes in the structures of partisan politics also created incentives to open discussion on the left. The coming of the Fifth Republic in 1958 brought a new electoral system and presidentialism (with direct election to the presidency as amended in 1962), which both undercut the amorphous centrist coalition building of the Fourth Republic and favored renewed left-right political polarization. Great pressure ensued for the French left to unite its disparate and quarreling forces and for the new constituencies created by modernization to choose clearly between left and right. The character of the right-center majority that formed around General de Gaulle in the early 1960s (and that ruled France in various forms until 1981) biased this latter choice. Gaullism, being possessed of considerable *dirigiste* modernism, pushed hard to prepare the French economy for international competition, beginning with the European Common Market. Yet progrowth attitudes and intelligent economic strategies coexisted with markedly conservative approaches to the social consequences of growth. Some parts of the new majority were taken in by American rhetoric that growth, in itself, would provide the solvents needed to avoid social problems. Others had more old-fashioned ideas and believed that social problems were a form of malingering to be dealt with in mildly authoritarian ways. Since the huge social changes fostered by the postwar boom were often painful, dislocating, and disorienting, this mixture of benign neglect and mild repressiveness was bound to fuel discontent from which the left was likely to benefit.

The Ephemeral Triumph of Autogestion

Autogestion . . . is not only the product of uneven development between structures of economic and political power. It is equally a calling into question of bourgeois concepts of democracy, defined as a formal system of representation, . . . a refusal of popular democracy characterized by the refraction of society into the state.[14]

While statist definitions of workers' control and liberation dominated large party politics on the French left into the 1960s, both major leftist families, the Socialists and the Communists, had tarnished ideological reputations and declining political stock. Social change was rapidly redrawing France's class map in ways that would oblige both of these families to rethink traditional appeals and approaches. The "big two" also faced a new institutional setting that pushed them toward some form of unification and theoretical and strategic innovation. French leftist politics was thus more open and more promising in the 1960s than it had been for a considerable time. It was into this climate that *autogestion* burst in May–June 1968.

Autogestion Announced

The major labor movement bearer of *autogestion* was the Confédération Française Démocratique du Travail (CFDT). Like Molière's M. Jourdain, who was astonished to learn he had been speaking prose, the CFDT had begun to "speak" *autogestion* before it was aware of it. In 1968 the CFDT was a recent descendant of what had been France's main Catholic union, the CFTC. The CFTC had persisted obstinately after 1945 with traditional Catholic labor doctrines about the essential harmony between classes, consequently behaving in very moderate ways. Opposition to such positions spread within the union in the 1950s, stemming in part from the leftward drift of parts of French Catholicism later abetted by Pope John XXIII. After extensive internal conflict the CFTC finally split in 1964. The great bulk of it, led by the progressive former minority, resolved to "deconfessionalize" and became the CFDT.[15]

The new CFDT wanted to abandon the class-collaborative meekness of its predecessor but beyond this was unsure of itself. CFDT leaders were aware of the effects of economic modernization on the French working class and perceived opportunities to tap new support from this group. In general, strategic movement was dictated by two factors. To begin with, the CFDT had to construct a new trade union identity different from that of its two major competitors, the Communist-controlled Confédération Générale du Travail (CGT) and the much weaker "business unionist" CGT–Force Ouvrière (CGT–FO). The CFDT wanted to be both militant and radical, therefore by definition unlike the CGT–FO. Yet it had to find ways to be both in order to distinguish it from the CGT, which was by far the most powerful union force in France. The CGT, subordinate to the PCF's politics, ordered its mobilizational goals around generating working-class support for the PCF and favored statist solutions to working-class problems. At least in the early 1960s it also believed in the liberating prospects of a French version of Eastern-style socialism.[16] It made sense, then, to compete with the CGT by devising a militant, decentralized, and nonpolitical strategic perspective. Secondly, this rough-and-ready guide derived from the CFDT's competitive position happened to fit rather well with the tone of the maturing leftist Catholicism shared by many CFDT leaders and organizers. Leftist Catholicism favored face-to-face mobilization of a decentralized and antibureaucratic kind that was solidly anticommunist.

Events, plus these strategic concerns, led the CFDT to 1968. A limited treaty of unified action with its rival the CGT was signed in January 1966, leading the CFDT to refine its new approaches. The CGT was concerned with shaping local union struggles to contribute to broad national union concerns—big, general demands and campaigns—and against local struggles that followed their own parochial logic. In the face of this the CFDT developed a passion for encouraging local militancy to the fullest. Whereas the CGT sought to shape general labor mobilization in ways that might pay off politically, the CFDT was resolutely antipolitical. As a result the CFDT began to acquire a reputation for eager militancy and almost reckless desire to fight local struggles to their ends, a reputation garnered from its leadership of highly publicized, rather desperate local strikes, with the CGT usually looking on disapprovingly and apprenhensively.[17]

To return to M. Jourdain, such strikes and tactics had no label until May 1968 when the CFDT, in the heat of the moment, officially discovered that they were *autogestionnaire.* The huge strike of May–June 1968—which may conceivably have been the largest strike in the history of modern capitalism—added more to the content of the term, since there was a modest number of individual movements in which workers' control over a plant or firm was posed as an issue.[18] *Autogestion,* at that point, was defined in terms that looked very much like old-style anarcho-syndicalism—struggles for point-of-production workers' control without much reflection on politics or general issues of economic coordination.

The other major *autogestionnaire* actor in May–June 1968 was the student movement. Here we need say much less, both because of the immensity of the literature on the 1968 student movement and because of the familiarity that most readers have with the general outlines of student movements.[19] Demands for "participatory democracy" or "co-management," particularly in universities and professional settings, were common to student-intelligentsia movements of this period almost everywhere. From such demands to their French translation of *autogestion* was not far. If the powerful antibureaucratic thrust of students was common everywhere, the response of the elite and the right-center majority in power gave the French case some of its particularity. Despite demographics and the expansion of universities, changes in policy, funding, facilities, and habits were slow. When the predictable student movement appeared, universities met the challenge with repressive ineptness. The result was a momentarily uncontrollable explosion of protest.

The specificity of the May–June 1968 student movement was the way in which it saw itself as revolutionary, in an anarcho-syndicalist way. One source of this was the sociology of the new middle strata (here the work of Alain Touraine is a useful guide). Equally important was the rebellion against the statist model of revolution proffered by the PCF. Because of its history of almost unbelievable ineptitude in dealing with intellectuals and students prior to May–June, the Communist party had managed to lose much of the great power and credibility that it had once exerted in French student politics. As a result many of the leaders and cadre of May–June 1968, if divided among themselves along the most esoteric of lines, were united in characterizing the PCF as a stolid, revisionist, Stalinized bureaucracy. The party's predictably brutal and incomprehensive response to the May events themselves reinforced such feelings. Thus vague longings for nonstatist and decentralized radicalism natural to students were powerfully reinforced by antipathy to the postures of the PCF.

There were, of course, a number of writers to which the May movement could refer—Serge Mallet, the *Socialisme ou Barbarie* team (Castoriadis, Lefort, Mothé, Naville), André Gorz, Marcuse. The events themselves produced a tremendous explosion of new literature along *autogestionnaire* lines (often by the same authors). New vanguards of change were announced—new working classes, new middle strata, cultural revolutionaries—mobilizing around new anti-statist and antibureaucratic concerns in the interests of an *autogestion* whose positive content beyond such generalities remained elusive. Despite such vagueness, this new writing was of great importance. The radical intelligentsia was weighing in in an emerging political struggle against the statist leftism, particularly its PCF variety, which had dominated French leftist debate for so long.[20]

Welcoming Structures: The Changing Political Scene

What was the essence of this more general political struggle? Here we reach the heart of the hidden history of *autogestion,* to be found in the workings of leftist political pluralism in France. From early in the Fifth Republic, the Communists had begun to urge *union de la gauche* (leftist unity) around a "Common Program of Government." After hovering for some time between leftist unity and a new centrist alliance strategy, the Socialists became more receptive to the Communist appeal, especially after the disastrous showing of a centrist Socialist candidate in the 1969 presidential election. With the coming of the 1970s a new episode of alliance between the two major leftist families was at hand.

Union de la gauche was designed to bring the left to power electorally. To do so, the left had to attract a substantial amount of new electoral support. Within the context of such general concerns, however, each major leftist party was betting on gaining the majority of this new support. The party winning this gamble would predominate in shaping the policies of the leftist government, which both parties were sure was in the offing. The PCF was much stronger at the outset of *Union,* yet it still operated in the shadow of its Stalinized, pro-Soviet past, demonstrating only the slimmest awareness of the need to change. The Socialists were substantially weaker than the PCF and burdened with an unattractive past. Since the general political situation after May–June 1968 favored the left, there was obviously a great deal of political hay to be made by the leftist force that would be best able to attract support from the newly radicalized intelligentsia and middle strata. The PCF's strategic, organizational, and theoretical conservatism and its unfortunate record in dealing with these social groups in the past meant that the Socialists, despite their lackluster image and reputation, had a better chance of recruiting from the new forces.

The Socialists were the key to the new political situation. Beginning in 1969 and culminating at the Congress of Epinay (1971), the old Section Française de l'Internationale Ouvrière (SFIO) became a new Parti Socialiste (PS). The old party was effectively taken over by new forces, some from outside the SFIO and some from its own internal rebellious minorities. After much back-room wheeling and dealing, François Mitterrand, an ex-centrist, became the new PS leader, bringing with him commitment to a strategy of Left unity that led quickly to the signature of the Left Common Program with the Communists in 1972. The new party also structured itself internally in pluralist ways, such that the distribution of leadership posts and control over strategy were the final products of struggle between a multiplicity of internal currents, each seeking power and advancing different strategic concerns.[21] The internal political system that emerged became byzantine in its complexity. More important, because of the existence of multiple currents whose relative strength varied over time, the balance of power, ideology, and program of the party were prone to change.

All of this meant that the new PS seemed open to influence by groups with determination and support, all the more so to the degree to which the complex balance of forces between internal currents was delicate. In fact, dissent existed from the outset to Mitterrand's choice of a Left unity strategy. Beyond this, considerable discomfort existed about the specific content of the 1972 Left Common program, a classically statist document reminiscent of the left's resistance program that when not ambiguous, favored Communist priorities. On both issues an infusion of *autogestionnaire* forces might tip the internal party balance. For *autogestionnaire* forces outside the PS in the 1970s, the prospect of entering or working with this evolving party held an opportunity to de-statize the non communist side of the French left while endowing it with new strategic energy. At their most ambitious, these forces even dreamed of taking over the PS.

If the CFDT had found itself speaking *autogestion* almost by accident in May–June 1968, it quickly learned to speak it on purpose thereafter. Many of the labor market factors that had made the vocabulary pay off in 1968 continued into the early 1970s. Thus the CFDT intensified its decentralized, hypermilitant, anarcho-syndicalist union tactics, reasoning that there were large receptive constituencies of the French work forces, particularly in newly industrializing areas and among newly proletarianized groups. To the degree to which these tactics worked, the CFDT hoped to gain ground on the CGT, its ally-competitor. What was new after 1968 was the CFDT's desire to formalize a body of *autogestionnaire* theory and practice, thereby making itself the principal carrier of *autogestion*.

Between 1969 and 1974 the CFDT made itself the champion of a large number of militant and often spectacular local strike movements, usually carried on under the banner of *autogestion*.[22] More often than not, these strikes occurred in less industrialized areas of the country where dynamic and exploitative small- and medium-sized capital had moved to tap cheaper sources of labor (often female). Sometimes they occurred among unskilled workers in mass production industry (in the work category the French call *ouvriers spécialisés*). Such strikes often spilled over into surrounding communities, giving them a workplace-town character that accentuated their uniqueness. In such struggles, which usually had a strong egalitarian antihierarchical tone, the CFDT, at local levels at least, was willing to contemplate illegal militant tactics, such as "sequestering" (locking in) employers and occupying plants.[23] The Lip strike of 1973 was archetypal. Here the CFDT led a movement in a dying Besançon watch factory in which the workers (mainly women) took over and "self-managed" the plant until it could be saved by refinancing.[24]

The CFDT's efforts to formalize its commitment to *autogestion* paralleled these labor market events. The central moment was the union's thirty-fifth congress in 1970 where it was announced for the first time that the CFDT believed in the class struggle and desired to help create a "socialist society," both conclusions implying that the union recognized the need for a political side to its *autogestionnaire* vision.[25] The model of socialism advanced by the CFDT was predictably a mirror image of statist and, more specifically PCF-CGT, positions, "founded on three indispensable and complementary pillars: *autogestion*, the socialization of the means of production and democratic planning." If the CFDT recognized the need for political action, however, it was adamant in asserting that movement toward socialism would follow neither from electoralism nor from the maneuvers of parties and leaders, but through *autogestionnaire* local struggles, primarily in the workplace but also in the community.

What *autogestion* would look like more concretely was left vague, however. As various leaders announced at the congress, *autogestion* "was not a security blanket, but imaginative and open toward change." *Autogestionnaire* struggle, rather than being aimed primarily toward the satisfaction of material demands of wages and hours and leaving the hard work of basic social change to political parties, ought "to begin to call into question the capitalist organization of the labor process directly."[26] Many speaking for the CFDT seemed to believe that the delegation of power and responsibility inherent in modern organizational life could be transcended. In the words of a young CFDT theoretician, "*autogestion* is a social dynamic before becoming a system, thus only the basic axes of reflection can be set out now."

The CFDT also engaged in public debate about its new strategy with the CGT in the early 1970s, in ways that both publicized and sharpened its positions. The CGT's postures at the time, more or less translated from the PCF program, were dismissive of *autogestion* as "vague formulae," reformist by definition because they neglected politics. The CGT itself persisted in advocating a statist definition of workers' control, which it called *gestion démocratique,* involving such elements as nationalizations with worker representation on boards of directors, planning, and strengthened union positions, but with the essential work of social change to come from party politics and national-level political reforms.[27] In response the CFDT asserted that a triptych of *autogestion,* democratic planning, and decentralization were the only ways to begin overcoming what it saw as the three evils of capitalism—economic exploitation, authoritarian domination, and alienation. Any schemes for change and workers' management that did not address all three of these issues simultaneously had a high risk of being exploitative, authoritarian, and alienating, as existing Socialism was and as France after implementation of the PCF-CGT program was likely to be. *Autogestionnaire* struggle, in contrast, would undermine workplace authoritarianism, generate new democracy, and create a "union of popular forces" pointing the way to a "new model of development."[28]

The other major organizational bearer of *autogestion* from 1968 into the 1970s was the Parti Socialiste Unifié (PSU), a small leftist party that had emerged from the amalgamation of split-off factions from both Communists and Socialists.[29] By the early 1960s it had become a railroad station for the "new" left, bustling with the most vibrant—but also diverse and contentious—currents of leftist thought. Because of its pluralism and openness to virtually any strain of leftist ideology, the PSU found itself drawn to May–June 1968 like a fish to water, playing an important role in the events themselves and becoming at least partially converted to *autogestionnaire* politics in the process. The May–June period also coincided with the assumption of PSU leadership by Michel Rocard. At this point Rocard, one of the more important leftist politicians of his time, was a young technocratic modernist looking for a vehicle to pilot on his way to the highest pinnacles of French public life. *Autogestionnaire* politics fit his needs of the moment.[30]

At its sixth congress in 1969, the PSU, despite congenital internal disagreement, officially became *autogestionnaire*. The mirror-image process of defining *autogestion* against the Communists tended also to prevail in the PSU. "The essential thing," stated thesis 6 of the 1969 Congress Declaration, "remains to organize effectively the power of workers collectively, and not that of state bureaucracy. Collective appropriation will progressively destroy the power of the existing possessing classes." The answer to the conundrum of bureaucratization lay in radical decentralization of power, particularly in the firms (which workers' councils would eventually run), with greater access to knowledge and "the socialist univiersity" helping to achieve the general level of competence needed to make such things work. As Michel Rocard himself announced, existing capitalist society destroyed "social man" by dividing and isolating him into specific producer, consumer, and citizen roles. "It is these divisions between civil society and political society, between concrete man and abstract citizen, that we must end . . . *autogestion* is the means."[31] The major difference between the CFDT and PSU was the added emphasis the PSU gave to *political autogestion* (usually translated as "radical decentralization").

After 1968 the significance of the PSU was much greater than either its actual size or internal disunity indicated. Rocard ran for president in 1969, for example, and won nearly as many votes (3.6 percent) as an admittedly weak Socialist candidate (together they won only about 10 percent). PSU activists were prominent in highly publicized strikes (Charles Piaget, the leader at Lip in 1973, was active in PSU, for example), in the renewal of grassroots politics through France's new social movements and associations (e.g., ecology, urban activism, regionalism, consumerism), in the CFDT itself, and in the influential press including the important *Le Nouvel Observateur.*

All of this pointed the PSU toward deals with the PS. The PS needed a new self-presentation that would allow it to appear different not only from its statist rival-ally, the PCF, but also from its pallid social democratic ancestor, the SFIO. Moreover, it was particularly important for the PS to tap the modernist fervor and electoral support of the new middle strata that flowed from 1968. Thus there was an obvious place within the new PS for *autogestion,* for the militant activism of the PSU, the prestige of Rocard, and important trade union links with the CFDT.

The moment in 1974 the PS chose to address such matters was carefully selected by its very clever first secretary, François Mitterrand. *Union de la gauche* had done reasonably well in the 1973 legislative elections, with the PS starting an electoral comeback. Then in the presidential election in springtime 1974 occasioned by Georges Pompidou's death, François Mitterrand, candidate of the United Left, missed winning by less than 1 percent. The stage was set for the autumn 1974 Assises du Socialisme call to integrate all, or as many as possible, of the *autogestion-naire* forces into the PS.

The Ironic Fate of Autogestion

> The pieces of the puzzle are easy to put together. The word *autogestion* was on everyone's lips . . . in the 1970s. Today it is absent from political vocabulary. Its disappearance has been as brutal as its rise was rapid.[32]

At the moment of the Assises, François Mitterrand was at the peak of his 1970s political strength. Mitterrand being Mitterrand, the Assises were designed as much to advance his personal goals as to do any favors for the advocates of *autogestion.* This was important, because the bulk of the PSU and CFDT *autogestionnaires* were hostile to both *union de la gauche* (Mitterrand's preferred strategy) and the statist Common Program of 1972 (the agreement with the Communists that cemented this strategy). How much *autogestion* could be gotten from a party leader who held fast to such basic options?

Autogestion in the Lion's Den

To begin with, the *autogestionnaires* who participated in the Assises (PSU members and other Rocard supporters, CFDT leaders and activists) were weakened by mixed goals and confused mandates. The PSU split about the Assises, for example, leaving Rocard, its leader, in a minority position where he could not officially speak for his own party. Moreover, some, if not the bulk, of new middle-strata agitation for *autogestion* had been dispersed into specific new social movements (e.g., feminism, an-tinuclear power, regionalism). The Assises therefore came to look more like a way of allowing Rocard and followers to join the PS than of integrating the PSU and *autogestion.* This, in turn, fueled well-founded suspicions in the PS that Rocard's purposes were more personal than doctrinal. His stewardship over the PSU, it was suggested, had much less to do with the promotion of *autogestion* (in fact, Rocard was politically a centrist) than with establishing himself as a national political leader. The situation of CFDT leaders was more complex. They wanted to influence the PS programmatically, both in a general *autogestionnaire* sense and in more specific pro-CFDT ways (such that the PS would take CFDT policy proposals more seriously as it approached power). Yet the leaders knew that they could not carry the bulk of CFDT troops toward any explicit ties with the PS, since such ties would contradict the union's commitment to trade union independence from politics. Thus they were not quite sure what they wanted from the Assises and, moreover, were unfamiliar with the shark-infested political waters they were entering. It rapidly became clear, for example, that Edmond Maire, the idealistic and rhetorical CFDT leader, and François Mitterrand, the florentine back-room log-roller *extraordinaire,* could make very little sense of one another, to the CFDT's detriment.

In contrast Mitterrand and his colleagues knew precisely what they wanted from the Assises. Mitterrand was determined to maintain the *union de la gauche* strategy, because as of 1974 it had begun to allow the PS to outdistance its Communist ally-rival in important ways. Embracing *autogestion,* at least rhetorically, would help the party bring in needed new middle-strata electoral support, which the PCF had itself begun to woo through its own timid Eurocommunism. However, as both the PSU and the CFDT defined it, *autogestion* clearly had an anti-statist, decentralizing, antibureaucratic (and anticommunist) core. The juggling trick for Mitterrand would be to both maintain *Union* around the Common Program and embrace *autogestion,* since they were largely contradictory. For Mitterrand the path was clear. The PS would speak *autogestion* without taking it very seriously.

Mitterrand also had internal PS goals for the Assises that also had little to do with embracing *autogestion.* Introducing the Rocardians into the complex internal life of the PS might give Mitterrand a new coalitional pawn for his internal tactics. Beginning at the Epinay Congress in 1971, the leftmost fraction of the PS, the CERES (Centres d'Études et de Recherches Socialistes) group, had been an essential component in the coalition that had allowed Mitterrand to run the PS. CERES (which also talked about *autogestion,* by which it mainly meant local activism) was persistently the strongest PS advocate of close-to-PCF programs. Mitterrand understood, however, that as the PS gained strength vis-à-vis the PCF within Left Union, it would gain greater freedom to cut loose from the PCF's programmatic desires. The first secretary also knew that such a cutting-loose process might well be the penultimate move needed to promote a Left victory led by a dominant PS. To take such external steps toward redefining *union de la gauche,* the internal coalition of the PS had to change. As long as CERES played a pivotal internal role, pro-PCF program positions would be well defended. The Rocardians, whose *autogestionnaire* politics barely masked anticommunism and anti-*union* centrism, would be useful new allies.

The Assises were a *grande messe* in true French leftist style, leading to a PS "project for society" embracing *autogestion* in vague and general terms.[33] Michel Rocard and his followers were duly admitted as a new current into the PS, even if not warmly welcomed by everyone in the party. The CFDT leadership felt misunderstood and left with bitter feelings about politics and politicians. The following June (1975) the PS itself held a special conference to adopt its "15 Theses for *Autogestion,*" which were also vague and general, if nonetheless clear endorsements of *autogestion.*[34] What would this mean in the greater scheme of socialist things? In the words of an astute former collaborator of Michel Rocard, "What is at issue is to know whether or not the PS actually accepts an *autogestionnaire* strategy as the foundation stone of an autonomous political logic."[35] Or, as the same author speculated, was all this just a way of taking tactical distance from the PCF as the PS got stronger?

Neostatism or Neoliberalism?

The answers were not long in coming. As the PS grew stronger electorally and as the left moved toward a majority, the PS began to claim predominance in *union de la gauche* over the Communists, with Mitterrand and others using *autogestionnaire* rhetoric liberally. The party began to succeed at winning new support from the uncommitted center and new middle strata, while also cutting into the PCF's traditional working-class base. To accomplish all this, Mitterrand manipulated a recast internal PS majority, with the Rocardians replacing the CERES group. When the Communists finally concluded that *union de la gauche* had turned against them, they promoted a showdown over program in the summer of 1977, which led quickly to the end of Left unity.[36]

The split cost the left electoral victory in 1978. In the process the PCF (followed by the CGT) itself officially adopted *autogestion,* which it combined with a new workerist sectarianism for attacking the Socialists for their "right turn." What the PCF meant by this was only marginally clearer than what the CFDT, PSU, and the PS had meant earlier. Communist *autogestion* would be a step-by-step movement to socialism via an accretion of local struggles. In an important sense, this also symbolized the PCF's belated abandonment of its generations-honored "united front from above" political strategy that had been theoretically informed by a Marxist-Leninist vision of the state.[37] With almost everyone on the left using the vocabulary of *autogestion* but with different meanings attached to it in each case, coherence had clearly been lost by 1978.

The left's failure in 1978 and the breakdown of *union de la gauche* reopened strategic debate in the PS as well. It was inevitable that minority factions in the PS would press to drop Mitterrand's strategy of leftist unity, along with Mitterrand himself. In contrast, Mitterrand insisted that the PS continue along much the same lines as before, being, as he said "unitary for two." By 1979 with a presidential election in the offing, Mitterrand's majority in the PS was weakening and he was increasingly portrayed as "archaic." A hard-nosed internal struggle over PS strategy and party leadership between Mitterrand and Michel Rocard followed. The basic question was whether to persist in a *union de la gauche* posture or to turn toward a new left-center alliance constructed ideologically around economic modernism and *autogestion*. Underneath this lay issues about the advisability of statist solutions—those set out in the 1972 Common Program—to France's problems, now greatly intensified by economic crisis, or the more localized initiatives urged by Rocard and his coterie. Something interesting had happened since the Assises to the Rocard position, however. *Autogestion* had lost its radical cutting edge and begun to move toward a de-statizing, decentralizing, deregulating perspective with clear ties to centrist American neoliberalism. The Rocardians were, in fact, labeled "the American left" by their CERES enemies. What was essential, however, was that the major spokesmen for the *autogestionnaire* current in the PS had redefined and deradicalized the meaning of *autogestion*. Henceforth, it was to mean little more than taking measures to allow French civil society to breath more freely against the state.

What was really at stake in this internal PS battle was the name of the Socialist candidate for the 1981 presidential elections. Here François Mitterrand ultimately outmaneuvered the Rocardians. But he did so only by renewed coalition manipulating inside the PS that resulted in a return to prominence and influence of CERES, the left-most current in the PS. The consequences of this involved reaffirming programmatic continuity with the 1972 Common Program—nationalizations, planning, and centralized economic voluntarism. Both the radical Projet Socialiste of 1980 and the list of promises in Mitterrand's 1981 election manifesto were strong assertions of traditional statist leftism.[38] Along with this came a renewal of "unitary for two" posturing toward the PCF (which, during the same period, was accusing Mitterrand and the Socialists of being agents of international capital). There were ritual mentions of *autogestion* in all this, but the bulk of pre-1981 Socialist politics was pre-*autogestionnaire*.

By 1981 the situation on the French left was full of irony. As a result of complex maneuverings, both major parties on the left had converted to *autogestion,* at least in language, by the later 1970s. Yet neither really took *autogestion* seriously on the eve of the left's great 1981 electoral victories (though the PCF did begin to do so later on). The PSU as the major vehicle for *autogestionnaire* politics in the earlier 1970s had split, with its "locomotives" moving into the PS as Rocardians (though the PSU did persist thereafter as something of a rump). Once inside the PS, however, the Rocardians lost their taste for *autogestion,* gradually adopting a technocratic, anti-statist neoliberalism. Thus *autogestion* was like a bee that had flown noisily about the French political left after May–June 1968 until, after stinging everyone in sight, it died.

The evolution of the major trade union carrier of *autogestion,* the CFDT, was analogous. In and around the Assises the CFDT had assumed a posture of grudging support for the left. After 1974 the CFDT was strongly buffeted by political and economic forces. With the left contemplating its first political success in over two decades, the political atmosphere in France was unusually frenetic between 1974 and 1977–78. The CFDT, despite itself, was propelled into substituting quasi-political activity for real trade unionism in these years. At the very same moment the end of the postwar boom undermined the hypermilitant local struggles that had been the CFDT's tactical launching pad. Thus there were fewer and fewer movements the CFDT could guide toward *autogestionnaire* protest. Swamped by politicization and coincidentally outmaneuvered by its rival, the CGT (which recaptured its title as the most militant French union in this period), the CFDT lost bearings and momentum.[39]

This, plus the collapse of leftist political unity, pushed the CFDT toward strategic reconsideration.[40] Beginning in 1978 with what its leadership labeled *recentrage* (recentering), the CFDT called for total depoliticization and a return to rigorous trade union autonomy. In a logical (but erroneous, as it turned out) calculation that the left's 1978 defeat would be long term, the union also began deradicalizing its identity away from the *autogestion* euphoria of earlier years and moving toward "pure and simple" unionism with much stronger stress on collective bargaining. Here the CFDT leadership was also responding to changes in the structures of trade union pluralistic competition. The CGT had itself begun to move toward pro-PCF sectarian isolation after the split of the political left. Because of this, might there not be new space for new "pure and simple" unionism? Finally, leftist Catholicism, which had pushed the CFDT forward for so long, was losing its creativity and energy.

The CFDT's internal recentering coincided with the return of hard times for French unionism more generally. The memberships and mobilizing power of the CGT and CFDT both declined. Under growing pressure, the CFDT leadership changed the name of recentering to *resyndicalisation* and began to place more and more weight on a largely unsuccessful search for new collective bargaining. *Autogestion* increasingly became a ritual incantation. For the CFDT, as for other unions, macroeconomic and industrial policy questions of a more immediate kind came to the fore, as the very existence of work for trade unionists was called into question by geographical and technological changes in French capitalism. The analogy with the processes undergone by the Rocardians was close. For the CFDT, as for the Rocardians in the PS, *autogestion* lost its corrosive edge and came to mean a desire to revitalize French civil society at the expense of the state—in the CFDT's case, through bargaining.

Conclusions

Autogestion had lived its time by 1981 when the French left finally did come to power. Derived from rejection of existing statist parameters in leftist strategy and tapping into familiar French working-class roots, *autogestion* had represented the radical dreams of significant forces in French society. Ironically, however, its adoption by first one and then the other major political force coincided with the beginning of its decline. Moreover, the social base for *autogestion* was moving on to other concerns. French new middle strata began to exchange collective political endeavors for individualistic cultural liberation. Where political urges persisted, single-issue focuses were the rule. The later 1970s, even as the left was about to come to power, were a time when powerful antileftist intellectual currents spread rapidly in the French intelligentsia. Leftist Catholicism also ran its course, with the CFDT, in particular, exhausting itself and changing its perspective.

In all this a strong new refrain arose from those who had once been the strongest believers in *autogestion*. Perhaps the problem in France was less capitalism than the fact that the state over generations had taken up so much space that French civil society had less and less room to breathe. If this was the problem, the solution was not *autogestion* but opening up breathing space. By the early 1980s Proudhon and Rosa Luxemburg had given way to Tocqueville! *Autogestion,* as a result, became a dead letter except in one rather unexpected place—the Communist party.[41]

The story of the French left in power after 1981 dramatically underscored this evolution.[42] The first period (eighteen months or so) of the Mitterrand presidency was a time of concentrated and radical change. In particular, during this period three different sets of substantial reforms—nationalizations, government decentralization, and the industrial relations system—were enacted. The precise definitions of these reforms provided the ultimate litmus test of the fate of *autogestion* in France.

There *were,* here and there, pieces of evidence that indicated to careful observers that the French left had very recently spent much of its time debating *autogestion*. The nationalization laws included provisions for worker "administrators" (in fact, union delegates) on public-sector firm boards of directors, who received limited access to important confidential information about basic company decisions.[43] Strictly speaking, however, this particular innovation and the structures of nationalization more generally owed much more to the left's traditional practices than to *autogestion*. Moreover, given the difficult economic circumstances of the 1980s, the left in power quickly abandoned even the reduced aspirations toward broader industrial democracy in public firms that it may have had and turned toward using public ownership as a tool for restructuring and rationalizing large French industry sector-by-sector to make it more internationally competitive.[44]

Union administrators on boards of nationalized firms did play more active roles in discussions of company strategy, particularly since the economic crisis has drawn unions more and more into detailed issues of investment choice, industrial location, and employment policy. However, management still managed on the basis of criteria that would not have been be out of place at General Motors or IBM. Indeed, after much early leftist rhetoric concerning the place of newly nationalized industry in an industrial policy that would ensure employment and "reconquer the domestic market," French public-sector firms were subsequently given strict orders to make profits and to behave like their private-sector multinationalized competitors. The right-center, which returned to power in 1986, began to denationalize and remove what little industrial democracy actually had come to exist under the left, rendering moot the issues of public-sector worker participation and *autogestion*.

The left's governmental decentralization would have been considered a modest measure altogether had it occurred anywhere else but in a country like France that was plagued by hypertrophied overcentralization. Still, decentralization was an important change. By 1986 it had already begun to regenerate local political life on the new regional levels, with new party activity, new interest groups, and new local associations emerging. More of this will undoubtedly follow. Thus far, the effects of decentralization have almost all favored the political right, but in time this may change as well. Nonetheless, when the left decentralized after 1982, it retreated from any radical and *autogestionnaire* approaches. Instead, it implemented what had become consensual about decentralization across the entire French political spectrum prior to 1981, which was essentially a significant degree of administrative deconcentration plus increased policy freedom for local and regional governments. Thus, however felicitous such movement may turn out to be for France, its relative meekness will bring no new *autogestionnaire* Jerusalems.[45]

The workplace had been the privileged locus for *autogestionnaire* visions. Given the nature of social relationships at firm level in France that prevailed into the 1980s, this ought not to have been surprising. French employers, more often than not imbued with authoritarian or paternalistic values, had traditionally regarded workers as second-class citizens and objects to be manipulated. Unions, in turn, regarded employers as exploiters to be resisted at all times and to be dispensed with at the earliest possible opportunity. Partly for these reasons, France, unlike most other advanced capitalist societies, had never really built the kind of institutionalized, collectively bargained system that had established new rights and duties in industrial relations elsewhere. As a result, conflicts between capital and labor were ill-regulated. Contracts, when they were signed, were understood on all sides as momentary truces to be dispensed with when the balance of power changed. Moreover, such regulation of industrial conflicts as existed in France tended to come from the state and politics, a situation that overpoliticized the workplace.

Changing all this was one of the left's main purposes after 1981. The left's 1982 industrial relations reforms—the four Auroux Laws, so called after the minister of labor—were heavily influenced in their conception by the CFDT (if by a weakened CFDT more concerned with *resyndicalisation* than *autogestion*).[46] Law I gave increased power and resources to firm-level union sections and personnel delegates while also reinforcing the position of works committees (*comités d'entreprise*). Law II contained provisions for obligatory annual firm-level wage bargaining and a clause that allowed majority unions to veto the implementation of minority union-signed contracts.[47] Law III amalgamated formerly separate works' committees on health, safety, and working conditions and endowed this new combined committee with greater powers. Law IV discussed workers' rights in the firm, defined the legal scope of internal work rules established by employers, and established new shop-level "rights of expression" (implemented as periodic open meetings between workers and management to discuss the process and progress of the firm). The public sector, in general, benefited from even stronger versions of the same changes, plus new provisions for the election of workers' representatives to boards of directors.

Four years is much too short a time to judge the effects of this kind of large change, of course. Industrial relations systems, and changes in them, are rarely a simple function of legislation, depending more profoundly on the attitudes of capital and labor and the balance of power between them over long years. Therefore, the various qualitative and quantitative indicators thus far gathered about the effects of the French reforms only reviewed the establishment of new procedures and habits rather than the workings of finished institutions.[48]

Some things were initially clear about the new worker "rights of expression," perhaps the most *autogestionnaire* provisions of the reforms. Workers themselves, perhaps because of the economic crisis and shifts of leftist government policy toward austerity, were timid and skeptical about their rights. Significant problems arose quickly because of the lack of information available to workers, uncertainty about the role of middle management in the process, excessive formality in the "expression" proceedings themselves, and worker disbelief that "expression" would have any serious consequences for the running of the firm. There was some enthusiasm, in contrast, about the positive effects of new "expression" on intra-firm communications and the general atmosphere. The other important indicator of the workings of the reform, the firm-level "obligation to negotiate," brought equally mixed results. Of the firms legally mandated to negotiate that had actually begun to do so in the first year of operation, only a minority had actually concluded a contract (since there was nothing like the Wagner Act's injunction to "bargain in good faith" included in the law). Beyond this, works' committees were getting more economic information about their firms and using such resources to accumulate more knowledge about firm decision making and strategies.

The ironies that accumulated in the first years of the Auroux Law indicated developments at a deeper level, however. Employers and their professional associations had initially regarded the reforms as a declaration of war. It rapidly turned out that an obligation to bargain with labor when it was weak, at a moment of economic crisis when little existed in company coffers to concede, and when no obligation to conclude such bargaining successfully had been enjoined posed few problems to capital. Perhaps more important, obligations to consult with workers meshed well with new firm-based neo-Japanese managerial strategies of the "quality circle" type. The Auroux Laws thus encouraged management to deal more directly with workers at that very moment in French managerial history when, in many sectors, French capital had decided that such direct dealing might be more rewarding than older authoritarian approaches. In many cases employers quickly turned new "rights of expression" sessions into tools to cut out unions on the shop floor and gain rank-and-file support for increasing productivity. In all, the Auroux Laws "were upsetting."[49] They most clearly did not introduce *autogestion*. They did, however, begin to move French capital-labor relationships away from high-level politicized conflict and toward a decentralized focus on firm-level issues. But rather than giving workers and unions a new foothold at firm level, the new laws seemed to have been quickly assimilated into a new management armamentarium of deregulation, pressuring unions and workers to assume greater responsibility for firm success. Few would maintain that the reforms have made no difference, of course. What is clear, however, is that the differences that the reforms have made and will make have little in common with the grandiose expectations for radical change held out in the *autogestion* debate but a decade earlier.

The meager *autogestionnaire* results of leftist reformism after 1981 were clear. Indeed, what was most obvious about the left's reformism was that it was rarely even presented in *autogestionnaire* terms, a sign of the degree to which the *autogestion* debate had disappeared by 1981. Only the PCF and CGT even used the term with any regularity. The CFDT had developed new concerns with macroeconomic policy and the promotion of "new solidarities" in crisis, by which it meant work and income sharing of one kind or another, both of which fell flat as policies very early on. The first wave of leftist reforms were in fact strongly weighted toward traditional statist approaches. Where this was not the case, one found relatively timid (if usually needed) measures to redress the balance between state and civil society. Statist reforms fell on publicly deaf ears and seemed able to resolve few of the problems to which they were purportedly directed—i.e., nationalizations to economic growth. The left's later and more modest moves, however tangible they might prove in the longer run, had long start-up periods and, in any case, could only have been labeled *autogestionnaire* by someone who had missed all of the radical debate of the 1960s and 1970s. By 1983 even this reformism had run out of gas. The leftist government leaned more and more toward the types of policies in vogue in other capitalist societies—industrial restructuring, higher unemployment, deregulation, allowing the market to decide, encouraging profitability—a major shift to neoliberal centrism, in other words. In this new posture *autogestion* was eclipsed, not by statism but by faith in the effectiveness of the market. What was most surprising in all this was how many people who had earlier sought profound change in *autogestion* had come to believe firmly in an anti-statist regeneration of liberalism.

Notes

1. Annie Kriegel, "Le pain et les roses," in *Le Syndicalisme révolutionnaire et Proudhon* (Paris: PUF, 1968).

2. An excellent general review is provided in Bernard Moss, *The Origins of the French Labor Movement* (Berkeley: University of California Press, 1976). See also Peter Stearns, *Revolutionary Syndicalism and French Labor* (New Brunswick: Rutgers University Press, 1971).

3. On leftist alliances, see André Donneur, *L'Alliance fragile* (Montreal: Nouvelle Optique, 1985).

4. Stephen S. Cohen, *Modern Capitalist Planning* (Cambridge: Harvard University Press, 1969). Cohen does a particularly good job at showing how labor was effectively cut out of the planning process.

5. There is no really good study, but the closest is Maurice Monluclard, *La*

dynamique des comités d'entreprise (Paris: CNRS, 1963). General information on resistance-liberation reformism is found in Jean-Pierre Rioux, *La IVe République,* vol. 1 (Paris: Seuil, 1984).

6. There are some fantastic hidden stories to be told about this. For example, the Central Works' Committee of Electricité de France (EdF), through hard-nosed dealings in the post-liberation period by Communist Minister Marcel Paul, found itself endowed with a budget of 1% of EdF's *gross* take each year. The result, given the geometric expansion of energy use in postwar France, was a staff of 1,000 with huge resources largely put to the use of the Communists and the Confederation Générale du Travail (CGT).

7. See Hugues Portelli, *Le Socialisme français tel qu'il est* (Paris: PUF, 1980).

8. Jeanine Verdès-Leroux, *Au service du parti* (Paris: Minuit, 1983), on the PCF culture and science policies; Irwin Wall, *French Communism in the Era of Stalin* (Boulder: Westview, 1983); and Philippe Robrieux, *Histoire Intérieure du PCF,* vol. 2 (Paris: Fayard, 1981).

9. Jean-Paul Sartre, "Les Communistes et la paix," in *Situations VI* (Paris: Gallimard, 1964) and more generally Frédéric Bon and Michel Antoine Burnier, *Les Existentialistes et la politique* (Paris: Gallimard-Idées, 1971).

10. For samples, see Jacky Beilleret, *L'Idéologie du savoir* (Paris: Gallimard, 1971).

11. *Socialisme ou Barbarie* was a nursery for the intellectual mentors of later *autogestion,* such as Cornelius Castoriadis, Claude Lefort, Daniel Mothé, Pierre Naville, and others.

12. The most accessible source is Hervé Hamon and Patrick Rotman, *Les porteurs de valise* (Paris: Albin Michel, 1979).

13. See Jean Fourastié, *Les trentes glorieuses* (Paris: Pluriel, 1984), for a quick review of the extent of such change.

14. Pierre Rosanvallon, *L'Age de l'autogestion* (Paris: Seuil, 1976).

15. See Hervé Hamon and Patrick Rotman, *La deuxième gauche* (Paris: Ramsay, 1982), esp. chs. 1-5, for much of this history.

16. See George Ross, *Workers and Communists in France* (Berkeley: University of California Press, 1982), for details on the CGT.

17. Ibid., chs. 6-7.

18. For a thorough survey of the 1968 strikes, including those where *autogestion* was raised, see Pierre Dubois et al., *Grèves revendicatives ou grèves politiques?* (Paris: Anthropos, 1971).

19. The best reviews of the May events are to be found in Lucien Rioux and René Backmann, *L'explosion de mai 1968* (Paris: Laffont, 1968); Alain Schnapp and Pierre Vidal-Naquet, eds., *The French Student Uprising* (Boston: Beacon Press, 1971); Charles Posner, ed., *Reflections on the Revolution in France* (London: Penguin, 1969); and Alain Touraine, *The May Movement* (New York: Random House, 1971).

20. Pierre Grémion, *Paris-Prague* (Paris: Julliard, 1985), provides a perceptive overview of such movements among the intelligentsia.

21. See Portelli, *Le Socialisme français tel qu'il est.* A. Duroy and R. Schneider, *Le roman de la rose* (Paris: Seuil, 1982) provides a spicy, journalistic

approach to PS internal life. In English see R. W. Johnson, *The Long March of the French Left* (New York: St. Martin's Press, 1981).

22. For a review of these years in organized labor, see Peter Lange et al., *Unions, Change and Crisis* (London: George Allen and Unwin, 1982), ch. 1, parts 3 and 4.

23. For a glimpse at such strikes, see Claude Durand et al., *La grève* (Paris: Armand Colin, 1975); Jacques Capdevielle et al., *La grève au joint français* (Paris: Armand Colin, 1975); and Danielle Kergoat, *Bulledor* (Paris: Seuil, 1975).

24. See Charles Piaget, *Lip* (Paris: Stock, 1973), and *CFDT-Syndicalisme* in the summer of 1973, especially June 14, June 28, and July 5.

25. The all-important report to this Congress by André Jeanson, then president of the CFDT, is reprinted in *La CFDT* (Paris: Seuil, 1971).

26. *CFDT-Syndicalisme,* Dec. 3, 1970.

27. Henri Krasucki, *Syndicats et socialisme* (Paris: Ed. Sociales, 1972), summarizes the CGT's positions. The CGT-CFDT debate is well-reviewed in Keitha S. Fine and Stephen Bornstein, "Workers' Participation and Self-Management in France: Recent Political Developments," in G. David Garson, *Workers' Self Management in Industry: The West European Experience* (New York: Praeger, 1977).

28. Edmond Maire, *Demain l'autogestion* (Paris: Seghers, 1976), is the best review of CFDT doctrine. See also Rosanvallon, *L'Age de l'autogestion,* for a more intellectualized version.

29. Guy Nania, *Le PSU avant Rocard* (Paris: Roblot, 1973).

30. See Charles Hauss, *Radical Politics in France: The Unified Socialist Party* (Westport, Conn.: Greenwood, 1978).

31. Michel Rocard, "Le PSU et l'autogestion," in *Revue Politique et Parlementaire,* Dec. 1972.

32. Pierre Rosanvallon, "Ou est passée l'autogestion?" in *Passé-Présent* 4 (1984): 186.

33. Assises du Socialisme, *Pour le socialisme* (Paris: Stock, 1974), esp. 29-32.

34. "Quinze thèses sur l'autogestion." *Le poing et la rose,* no. 45 supplement (Nov. 15, 1975).

35. Roland Cayrol, "Le PS et l'autogestion, un beau texte ou un choix politique." *Projet* 98, Sept.-Oct. 1975.

36. Interestingly enough, it was the issue of nationalizations that was central in the split, with the PCF asking for more and the PS moving away from those it had already agreed to promote.

37. We have tried to capture the turbulence and confusion of the PCF in this period in Jane Jenson and George Ross, *The View from Inside: A French Communist Cell in Crisis* (Berkeley: University of California Press, 1984).

38. For a more detailed review, see George Ross and Jane Jenson, "Strategy and Contradiction in the Victory of French Socialism," in *The Socialist Register 1981,* ed. Ralph Miliband and John Saville (London: Merlin Press, 1981).

39. See Ross, *Workers and Communists in France,* ch. 9.

40. Ch. 10 in Hamon and Rotman, *La Deuxième gauche,* contains the best review of this process at the elite level. See also the "Moreau report" introducing

recentering in *CFDT Syndicalisme,* Jan. 12, 1978, and the CFDT Congress documents from later in 1978 published in *CFDT Syndicalisme,* Dec. 1978.

41. For a most interesting theoretical illustration of this, see Philippe Herzog, *L'Economie nouvelle à bras le corps* (Paris: Ed. Sociales, 1984).

42. For interesting beginnings see John Ambler, ed., *The French Socialist Experiment* (Philadelphia: ISHI Press, 1984); Philip Cerny and Martin Schain, eds., *French Socialism and Public Policy* (New York: St. Martin's Press, 1985); and George Ross, Stanley Hoffmann, and Sylvia Malzacher, *The Mitterrand Experiment: Continuity and Change in Socialist France* (London: Polity Press, 1986).

43. See A. G. Delion and M. Durupty, *Les nationalisations 1982* (Paris: Economica, 1982), for an exhaustive description of the legislation.

44. David Cameron has done a good general review of this in *French Politics and Society,* no. 14 (Spring 1986). See also Jean-Louis Moynot's "The Left, Industrial Policy and the *Filière Electronique,*" in Ross, Hoffmann, and Malzacher, *The Mitterrand Experiment,* ch. 12.

45. There are few sources where one can find out much about the effects of decentralization to this point. For one, see Jacques Rondin, *Le sacre des notables* (Paris: Fayard, 1985). See also Mark Kesselman's "The Quiet Revolution at Clochemerle," in Cerny and Schain, *French Socialism and Public Policy;* and Catherine Gremion's "Decentralization in France: An Historical Perspective," and Yves Meny's "The Socialist Decentralization," in Ross, Hoffmann, and Malzacher, *The Mitterrand Experiment,* chs. 8 and 9, respectively.

46. See Jean Auroux, *Les droits des travailleurs* (Paris: Documentation Française, 1981) and "Les nouveaux droits des travailleurs," *Le Monde, dossiers et documents,* June 1983, for the original report and a review of the final texts.

47. France has had a pluralistic union movement, which has usually meant more than one union competing for precedence in a specific sector. This situation, in turn, has allowed employers to divide and rule by, among other things, signing contracts with the most pliable union it can find, hence this provision of Law II.

48. See the "Rapport d'information" submitted to the French National Assembly in early 1985 by the Commission des Affaires Culturelles, Familiales et Sociales (document 2681) for an early overview. See also Anni Borzeix, Danièle Linhart, and Denis Segrestin, *Sur les traces du droit d'expression* (Paris: CNAM, 1985), for a series of case studies.

49. The expression is from Michele Millot and Jean-Pol Roulleau, "Les relations sociales depuis les loix Auroux," *Projet,* Nov.–Dec. 1985.

8

INDUSTRIAL RELATIONS AND ECONOMIC REFORM IN SOCIALISM: HUNGARY AND YUGOSLAVIA COMPARED

Ellen Comisso

Industrial relations systems both reflect and influence larger political structures and power relations within states and economies everywhere, and East Europe is no exception. It is hardly accidental, then, that since 1979 advocates of economic reform in Hungary have sought to modify the industrial relations system of the state sector of the economy. This has been done as part of a program to decentralize one of the most highly concentrated industrial structures in the world.

Two recent changes are particularly noteworthy. The first, allowing for the establishment of Enterprise Contract Work Associations (ECWAs), affects the organization of work in the firm. ECWAs are groups of workers—two to thirty people—who contract with their own firm to carry out tasks the enterprise cannot otherwise perform or that can be done at a lower cost through the new arrangements. ECWAs neither employ independent means nor bear risks; instead, they use enterprise facilities and inputs the firm provides. Nevertheless, participating in them allows workers to earn far more than they can even by working overtime; at the same time, their establishment permits management to allocate labor and rewards more efficiently and flexibly than it can during normal working hours.

The second change was initiated by the Hungarian Socialist Workers' Party (HSWP) in 1984 and enacted into law in 1985. The law will be implemented gradually over the next few years and affects enterprise governance itself. Many of the functions of ownership in all but the largest firms are being transferred from the supervisory ministry to enterprise councils elected at least in part by employees. Such boards will have the right to select and evaluate enterprise directors (subject to ministry veto) as well as define enterprise plans, approve annual financial statements, determine the allocation of profits between investment and personal incomes, set up subsidiaries, and decide on mergers.

Such reform innovations accompany other measures affecting prices, investments, taxes, wages and the like.[1] These broader, macroeconomic changes are direct descendants of the New Economic Mechanism (NEM), Hungary's "original" economic reform enacted in 1968, many principles of which were ignored after 1972. In fact, many of the 1979 reforms were simply changes that had been scheduled in 1968 and were never made, or measures that were introduced a decade ago and subsequently reversed. Taken as a whole, then, the "new" NEM represents as much a return to a set of policies that had been abandoned as a completely new departure in economic policy. Hence, in order to assess the significance of the current reform wave, it is worth analyzing why so many of the original provisions and expectations surrounding NEM were put aside in the 1970s, and what were the causes for the ensuing recentralization of the economy.[2] Moreover, since the NEM of 1968 did not include any of the changes in the industrial relations system the measures of the 1980s initiated, it is important to assess the degree to which the industrial relations system in effect at the time contributed to the "rearrangement backward" that took place in the 1970s.

One way of gauging the impact of the industrial relations system on the ability of central governments to introduce economic decentralization and structural reform in socialist economies is by comparing Hungary's experience under NEM with developments in Yugoslavia in the 1950s. The planning model, whereby central development preferences were to be communicated to firms via market manipulation rather than direct instructions, was fundamentally similar.[3] In both cases, enterprise autonomy was restricted by high taxes on profits (in fact, Yugoslav firms in those years paid an even higher portion of their profits to government bodies than their Hungarian counterparts in the 1970s did), accounting rules limiting firms' discretion over the funds left at their disposal, supervision of enterprise financial arrangements by the national banks, and politically determined wage and bonus regulations. Price controls, differentiated turnover taxes, and multiple exchange rates were also among the armory of instruments both governments deployed to actively shape the economic environment; in both cases foreign trade was conducted largely through licensed trading companies, and arrangements were punctuated by quantitative controls as well. Finally, the linchpin of both the Yugoslav and Hungarian systems of "visible hand" planning was centralized investment allocation. In both countries, the rate of investment was set centrally; part of investment funds came directly from budgetary sources and went to specific projects earmarked by the national government, while the remainder was allocated through central banks according to criteria set by national planning authorities. Moreover, investment funds in Hungary and Yugoslavia alike were loaned at quite varied but normally subsidized rates.

Similar patterns of economic behavior matched the similarities in the overall economic framework. Investment cycles were the name of the game in both Hungary and Yugoslavia; bankruptcy was unheard of in either. On domestic markets, firms were typically price makers rather than takers; in both cases, manufacturing activities tended to expand quite independently of the raw material base or import capacities of the economy to support them. Meanwhile, firms faced greater uncertainty trying to predict the next round of government regulations than in assessing market conditions. Production and investment programs were designed around the expectations of the political and bureaucratic figures whose approval was required for their adoption. As much energy was devoted to haggling with officials for access to foreign currency for imports, special tax exemptions, favorable price rulings, and hidden subsidies as was given to addressing questions of productivity, costs, and efficiency.

Nevertheless, the outcome of the tensions between center and periphery in Yugoslavia was a major economic reform in 1965, radically curtailing the regulatory and redistributive role of the central government and marking the abandonment of effective planning altogether. In Hungary, in contrast, similar pressures led to the extension of central controls, a decline in the orienting function of prices, and a gradual erosion of enterprise autonomy. Indeed, despite the attempt of NEM to decentralize and deconcentrate the economy, the number of independent enterprises and cooperatives in 1978 was actually a good deal lower than in 1967, while their average size had increased.[4]

Certainly, there are great differences in both the international environments of the 1950s and the 1970s as well as in the two countries themselves (from their levels of development to the degree of ethnic homogeneity) that help to explain such contrasting outcomes. Not the least of these are differences in the international alignments and domestic political structures of the two states, contrasts which, at the microeconomic level, materialized as two very different industrial relations systems.

In Yugoslavia, the introduction of socialism was an integral part of a strategy for creating an autonomous nation-state.[5] For one, a socialized economy could supply state-building political elites with resources to build state structures able to withstand the pressures of rival states in the international system. For another, the institutional network thereby established could serve to incorporate a heterogeneous, conflict-prone, and highly parochial population into a setting that would bind its loyalties to a larger (multi) national community.

Hence, popular allegiance was to be to the new Yugoslav state, not to the class mission of a universalistic party. The effective political community thus consisted of all Yugoslav citizens, whose loyalties were to be formed through their involvement in new state institutions: the more people worked in socially owned firms, sent their children to public schools, or received medical care from socialized hospitals, the more the nation-state in which these institutions were embedded would become a part of their daily life. And their commitment to defending them would be greater.

Claims on the larger national community—whether for higher wages, instruction in the native tongue, or vaccination against smallpox—were thus made through participation in state organizations,[6] whose activities, in theory, would reflect the preferences of the specific constituencies they incorporated. The task of the League of Communists (LCY), in turn, was to selectively articulate and mobilize those preferences in ways that contributed to the state-building enterprise itself. The party thus played a critical role in defining, filtering, and delimiting the use of political power and the claims state institutions could make. Nevertheless, insofar as the nation-state defined the Yugoslav political community, the party's own ability to mobilize resources to achieve its objectives depended heavily on the cooperation it could exact from state bodies with a far more inclusive and much less disciplined membership.

In contrast, the initial establishment of socialism in Hungary was primarily for the purpose of restructuring class relations. Moreover, it was the platform of a political party whose power base was not, for the most part, national or domestic at all. Rather, the Hungarian communist party's ability to achieve its objectives depended on the political and military backing it had from a foreign power—namely, the Soviet Union. With such support, power was taken away from society, and social groups formed on the basis of the traditional social order and then concentrated in the hands of political elites committed to wholesale social transformation. Introducing centralized economic planning was a critical tool in this effort. Placing an enormous quantity of resources in the hands of political leaders, it allowed them to subordinate state, society, and economy alike to the goals of rapid and extensive industrialization, rural transformation, class mobilization, and maintaining the international strength of the Soviet Union, whose support and protection was vital for defending the socialist project in Hungary itself. Thus, state structures in Hungary were never designed to compete with other states in the international arena; moreover, consciously creating a standardized socialist state that could not reflect national specificities or particularities made it incapable of commanding much popular allegiance.

In effect, the Hungarian transition to socialism narrowed the effective political community from the citizens of the nation-state to the members of a highly centralized Leninist party, a party whose priorities were ordered as much by the international exigencies of the Soviet alliance as by the national goals of its domestic population. The state and the mass organizations consequently became vehicles for implementing party preferences rather than mechanisms for articulating society's wishes.

Unlike Yugoslavia, then, claims on collective choices in Hungary were not made through participation in state bodies, whether they were the national Parliament or the industrial firms. Rather, they could be advanced through involvement in and appointment to party committees whose decisions state institutions carried out. Moreover, within the party itself, power flowed from top to bottom. As a result, access to genuine political influence depended on the support leaders enjoyed in higher party bodies, and not on their ability to mobilize a constituency below, whether among grassroots party members, employees of (nonparty) state organizations, or residents of local communities.

In Hungary, political power remained the monopoly of a hegemonic party able to command obedience from a state administration without power of its own. Accordingly, even when NEM was adopted in 1968, it was not because social groups or state organizations pushed for it, but because the party itself—after several years of low growth rates, stagnating living standards, and balance-of-payments difficulties—felt its ability to steer the economy would be enhanced if its preferences were communicated to microlevel state or economic actors via economic parameters rather than through detailed instructions.

The Hungarian industrial relations system reflected this power structure as much as its Yugoslav counterpart mirrored very different political exigencies. In Yugoslavia, the LCY's need to rely on domestic support following its expulsion from the Cominform led to the adoption of "visible-hand" planning in the economy and self-management in the firms. Moreover, branch ministries were eliminated and plans were formulated and implemented on a geographic basis, with local and national governments playing the major roles.

In Hungary the initial transition to central planning was accomplished only when the party emancipated itself from the need for domestic support. It was accompanied by adherence to the Soviet model of "one-man" management in the firms. Accordingly, a director's authority did not depend on an ability to forward the interests of the firm or its employees, but on carrying out the instructions of superiors; elaborated within the state bureaucracy, such instructions ultimately reflected the priorities of top party leaders. NEM saw an important change in these priorities and instructions, but not in the political status of the enterprises themselves. Consequently, "one-man" management remained intact. Moreover, if plans were less detailed and no longer binding, local governments did not play a role in them; rather, plans continued to be made and coordinated through vertical and horizontal ministries that, after 1968, were legally responsible for implementing NEM within their respective spheres of jurisdiction.

At the enterprise level, directors and high-level executives in Hungary continued to be appointed by a branch ministry with the approval of the party committee within whose *nomenklatura* the position fell.[7] In contrast, after 1950, managerial personnel in Yugoslavia were selected by a workers' council representing the labor force of the enterprise and a committee of the local (commune) government, together with the endorsement of local party officials. Equally important, formal authority for enterprise decisions in Yugoslavia was shared with the workers' council, which had to approve all production, financial, and investment plans as well as enterprise statutes regulating salaries, work relations, and similar matters. In Hungary, however, despite the existence of committees for consultation with the labor force and even a campaign for "workshop democracy" in 1975–76, decision making remained a managerial prerogative.

Not the least of the decisions Yugoslav workers' councils were authorized to make concerned the allocation of yearly net profits between investment and consumption and the distribution of the share marked for consumption among members of the firm's labor force. In Hungary, however, wage determination and profit distribution were products of agreements concluded between management and enterprise-level trade union branches.[8] Executive bonuses were awarded by a workers' council in Yugoslavia; in Hungary they came from the ministry with jurisdiction over the firm.

Last but hardly least, self-management in Yugoslavia signified not only a set of decision-making arrangements within the firm but also a basic ideological tenet of the politico-economic system. Consequently, enterprise sociopolitical organizations (particularly the LCY and the trade unions) had the task of making it function: namely, making sure meetings were called, that quorums were present, that proposals were approved by the appropriate bodies, and that neither they themselves nor the management usurped the decision-making rights of the workers' councils. In Hungary, in contrast, the task of the party and trade union branches in the firm was to control management and protect workers by ensuring that general political priorities were respected and centrally determined statutes were enforced in the firm.

The consequences of these arrangements were twofold. First of all, Yugoslav firms—and especially the managerial and "self-managerial elites" within them—developed a much stronger interest in enlarging their sphere of autonomy than Hungarian enterprises ever did. Second, labor-management relations in Yugoslav firms allowed enterprise elites to mobilize the labor force itself in support of this goal; in Hungary, however, management had neither a constituency nor allies within the firm to organize on behalf of expanded enterprise independence, and indeed, labor-management relations militated in precisely the opposite direction. In short, the operation of the two industrial relations systems not only made the objectives of enterprise elites very different, but it also provided them with very different sets of political resources with which to realize those goals.

Self-management in Yugoslavia, 1950–65

Factors Shaping Enterprise Objectives

An insight into the dynamics behind these outcomes requires a preliminary understanding of the background and role of Yugoslav management in the 1950s. Certainly, Yugoslav executives in these years were a far cry from the sophisticated business people they evolved into by the 1980s. For the most part they lacked as much in qualifications as in managerial experience, knew little of entrepreneurship, and were distinguished mainly by their political reliability and commitment to building a uniquely Yugoslav model of socialism.[9] They enjoyed close and cordial relationships with local political leaders,often having fought together with them in the war and typically having come to the enterprise in the first place via the local government or party organization rather than through an independent search by the workers' council that became characteristic in later years.

Yet once installed as enterprise director, an executive's power base—that is, the ability to mobilize resources inside and outside the firm on behalf of his own goals—was very much his firm, its labor force, and its economic contribution to the surrounding area. And although offering employment, supplying free labor for community projects, and lending enterprise facilities for social purposes all won the director recognition for good citizenship, the bottom line of good performance was the revenue the enterprise could generate for Yugoslavia's fiscally hungry communes[10] and the earnings it could pay its employees.

The problem, of course, was that enterprises frequently could neither produce the income local governments wanted and needed nor the wages workers desired while simultaneously performing all the civic obligations local governments expected from them. If firms were to employ as many workers as political leaders thought desirable and charge prices political leaders thought fair, profitability and local taxes on profits were likely to be the victims. If firms produced the wide variety of products local elites wanted to make available to residents and enterprises in the area, production runs were bound to be short, specialization minimal, and competitiveness outside the local market weak. Despite the political commitment of the native son, the close friendship, and the constant collaboration with regional political figures, then, enterprise directors increasingly found themselves forced to choose between good citizenship and good management as the 1950s progressed.[11]

Critical to the choice many managerial elites made was the presence and role of the enterprise self-management bodies. Here, as already noted, the first generation of Yugoslav executives had but minimal qualification. Even in traditionally urban areas, a large number of small shops were suddenly transformed into factories gearing up for mass production with only former skilled workers trained in artisan methods and work rhythms at their helms. Needless to say, in less industrialized areas the shortage of trained cadres was even more severe.

Nevertheless, precisely because managers did not know how to manage, they turned elsewhere for help. One gets the sense of the early workers' council as a body composed of the more ambitious and educated members of the workforce that functioned as a kind of managerial committee forced to collectively resolve the issues no one was individually qualified to decide.[12] Managers also came to rely on the workers' councils insofar as their members were also informal leaders of the work collective. On the one hand, their approval of a managerial recommendation would facilitate its acceptance by the labor force as a whole, and on the other, they served to communicate demands from the labor force to the management.

Significantly, as workers' councils were elected by and accountable to the enterprise labor force, they had none of the divided loyalties between firm and locality that often characterized the management. Their perspective was uniquely that of the firm, and their very raison d'etre was to mobilize solidarity around the plant.[13] Moreover, though an enterprise director typically had standing in the region or the local community even prior to assuming leadership in the firm, this was much less likely to be the case of an individual member of a workers' council. The latter, more often than not, was an individual rising from the ranks of the labor force, whose chances for advancement depended heavily on the opportunities—in salaries, bonuses, and promotions or in housing and training—the enterprise could provide.[14]

But it was not only the individual motives of council members that made enterprise self-management bodies jealous of their authority. Institutionally, the power of the workers' council itself depended on its ability to make decisions for the firm and see them carried out, and when its already enterprise-oriented membership convened as a group, the whole was typically greater than its parts.

The suspicions of the self-management bodies were not, for the most part, directed at enterprise executives. As many have pointed out, power in the self-managed firm is not played out as a zero-sum game between management and labor. Rather, it is a positive-sum game, in which the ability of a workers' council to make effective decisions depends on having a strong management and vice versa.[15] Furthermore, barring occasional cases of corruption and nepotism, management's interest in enterprise welfare did not diverge from that of the enterprise labor force; executives typically wanted higher wage scales as much as workers did, and everyone was in favor of more and better equipment and work organization.[16]

Rather, the suspicions of enterprise activists turned toward outside agents—political or economic—that constituted barriers to making decisions they (rightly or wrongly) judged best for the firm. In this regard, simply because workers' councils had decision-making rights on a wide range of issues did not necessarily mean they could do what they wanted. A host of regulations restricted their discretion on everything from management selection to wage regulation, and it was the local government's responsibility to enforce them. Equally important were the financial constraints imposed on the firm by heavy taxes on profits and the need to finance investment and imports with funds from outside sources. In this, not only commune approval but the personal and political clout local officials could bring to bear on central authorities often proved critical to the success of enterprise plans. These powers formed the material base for much of the "meddling" in enterprise affairs so common among local governments in the 1950s. Moreover, even the most stridently independent work collectives could hardly put up much resistance when they depended on such meddlers for the funds and flexibility vital for enterprise development.[17]

Hence, the key issue the establishment of self-management posed in Yugoslavia in the 1950s was not whether workers and workers' councils could control enterprise management, but whether workers' councils and management together could control enterprise operations, as opposed to sharing that control with various external political bodies charged with regulatory tasks. In this context, workers' councils constituted a steady source of enterprise-centered pressures on a management that otherwise might have been tempted to look for its cues outside the firm entirely.

Management thus came to play a critical intermediary role between the enterprise and political authorities, and a variety of strategies emerged.[18] Ideally, a clever director could have cake and eat it too: make external authorities and ambiguous regulations the eminence grise for plans the director wished the firm to pursue, and at the same time utilize the "demands and needs of the working class" in the firm to get what he wanted out of political bodies—who, especially in the case of the communes, were far from adverse to aiding local firms in any case. A second strategy was to fashion enterprise plans in collaboration with political elites outside the firm and present them to the self-management bodies—who had no alternative plans to use as a standard for judgment—as being in the enterprise's own interest as well. Both strategies depended on the support and confidence management enjoyed from the workers' council, but in the expansionary climate of the 1950s, these were normally forthcoming.

More importantly, however, such strategies depended on both the willingness and ability of local political elites to cooperate. If local leaders were unsympathetic to the firm for whatever reason (for example, it might be a small enterprise surrounded by large ones, or the director may have sided with the losers in a local power struggle), if they looked askance on the ambitions a director entertained for the enterprise (as when firms tried to expand to other regions, and communes feared a loss of tax revenues), if they lacked strong ties to central allocation networks (and so could not lobby effectively for investment funds), or if local political elites themselves disagreed over what they wanted from local firms (such that no predictable or consistent reaction to enterprise requests was possible), the feasibility and desirability of either strategy were greatly reduced.

But enterprise self-management created a possibility for managerial elites to pursue a third strategy. Here, management identified its own fate with that of the enterprise, based itself politically on the support of the workers' council and the work collective, and used its position in the locality to advance its own definition of enterprise interests and resist the incursions of local political leaders in enterprise affairs. For several reasons, such a strategy was particularly appealing to larger firms located in the more developed and urbanized areas.[19]

First of all, the local economy itself was less dependent on the employment and free services of any single firm. At the same time, the local political leadership was far more interested in the revenues the enterprises could generate to cover the infrastructure needs rapid urbanization created than in their fulfillment of particular community tasks. Thus, the political outlook of local authorities itself reinforced the "enterprise first" propensities of the self-management bodies.

Second, not only were directors more likely to be better qualified for their managerial roles in these areas, but even if they weren't, it was far easier to recruit a qualified staff and middle management to compensate for the lack of expertise at the top. Thus, directors could utilize enterprise resources to fashion business policies and, as a result, such policies tended to reflect enterprise rather than regional priorities.

Third, even with—and in large part, because of—the workers' councils, directors had much greater control over the use of enterprise resources than over the actions of political authorities. In the firm they stood at the top of the organizational hierarchy and easily constituted the natural leadership of the work collective.[20] In the local political community even a politically prominent director was only one among equals in a context where government and party bodies alike were beset with a multitude of problems and conflicting claims, all demanding urgent attention.

Finally, pursuing an enterprise-based strategy that management itself could have a heavy hand in shaping meant that rather than finding himself on the defensive vis-à-vis the autonomist sentiments of the self-management bodies, a director could mobilize and exploit them to channel enterprise solidarity to his own and the firm's advantage. And indeed, strengthening a firm economically was often the best route to political clout as well: if a director became a success to be emulated by others and could point to the contribution his firm made to the economy, he was also likely to be a man heeded in wider political bodies as well.[21]

For such reasons, a strategy that called for differentiating enterprise interests from local and regional ones and giving the former priority became increasingly popular among enterprise elites outside the developed regions as well.[22] In some cases, managerial elites who had initially expanded their firms through political cooperation began to find the major barriers to further growth were precisely the taxes, regulations, and officials that had once been so helpful. In other cases, centrally initiated campaigns against excessive localism drove a wedge into local political elites, creating conflicts within them over how much independence local firms should have. There was a material basis for political conflicts among local elites as well that was exacerbated with economic development. That is, it became increasingly difficult to tailor enterprise operations to local community needs while expanding enterprise income to use as a tax base. Likewise, it became increasingly difficult to reconcile the desire to maintain local markets as a monopolistic outlet for local firms with the goal of providing the wide assortment of goods that higher living standards demanded.

With divided authorities on the one hand and the solidaristic pressures of the self-management bodies on the other, directors quite understandably began to turn to their own work collectives as a more reliable and predictable—not to mention controllable—ally and source of support. And by mobilizing their own distinct constituency, they could exert independent influence on the local balance of political forces as the debate over development strategies heated up at the start of a new decade.

Thus, expanding the sphere of enterprise autonomy was very much in the political interest of both managerial and self-managerial elites in many areas, as it seemed to simultaneously promise greater power over enterprise operations and increased influence within the region. Moreover, increasing enterprise control over the resources it produced was in the economic interest of many firms as well. This was particularly the case with larger, more prosperous, and dynamic firms producing commodities in high demand. Such firms understandably resented seeing 70 percent of their profits drained off each year in taxes. Equally understandable, they disliked the barriers to their expansion caused by the lack of uniform market conditions widely varying local regulations gave rise to, by the attempts of local elites to close off markets to outside firms altogether, and by the price controls, wage regulations, import quotas, and other administrative measures erratically applied to them. In addition, insofar as expanded use of the market for allocative purposes presaged a price reform as well, even firms who were not doing so well in the hothouse development conditions of the 1950s began to feel that they would fare better if they were free to charge prices that reflected their real costs of production.[23]

Political Resources for Realizing Enterprise Goals

Enterprise elites in Yugoslavia, then, had real incentives to expand the firm's sphere of autonomy. In addition, the labor-management relations that self-management brought into being meant they could do something about it as well: the work collective itself could be mobilized by management and its support used as a political resource with which to pursue enterprise goals.[24]

Self-management enshrined the workers' council as *the* representative of workers in the enterprise, thereby creating a direct link between management and the labor force, in which both shared an interest in the successful operation of the firm.[25] It was this institutionally created community of interest, reinforced after 1957 by legislation that tied workers' incomes more closely to enterprise performance, that encouraged workers' councils to take their cues from management as to what business policies were in the interest of the work collective. And it was this same institutionally created community of interest that made them all too willing to rally their constituency around demands for greater autonomy once managerial preferences shifted in that direction and provided them with a source of leadership.

As for the enterprise LCY and trade union branches, they were not organizations based in the firms. Rather, the LCY and other sociopolitical organizations were merely units of larger, national associations, and the directives they conformed with politically were formulated at national levels. Hence, they had no particular stake in enterprise autonomy per se. But to take the case of the League, although its individual members who were elected to the self-management bodies might argue for its positions at workers' council meetings, the LCY branch itself had strict directives not to replace the council as the representative of the labor force. Consequently, unless League members could convince others to follow their lead, it could not maintain its influence within the firm. Not surprisingly the easiest way to do this in many cases was by tailoring its own preferences to those of the self-management bodies.

Moreover, the task of the party and trade unions to strengthen the self-management bodies typically meant articulating their demands in wider party and trade union forums. Significantly, the LCY organizations most able to convince enterprises to follow their lead were precisely those most adept at satisfying the demands the latter would make in their own interest. Consequently, once a coalition between management and the workers' council emerged, it was not only able to mobilize the work collective on behalf of "augmenting the material base of self-management," but could also find allies in the enterprise sociopolitical organizations as well.

Pressures from enterprises for greater control over their earnings took their clearest form in the debate over incentives, a discussion that became increasingly heated at the start of the 1960s. For the firms, diminishing the scope of political decision making and administrative intervention seemed to promise a more rational allocation of capital, a real incentive to cut costs and increase productivity, and an opportunity to expand in ways of their own choosing. In particular, greater control over profits meant lower taxes (and hence, a greater incentive to make profits in the first place), a more predictable source of funding (their own reserves), and prices more reflective of supply and demand than of the prejudices of government officials. For workers, if their enterprises were no longer subjected to a politically determined high rate of forced savings, a greater share of earnings could be devoted to wages, putting teeth into income-sharing plans and stimulating productivity.

But if widening the scope of the market promised benefits for the enterprises, elites based in the state administration and party apparatus took a less sanguine view of increasing enterprise autonomy. For the latter, there were serious doubts of the actual ability of the market to produce results consistent with the development goals they were committed to achieving. Higher wages could lead to inflation as much as increased productivity; cutbacks in bureaucracy might in practice lead to lowering the social standard of living and widening still pronounced regional inequalities.

Equally important, the end of command planning and the inauguration of self-managed socialism had made discretion in disposing of economic resources a vital determinant of political power. With resources, one could reward one's followers, punish one's detractors, redeem promises to one's constituency, bargain with others on an equal footing, and see one's own vision of a better life materialize. Hence, the same factors that made enterprise elites anxious to enlarge their access to resources and their ability to dispose of them independently made central authorities and political elites in national government and party bodies reluctant to cooperate. For national political elites, the loss of discretionary funds and regulatory authority meant losing a key set of rewards and penalties at their disposal for disciplining the political behavior of enterprise and political elites in the provinces. Thus, the debate over the relative economic merits of "plan" and "market" was as much over who would control resources as over how they would be allocated and what would be done with them. Not surprisingly, elites based in central organs not only resisted local incursions on national power, but as long as they were united in that resistance, the control over resources they exerted made them a force to contend with.

In fact, if the conflict between enterprises and political authorities had been the only conflict over economic policy in Yugoslavia in the 1950s and 1960s, it is doubtful that the 1965 economic reform would ever have taken place. Given the center's actual control over resources, enterprises simply lacked the political clout to push through a reform of that magnitude. Moreover, they were far from united on what autonomy should mean and the degree to which it was desirable. Many enterprise elites—managerial and self-managerial—were well aware that they might have less control over resources and fewer resources to dispose of once their ties to political authorities allocating capital and favors lost their importance. Indeed, it was only a split in the national political elite itself over what was the most effective way to control both the provinces and the enterprises within them that finally produced the 1965 reform. If that split did not occur independently of self-management in enterprises and local governments, it was hardly determined by it either.[26]

Yet what the autonomistic aspirations of enterprise elites did mean was that once the economic reforms did go into effect there was a real constituency to support them that was strategically placed to exploit the new economic and political opportunities they offered. This was not to be the case in Hungary.

"One-man" Management and Economic Reforms in Hungary, 1968–78

Factors Shaping Enterprise Objectives

In Hungary, the industrial relations system of the firm led to a set of outcomes quite different from those in Yugoslavia.[27] Not only did Hungarian management derive few political or economic advantages from enlarging the sphere of enterprise autonomy to start with, but it had no constituency or allies inside or outside the firm to mobilize on behalf of such a goal.

For one, none of the tensions caused by Yugoslavia's "social ownership" formula appeared in Hungary, even after 1968. In Yugoslavia ownership rights were shared by local governments and self-managing work collectives, each with its own set of priorities, interests, constituencies, and political resources. Predictably, conflicts arose without any clear authority to settle them. Disputes could then be resolved by a variety of means, including direct bargaining among the actors involved, negotiations mediated by local party leaders, and tests of strength among disputants in which the victor dictated the terms of the settlement. In all cases, however, conflicts created political opportunities for those involved in them to forward their own goals for their own institution and even for the wider community. As a result, exercising the legal rights of ownership in Yugoslavia was itself a political action, entailing building alliances, accumulating political resources, and making strategic calculations.

In Hungary, however, no such ambiguity surrounded ownership rights.[28] They were clearly lodged in the state, and formal ownership functions were exercised exclusively by a supervisory ministry. If such ministries were legally accountable to the government, they were politically accountable to the HSWP, which in practice appointed the government, prescribed its program, and exercised checks (*"kontrol"*) on the state bureaucracy to ensure proper implementation.

The situation was thus quite different from that of Yugoslavia. There, state organizations were genuine political actors, able to formulate their own objectives and mobilize political and economic resources to achieve them. In Hungary state bodies were essentially bureaucratic agencies, whose competences were defined juridically and whose tasks and goals were prescribed politically by the highest echelons of the HSWP itself. Unlike Yugoslavia, therefore, the tasks and priorities that state and economic organizations carried out were determined *outside* the state bureaucratic and industrial structure itself. Within it, a legal and bureaucratic chain of command was established, such that the interests of its hierarchically ordered components (e.g., ministries and enterprises) basically consisted of satisfying the expectations of the next highest level of authority—ultimately, the top political leadership of the HSWP.[29]

As the lowest link in a bureaucratic chain of command, enterprises could certainly bargain with their administrative superiors, but only within arenas and over issues defined outside the state itself. Such bargaining could not reflect any interests enterprises or ministries had that were independent of the HSWP. It typically took the form of lobbying for exceptions should a strict application of the rules jeopardize an organization's ability to satisfy its superiors. Moreover, since exceptions were granted on an individual, case-by-case basis, their logic militated against forming organizational coalitions—a genuinely collective and political action—to alter the rules themselves, as could occur in Yugoslavia.[30]

Although state officials do not have access to political power in the course of exercising legal authority during their full-time jobs, they can achieve political influence by participating in the hierarchically arranged party committees that approve their appointments. But in that context, the political resources they can deploy to forward their policy preferences are not the demands of subordinates within their organization but the support they can rally from higher echelons in the HSWP. The availability of such support, in turn, depends on factors such as the substance of the proposals officials advocate (i.e., whether they accord with generally accepted party priorities), their standing within the HSWP itself, their personal connections, and the degree to which the organizations they legally manage perform to the administrative standards of the day— regardless of whether or not the officials personally agree with them. Such support, then, may well be *inversely* related to the attempts to pursue organizational objectives different from those superior authorities select for them. Moreover, support from above is quite independent of officials' popularity within their own organizations. In short, where Yugoslav directors located a constituency in the firm itself and sought to articulate (their vision of) its interests in wider political forums, the constituency of their Hungarian counterparts was the HSWP, and its was the party's (version of its own) interests they represented in the firm.

Hence, after 1968 Hungarian enterprises did not seek to realize profits because they themselves had any intrinsic advantage or independent interest in doing so. Rather, they did so in conformity with new political priorities and changed expectations of administrative superiors; in effect, profits merely replaced high outputs or lower costs as a basis for managerial bonuses.

The situation was thus quite different from Yugoslavia. There, profits were the means through which enterprises and the elites within them could achieve goals the firm itself defined. Consequently, realizing and controlling profits were frequent causes of conflicts between enterprises and political bodies. In Hungary, however, profits were merely an indicator of the degree to which an enterprise achieved the objectives its administrative superiors determined. If those objectives were such that profitability suffered, it was the objectives, not profitability criteria, to which the firm conformed.

With the adoption of NEM, then, Hungarian managers initially concentrated their efforts on creating the conditions in which their enterprises could now show an annual profit, just as they had previously concentrated their efforts on creating capacities to satisfy quantitative targets. In many cases this entailed making exactly the kind of changes NEM envisioned: altering production programs to meet buyers' needs, making better use of plant capacities, modernizing production processes, and expanding exports. In other cases it simply involved lobbying for investment funds at subsidized rates, expanding output at favorable prices, or getting special subsidies and premia. But in either case, an enterprise's major ally in its pursuit of profits was its supervisory ministry.[31]

Thus the cost-benefit tradeoff associated with enterprise autonomy was quite different in Hungary and Yugoslavia. In the former, management and enterprises had little to gain from acquiring greater independence from central control, if only because it was the center itself that defined what a "gain" was in the first place. At the same time, given what enterprises required in the way of resources to show a profit (or perform whatever other tasks they were assigned), they stood to lose a great deal by cutting their ties to the only agencies who could procure these resources for them.

The procedures for handling the shortages that continued to plague the Hungarian economy after 1968 graphically illustrate the contradictory relationships that developed between enterprises. Frequently, enterprises had to continue unprofitable lines of production simply because they were the only domestic supplier of the commodity in question. If many enterprise directors did not appreciate the burden their monopoly position placed on them, they nevertheless depended on ministry intervention to guarantee inputs (from investment to raw materials) for their more lucrative lines of production. Therefore, the benefits that would be derived from leaving the ministry's fold were slight. Likewise, ministry support before the Price Commission could be crucial, and it also could provide special subsidies to firms whose profit pictures were negatively affected by their performance of social obligations.

To take an empirical case, the steel boom of 1974 encouraged Hungarian steel companies to increase the quantity of output available for export. Exporting steel was particularly appealing since world market prices were at an all-time high while domestic prices were under strict control. For the same reasons Hungarian steel consumers sought to avoid purchasing imports and proceeded to hoard in the grand style: while steel consumption in 1974–75 increased by 9 percent, steel orders shot up by 20 percent. The industry, under an injunction to satisfy domestic requirements prior to exporting, ran to its ministry in protest. Its efforts on behalf of its clients proved successful when the Finance Ministry imposed a special inventory tax on steel to discourage hoarding.[32]

In such a case all parties might well have been better off had steel companies been able to choose their markets and had prices been decontrolled and imports liberalized. Nevertheless, unless such conditions applied to *all* enterprises, it was not in the interest of any one of them to create such conditions for itself. In Yugoslavia, enterprises competed for markets, and greater freedom from supervision, taxes, and regulations carried individual benefits for firms. Hungarian firms, in contrast, competed for supplies and inputs on a sellers' market; in such a context independence on the part of an individual firm literally placed it at a disadvantage vis-a-vis its competitors with strong ministerial allies.

Moreover, if the vertical industrial ministry had legal responsibility for enterprises in its jurisdiction, it was far from the only central agency regulating them, as the intervention of the Finance Ministry in the steel case indicates. But because of its special position vis-a-vis the firms, the branch ministry was a critical mediator and partner when it came to persuading other central regulators to adapt their own rules to a particular case. Such support was particularly vital for enterprises who struck out in new directions, where existing rules did not cover the new circumstances. Not surprisingly, then, directors who sought to introduce innovations in their firms drew closer to their ministry in Hungary, whereas the more dynamic and innovative Yugoslav enterprises sought independence from regulatory authorities.[33]

For example, in 1976 the Hungarian shoe industry found itself facing the evaporation of its export markets along with widespread complaints from foreign and domestic consumers alike over the quality and assortment of its output. One firm began to consider the possibility of altering its production assortment to produce more stylish shoes of a higher quality in smaller lots. It found that diverting capacities for these purposes would have entailed reducing the quantity of cheap, mass-produced shoes it normally manufactured for the domestic market, requiring a special dispensation from the Ministry of Internal Trade. At the same time, wage norms would have to be modified to give additional premia to workers engaged in producing the new shoes, since existing piece rates were geared to shoes requiring less workmanship and labor time. Accordingly, the special assent of the party branch, the trade union, and the Ministry of Labor would have to be obtained. Next, since labor and raw material costs would be higher per unit produced, existing price regulations would have to be altered, an exception only the Materials and Price Commission could grant. Nor was this the end of the story: special import arrangements would have to be made, retail outlets modified from a self-service to a salon format, and penalties for a profit above what was considered an honest level rescinded. The Quality Shoe Factory finally did succeed in producing 200,000 pairs of specialty shoes for export in 1977, but even then, the Price Commission balked and none of the new production could be marketed domestically at a profit.[34]

It is hardly surprising, then, that even enterprises seeking to increase their competitiveness on the market cooperated closely with tutelary authorities. Indeed, the cases in which Hungarian enterprises did establish some distance from supervisory ministries were exceptions that proved the rule. One set of cases was the occasional firm singled out by the government for a special, high-priority central program where the director was an important political figure in his own right. The RÁBA Motor Works, commissioned to participate in a special CMEA (Council for Mutual Economic Assistance) vehicle program, is such an example. Here, the necessary capital and inputs were assured from the start, and between the importance of the program and the prominence of the director, the enterprise literally overshadowed the ministry.

Another area in which enterprises were left more to their own devices was among smaller firms in light industry. The cause was not the strong position of the firms or the directors, but their marginal importance in the economy as a whole and the weak position of the ministry. The firms were thus forced to finance their development out of their own resources, borrow from the bank at (for Hungary) competitive rates, and search out their own markets since the ministry lacked the clout to garner special privileges for them. Yet far from making the enterprises jealous of their autonomy, it simply made them envious of industries enjoying a position closer to central authorities. Significantly, when the textile industry had its chance to corner investment capital for modernization in the early 1970s, it opted for the most centralized form of capital allocation available—the central development program—despite the fact that the large number of firms in the industry and the great diversities among them made such a format least appropriate from an economic point of view.[35]

The fate of small-scale local plants and cooperatives also illustrates the perils of standing on one's own. After the adoption of NEM local governments were encouraged to set up small industrial workshops out of their own revenues, utilizing local facilities and supplementary funds supplied by the National Bank. Since taxation was a prerogative of the national government, local governments did not enjoy increased tax revenues from these economic activities, as in Yugoslavia. Nevertheless, small workshops helped employ local residents and stem migration to urban agglomerations. For the economy at large, they provided flexibility and products that were unprofitable to be manufactured in large quantities. As such, along with small workshops in the cooperative sector, they complemented and competed with larger enterprises in the socialist sector proper. Moreover, precisely because they were small, they were not supervised by an industrial ministry. So they did not face the strict regulations that covered pricing, production assortment, labor practices, and other operations that characterized the large firms in the socialist sector.

The very success of the small firms under NEM was the main cause of their downfall. If they regularly supplied large firms with inputs or services, the enterprises eventually sought to absorb them. Or, when they competed successfully with large enterprises on either labor or product markets, the socialist firms would try to take them over.

On the one hand, given enterprise ties to the ministry and central authorities and the legal obligation all had to maintain profitability in the socialist sector, the argument that this objective could be better realized by absorbing a well-run, small plant in a related field of production was an attractive one for all concerned. Ironically, the rationale for such mergers was often that large firms, with the resources of the socialist sector behind them, would be more adept at expanding the more lucrative activities of their smaller counterparts or realizing economies of scale (and/or lower subcontracting costs) by merging capacities and labor forces, despite the fact that it was typically small size, small lots, and labor flexibility that made the small firm more profitable in the first place.

On the other hand, the large socialist enterprises were saddled with so many political and administrative constraints that small firms either lacked or could easily evade, they necessarily competed at a disadvantage and were literally disallowed from adapting their own operations appropriately to meet the challenge. The Quality Shoe Factory is a case in point, and its experience was hardly an isolated one. But given the political and administrative resources enterprise elites did have at their disposal, a strategy of absorbing the small firms to meet the expectations demanded of them was an eminently rational one. Similar dynamics prevailed in the cooperative sector of the economy as well: the result was the Great Hungarian Merger Movement of the 1970s.[36]

Significantly, small firms put up little resistance to their incorporation into larger units, nor was much protest lodged by the local government who founded them. The contrast with the behavior of Yugoslav firms and communes, who aggressively resisted central pressures to amalgamate enterprises across regional boundaries, is striking.

Equally dramatic are the differences in the behavior of larger firms in the two countries. Where Hungarian firms sought to absorb their competitors, Yugoslav enterprises often reacted to competition by pressuring local authorities to close off regional markets to new entrants. When Yugoslav firms depended on inputs from a distant supplier, they would try to duplicate its capacities within their own walls or locality; in Hungary, merger activity was the response. Likewise, Yugoslav enterprises deployed the threat of competition politically, seeking to emancipate themselves from regulatory constraints or to extract political favors to meet it. In Hungary, however, the reaction was a classic bureaucratic one: firms abided by their regulatory constraints and helped extend them to other sectors of the economy, following rather than influencing the political cues to which they responded. Finally, the nature of competition itself differed in the two economies. In Yugoslavia, enterprises competed for sales and markets; in Hungary, they competed for supplies and inputs. Hence, even small firms could find their access to resources improved as their profitability declined thanks to incorporation into a major enterprise.

Thus where expanded autonomy in Yugoslavia appeared to promise enterprises increased opportunities to create and control their own operations and finances, from the perspective of the Hungarian firm, autonomy promised precisely the opposite: responsibility for losses and bad performance in administratively determined conditions very likely to lead to them. Likewise, increased control over economic resources in Yugoslavia could be translated by enterprise elites into increased political influence within both the firm and the larger community. In Hungary, in contrast, increased size and resources meant that firms could meet the expectations of superiors but that their control over their own operations declined. In effect, the more resources a firm had access to (e.g., the more monopolistic its market position was), the less discretion it had over how to dispose of them.

No matter how much Hungarian directors lamented the effects of supervision from above, they never developed any real interest in emancipating themselves from it. Accordingly, where the enactment of the Yugoslav economic reform of 1965 found a constituency among the firms ready and willing to take advantage of their new freedom, recentralization in Hungary was accompanied by passive acceptance from those whose active opposition would have been most necessary to halt it.

Intrafirm Power Relations and Enterprise Autonomy

The structure of power within the Hungarian firms was hardly coincidental to management's lack of interest in autonomy. In Yugoslavia enterprise self-management bodies played a critical role as a source of pressure and support for reducing external political and administrative constraints on their freedom of action. Though management was needed to supply leadership and articulation to the solidaristic sentiments of the workers' council, it would undoubtedly have been highly reluctant to do so without the presence of such a highly legitimate ally in direct contact with the labor force.

In Hungary, however, there was never any workers' council (or, indeed, any other body whose institutional loyalties were solely within the firm) to either form a source of constant pressure against the incursions of external authorities or constitute a vehicle for mobilizing the labor force to this end. Instead there was no direct link between management and labor, and executives dealt with workers through the enterprise-level branches of the party and trade unions.

For example, the campaign for "workshop democracy" in the 1970s was led and managed by the trade unions, who set up "consultation committees," canvassed the workers, ensured attendance at meetings, and interpreted and transmitted the discussions to both enterprise management and wider political forums.[37] Not surprisingly, where wage pressures from Yugoslav workers came to be articulated as a claim for greater enterprise control over the value it produced, wage pressures in Hungary either strengthened the union and party's ability to control management (and so reduce enterprise independence and flexibility) or pushed management back up into the arms of the ministry in search of special "wage preferences."[38]

There were other consequences to these contrasting internal arrangements. Management had no internal pressure on it to resist ministry "suggestions" it felt were unwise for the firm, and even if management did seek to expand the issues over which the enterprise could decide independently, it also had no organizational means of its own to mobilize the labor force in support.

For example, let us assume a director sought a grant of discretion from tutelary authorities to reorganize production and redefine jobs, as the Lenin Steel Mill did in response to the international steel crisis of 1980. Even if the reorganization promised higher wages for workers, there was no way the director could show workers were willing to make the changes unless the trade union and party branch also supported the restructuring. Not surprisingly, the first step the director of the Lenin Mill took was to call a meeting of the enterprise political *aktiv;* with its support, he then turned not to the enterprise labor force, but to the county party committee to back up his proposals to the supervisory ministry.

Meanwhile, conflicts between management and enterprise social organizations may have been infrequent, but they certainly occurred.[39] Their presence in the firm could be a real threat to an innovative executive, and in cases of conflict, the support and solidarity ministry personnel provided to management could be crucial to the outcome. Alternatively, a director could turn to the city or county party committee for support, lest he encounter opposition from internal social organizations. As a result, management had an incentive to maintain close ties to external political bodies and ministerial authorities to maintain its position *within* the firm as well as to protect its status in the larger economy. In effect, the industrial relations system in Hungary created a community of interest between management and ministry and management and party, whereas in Yugoslavia a community of interests shared by management and labor emerged.

Both enterprise party and trade union organizations in Hungary were similar to their Yugoslav counterparts in that they were low-level branches of larger national organizations. Like Yugoslav party and trade union branches, they had no interest in enterprise autonomy per se. But in Yugoslavia the mass organizations and party cells had the task of strengthening the self-management bodies, who, as the legitimate representatives of the enterprise labor force, could exercise power in the plant quite independently of them. In Hungary the task of party and trade unions in the firm was to control both management and labor force so that neither exercised power independently of the working class as a whole—or more precisely, to maintain its interests as interpreted by the top echelons of a vanguard party.

Consequently, they were far less subject to managerial manipulation on behalf of purely enterprise-centered interests than were either the Yugoslav sociopolitical organizations or the enterprise-based self-management bodies. Yet for the same reason, they were also far less likely to take up the immediate demands of workers in particular firms. Thus, when workers would seek to bargain over norms and premia, they typically turned to their supervisor rather than the shop steward for support.[40] Likewise, responding to a survey asking how to increase managerial effectiveness, a large majority of workers suggested that "listening more to the workers and not only to the leaders of the social organizations" would make a major improvement.[41]

In the case of enterprise party organizations, such insulation from the immediate claims of workers follows logically from the HSWP's adherence to democratic centralism. In a party where power flows from top to bottom, the ability of low-level branches to exercise power within state organizations depends on the backing their leaders have from higher party bodies and not from the support they derive from the grassroots membership—let alone employees of the organization who are not even HSWP members themselves.

But neither do Hungarian trade unions necessarily use their discretion to advance their membership's subjectively perceived interests either inside or outside the firm. Like state officials, union leaders are approved for their positions by the party, whose policies they implement within their organizations. And like enterprise directors, union leaders' constituencies is the HSWP, not the members of the organizations they lead, who have no means to keep them accountable in any case. Thus, when NEM awarded the trade unions an enlarged voice in the enterprise, it was not because the unions or their members demanded these rights, but because the party thought they should have them.

Significantly, the so-called union opposition to NEM that arose in the 1970s was hardly a product of *worker* pressures or membership "interests."[42] By and large, workers were not negatively affected by NEM, especially once a bonus system highly preferential to management was revised in 1969. Indeed, to the degree the supply of consumer goods improved because of the reform, the qualitative value of workers' incomes (i.e., what they could actually buy with their earnings) rose. Moreover, although income levels in the cooperative and private sectors—particularly in agriculture—rose more rapidly than in the state industrial sector after 1968, wages in the large enterprises remained relatively high, especially in industries given preferential treatment by state planners.[43] Rather than threatening egalitarianism, allowing incomes outside the socialist sector to increase above previously depressed levels may very well have decreased differentials among labor in the different sectors of the economy.

Equally important, a substantial proportion of the Hungarian proletariat works in both the private and state sectors, and this proportion increased with the expanded opportunities NEM provided.[44] While such labor mobility benefited workers making a move, it posed serious implications for the political clout of union leaders: should a significant segment of the labor force fall outside normal union channels, the leadership's influence in party policy-making forums could be severely compromised.

Even workers employed exclusively in the socialist sector could have benefited from the expansion of private and cooperative activities had labor shortages been exploited to raise wages in the firms. But for the unions to have led them in this endeavor would have put the former on a collision course with central authorities and the larger political leadership anxious to restrain inflationary pressures. Rather than mobilizing their following, then, union leaders pushed for an across-the-board wage increase in 1972, the maintenance of central wage controls, and measures that restricted the activities of cooperatives and taxed private incomes more stringently. In sum, the union leadership sought to *ease* the labor shortage for its own reasons rather than taking advantage of it to benefit union members.

Placing social organizations responsive to cues generated independently of particular enterprise and labor force exigencies between management and labor in the firm thus gave Hungarian management a structurally weak base from which to inspire loyalty and cooperation from the enterprise labor force. Unlike Yugoslav directors, Hungarian managers were institutionally incapable of playing the inherently political role of leading the work collective and articulating its interests to influence larger processes of collective choice. Rather, politics—the autonomous formulation of collective objectives and the mobilization of resources to achieve them—remained the monopoly of the centralized and hierarchical HSWP, while enterprise managers accomplished the objectives administrative superiors assigned through their use of legal authority over enterprise business operations. Industrial relations in Hungary were therefore bureaucratic rather than political, and management's relationship to the enterprise labor force was that of a superior to subordinates, not that of a representative/leader to constituents/followers.

For workers in state-owned firms, they had the same "rights" all other units of the state administration enjoyed: the right to become an "exception" to a rule whose strict observation jeopardized the probability of carrying out the purpose for which the rule was adopted. Hence, just as enterprises could bargain with ministries over issues and in arenas they themselves did not define, workers could bargain with management in arenas and over issues that were delimited by the genuine political actors who often did not participate in the bargaining at all. While a firm's petition for an exception would involve a request for a special tax exemption, export premia, pricing rule, or investment decision in order to better meet objectives it did not select, exceptionalism for workers involved an adjustment of norms, an increase in overtime, and special wage preferences in order to facilitate enterprise plans they played no role in formulating. In both cases exceptions were justified by the special circumstances of the individual or group requesting them, and in both cases exceptionalism militated against forming wider, genuinely political coalitions to change the rules themselves.

Moreover, just as the ability of an enterprise to become an exception to a rule in no way indicated an excercise of genuine *political* power, neither was endemic workshop bargaining a sign of any independent political power workers had acquired. For example, despite serious labor shortages, high turnover, absenteeism, and widespread shopfloor bargaining in the 1970s, personal incomes by and large followed plan projections; inflationary pressures came from overinvestment, *not* workers' ability to achieve wage increases.[45] The latter was indeed the case in Poland. But there, workers achieved a considerable degree of autonomous organization after the 1970–71 strikes, in direct contrast to Hungary where no challenge to the HSWP's monopoly of the means of collective action appeared after 1956. In effect, then, the ability of small groups of workers to become an exception to existing work rules is (like the ability of enterprises to be exempted from ministry regulations) more an indicator of the lack of independent clout both workers and enterprises have, when rules are made to start with, than a sign of labor strength.

To the degree workers' preferences do enter the political arena, it is normally through individual actions taken outside organizational frameworks rather than by coordinated group efforts. Yet a large number of individual exits do not a collective voice make, and political leaders have a wide latitude for response. Thus high labor turnover can lead to higher wages, but it can also be countered by hiring freezes and making job changes more difficult. Likewise, high demand for a consumer good—be it meat or telephones—may cause its output and availability on domestic markets to rise, but it can also result in price hikes, rationing, or the disappearance of the product from domestic markets entirely. Hence, the fact that an exit option is more freely available to Hungarian workers than to Yugoslavs, where the economy is marked by high unemployment rates, certainly does mean workers' welfare is greater in the former. Yet welfare is in no sense an indication of political power; it is simply the result of the priorities Hungarian party leaders have endorsed quite independently of workers' subjective demands and preferences. As one Hungarian economist quipped, political leaders find out what workers want by reading Marx and Lenin; they can hardly ask workers themselves given the lack of any autonomous worker organization.

Some note should be made of the effect of labor shortages on the distribution of power in Hungary. In economies with active price mechanisms, suppliers of scarce commodities gain discretion over their allocation. They may raise their price, engage in discriminatory practices against buyers, or use market power to discipline suppliers of inputs. Moreover, such economic power can often be translated into political influence as well: monopolistic producers or suppliers, for example, may use economic threats or inducements to pressure political elites to enact legislation (from tariffs to regulation and licensing arrangements) preserving their market position. Thus the presence of a labor market in conditions approaching full employment allows workers to raise the price of labor while strengthening the ability of unions to bargain collectively with employers and politically with government leaders.

Hungary, however, lacks an active price mechanism and even in the heyday of NEM, the best that could be done was to simulate what might be the effect of active prices through administrative decisions. Meanwhile, however, the lack of real markets meant that suppliers of strategic commodities—enterprises supplying goods, banks supplying capital, or workers supplying labor—*lost* discretion over their allocation when shortage conditions prevailed. The steel industry's dilemma in 1974 was a case in point: not only did the industry have no control over the prices it charged on the domestic market, but it was prevented from taking advantage of favorable opportunities abroad until domestic needs had been met. And it faced such restrictions, not *despite* its monopolistic position but *because of it*. Moreover, if being a monopolistic producer increases the amount of administrative constraints on a supplier's sphere of action, supply shortages enhance the amount of external political constraints on its activities as well. That is, when resources are overcommitted, it is the party's task to ensure that projects with political priority get their necessary share, and it has the power to cut red tape and intervene directly in administrative routines precisely for this purpose.

Hence, economic shortages enhance the strategic role of the party and not the suppliers of scarce commodities. This is no less true for labor, insofar as an active labor market does not exist in the socialist sector either. Tight labor markets have not acted to give Hungarian workers more economic power; in the 1980s, for example, real wages have stagnated despite the persistence of full employment. Nor do labor shortages act to give workers political power: nothing remotely approaching Poland's Solidarity emerged when austerity was imposed in Hungary. Tight labor markets in the 1970s, however, did have the result of greatly increasing the discretion local party officials exercised over regional employment practices.[46]

Given the political context and the industrial relations system within which NEM was introduced, then, it is hardly surprising that Hungarian enterprises did not protest the erosion of their autonomy that ensued in the 1970s. For management, greater enterprise autonomy promised few economic benefits for the firm and political and administrative problems for its directors. For directors who attempted to meet the challenge of the market, ministry support could be even more important than for those who tried to shield themselves from it. Indeed, had industrial ministries been abolished in 1968, the lack of genuine markets would have forced enterprise management to invent a substitute for them. Nevertheless, the fact that management's main partner was located in a central bureaucracy (or alternatively, within the hierarchy of a hegemonic Leninist party) was as much a factor militating toward economic recentralization in Hungary as was management's coalition with a body based within the firm an important factor strengthening pressures for economic decentralization in Yugoslavia.

In addition, not only did management have little interest in preserving enterprise independence, it also had no political resources available to advance such an objective. The fact that it relied on organizations whose loyalties and constituencies lay outside the firm to communicate with the enterprise labor force meant it lacked any mechanism to mobilize the labor force around purely enterprise-centered goals. At the same time, the fact that workers had no effective political power in any case meant management had scant incentive to invent such a mechanism either.

Conclusion

The reforms enacted in Hungary in the 1980s have indeed made major changes within the state administration. The industrial ministries were consolidated and streamlined, a number of very large firms were broken up, and new rules for price determination, wage regulation, and capital allocation were put into effect. Moreover, the new NEM has included changes in the industrial relations system within the firm as well, as evidenced by the ECWAs and plans to introduce self-management.

Although economic and administrative relations within the state have been modified, the political relationship between the state as a whole and the HSWP remains intact. The latter retains its monopoly of political power as in the past, and state organizations—from self-managed firms and local governments to ministries and Parliament—remain essentially apolitical, bureaucratic actors who bargain with each other over how to accomplish objectives the HSWP selects.

The question, then, is whether changes in the state administration can have any effect on the distribution of power within the HSWP or on the way the HSWP uses the power it commands (i.e., on the development strategy and priorities it actually selects).[47] That is, are the new reforms likely to strengthen the influence of reform advocates within the party, thereby creating new political barriers to a replay of the 1970s scenario of recentralization? Further, do the changes made in the industrial relations system act to increase both the commitment and the political capacity of enterprises to preserve their own autonomy? And finally, to what degree is advancing the cause of economic reform synonymous with advancing the political power and economic welfare of workers?

Let us first consider the new ECWAs.[48] A popular innovation, they included approximately 200,000 workers by 1984. At the same time, numerous problems with their operation have also appeared. For example, because work "on contract" is so well paid, the establishment of ECWAs can easily be regarded by employees not included in them as little more than managerial favoritism. Likewise, ECWAs were intended to organize work in the firm on a spontaneous, economic basis, rather than on the traditional, bureaucratic, and hierarchical one. Yet, since ECWAs can only contract to do work that enterprise management authorizes, they have often simply become a device through which firms can short-circuit highly regulated labor relations to perform their traditional activities rather than being a means for introducing innovation and new lines of activity. As a result the actual work individuals perform within ECWAs is frequently the same work they do on their regular jobs, but the fact that it is better paid creates rivalries and jealousies within the labor force. Furthermore, their contribution to efficiency must still be established. Although individual labor productivity is clearly higher in ECWAs than in the traditional work organization, in many cases they may operate to simply deter workers in the state enterprises from moving to jobs in private or cooperative sectors where their labor could be deployed far more efficiently.

Meanwhile, ECWAs are purely economic entities. Certainly, the more flexible, contractual format gives workers increased autonomy in their jobs: "It is an undebatable achievement of the [ECWA] that while during the regular hours of work the worker has no active role in organizing his own work, in the [ECWA], where time is money for him, he does have such [a] role. The rational organization of his work becomes the immediate interest of the [ECWA] member."[49]

In addition, ECWAs increase labor's bargaining power with management and in this sense represent an important, politically approved extension of the arenas and issues over which intrafirm bargaining can occur. They do not, however, give workers any political power, and existing or would-be ECWA members have no role in determining the rules governing their formation. Significantly, the imposition of a 10 percent surcharge on firms with ECWAs in February 1985 did not bring about protests from either management or labor; on the contrary, "many managers consider[ed] the introduction of the surtax as a kind of signal and exhibited[ed] a cautious behaviour towards small ventures."[50]

The surcharge was part of a package of measures regulating small ventures in Hungary to prevent unfair economic competition—the same accusation that presaged the reversal of NEM in the 1970s. Not surprisingly, significant opposition to ECWAs and other new forms of economic activity materialized at high levels of the HSWP, and they became a major issue of debate at the 1985 Party Congress. If efforts to impose further limits on their formation were beaten back by reformists, this was due more to the difficult circumstances under which the economy is still operating, and *not* to any explicit political support ECWAs or their members provided. As we have seen, support from below and demands originating outside the HSWP itself are simply not very valuable political resources in Hungary. Indeed, if managers saw the surtax as a signal and reacted with caution, workers did not respond at all.

Interestingly enough, reformists have countered the opposition by proposing that *all* work within enterprises be organized on an ECWA-contractual basis, a move that would strike at the traditional enterprise hierarchy from within. Moreover, they suggest finding a way to give ECWAs and other small-venture forms political representation as well.

Political representation would certainly help institutionalize ECWAs as a permanent fixture of the Hungarian economic scene, but it need not constitute a radical political innovation—much less a way of giving ECWA members real political power. All politically recognized social interests in Hungary have a form of political "representation": workers have unions, young people have KISZ, the youth organization, even enterprises have a chamber of commerce. As we have seen in the case of the trade unions, such organs of social representation operate according to standard "transmission belt" formats. They thus act more to control and manage their members than to voice their demands, participating in the definition of members' "objective" interests within the HSWP much more than articulating and mobilizing their subjective interests outside it.

If ECWAs become members of such a transmission-belt organization, several consequences will follow. First of all, one can indeed expect its leaders to be committed to the expansion of ECWA activity in Hungarian firms, since—like all leaders—their influence will depend on the size and strategic value of the activities for which they are responsible. Moreover, such a leadership—like that of the unions and the other mass organizations—will have clout where it counts: in the HSWP. To the degree ECWAs are genuinely in workers' interests, this would not be an insignificant development. Likewise, insofar as the propagation of ECWAs and small ventures is part of a broader reformist program, such an organization would give it an additional base of politically relevant support.

One can also expect such a leadership—again, like that of all mass organizations—to be accountable to the HSWP and its top echelons in particular, and not to the ECWAs or their members. Hence, one can expect it to regulate and routinize their formation, despite the fact that such bureaucratization need not be in the interests of ECWA members and indeed is antithetical to the entrepreneurial functions reformists intended them to have. In effect, one would get an expansion of the use of ECWAs qua collective teams and work brigades along with an atrophy of ECWAs qua in-house entrepreneurs. From that, it would be a small step to regulating the incomes ECWA members generate much along the lines wages are currently regulated, strengthening the clout of national ECWA leaders within the HSWP while eroding the grassroots bargaining power ECWA members currently enjoy.

One can, however, imagine an alternative mode of political representation for ECWAs and small ventures that would simultaneously reinforce the HSWP's hegemonic political position and allow it to take the real preferences of ECWA members (as opposed to leaders) into account in determining its own priorities.[51] That is, rather than following the traditional pattern of establishing *one* transmission belt organization with a monopoly of representation of all eligible to join it, the HSWP could set up several transmission belt organizations that would compete for members.

Their leaders would still be approved for their positions by the party and would thus remain accountable to it. Hence, they would continue to implement party directives within their own organizations. Nevertheless, once organizations must compete for members, leaders have an incentive to use their discretion in interpreting directives in ways that would maximize their organization's following. Moreover, insofar as mass organization leaders often play critical roles when the HSWP adopts directives that apply to their own functions, such leaders would also have a reason to use that influence on behalf of expanding and retaining their membership, as opposed to simply equating their own views and interests with those of a captive following.

Workers would certainly still be prohibited from forming their own organization, but they would be able to shift support among party-approved rivals with at least slightly different bases of appeal. By doing so, they would not only have more bargaining clout within the firm, but competing ECWA representatives would have an incentive to articulate their more general preferences within the party as well. For example, if there is genuine interest among workers to engage in "intrapreneurial" activities within their own firms, one could expect that interest to be reflected by even a transmission-belt organization, once it became anxious to recruit such individuals and groups into its own ranks.

ECWAs, then, appear to promise substantial economic benefits to workers and possible political advantages, too. Economically, they may increase income differentiation among workers, but significantly, such differentiation does not occur at the expense of non-ECWA members, who retain the traditional protections employment in the state sector provides. Moreover, to the degree the use of ECWAs enhances enterprise profitability, they can also increase a firm's ability to raise overall wages; in that case, their operation indirectly benefits even those who are not themselves ECWA members.

Politically, if there were competing ECWA transmission-belt organizations, they would have the same incentive to generalize ECWAs to the labor force as a whole that a single, monopolistic representative would have but without the temptation or ability to impose a uniform model on all small units. Moreover, even if such organizations cater their appeals exclusively to ECWA members, this need not imply that the rest of the labor force go unrepresented. Indeed, trade union leaders might, for the first time, have a real cause to bargain on behalf of their members.

As for the introduction of self-management, if enterprises (or enterprise elites) turn out to be willing and able to translate what is in fact a considerable grant of legal autonomy into genuine political influence, the consequences could be important. Although the absence of any real change in either the relationship between the state and the party or in the organization of the highly centralized HSWP makes such a development unlikely, both the provisions of the new law and the political climate surrounding its adoption do, for the first time, at least make it possible.

In this regard, it is important to note that the law adopted in 1985 created a significantly stronger version of self-management than could have been anticipated on the basis of proposals and discussions aired in 1983–84.[52] Not only were more enterprises affected by the new law than originally envisioned, but the sphere of authority of the new enterprise councils was enlarged to the point where it was roughly comparable to that of a capitalist board of directors.[53] At the same time, the councils' composition was narrowed to include only individuals employed within the enterprise, thereby excluding representatives of outside agencies (like the Chamber of Commerce, independent experts, and ministry officials) with no strong ties to the particular firm. Certainly, representational arrangements in Hungary provided enterprise management with a much stronger and more legitimate presence on enterprise councils than it ever had in Yugoslavia.[54] Yet interestingly enough, in Yugoslavia, it was precisely enterprise management who turned out to be the intra-enterprise group whose position in the firm and society gave it the greatest stake in expanding enterprise autonomy and made it most capable of mobilizing the labor force to this end.

Hungarian firms in the 1980s have thus acquired both a very different legal status and industrial relations system from the ones they had in 1968, when the first economic reform measures were enacted. Equally significant, many of the new powers of the enterprise councils—in planning, investment, finance, and personnel and organizational questions—have been awarded at the expense of the industrial branch ministries upon whom enterprise management had been so dependent in the past. Even in the selection of enterprise directors, the traditional rights of ministries to nominate chief executives has been reduced to the weaker power of vetoing an enterprise council's choice. All in all, then, the new legislation gives Hungarian firms considerably more formal control over their own operations than their Yugoslav counterparts had in the 1950s.

Nevertheless, although altering the legal status of enterprises and redefining labor-management relations within them may be necessary conditions of economic decentralization, they are far from necessary and sufficient. The larger politico-economic system must also work to make it worthwhile for enterprises to operate independently and to endow firms with the political resources needed to resist central incursions into their internal affairs.

In Yugoslavia this was indeed the case, and controlling a state institution like a firm or a local government allowed its leaders to utilize the resources it generated and the constituency it encapsulated to make claims on larger collective choices—from demanding specific resources to shaping the resource allocation mechanism itself. Independent organizations were a power base, and leaders within them had incentives to resist incursions into their autonomy as well as the political resources to make such resistance into a political issue.

In contrast, organizational independence in Hungary in the past has typically entailed renouncing access to centrally allocated resources and encountering stiffer obstacles to generating resources on one's own. Moreover, political power has been monopolized by the HSWP, and leaders in state organizations have had as little incentive to protect their independence as they have had political capacity to do so. The fate of Hungarian cooperatives in the 1970s is illustrative in this regard. In both agricultural (collective farm) and small industrial and service cooperatives, the labor force had representation in managerial organs that was at least as strong as it will be in the new self-managed firms. The cooperatives were not under ministry supervision either. Nevertheless, when the HSWP decided to consolidate them and restrict their activities, there was very little they could do about it.[55] As for the Association of Cooperatives, rather than come to the defense of its affiliates, it helped supervise the merger movement and regulate the new, enlarged units much in the manner of a ministry.[56] Meanwhile, since mergers expanded the number of cooperative members, they watered down individual voting strength and hence interest in cooperative decisions; they thus freed the management from internal pressures while increasing its responsiveness to and dependence on external political and administrative bodies. Not surprisingly, by 1978 the difference between working in a cooperative and a state firm was minimal.[57]

The question, of course, is whether anything today would prevent the same scenario from occurring in the 1980s among the self-managed firms. That is, do enterprise elites now have the kind of incentives to preserve their organizational independence that were present in Yugoslavia and which the cooperative leaders lacked? And if so, do they have the political resources to deploy for such a purpose?

Certainly, leaders in Hungarian firms will continue to differ from those in Yugoslavia insofar as they will not benefit politically from organizational autonomy. In Hungary, nonparty organizations will not function as a power base, and an enterprise's ability to generate resources or attract investment will not necessarily increase the political influence of the responsible management. Nevertheless, if an increasing share of resources is in fact allocated by market mechanisms (as the macro-economic reform measures seek) rather than through administrative channels, more efficient Hungarian firms should find their efforts rewarded by easier access to investment, working capital, imports, and the like as well as by the ability to pay higher wages and bonuses. Hence, Hungarian firms may have an economic incentive as strong as the political incentive Yugoslav enterprises had to resist centralization and external intervention in their decisions. For example, Hungarian directors may find themselves no freer to play a major political role in local or national affairs, but they may instead find they can pursue what they judge to be wise business strategies with far less restriction. Similarly, workers would not acquire greater power in perhaps shaping national housing policy but they might find their enterprise with more funds with which to purchase apartments and themselves with more influence over their distribution.

Clearly, the efficacy of such economic incentives will depend on a number of factors, not the least of which is the quality of the management selected by the enterprise councils and the degree to which it is committed to and rewarded for good entrepreneurship. Equally important will be the extent to which the enterprise councils can be used to create a community of interest among management and labor based on advancing the interests of the individual firm. If party and union branches coopt worker representation, the self-management bodies will reflect party and union priorities rather than those of the enterprise labor force. Needless to say, the former are far less likely to place a premium on enterprise autonomy, profitability, and wage levels, and far more likely to emphasize coordinating enterprise activities with general economic goals and maintaining solidaristic income policies. The fact that the introduction of self-management was delayed in 1985 partly to allow enterprise social organizations to educate workers not to use the new arrangements to vote themselves wage increases suggests such a possibility is real.

More profoundly, the impact of economic incentives on enterprise behavior depends heavily on whether or not market mechanisms actually govern resource allocation in the economy. Certainly, the reduction of the branch ministries' jurisdiction suggests enterprises will be less shielded from market forces than in the past. Yet the change should not be exaggerated, since many of the industrial ministries' responsibilities have in practice simply been shifted to other agencies of the central government (e.g., the Materials and Price Commission, the Planning Office, the finance and foreign trade ministries). Nor is the continuation of heavy and relatively detailed regulation particularly surprising, given the high degree of concentration that characterizes the Hungarian economy. With competition virtually nonexistent on so many product markets, it is doubtful that simply giving enterprises greater control over their own operations will lead to greater efficiency in the economy as a whole. And if it is difficult to imagine enterprise councils of socialist firms even closing down unprofitable operations, it is even more difficult to imagine their consenting to having their firms broken up into smaller units merely for the sake of introducing greater competition. Yet in the absence of real competition, the economic lives of enterprises will necessarily continue to depend on their subordination to administrative authorities, giving firms greater incentives to let their objectives be defined for them in the central government, than by them, in the enterprise councils.

Whether enterprises will have the political capacity to defend their legal right to control their operations in substantive terms is equally unclear. In Hungary changing the industrial relations system within the firm has not been accompanied by altering the relationship between the party and the state, which began to occur in Yugoslavia with the 1952 Party Congress there. The degree then to which enterprises can really make their own decisions will again be more heavily influenced by the political winds prevailing in the HSWP than by the aspirations of enterprise leaders and councils.

Working in the enterprises' favor is the fact that the adoption of such a strengthened version of self-management in Hungary suggests that the constellation of forces dominating the HSWP is at least temporarily composed of leaders determined to provide "scope for socialist enterprises to operate as true ventures" and to replace "hierarchical dependence" with "democratic responsibility."[58] With such political backing, even if the support of work collectives is insufficient to overcome administrative barriers to innovative business strategies, enterprise elites have an alternative constituency to turn to for aid—one within the HSWP itself. Likewise, the enterprise labor force may find its enterprise council too weak politically to enforce claims made on its behalf. But to the degree the councils even articulate a version of worker aspirations different from that traditionally espoused by the party and trade unions, the result could be to force enterprise social organizations to take serious account of rank-and-file preferences in order to compete effectively for worker loyalty and retain control of their membership.

If the scenario described above is what actually occurs, it will be no small change indeed on the Hungarian economic and political landscape. Yet many factors suggest it is highly improbable. For one, even if the introduction of self-management creates an economic community of interest between elected executives of self-managed firms and the enterprise labor force, the fact that the labor force enjoys no more political power than before means that preserving enterprise autonomy may not necessarily be a means for advancing those interests in what remains a highly politicized and bureaucratized allocation process. In effect, all self-management in Hungary may do is loosen the ties of enterprise management to ministries while tightening the dependence of both management and enterprise councils on the HSWP.

Moreover, influence within the centralized and hierarchic HSWP continues to depend on the strategic value of activities for which leaders are politically responsible. Significantly, strategic value is not equivalent to economic value, and an enterprise producing a necessity at a loss is far more valuable politically than one producing nonessential items at a profit. Likewise, large firms whose operations affect the national economy are preferable to small ones of marginal importance. Consequently, to the degree self-managed firms may require political intervention to forward their economic interest, they have an incentive to increase their size, engage in merger activity, and acquire monopoly status even if this implies increased regulation and compromises the ability of the enterprise labor force to influence enterprise business strategy.

In addition, if Hungarian firms do use their new legal power to respond more to market cues, greater differentiation in profits and personal incomes will undoubtedly develop among them. The political reaction to such differentiation in the past has been to amalgamate weaker and stronger economic units, often to the detriment of both and with scant concern for the preferences of employees. It is entirely possible for this pattern to repeat itself in the future, particularly since the persistence of a highly monopolistic and regulated economic environment makes the charge of unjustified profits a telling one.

Finally, although the tendency of labor-managed firms to guard their autonomy may create serious obstacles to the continuation of central planning, it is no guarantee that enterprises will use that autonomy in economically optimal ways. If the establishment of self-management is followed by a new round of overinvestment by firms, widespread price increases, and inflationary wage pressures, the experiment is likely to harm reformist efforts to bring modified market socialism to Hungary rather than to forward the cause. In that case one can expect reformist influence in the HSWP to erode not only together with enterprise autonomy but because of it.

In both Yugoslavia and Hungary, then, the political and economic impact of the industrial relations system depended heavily on the politico-economic structure within which it was situated. In Yugoslavia self-managed enterprises were part of a project for creating a national political community.

Hence, they had both an interest and a political capacity to protect their economic autonomy. At the same time, precisely because self-managed firms had the power to preserve their independence, political considerations easily eclipsed market cues when they made their economic decisions. As a result, if it proved impossible to coordinate their activities through administrative and political means, after 1965 it proved no less difficult to coordinate their activities through a price mechanism.

In Hungary the introduction of self-management in socialist-sector firms is part of a project for creating a more efficient economy. Although such firms and their labor force may well acquire an economic interest in preserving their rights to make their own decisions, they lack the political power to enforce it. Their future will thus depend heavily on political winds within the HSWP that they will have little opportunity to shape.

And ironically, the political consequence of enterprises' using their autonomy to pursue their economic interests in a highly monopolistic and protected economy may be to reinforce pressures from the center to take that autonomy away.

Notes

Acknowledgments: The fieldwork on which this article is based was generously funded during 1981–82 by the International Research and Exchange Board and the German Marshall Fund. The article was completed while the author was a fellow at the Center for Advanced Study in the Behavioral Sciences. I am grateful for the financial support provided by the Exxon Educational Foundation during my stay there.

1. For a summary of recent reform measures, see Paul Marer, "Economic Reform in Hungary: From Central Planning to a Regulated Market," in U.S. Congress, Joint Economic Committee, *East European Economies: Slow Growth in the 1980s* (Washington, D.C.: U.S. Government Printing Office, forthcoming); idem and Ellen Comisso, "Explaining Economic Strategy in Hungary," *International Organization* 40 (Spring 1986):421–54; Marton Tardos, "How to Create Efficient Markets in Socialism" (paper presented at the Conference on the Soviet Union and Eastern Europe in the World Economy, Kennan Institute, Washington, D.C., Oct. 18–19, 1984); and Xavier Richet, "Politiques d'ajustement et réformes institutionnelles en Hongrie," in Marie Lavigne and Wladimir Andreff, eds., *La réalité socialiste* (Paris: Economica, 1985), 169–83.

2. For some analyses of the causes and dimensions of the reversal of the 1968 reform, see Comisso and Marer, "Economic Strategy;" Edward Hewett, "The Hungarian Economy: Lessons of the 1970s and Prospects for the 1980s," in U.S. Congress, Joint Economic Committee, *East European Economic Assessment,* vol. 1 (Washington, D.C.: U.S. Government Printing Office, 1981), 483–525; Richard Portes, "Hungary: Economic Performance, Policy, and Prospects," in U.S. Congress, Joint Economic Committee, *East European Economies Post-Helsinki* (Washington, D.C.: U.S. Government Printing Office, 1977), 767–815; János Kornai, *The Economics of Shortages,* vol. 2 (Amsterdam: North Holland, 1981); Marton Tardos, "Enterprise Independence and Central Control," *Eastern European Economics* 15 (Fall 1976):24–45; Teréz Laky, "The Hidden Mechanisms of Recentralization in Hungary," *Acta Oeconomica* 24, nos. 1–2 (1980):95–109; and László Antal, *Fejlödés—Kitérövél* (Budapest: Pénzügyi Kutatási Intézet, 1979).

3. Descriptions of NEM are numerous. See Portes, "Economic Performance," 766–75; David Granick, "The Hungarian Economic Reform," in Morris Bornstein, ed., *Comparative Economic Systems,* 3rd ed. (Homewood, Ill.: Irwin, 1974), 218–33; Istvan Friss, ed., *Reform of the Economic Mechanism in Hungary* (Budapest: Akademiai Kiadó, 1968); O. Gadó, ed., *Reform of the Economic Mechanism in Hungary, Development 1968–71* (Budapest: Akademiai Kiadó, 1972); and Alec Nove, "Economic Reforms in the USSR and Hungary: A Study in Contrasts," in A. Nove and D. M. Nuti, eds., *Socialist Economics* (Baltimore: Penguin, 1972).

On Yugoslav planning of the 1950s, see Deborah Milenkovitch, *Plan and Market in Yugoslav Economic Thought* (New Haven: Yale University Press, 1971); Albert Waterson, *Planning in Yugoslavia* (Charlottesville, Va.: University of Virginia Press, 1964); Rudolf Bićanić, "Economic Growth under Centralized and Decentralized Planning: Jugoslavia—A Case Study," *Economic Development and Cultural Change* 6 (Oct. 1957); idem, "Interaction of Macro and Micro-Economic Decision in Yugoslavia, 1954–1957," in Gregory Grossman, ed., *Value and Plan* (Berkeley: University of California Press, 1960); and Ellen Comisso, *Workers' Control under Plan and Market* (New Haven: Yale University Press, 1979).

4. See Mihály Laki, "Liquidation and Merger in the Hungarian Industry," *Acta Oeconomica* 28, nos. 1–2 (1982):87–108.

5. On state building, see Charles Tilly, ed., *The Formation of National States in Western Europe* (Princeton: Princeton University Press, 1975); Perry Anderson, *Lineages of the Absolutist State* (London: New Left Books, 1974). In effect, socialism could perform in the twentieth century many of the functions capitalism performed in the sixteenth. On Yugoslav aims, see Vladimir Dedijer, *The Battle Stalin Lost* (New York: Grosset and Dunlop, 1973).

6. By state organizations I mean public institutions established under law. In Yugoslavia state organizations are normally self-managed in one way or another (the armed forces is the major exception). Their functions, however, differ. Some are directly engaged in economic or productive activity; these are "enterprises." Other supply social services (e.g., schools, hospitals). Others perform regulatory functions (e.g., local, republic, and national governments); in the Yugoslav jargon, these constitute "socio-political communities." Yet others are largely concerned with financial transactions (e.g., banks). All, however, are public bodies. The mass organizations (e.g., the League of Communists, the trade unions) are secondary associations whose purposes are self-defined, in contrast. In Yugoslavia they are called "sociopolitical organizations."

Readers should note that I employ the same terminology in describing Hungarian arrangements. There, state organizations are not self-managed, however. But they include both economic organizations (e.g., enterprises and banks) as well as administrative hierarchies (e.g., the various ministries), and local and national governments. All must be distinguished from the party and its apparatus, which operates distinct from but parallel to the state administration. Whereas the state administration operates according to public laws government bodies adopt, the party operates by its own statutes.

7. This did not necessarily mean the executives themselves had to be party members, although normally this was the case. See Bennett Kovrig, *Communism in Hungary* (Stanford: Hoover Press, 1979):340–53.

8. It must be stressed, however, that in both cases, the determination of income levels and salary differentials was made within the framework of centrally determined regulations. On the role of trade unions in Hungarian firms after 1968, see William Robinson, *The Pattern of Reform in Hungary* (New York: Praeger, 1973), 235–50. On wage determination in Yugoslavia in the 1950s, see Howard Wachtel, *Workers' Management and Workers' Wages in Yugoslavia* (Ithaca: Cornell University Press, 1973).

9. Author's interviews, 1981. See also Slobodan Bosnic, "Profesionalna struktura i pokretljivost," in M. Ilić, ed., *Socijalna struktura i pokretljivost*

radničke klase Jugoslavije (Belgrade: Institute za društvenih nauka, 1963), 397–406; S. J. Rawin, "Social Values and the Managerial Structure: The Case of Yugoslavia and Poland," *Journal of Comparative Administration* 2 (Aug. 1970):130–50; A. Barton, B. Denitch, and C. Kadushin, *Opinion-Making Elites in Yugoslavia* (New York: Praeger, 1973).

10. Unlike Hungarian local governments, whose budgets were funded by taxes levied by the national government and allocated by centrally set formulas, Yugoslav communes derived a large share of their revenues from local taxes they themselves levied. In addition, they performed many of the regulatory tasks (e.g., controlling prices and wages) that were performed by central branch ministries in Hungary. On the functions of the commune, see Comisso, *Workers' Control*, 44–50; J. Dordević and N. Pasić, "The Communal Self-Government System in Yugoslavia," *International Social Science Journal* 63 (1961):399–408.

11. See Albert Meister, *Socialisme et autogestion* (Paris: Editions du Seuil), 65ff.; Juraj Hrženjak, "Neki problemi radničkog samoupravljanja," *Ekonomski Pregled* 8, no. 5 (1957):311–18.

12. See Comisso, *Workers' Control*, 234–36; Živan Tanić, "Neke tendencije u dosadašnjem radu radničkih savjeta," *Sociologija* 2 (Feb. 1961):101–12; Meister, *Autogestion*, 89–90; Rawin, "Social Values," 140; Jiri Kolaja, "A Yugoslav Workers' Council," *Human Organization* 1 (1961):27–31; J. Brekić, "Pokretljivost u organima radničkog samoupravljanja," *Sociologija* 3 (Jan. 1961):61–70.

13. See Miloš Ilić, "Radnička klasa Jugoslavije i globalno jugoslovensko društvo," in Ilić, ed., *Socijalna struktura*, 100; Comisso, *Workers' Control*, 9–23; Adizes, *Industrial Democracy*, 200ff.

14. See Brekić, "Pokretljivost," 67; Ašer DeLeon, *The Yugoslav Worker* (Belgrade: Yugoslav Trade Unions, 1962), 18. Peasant workers, whose incomes did not depend entirely on their wages, were typically underrepresented in the self-management bodies.

15. See Josip Županov and Arnold Tannenbaum, "Control in Some Yugoslav Industrial Organizations," in A. Tannenbaum, ed., *Control in Organizations* (New York: McGraw-Hill, 1968), 91–112; Ellen Comisso, "Workers' Councils and Labor Unions: Some Objective Tradeoffs," *Politics and Society* 10, no. 3 (1981):251–79.

16. See DeLeon, *Yugoslav Worker*, 27, 72; Slavko Luković, "Ekonomsko poslovanje radničkih savjeta," in A. DeLeon and L. Mijatović, eds., *Kongres radnickih savjeta* (Belgrade: Rad, 1957), 255–95; R. Radosavljević, "Radnici o nekim pitanjima čistog prihoda i ličnog dohotka," *Sociologija* 3 (Jan. 1961):70–9.

17. On meddling, see Meister, *Autogestion*, 79–90; and "Discussions," in DeLeon and Mijatović, *Kongres*.

18. See Meister, *Autogestion*; "Discussions," in DeLeon and Mijatović, *Kongres*; Josip Županov, *Samoupravljanje i društvena moć* (Zagreb: Naše Teme, 1968); and Joel Dirlam and James Plummer, *An Introduction to the Yugoslav Economy* (Columbus, Ohio: Merrill, 1973).

19. On regional variations in enterprise-government relations, see Paul Shoup, *Communism and the Yugoslav National Question* (New York: Columbia University Press, 1968); and Dennison Rusinow, *The Yugoslav Experiment* (Berkeley: University of California Press, 1977).

20. See Comisso, "Councils and Unions," 251–79; Emerik Blum, "The Direc-

tor and Workers' Self-management," in M. Broekmeyer, ed., *Yugoslav Workers' Self-Management* (Dordrecht, Holland: D. Reidel, 1970), 170–200; and Mladen Zvonarević, "Socijalna moć, informiranost i motivacija u procesu samoupravljanja," *Naše Teme* 13 (June 1969):900–918.

21. The case of Energoinvest's Emerik Blum is illustrative. See his "Director and Self-management," in Broekmeyer, ed., *Yugoslav Workers' Self-Management*, 170–200.

22. See Rusinow, *Yugoslav Experiment*, 81–138.

23. See ibid., 81–138; Milenkovitch, *Plan and Market*, 100–200; Shoup, *National Question*, 227–61.

24. Political resources can be thought of as sources of support "valuable" for advancing claims on collective choices.

25. See Comisso, "Councils and Unions," 253–62; Županov *Samoupravljanja*, ch. 1; and Branko Horvat, *An Essay on Yugoslav Society* (White Plains, N.Y.: International Arts and Sciences Press, 1969). The point here is not that all interests of labor and management in Yugoslav firms coincided, which in fact was not the case. Rather, the point is that self-management created an institutional structure strongly skewed in favor of strengthening and representing interests they shared while weakening and delegitimizing the bases of conflict. Thus, interests workers shared with management were easily articulated by workers' councils; interests whose satisfaction management opposed typically could only be advanced through strikes and other actions much more difficult to organize.

26. See Rusinow, *Yugoslav Experiment*, 108–38; Josip Županov, *Marginalije o društvenoj krizi* (Zagreb: Globus, 1983); Branko Horvat, *Privredni sistem i ekonomskih politika Jugoslavije* (Belgrade: Institut Ekonomskih Nauka, 1970).

27. Most descriptions of "one-man" management describe the Soviet experience. See Joseph Berliner, "Managerial Incentives and Decision-Making: A Comparison of the United States and the Soviet Union," in Bornstein, ed., *Comparative Economic Systems*, 396–427; Jerry Hough, "The Soviet Concept of the Relationship Between the Lower Party Organs and the State Administration," in R. Cornell, ed., *The Soviet Political System* (Englewood Cliffs: Prentice-Hall, 1970), 250–71; David Granick, *Management of the Industrial Firm in the USSR* (New York: Columbia University Press, 1955).

28. On ownership rights in Hungary, see Lajos Ficzere, *The Socialist State Enterprise* (Budapest: Akademiai Kiadó, 1974); Geza Peter Lauter, *The Manager and Economic Reform* (New York: Praeger, 1972); Tardos, "Efficient Markets"; and Wlodzimierz Brus, *Socialist Ownership and Political Systems* (London: Routledge and Kegan Paul, 1975).

29. The relationship between the state and the party is described in greater detail in Comisso and Marer, "Hungary," and in Ellen Comisso, "Introduction: State Structures, Political Processes and Collective Choice," *International Organization* 40 (Spring 1986):195–238.

30. James March and Herbert Simon make the following distinction between politics and bureaucratic bargaining: "Politics . . . is a process in which the situation is the same as in bargaining—there is intergroup conflict of interest—but the arena of bargaining is not taken as fixed by participants." In *Organizations* (New York: Wiley and Sons, 1958), 130.

In Hungary, the "arena of bargaining" among state organizations is very much "taken as fixed by participants." For example, legislation passed in 1971 allowing young mothers to be paid to stay home with infants had a crippling effect on an already labor-short textile industry. Nevertheless, the industry made no attempt to oppose the legislation: "It was demographic policy," an executive explained. (Author's interviews, 1981). Such passivity can be contrasted with the aggressive lobbying efforts of the American textile industry when minimum wage proposals are debated in Congress.

More recently, austerity hit the steel industry in 1978–79. The firms and the metallurgical ministry proceeded to scale back previously ambitious expansion plans. Bargaining was certainly intense, but it was over how much to cut back, and how much investment (as opposed to, say, employment or wages) to reduce in particular, quite in accord with overall party priorities. Author's interviews, 1981. See also "Milliardos Fejlesztés—Gondokkal," *Figyelő*, March 14, 1979.

31. Case studies of both successful and unsuccessful enterprise adaptation to NEM appear in Marton Tardos, ed., *Vállalati magatartas—vállalati környezet* (Budapest: Közgazdasági és Jogi Könyvkiadó, 1980). See also David Granick, *Enterprise Guidance in Eastern Europe* (Princeton: Princeton University Press, 1975).

32. Author's interviews, 1981. See Endre Megyeri, "A magyar vaskoházsat iparpolitikai irányelvel," MKKE Department of Industrial Economics, Oct. 1975 (mimeo).

33. See Mihály Laki, "Az állam szerepe az új termékek gyártásában, as új technologiak alkalmazásaban," *Kösgazdasági Szemle* 7–8 (1978):807–19; Granick, *Enterprise Guidance*, 282–316.

34. See Judit Hamar, "A magyar cipöexport strukturája, ipari és villágpiaca háttere," Konjunktúra és Piackutáto Intézet, April 1980 (mimeo), 53–56.

35. Author's interviews, 1981. See also Béla Greskovits, "A 'kvási-Vállalatol' a 'Szivásos Monopoliumig': A vállalati szervezet fejlödési útja az 1950-és, 1960-és, es 1970-és évek magyar textiliparban" (Ph.D. diss., MKKE, Budapest, 1979); and György Moldova, *A Szent Tehén* (Budapest: Magvetö, 1980).

36. See Mihály Laki, "Liquidation and Merger in the Hungarian Industry," *Acta Oeconomica* 28, nos. 1–2 (1982):87–108; Gábor Revész, "Enterprise and Plant Size of the Hungarian Industry," *Acta Oeconomica* 22, nos. 1–2 (1979):47–78.

37. The kind of worker consultation that occurred in traditional production conferences is described in Miklos Haraszti, *Salaire aux pieces* (Paris: Seuil, 1973); on "workshop democracy," see Mrs. Aladar Mod and Gyúla Koszak, *A munkások retégzödése, munkája, isméretei és az üzemi demokrácia* (Budapest: Akadémiai Kiadó, 1974).

38. See Dominique Redor, "Le'économie du travail en Hongrie," CNRS report of research sponsored by the Hungarian Academy of Sciences, Oct. 1980 (mimeo), 40–42.

39. See Granick, *Enterprise Guidance,* 298.

40. See Lajos Héthy and Csaba Makó, *Munkasok, Érdékek, Erdékegyeztetés* (Budapest: Gondolat, 1978), 53–99.

41. See Mod and Kosza, *Üzemi demokrácia,* 67.

42. Such an interpretation of union opposition to NEM is suggested in Robinson, *Pattern of Reform,* 310–45, and Portes, "Economic Performance," 786.

43. See E. Szalai, "The New Stage of the Reform Process in Hungary and the Large Enterprises," *Acta Oeconomica* 29, no. 102 (1982):35n.

44. According to one estimate, in 1975 half the working class lived in villages. See Rudolf Andorka, "Hungary's Long-Term Social Evolution," *New Hungarian Quarterly* 20 (1975):88. Labor turnover apparently jumped from 20–25 percent to 41 percent in 1970. See Julius Reszler, "Recent Developments on the Hungarian Labor Market," *East European Quarterly* (Summer 1976):255–67; and Révész, "Enterprise Size," 47–68.

45. See Hewett, "Hungarian Economy," 491.

46. Author's interviews, Dec. 1983. See K. Fazekas et al., *MTA Közgazdaságtudományi Intézet Közleményei* 29 (Budapest: MTS Közgazdaságtudományi Intézet, 1983).

47. For example, Hungary elected its first parliament by contested elections in 1985. Certainly, competitive elections do not necessarily mean the Parliament itself has any more power than it did when single slates were presented. However, the fact that several major party figures lost elections in their district will presumably diminish their influence in the HSWP itself. Likewise, György Aczél may yet stage a political comeback within the HSWP thanks to his successful electoral campaign for parliament.

48. My information here is drawn by György Varga, "Small Ventures in the Hungarian Economy" (paper presented at the Ninth Hungarian-U.S. Roundtable on Economics, Berkeley, Cal., June 9–12, 1985, mimeo). See also David Stark, "The Dynamics of Organization Innovation and the Politics of Reform in Hungary" (paper presented at the Conference on the Social Consequences of Market Reforms in China and Eastern Europe, Santa Barbara, Cal., May 8–11, 1986, mimeo).

49. Varga, "Small Ventures," 21.

50. Ibid, 36.

51. The following proposal is my own and is not under active consideration in Hungary.

52. My account of the new law is drawn from Bela Balassa, "The 'New Growth Path' in Hungary" (unpublished, Oct. 1985); and Tamás Bauer, "The New Hungarian Forms of Enterprise Management and Their Economic Environment" (working paper for the 1985 Radein Research Seminar, Summer 1985). Their descriptions can be compared with the one given by Marer, "Economic Reform," and in László Csaba, "New Features of the Hungarian Economic Mechanism in the Mid-Eighties," *New Hungarian Quarterly* 24 (Summer 1983):1–20.

53. Initial accounts suggested that only firms with less than 500 employees would elect councils. In the final law, well over two-thirds of all Hungarian firms (and a similar proportion of industrial workers) will have some form of self-management. In firms with less than 500 employees, the director will be elected by a general assembly of the entire workforce; in larger enterprises directors will be selected by an enterprise council. Only public utilities in the wide sense of the word (e.g., power plants, mines, oil refineries, gas and water companies), trusts, and enterprises classed "under administrative control" for special reasons will

continue to be subordinated to branch ministries. The latter group is expected to be composed of about one-sixth of all firms and one-third of the workers.

Enterprise councils define enterprise plans, determine the allocation of profits between investment and incomes, approve financial balances and annual reports, and decide on modifications in the enterprise's line of activity by approving mergers, new subsidiaries, membership in associations, and the like. Last but hardly least, they elect the director, subject to ministry veto. Originally, it was proposed that about one-third of council members be drawn from outside the enterprise itself.

54. Tamás Bauer's account is as follows: "The council should have not more than 50 members, at least the half of whom should be elected by the staff. No more than one-third of the other half is to be nominated by the director, while the rest are executives, heads of divisions, establishments, etc. who are ex officio members of the council as stated in the statutes of the firm." Bauer, "New Forms," 5.

55. See Julia Varga, "Egy ipari szövetkezeti fúzió története," *Szociologia* nos. 3–4 (1980):413–25; Laki, "Liquidation and Merger," 90.

56. See Mihály Laki, *Vállalatok megszünése és összevonása* (Budapest: Közgazdasági és Jogi Könyvkiado, 1983); Tardos, "Efficient Markets," 10–12. Regarding the merger movement that took place among collective farms, see Nigel Swain, "The Evolution of Hungary's Agricultural System Since 1968," in Paul Hare, Hugo Radice, and Nigel Swain, eds., *Hungary: A Decade of Economic Reform* (London: Allen and Unwin, 1981), 225–52.

57. Author's interviews, 1981.

58. F. Havasi, head of the Economic Department of the Central Committee, cited in Bauer, "New Forms," 7.

9

SELF-MANAGEMENT AND THE POLITICS OF SOLIDARITY IN POLAND

Henry Norr

When massive strike waves broke over Poland in the summer of 1980, few predicted that the workers would succeed in building a genuinely independent and democratic trade union. Even fewer could have anticipated that the popular upsurge would also evolve into a mass movement demanding that the management of industry be put into the hands of elected workers' councils.

Farfetched as it sounded in a country ruled by a Leninist party, the idea of free unions had been in the air among the militant workers of the Baltic Coast at least since 1970. Industrial self-management, on the other hand, was a concept almost no one in Poland cared about in 1980. There was—as there continues to be—a broad consensus in favor of some variety of workers' democracy as a feature of an ideal economy.[1] But in the grim reality of "actually existing socialism," veteran activists and newly mobilized workers alike regarded direct participation in the management of enterprises as at best a second- or third-rank objective, and at worst a trap that might divert and coopt the movement. The fate of the workers' councils that had arisen in 1956 seemed to show where such forms of "socialist democracy" would lead: within months of their origin the councils began to be stripped of their powers, and in 1958 they were involuntarily incorporated into umbrella entities (called Conferences of Workers' Self-Management, or KSR) that were almost universally perceived as powerless ornaments dominated by management, by its allies in the party and in the discredited official trade unions, and by a handful of white-collar toadies.

As every close observer of the Polish scene has reported, the political consciousness of the Polish working class was centered on the "we"/"they" dichotomy, with the workers and "society" in general on one side and "the authorities"—the narrow elite of politicians, bureaucrats, and policemen—

on the other. In this framework the idea of building an independent organization—"ours"—to stand up to "them" had a powerful allure, as the explosive growth of Solidarity in the months after August 1980 demonstrated; joining "their" institutions, helping "them" to run the system they had created and still controlled, had scarcely any appeal. And in 1980, with the Polish economy in a deepening debacle, the prospect of assuming responsibility for the organization of production was particularly uninviting.

True, in response to the spreading August protests, the official press had begun to hold out the possibility of a revitalization of the moribund self-management system, and the Gdansk Agreements included a provision committing the new unions to take part in formulating laws to that effect. But self-management had not even been mentioned in the Gdansk workers' own Twenty-One Demands; the accord's reference to the subject was proposed by government negotiators and incorporated into the document with little discussion. The emerging union's orientation was more accurately reflected in the "Draft Program of Current Action," a proposal that circulated in Gdansk in the first weeks of Solidarity's existence: the union, the document declared, "has no intention of interfering with affairs under the competence of management, nor of replacing it, nor of taking responsibility for its activities."[2]

The new organization's leaders insisted repeatedly that the "partnership" with the authorities that they had in mind was to be an adversarial, not participatory, relationship. As a union in the strict sense, Solidarity wanted to compel the authorities to bargain with it on matters of immediate economic significance to it members. As an independent advocate of the interests of society, it would also demand the right to be consulted over broader issues of economic and social policy. But neither at the enterprise nor at the national level would it allow itself to be entangled in the apparatus of power.

Within a year, however, Solidarity had executed a dramatic turnaround in its approach to the question of self-management. From the grass roots of the union had arisen a vigorous popular movement with slogans like "Give us back our factories!" and elaborate plans for a reorganization of Polish industry that would put the management of each enterprise under the authority of its workforce. This new movement garnered support first from junior technocrats impatient with the waste and inefficiency that management by the party and the bureaucracy had produced, and from factory- and regional-level activists chafing at a model of reactive trade-unionism that seemed to be leading Solidarity into a dead end. In the tense summer of 1981 the idea of self-management started to catch on among rank-and-file workers as well, and before long the movement proved strong enough to force the issue upon Solidarity's hitherto hesitant national leadership. By September, when union delegates assembled in

Gdańsk for Solidarity's first national congress, self-management had emerged as the union's foremost demand, the centerpiece of its program for a self-governing republic.[3]

Ironically, however, the very anxieties and tensions that gave rise to the self-management movement soon began to sap its strength. With the economy in shambles and the political climate deteriorating, self-management could not be the panacea some of its champions had advertised, and popular enthusiasm waned almost as fast as it had arisen. Compromise legislation accepted by the union leadership in the fall of 1981 was far-reaching in comparison with previous workplace participation schemes in Poland and elsewhere in the Soviet bloc, but fell far short of the radical objectives on which the self-management movement and, more recently, the union congress had insisted. The result was division and confusion. Dedicated activists continued to agitate over the issue, but the movement had already lost much of its momentum before the coup of December 13, 1981, brought the struggle—or rather, this phase of it—to an abrupt end.

In this essay space does not permit full discussion of the Poles' attitudes toward and previous experiences with self-management, nor of the evolution of the situation during and since the "state of war." The focus here will be on 1981. Through analysis of the complex coalition that gradually assembled under the banner of self-management, the motives of various strata drawn to the demand, and the ideological and political specificity of this Polish version of industrial democracy, I shall attempt to explain the unexpected and dramatic rise of the self-management movement, as well as its subsequent decline.

Attitudes toward self-management were generally measured only tangentially in the many official and unofficial surveys of opinion carried out during the Solidarity period,[4] and hard sociological data about the orientation and composition of the movement are lacking. The interpretation presented here was extrapolated originally from the documentary record left by Solidarity and the self-management movement itself; their voluminous press, the protocols and resolutions of their meetings, and the testimony of their leaders.[5] Subsequently, my understanding of the movement has been much enriched by conversations in Poland during 1984 with a number of participants in and advisers to the movement.[6]

Origins

The Polish upheaval of 1980–81 is sometimes, and with good reason, called the first social revolution actually led by the working class.[7] In fact, of course, Solidarity was the product of a complicated interaction among the traditional proletariat, technical and white-collar employees, and professional intellectuals. So too was the movement for self-management. Production workers in heavy industry were ultimately the decisive force. From the very first months of Solidarity's existence, scattered groups of them implemented a rough-and-tumble kind of self-management, by driving particularly tyrannical or inept bosses out of their enterprises.[8] The grouping within Solidarity that later spearheaded the struggle for self-management (its cumbersome formal title was the Network of Solidarity Workplace Organizations of Leading Workplaces, but it will be referred to hereafter, as in Poland, simply as the Network) was made up of representatives from Poland's largest industrial enterprises. And it was when significant numbers of ordinary workers at such plants became convinced that self-management was a necessity alongside the independent union that the issue moved to the center of the political stage.

But until mid-1981 rank-and-file workers did not mobilize in large numbers around the demand for self-management, and disproportionately few of the pioneers who built the movement came from proletarian ranks. It was among the intellectuals aligned with Solidarity that self-management had the broadest support, and it was chiefly members of the intermediate technical stratum in the factories—what may be called the "production intelligentsia"—who led the developing struggle.

The Intellectuals

Workplace self-management had long been part of the program of most opposition-minded intellectuals in Poland. In Catholic circles the idea was rooted in the doctrine of Personalism, the Christian social philosophy that has deeply influenced the thinking of Polish church (including that of Karol Wojtyła, now Pope John Paul II) in recent decades.[9] For those of secular democratic orientation—notably members and supporters of KOR, the Committee for the Defense of the Workers/Committee for Social Self-Defense (the vanguard of the intellectual opposition since 1976)—self-management was an element of a much broader strategy and vision. It had been articulated over the course of the 1970s by Michnik, Kuroń, and their associates: winning a voice in the management of the enterprise was to be part of the process of self-organization through which Polish civil society would gradually restrict the scope of party power and regain at least partial control of its destiny.[10]

Among the economists who advised Solidarity about the reform of Poland's disintegrating system of planning and management, support for self-management was likewise widespread. Some of them recalled the ideals of 1956 and of reformist Communists like Oskar Lange, who assigned an important role to the workers' councils in proposals for restructuring the Stalinist economy that he drafted at that time. Other economists were drawn more toward managerialist models but supported self-management for instrumental reasons: they saw it as a concession that might be offered in exchange for the assent of workers to price increases, manpower redeployment, and other unpopular but necessary moves to rationalize the Polish system; over the longer haul they hoped it could serve as a mechanism for improving motivation and productivity and as a lever for prying the enterprises free from the grip of the central bureaucracies that had for so long mismanaged them.

Such broad-based intellectual endorsement for the notion of self-management undoubtedly contributed to its vague legitimacy, at least as a long-term objective, even in the first months when most of Solidarity was wary of any concrete involvement with the issue. Moreover, a few of Solidarity's advisers—like Szymon Jakubowicz, an economist and former party journalist who worked for the union's research center, and a handful of young intellectuals of radical Marxist persuasion, like Henryk Szlajfer (a leader in the 1968 student protests, and now an economist) and Zbigniew Kowalewski (an anthropologist who had spent several years in Cuba)—early on undertook a campaign to promote self-management as an important strategic goal for the union. Later, as the issue caught on, these men were to play highly visible parts as advisers and publicists in the cause of self-management. And, as we shall see, another adviser from academe, Jerzy Milewski, had a critical role in the entire history of the self-management struggle.

Still, it is important to resist the conclusion—prominently featured in official Polish and Soviet propaganda, and echoed in some Western treatments—that Solidarity's intellectuals bear responsibility for the union's evolution during 1981 toward a more radical strategy, and specifically for its turn toward the self-management program.[11] Nearly all of the principal advisers shared the prevailing tendency to regard self-management, however desirable, as a demand to which Solidarity could not or should not actively attach itself. Most of them greeted the emergence of the Network and its program with some reserve; only a few of the leading advisers—and none of the most prominent—were directly linked with the new movement. The caution of the mainstream union intellectuals is apparent in the draft program that Solidarity's "brain trust" (formally, the Center for Socio-Occupational Studies) prepared for discussion in the union in the late winter of 1980–81: under the heading of "The Character of the Changes Expected," self-management is there endorsed as "indispensable," but the language used is notably moderate compared with the proposals the Network was soon to offer, and the document insisted that it was not the union's role to draft specific plans for reform.[12]

Because friends and foes alike often exaggerate the role of KOR, the group deserves special attention in this context. Despite the philosophical affinity of its main currents for the concept of self-management, its members (by 1981 the group had ceased to function as a unified organization) played no direct role in promoting the demand as a strategy for Solidarity. *Robotnik,* the influential bulletin for workers that KOR helped to support, had decided, even before 1980, to emphasize trade-union independence in preference to self-management as the central plank of its platform.[13] Although Jacek Kuroń and his associates eventually played an important role in making self-government in a more generalized sense the keynote of Solidarity's visionary program, they continued to express considerable doubt about emphasizing control at the enterprise level. "For me," Kuroń remarked in a public debate in August 1981, "the main function of the self-management movement is not managing the factories—after all, that's impossible in present conditions. I'm talking about a self-management movement that would create, through its central structure, a new mechanism for making decisions . . . on the scale of the whole economy."[14]

The "Production Intelligentsia"

The sympathy for self-management that was prevalent among Solidarity's intellectuals thus had little direct impact on the union's strategic posture. It was only when other elements in the Solidarity coalition—beginning with the industrial engineers and technicians—began to take up the cause that self-management emerged as a pressing issue. In this light the case of Jerzy Milewski is a revealing one. At first glance it seems to support the argument that the self-management movement was a creation of the intelligentsia in the usual sense: Milewski, a member of the research staff and Solidarity leader at the Polish Academy of Sciences' branch in Gdańsk, cofounded the Network; as its secretary and coordinator, he became the movement's key strategist and propagandist; and in the end he rode its momentum to a position of some prominence in Solidarity as a whole.[15] Milewski, however, was not a traditional political intellectual, but, significantly, a technologist, an expert in fluid-dynamic machinery. His success in bringing self-management to the top of Solidarity's agenda stemmed not from his direct influence on the union's leaders (though he had served as an adviser to the Lenin Shipyard local) nor from the eloquence of his political writing (the pamphlets he wrote about his pet project, a new political organization to be called the Polish Labor Party, were something of an embarrassment to many in the movement), but rather from the ties he established with a remarkable group of young activists from regional and factory-level Solidarity committees.

Aside from their union responsibilities, most of the group were engineers, employed at low-level, nonmanagerial positions. Frustrated by

Solidarity's reluctance and the authorities' apparent inability to develop an effective program to combat the deepening national crisis, they were hungry for bold new approaches. In conversation with Milewski, they fastened on to the idea of a Solidarity initiative in the field of self-management, and it was they and others like them who organized the Network and quickly made it a powerful force in the politics of the union and the nation.

The production intelligentsia is ordinarily overshadowed in our perceptions of Solidarity. The pictures transmitted from Poland in 1980-81 were typically of the classic Proletariat of mine, mill, and production line: hard-hatted shipyard workers from the Baltic ports, grimy Silesian coal-haulers, occasionally a weary woman from the textile mills. "Crisis of Marxism" notwithstanding, such images still evoke spectres that loom powerfully in the smoggy depths of the Western political imagination. The intellectuals who stepped forth from the democratic and Catholic opposition to articulate the movement's aspirations and advise its leaders also captivate our attention, though for other reasons: linguistically and politically, they speak in Western tongues, and foreign journalists and scholars, relying on their insights and admiring (perhaps even envying) their eloquence, courage, and influence, tend unwittingly to attribute to them a role even larger than the undoubtedly significant one they actually played. Even in the age of high technology, the manufacturing engineer and the quality-control technician are less compelling figures, but their significance in Solidarity—especially at the enterprise and regional levels of the organization—was enormous, and nowhere was it more visible than in the movement toward self-management.

These young technicians and engineers were part of an army of cadres trained under Communist rule to staff Poland's expanding industrial base.[16] Often of peasant or worker origin, and posted to jobs where they earned no more than many of the production workers around them, they shared the full range of economic, political, and cultural grievances that inspired the rise of Solidarity. But temperament, education, and experience gave them some special sensitivities; like the engineers Veblen expected to find in the American corporation, they were appalled at the chaos and irrationality festering behind the facade of orderly planning in the economy, and they were positioned close enough to management to see that the strategic mistakes and venality of the Gierek team had only exacerbated the problems of a system desperately in need of structural reform. In the technical colleges they had attended they had studied rationalistic disciplines and, typically, adopted the technocratic outlook that all the Soviet-style regimes now promote (nominally, at least) under the rubric of "scientific-technical revolution"; on the job they faced the reality that in "actually existing socialism" political subservience and bureaucratic back-scratching count for more than technical competence or economic rationality.

In the 1970s as stratification patterns created by the postwar transformations began to rigidify, rates of social mobility had slowed. Younger engineers and technicians in particular found paths to career advancement blocked, often by senior colleagues with inferior educations and little expertise in the new technologies imported from the West; indeed, contrary to the image of technocracy the previous Polish administration had tried, with some success, to give itself, the tendency for key posts in economic enterprises to go to older people with lower qualifications "became more pronounced than attenuated under the Gierek regime."[17] Most galling of all, promotion continued to depend in large part on political criteria: under the *nomenklatura* system, all key personnel decisions remain subject to the approval of the pertinent party body.[18]

Before Solidarity, a large proportion of the young technical cadres—including many who later became active in the self-management movement—had responded to the situation by joining the party, sometimes as a purely pragmatic effort to "play the game," sometimes in hopes of fostering rationalization from within the system. (Some of the Network's key leaders even now confess that personally they are drawn more to technocratic and managerialist visions of the social order than to syndicalist or participatory models.) But by 1981 the incumbent authorities were so thoroughly discredited—so widely identified as defenders of a system irrational to the core—and the workers' movement so powerful and hungry for change, that support for reform seemed more likely to come from below than above. As part of the "socialist renewal" it was promising. The party leadership had made rhetorical commitments to economic reform and self-management, but the seemingly paralyzed regime had been unable to agree on any concrete proposal for serious reform; the draft plans slowly making their way through official channels in the winter and spring of 1981 were not notably bold or coherent to begin with, and the conservative bureaucratic apparatus was already succeeding in watering down their key provisions.

It was in this context that the Network was born and the self-management movement began to gather momentum. In March 1981 Milewski started to meet regularly with acquaintances from the Baltic shipyards and other large plants. They quickly agreed to challenge the notion that economic reform was not Solidarity's business by preparing and promoting a series of proposals for industrial reorganization. (In the original conception the self-management plan was to be only the first of many projects.) While most of the union was caught up in the crisis provoked by the police beatings at Bydgoszcz, the Network's founders—"a circle of enthusiasts," they called themselves—began crisscrossing Poland to seek out like-minded colleagues. A formal structure was established, with one flagship plant to represent each region of the country. With Milewski coordinating, the emerging group was soon churning out an imposing collection of documents about self-management—position papers, model by-laws and electoral statutes for workers' councils, and, most importantly, a "Draft Bill on the Social Enterprise," proffered as an alternative to the legislation the authorities had under consideration.

The Network's Plan

The keynote of the Network proposal was the concept of the "social enterprise," to contrast with the official category of "state enterprise" for the basic unit of the industrial economy.[19] The distinction gave rise to an extensive theoretical debate—full of references to old laws and the Polish constitution, but only rarely to the Marxist classics—between the movement and its official critics. The discussion was often obscure, but the underlying issue was clear enough: the Network wanted control of the means of production to rest in the hands of each enterprise's workforce, not those of the vanguard party or the state bureaucracy. The authorities were therefore right to regard this concept as a fundamental challenge to the system of authority on which their regime, like all the others descended from the Bolshevik Revolution, rested.

The enterprise envisioned in the Network's plan would have been governed, formally at least, in a highly democratic way. Solidarity as such would have had no privileged position within the self-management system. The ultimate authority was to be the plant workforce as a whole, expressing itself by majority vote—at a general meeting of all employees or (in large enterprises) of their elected delegates, or through a referendum. Ordinarily, the crew would delegate its authority to an employee council chosen in general, direct, and secret elections. (The traditional term "workers' council," which in Polish as in English has blue-collar connotations, was forsaken in favor of the more inclusive "employee council.") The councils would have had wide powers over all aspects of the enterprise's economic activity, organizational structure, and future development. The enterprise director would be hired by the council and could be fired by it or by referendum of the entire workforce: the director's role would, in principle, be that of "executor of the decisions of the organs of employee self-management."

The statute the Network drafted thus combined representative, plebiscitary, and participatory procedures. But the element of direct democracy—the active participation of rank-and-file workers in the governance of the enterprise—got little emphasis in the Network's discussions and appeals. One of the most striking features of the whole movement was the almost total absence of references to such lofty objectives as overcoming alienation, transcending the mental-manual division of labor, or enhancing the citizen-worker's sense of social efficacy—themes featured prominently in recent Western theoretical discussions of participatory democracy, as well as in the discourse of the New Left.[20] Neither the technocratically minded founders of the movement nor, it appears, the other activists and ordinary workers who came to support it gave much weight to the purportedly uplifting effects of collective decision making.

The emphasis, rather, was on rationality and effectiveness: the Network's case was built from the start on the premise that, in Polish conditions at least, enterprises would be run more sensibly and economically under workers' control than under the party-state's. In the West there is a widespread suspicion, shared even by many advocates of industrial democracy, that implementation of the idea in any large sense—that is, establishment of a system that would give workers power, not just influence, over "higher-level" (enterprise-wide and long-term) decisions as well as "lower-level" activity (day-to-day shopfloor operations)[21]—would necessarily entail some sacrifice of the efficiency expected of a well-ordered hierarchical structure. In Poland, as the Network saw things, the situation was reversed: there was nothing to lose, no existing efficiency to be jeopardized. Hierarchical control meant subordination to the party and state bureaucracies, which had come to represent nothing so much as corruption, incompetence, and waste. Managers appointed from above had stronger incentives to be loyal and submissive to their superiors than to run an effective operation, and even a dedicated executive could accomplish little when the enterprise was enmeshed in a "command economy" that no longer responded to commands but lacked any other effective steering mechanism.

The workers, on the other hand, were more likely (or so the proponents of self-management argued) to understand and respect the claims of rationality. They were, in the first place, beholden to no outside force putting its organizational or ideological interests above the collective's and society's welfare. Having learned from the crisis how high the price of poor planning and sloppy management could be, and who ultimately would pay it, they would be ready—or at least could be persuaded—to swallow the bitter pills that had to be taken to restore the economy's health. And since the Network's plan would make every enterprise financially as well as organizationally independent, each worker would have a direct material stake in making responsible decisions. (The economics of the Network proposal will be considered briefly below.)

For most participants in the struggle, then, self-management was above all a means, not an end—a means to overcoming the crisis of the Polish economy. To treat the Network's program as a call for "participatory democracy" is literally correct but many be misleading as to the movement's concerns. "Democratic managerialism" is a more apt characterization, for the assumption was always that the most important task of self-management would be to select the most competent professional available as enterprise director, and that the director would, in essence, run the enterprise. The movement's position was not that the masses possessed the expertise necessary to run an industrial economy effectively, but only that they had the ability and the motivation to recognize those who did. Few believed that the primary object—economic rationality—could be attained by entangling the workers in technical and financial discussions for which they had little preparation. The Network's draft law did put a long list of powers (including control over the enterprise's annual plan, acquisition and disposal of fixed assets, distribution of enterprise income, social welfare programs) within the competence of the employee councils, and had the plan been enacted as written, council delegates in some plants would no doubt have attempted aggressively to exercise these powers themselves. In most cases, however, the role of the council would probably have been primarily one of oversight (backed by the latent threat of veto) over policies developed by full-time managers. Self-management activists were especially anxious not to get stuck with responsibility for routine enterprise operations; at the Lenin Shipyard the committee laying the groundwork for self-management even modified the wording of the model plant code that the Network had drafted, in order to make clearer that such burdens would still fall on the shoulders of the administration, not of the workers' representatives.

Because the plan foresaw such a critical role for the factories' professional staff, the question of who would have the power to appoint or dismiss the enterprise director from the start overshadowed all other issues. From the point of view of a society all too familiar with the regime's cynical manipulation of the rhetoric of socialist democracy, the new councils seemed likely to end up as powerless as their post-1956 predecessors, no matter what other rights they might have on paper, if they lacked the power to hire and fire the plant's chief executive. The ruling party in effect shared the same assumption: it too treated the power of appointment as the crux of the controversy, even though much of its propaganda took the form of ideological disputation about the theory of ownership and the menace of what it called "group property." Both sides knew that whichever could choose the director would control the decisive voice in the life of the enterprise. A director indebted to the workers for his position would ultimately have to respect their preferences; one chosen through the usual procedures of the *nomenklatura* might make a more or less sincere effort to cooperate with the crew's representatives, but in the end could be expected to come down on the side of bureaucratic superiors.

The Network plan allowed the workers' council to choose the director on the basis of an open *konkurs,* a competition in which the qualifications and proposals of every candidate would be evaluated by representatives of the workforce. The designated director would be given a contract for a fixed period, but the council could remove the director before its expiration by rejecting the annual report, or at the end of the term by simply refusing to renew the contract; the enterprise workforce itself could remove the director at any time by referendum. The official draft law, on the other hand, stated that "the director of an enterprise is appointed and dismissed by the founding organ [ordinarily, the relevant industrial ministry], with the agreement of the Workers' Council"; the council could present its own nominees when the directorship was vacant, or request the removal of an incumbent with whom it was dissatisfied. While the somewhat ambiguous wording held out the prospect of negotiations over managerial appointments, it was clear that final authority would remain with the party-dominated central bureaucracy.

Economically, the Network's plan embodied what one Western economist has called an "almost [Milton-]Friedmanite faith in the virtue of markets and prices."[22] Most of its supporters saw self-management not as a necessary complement to the system of central economic planning, but as the foundation of an alternative to that system. That alternative was definitely not restoration of private ownership of the means of industrial production; most Polish workers, despite their pronounced distaste for what they had experienced as "socialism" and their envy of the living standards generated by the developed market economies, still viewed capitalism with considerable reserve, and restoring it was for almost everyone unimaginable in light of Poland's geography and history. (As a quip popular at the time put it, "Who would take over the Lenin Shipyard—the Lenin family?") Yet in its haste to get rid of the bureaucratic command economy, the Network would have made the free market the primary, if not the sole, mechanism of economic coordination. Enterprises were to function as independent entities, free of any direct state control. The operative principles were called the "three S's": *samorządność* (self-management), *samodzielność* (independence), and *samofinansowanie* (self-financing). Investment and production decisions were to be made with profitability as the chief criterion; they would be compiled and codified only in the enterprise's own plan and in its contracts with customers and suppliers.

The state would influence the economy solely by way of laws and "economic parameters" (taxes, tariffs, credits). Although the experts who prepared Solidarity's draft program had advocated a combination of self-management and democratized central planning, the Network, in its early pronouncements, scarcely mentioned the plan (or the party!). The Network's later and more elaborate position papers did call for a central plan to be established by a democratically elected parliament. But the plan would have been purely "indicative," as in the Western European economies; it was emphasized that "the central plan is a plan only for the government and cannot include any direct orders for the enterprises."[23]

In 1981, with the old economic mechanisms teetering on the brink of complete disintegration, "marketization" was in the air. Rooted in several generations of Polish economic thought, it was, to some degree, a feature of each of the more than half-dozen full-scale reform proposals then in circulation, including the state's. (Official publications even today present the "three S's" as the core of the reform.) The Network did not go as far as one group of Solidarity's economic advisers, who were calling for the activization of private capital. In insisting on absolute enterprise autonomy and downgrading all central mechanisms, the Network proposal did, however, constitute an extreme version of "market socialism."

From a strictly economic point of view, even advocates of the market might question the wisdom of an abrupt transition, especially at a moment of extraordinary economic dislocation. With hard currency, energy, and materials of all sorts in desperately short supply, it is not clear, to say the least, that throwing the task of resource allocation to the market would have produced economically or socially optimal results. Capitalist states typically move in the direction of increased central control during situations of crisis, and it could be argued that for all the failings of the central planners and ministries, the same logic held for Poland, at least until a modicum of stability could be restored to the economy. But the activists of the Network were not thinking in such categories and still reject the logic of this argument. In their view the center had shown itself incapable of mastering the situation. Once the enterprises were liberated from the tutelage of the bureaucracy and the good sense and energy of the workers were unleashed, the situation could only improve. Besides, politics, not economics, was the fundamental problem, as the activists saw it. They believed that they were facing a rare opportunity to displace a system that had failed them and the nation, and they could not afford to squander it in the probably vain hope of finding a better opportunity later.

Solidarity's Activists Take Up the Cause

The Network's initiative found a wide response, for others in Solidarity had been moving independently in the same direction. In Łódź, one of Poland's oldest industrial cities and the center of its textile industry, union leaders had been expressing interest in electing new workers' councils since the fall. Over the winter Zbigniew Bujak, leader of the Solidarity's Mazowsze (Warsaw) branch, did the same, and his regional organization sponsored a conference on the subject in early March. In the union press Jakubowicz and some of the other economic advisers began to publish articles and proposals about self-management. Party propaganda, too, had an effect: the official media were now actively promoting self-management as the key to the forthcoming economic reforms, and in a number of enterprises party organizations—hoping in some cases to enlist Solidarity's cooperation, in others to outflank the burgeoning union—were moving to create new councils or revive moribund ones.

So long as most union activists remained committed to the original conception of Solidarity as a trade union eschewing participatory entanglements and leaving policy initiatives to the authorities, the union's official bodies on the national level and in most regions continued to react warily to the rising discussion of self-management. But in the spring of 1981 Solidarity found itself at a strategic impasse. The police beating of union activists at Bydgoszcz in March had brought passions to a peak, but the expected climax never came: the last-minute agreements that averted the general strike for which the whole movement had mobilized were undoubtedly a relief to most Solidarity supporters, but they left the issues unresolved and the union frustrated, divided, and uncertain. In the aftermath a "crisis of identity" set in, in Jadwiga Staniszkis' phrase,[24] and more and more of the Solidarity's members and activists began to question the assumptions that had so far oriented its activity. With production figures plummeting, it seemed futile, if not downright counterproductive, to press short-term economic demands and to rely on the now familiar strike tactic. On the other hand, the political function Solidarity had envisaged for itself seemed equally unrealistic: Bydgoszcz was widely taken as confirmation that the authorities were more interested in obstructing and provoking the union than in dealing with it as a genuine partner entitled to a voice in the formulation of state policy and institutional reforms. In the eyes of most of the population, the legitimacy of party rule had all but disappeared, yet there was no plausible way to replace it. Solidarity seemed to be standing by passively as the fate of the nation hung in the balance: as Staniszkis argues, its power was enormous but useless, its day-to-day activities seemed to make little contribution to its long-term goals, and "self-limiting revolution" was becoming a formula for frustration.

For union officials at the factory and regional levels, the problem had an acute and personal dimension. In preparation for Solidarity's upcoming national congress, elections to lower leadership levels were getting under way, and the leaders who had emerged more or less spontaneously at the union's birth now had to face constituents wondering when and how the the August victory would yield some tangible improvement in their lives. For some ambitious militants—both incumbents and challengers—self-management provided an ideal platform: it allowed them to make a name for themselves at the local level (Solidarity-backed "founding committees for self-management" were now springing up in the factories); it addressed the most immediate source of popular frustration, the deteriorating economic situation; and, without explicitly challenging the principle of Communist rule (a step most Poles—whatever their private sentiments—would still at this time have considered dangerous) it gave vent to anti-party resentment.

By June of 1981, although Solidarity's national leadership still had no clear-cut position on the question of self-management and had made only half-hearted acknowledgment of the Network's existence, each day brought news of some new union body getting on board what was fast becoming a bandwagon in support of the Network's initiative. In Lower Silesia the regional committee countermanded a resolution (passed only months earlier) denouncing self-management as a sham and explicitly endorsed the Network. From regional conventions in Warsaw, Łódź, and elsewhere came programmatic proposals putting the struggle for self-management at the top of Solidarity's agenda. Resolutions in support of the idea poured forth in all directions—to the Sejm, to the Network, to the union leadership, to no one in particular. By the end of the spring, Alain Touraine's sociological teams discovered, self-management had become the principal topic of discussion among Solidarity activists.[25]

Even the authorities were forced to respond to this unanticipated change of mood among the unionists: in June the Social-Industrial Department of party Central Committee's staff sent out a secret (but soon leaked) bulletin warning party functionaries that the Network's ideas were taking hold in Solidarity and that it was "impossible to overestimate the dangers inherent" in them.[26] In a striking mixture of bureaucratic jargon and dogmatic rhetoric, the authors called for an immediate "politico-organizational and program-agitational counter-offensive" against a movement that, they spluttered, smacked of the Soviet Workers' Opposition, Yugoslav and Czech (1968) revisionism, contemporary bourgeois theory, and various other deviations. The columns of most official papers were soon filled with vituperative denunciations of a movement that the obviously frightened rulers plainly considered a serious threat.

In a few short months, then, self-management had moved from the fringes to the foreground of Solidarity's, and thus of Poland's, political stage. The idea had caught the fancy not only of young technical cadres like the Network's founders, but also, increasingly, of Solidarity activists from diverse backgrounds. For all the excitement, however, it was still not clear that the rank and file had been won over to the new cause. Among ordinary production workers, most observers agree, there remained considerable wariness about any form of institutional participation in the system of power. But as the movement developed, self-management's advocates found that some of their themes did strike a chord even among the skeptics, and these they began to emphasize more and more.

One such theme was the argument that self-management—and self-management alone—could stem the collapse of the national economy. By mid-1981, with lines growing ever longer and even necessities sometimes simply unavailable, economic reform was no longer just an abstract *desideratum,* the specter (if not yet the reality) of hunger now hung over the land. Public confidence in the capacities of the authorities, which had risen somewhat when the reputedly sincere and efficient General Jaruzelski had taken over as premier in February 1981, faded again as one official commission after another studied the crisis but no consistent policy seemed to emerge. Solidarity members debated whether it was unwillingness or inability (or both) that kept the regime from breaking with the old system of central control and allocation of resources, a system that was perceived with increasing clarity as the root of the crisis. The Network's original declarations had been remarkably dry and almost technical in tone, but with frustration mounting its spokesmen began to play on public emotion: "Without self-management," an orator at one of its sessions warned, "each of us, together with our families and loved ones, will fall into such hunger and destitution, dependence and servility as we have not known in the entire thousand years of our history."[27] The slogan of self-management was repeated over and over like an incantation; the concept seemed to take on almost magical properties as if it were some panacea for the Polish economy's many ills. The proclamation of a national conference of self-management activists called it "the only guarantee of Poland's escape from the crisis, the only way to relieve society from its daily uncertainty about the next day . . . . Self-management means a quick increase in the effectiveness of the economy, the liquidation of the total waste which as before remains the nightmare of the economy. . . . Self-management lets us see things as they are, not as they appear. Self-management is economic *raison d'etat.*"[28]

A case from Wrocław, in Lower Silesia, exemplifies the shift in the movement's tone. The struggle for self-management had begun there in the spring with a controversy over the appointment of a new director for one of the city's major factories. The plant's Solidarity committee and its experts had devised an elaborate scheme for screening candidates: each was subjected to a grueling round of psychological testing, expert evaluation, and public oral examinations, before a commission representing the workforce voted on a final choice. By midsummer, however, the emphasis had shifted from this meritocratic mania to more mundane matters. The regional union took up the struggle to force a hesitant ministry to approve the workers' choice (who turned out, after all the testing was completed, to be a popular engineer already serving on the factory's Solidarity committee), but the headlines on the leaflets with which local activists plastered the city revealed the pitch the union was now taking: "Hunger won't let us wait—" they read. "Self-management is our chance." (The enterprise in question made heavy construction equipment.)[29]

The other thread increasingly prominent in the campaign was the notion of self-management as a blow against the *nomenklatura* system and, by extension, against the party's monopoly of power. As the crisis sharpened, long latent antagonism toward the "reds" became ever more open and radical. Self-management's advocates found that even audiences otherwise unmoved began to respond when they raised the once-taboo question of the *nomenklatura*. And it was no longer simply a question of appointing qualified managers, instead of political hacks; now people were seeing self-management in a broader perspective, as a move against party rule as a whole. Even if the rulers could not be displaced altogether, there was growing sentiment that the crisis made it necessary and possible to put new limits on their power. Self-management was presented as a further step in what Western commentators have called the reconstruction of civil society, beyond the reach of the political apparatus.[30] In 1980 the party had been stripped of control over the unions; now the time had come to push it out of the industrial economy altogether. The official media's intemperate response to the Network's proposal seemed to confirm that the party was vulnerable to such an attack on its "material base." In the eyes of a deeply anti-Communist population, the reaction only enhanced the proposal's appeal.

Solidarity's National Leadership

The absence of other strategic alternatives, the manifest appeal of self-management to many activists, and the inroads the movement seemed to be making among the rank and file of the union finally pushed Solidarity's national leadership to endorse the Network's approach. In May and June the National Coordinating Commission (KKP) of Solidarity and its Presidium had issued several statements noting the growing movement and expressing a "positive attitude toward the creation of authentic self-management," but these conspicuously vague declarations had fallen short of the clear-cut endorsement the Network sought. In response, Network leaders, working behind the scenes with some of the many journalists and economists who were now gravitating toward their movement, organized a systematic campaign of pressure on union headquarters. Heeding a Network summons, regional union committees started binding their KKP delegates to fight for the self-management program, and in early July the Network flexed its new-found political muscle right at the leaders' doorstep by staging a conference-rally that drew some 1,000 activists from factories all over Poland to the conference hall of the Lenin Shipyard in Gdansk. Lech Walesa was invited to address the gathering, but the otherwise enthusiastic crowd was not pleased with his brief and uninspired address; in the discussion that followed the union chairman and his associates were roundly criticized for their "inertia" and "equivocation" over self-management. That very night Walesa personally telephoned a Gdansk acquaintance who was influential in the Network to ask for information about the growing movement and for advice about responding to it. Two days later the union chairman issued an unusual personal statement acknowledging criticism of the leadership's approach and suggesting a considerably more positive attitude toward self-management.

Meanwhile, a labor-management conflict at the Polish national airlines, LOT, raised the prospect that a full-scale national crisis over self-management might blow up spontaneously, in a way Solidarity's wary leaders (and the Network's as well) considered intolerably risky. The airline's managing director had recently retired, and its self-management body—in this case a pre-1980 "KSR" that had survived—won the backing of the local Solidarity for a plan to have the staff select his replacement. The government, referring to LOT's potential "strategic significance" (to the amusement of Poles familiar with the line's antiquated Soviet-made equipment), insisted on its own candidate, a general. When prolonged negotiations and a highly publicized warning strike that shut the airline down for four hours failed to break the impasse, the LOT workers scheduled an open-ended workstoppage.

A compromise designed to save face on both sides finally prevailed: the general got the job, the employees' choice was installed as his deputy and de facto chief executive officer, and the strike was averted. But the incident was yet another reminder to Solidarity's leaders that the self-management issue was becoming explosive and that the union still lacked a strong, coherent policy that would allow it to get out in front of a now-surging movement.

In this context the KKP assembled in late July for an unusually comprehensive review of the "the situation in the country and the union." By then a consensus had developed among most of the union's chief leaders and advisers: Solidarity would have to abandon its hesitations and make self-management the cornerstone of a more aggressive program for combating the crisis. There was little concrete political planning for the new initiative, and in the long discussion there were considerable implicit differences about the scope and meaning of the shift in policy, but nearly everyone addressing the session agreed that the old model of reactive, nonparticipatory trade-unionism had exhausted itself, and that self-management promised a new way out of the current impasse between union and society on the one hand and the party-state on the other.[31]

Culmination

Thus the construction of the self-management coalition was complete. An idea that had originally had little active support in Solidarity had now swept through the organization—first to disgruntled engineers and technicians, to other activists looking for new programmatic approaches, then down the hierarchy to the rank and file and finally up to the union's national leadership. The breadth of support self-management had acquired was reflected at Solidarity's National Congress in September 1981. With union representatives getting nowhere in their efforts to negotiate with the authorities over the shape of the forthcoming reform, the congress approved a militant resolution on the subject. By a vote of 856 to one, with one abstention, the delegates called on all union members to rise to the defense of self-management, demanded a national referendum on the issue, and threatened to challenge any plan the Sejm might adopt that did not live up to the union's expectations.

Broad as it had come to be, however, the self-management movement rested on what proved a fragile foundation. Behind the appearance of unity in support of the Network's demands lay some troubling contradictions, for the social forces that had converged around the slogan of self-management in fact had diverse priorities and some conflicting orientations. For the technocratic types who had played such a key role in launching the movement and for its economic advisers, self-management was above all a vehicle for rationalization, and to most of them rationality meant increased wage differentials, more realistic (i.e., higher) prices for many consumer goods, and the elimination of superfluous positions on factory payrolls—an objective that raised the specter of large-scale unemployment. Among the rank and file, however, an often uncritical enthusiasm for market mechanisms in the abstract coexisted uneasily with a deep-seated egalitarianism and an understandable fear of price increases and layoffs, whatever the rationale behind them. In 1981 these differences were scarcely acknowledged, let alone debated fully.[32] Had the Network's program somehow been implemented, however, they would inevitably have surfaced; it is easy to imagine a popular reaction against the reform, and with it bitter divisions within Solidarity or, at the enterprise level, between the union and the workers' councils.

None of this, of course, came to pass; self-management never got that far. The problems that the movement faced in the fall of 1981 were of a different order: they involved self-management not as an institution, but as a strategy. Even as the delegates to the union congress were enshrining self-management in Solidarity's program, the movement that had put the issue on the agenda was already slowing. In the union's last months of legality, interest in the issue of worker participation in factory management cooled noticeably. No one repudiated the idea, and a hard core of enthusiasts continued to organize around it. Self-management, however, had been advertised as something more than just another desirable reform—it had been packaged as the key that would open to resolution of the union's and the nation's dilemmas. When this promise began to lose its plausibility—as, I believe, it was bound to—enthusiasm for self-management waned.

The problem that began to catch up with the self-management movement was that in the face of a crisis as profound, multifaceted, and intractable as Poland's, it was simply unable to fulfill the claims on which its appeal was based. As we have seen, few in Poland had shown much interest in employee participation as an end in itself; most of the movement's supporters had been drawn to the Network's proposal on instrumental and conjunctural grounds as a remedy for a collapsing economy and as a strategem for liberating new social space from the party. By late summer of 1981 it was becoming clear that in both respects the hopes vested in the self-management plan had been misplaced, or at least exaggerated.

The first difficulty was economic. Contrary to the rhetoric of some of its advocates, self-management was no cure-all, certainly not in the short run; letting workers elect directors would not put meat on Polish tables, or pay off the nation's crushing foreign debt, or restore the flow of imported parts on which the manufacturing sector had grown dependent. At best, self-management, and the shift to market mechanisms that the Network's version of it entailed, could produce positive results over the medium term, and even then only as part of a more comprehensive program of economic stabilization and reconstruction. But with conditions deteriorating palpably over the summer, the patience of the Poles was wearing thin and tempers were growing short. In an account that appeared in the Solidarity weekly,[33] a union leader from Wrocław presents a revealing vignette. Returning home from the late-July session at which the KKP had made the momentous decision to adopt the self-management strategy, and setting out to mobilize the rank and file behind the new approach, they found the atmosphere in the factories explosive. Union offices were deluged with phone calls, but it was not in fact self-management that the unionists' constituents were exercised about—it was the latest round of food-ration cuts the authorities had just announced.

The Wrocław leaders, like other Solidarity activists all over Poland, struggled to channel popular anger away from the supply situation and to turn it into enthusiasm for the management reforms the union was now backing, for there was a consensus among responsible unionists that direct confrontation over the food question would be dangerous and unproductive. In this sense self-management was yet another of the "surrogate conflicts" that marked the whole history of Poland's "self-limiting revolution."[34] But the substitution did not work very well, for self-management was a demand too abstract and indirect to engage for long the emotions of people exhausted and enraged by an economic crisis that was now all too immediate.

The other dimension of the problem was political. Neither the Network nor the Solidarity leadership had devoted much thought to the likely reaction of the beneficiaries of the *nomenklatura* to what was openly advertised as a program to break that system's back; the specific strategies and tactics that would be needed to win such a radical reform had not been developed. Perhaps because official inertia in the face of crisis had convinced Solidarity's strategists of the regime's impotence, they paid little heed to its repeated and unequivocal insistence that self-management in the Network's sense could never be accepted. Implicitly, the popular assumption was that a movement that had already won one "impossible" concession—free trade unions—could surely win another the same way, by the sheer force of its determination, solidarity, and moral authority.

This time, however, the party's prerogatives were on the line: self-management in the form Solidarity now sought threatened the power and privileges of the ruling elite and its dependents even more directly (if not ultimately more seriously) than independent unions. Though many rank-and-file Communists and some local party organizations supported the Network's initiative, the party elite closed ranks against the threat. On this occasion the usual intra-organizational splits were scarcely visible; even prominent party "liberals" denounced the Network's line as "demagogy, an anti-worker trick of anti-socialist character."[35] And while Soviet commentaries at this stage did not focus in detail on the self-management issue, it is safe to assume that the qualified backing the Kremlin offered the Polish leaders after the July congress of the PUWP would have evaporated quickly if the Polish comrades even contemplated serious concessions over something as fundamental to the structure of Soviet-type systems as the *nomenklatura*.

Thus the notion that self-management might serve as a roundabout way of setting new limits on party power, without a direct confrontation over control of the state, came to seem steadily less realistic as the weeks went by and the authorities showed no sign of caving in on the issue. One might, of course, argue that the strategy had *never* been a realistic one; the important point here is that some who had previously been willing to try it were now losing their faith. In the Sejm work continued on legislation about self-management and the state enterprise—official proposals that would have given workforce councils wide but largely consultative powers and left the appointment of managers in the hands of the bureaucracy. The parliamentary subcommittee hearing the bills did allow the participation of representatives of Solidarity, the Network, and other organizations, and informally some of the committee's more independent members expressed sympathy for the Network's bold and direct approach, but on fundamental issues no concessions were forthcoming. In September, after the first half of the Solidarity congress, its all-but-unanimous endorsement of self-management, and its provocative call to workers elsewhere in the Soviet camp to follow the Polish example, the party's position seemed even to stiffen. The Soviets, meanwhile, attacked the congress as an "anti-Soviet orgy,"[36] and new rumors of economic blackmail or military intervention from the East began to bubble up.

In the face of these hard realities, moods in Solidarity were evolving quickly. The movement's most outspoken activists—both nationalistically inclined "fundamentalists" and secular radicals—moved closer to advocacy of an outright challenge to the party's political monopoly, while "pragmatists" committed to the strategy of self-limitation redoubled their efforts to find some common ground with the authorities. Self-management, in a sense, fell between two stools; both of these broad currents within the union were in support of the Network's plan, but for neither of them was it an issue that justified a full-scale confrontation.

Sizing up the situation, Wałesa and his closest associates decided in effect to disregard the resolution of the Solidarity congress and to settle the issue on the best terms practically available. With the Sejm on the verge of approving a proposal close to the government's draft, the union's negotiators abruptly proposed a compromise, one that fell well short of the Network's demands. In particular, they agreed to a clause that allowed the government to retain the power to name the management in enterprises "of fundamental significance" in the national economy. The list of such enterprises was to be negotiated between the Council of Ministers and the union, and in other enterprises the workforce would hold the initiative in the selection of the plant director, but it seemed clear to most observers that the compromise meant that the authorities would keep control of key firms throughout the heavy industrial and extractive sectors. And these, of course, constituted the backbone of Solidarity and of the self-management movement.

The settlement, approved at a poorly attended meeting of the Presidium of Solidarity's National Commission between sessions of the union's congress, provoked a storm of controversy.[37] Whatever its merits in terms of political realism, the deal failed to take account of what Karol Modzelewski called the "psychic engagement" that the union, and especially its activists, had made over the preceding months in the Network's radical plan. After several days of heated rhetoric, the union congress stopped just short of repudiating the deal, but it did denounce several aspects of the new legislation and issue a vague call for a referendum in the factories on disputed provisions. The most important political result, however, was a widespread sense of disappointment and disorientation among the movement's activists.

As suggested above, the struggle for self-management was flagging even before the compromise; afterward, it faded quickly from the headlines. The new system was to come into being at the start of 1982, and workers in some plants did begin to elect their councils and make preparations for taking over management. In surveys support for the idea of a self-managed economy remained high,[38] but the cause no longer commanded the enthusiasm it once had: in many enterprises in the last months of 1981, the workers' committees charged with preparing for self-management had trouble mustering a quorum for meetings. A National Federation of Self-Managements, more radical and more independent of the Solidarity leadership than the Network, attempted to coordinate what was left of the movement and to push for the referendum the union congress had proposed, but its success in most areas was limited. Some of its leaders—notably the anthropologist Kowalewski (who has since become a Trotskyist activist in the West) tried to give the movement a more revolutionary thrust as the process of political polarization accelerated; indeed, his proposals for "active strikes" (wherein workers would not shut down their workplaces, but instead maintain production and decide for themselves how the output would be distributed) and for "workers' guards" to defend occupied plants from interference attracted considerable attention.[39]

On the whole, however, participants in a conference on self-management convened in November 1981 by the Solidarity leadership agreed that the movement was in trouble. Only in some 15–20 percent of workplaces, their reports suggested, were the workers making concrete preparations to use such powers as the new laws gave them, and little enthusiasm was to be seen. Henryk Wujec, the mathematician and former KOR activist who reported to the gathering from the Mazowsze (Warsaw) region, summed up the situation: back in the summer, he recalled, "it seemed to us that self-management would begin to develop on its own, as had happened in the case of the union. It turned out that it's not so simple. The idea has, as it were, lost its dynamism." Jacek Merkel, a cofounder of the Network, newly elected member of Solidarity's National Commission, and organizer of the conference, concluded that what was most important was that "the National Commission understand that it has lived up to now in the grip of the myth of self-management. Sometimes it seems as if the very word self-management would automatically resolve a lot of issues. That way things are a lot more comfortable and seemingly more secure, but reality is what it is."[40]

Afterword

Although some of Jaruzelski's moderate advisers apparently urged him to leave the new self-management system intact when he launched the assault on Solidarity on December 13, 1981, in fact the general was not so foolish. The proclamation of martial law limited the implementation of the September 1981 laws, putting the workers' councils, like every other independent social organization, in a state of suspension. The legislation was not repealed, however, and beginning in 1983 the councils were gradually permitted to resume activity. Today the authorities report that councils have been installed in over 90 percent of the eligible enterprises.

But in a political context transformed by the suppression of Solidarity, self-management is not at all what the 1981 movement envisioned. Amendments to the legislation have enhanced the directors' power to overrule the decisions of the councils, and the list of firms where the regime retains the right to appoint the director—a list that was supposed to be negotiated with the unions—was imposed unilaterally by the state: it totals no fewer than 1,400 enterprises. Recently some of the councils' powers over enterprise social-welfare programs have been transferred to the new official unions, which the regime is blatantly attempting to bolster as an alternative both to Solidarity and to the less reliable self-management groups. The authority of the councils has been further undermined by a renewed campaign to recombine enterprises into larger bureaucratic entities, where the work crews have no effective voice.

Although it is difficult to generalize—there has been considerable fluidity and diversity in the situation, and detailed information is hard to come by—the consensus among independent observers is that most of the councils permitted in the post-Solidarity period are as much a sham as those that preceded them before 1980. According to a report issued by the Polish Sociological Association in 1985, the majority of new self-management bodies have adopted an "attitude of passivity and submission to management,"[41] and one of the best-informed of the Western correspondents in Warsaw estimates that only 10 percent of the elected councils, nationwide, have "shown the will to use their wide-ranging management prerogatives."[42] Solidarity's experts compare the councils they call "decisionally inactive"—in their view, the large majority—to the discredited institutions of the 1960s and 1970s:

> There is not much one can say about the role and functions of the councils dominated by the party and administration beyond what we already know from the KSR-ian past. . . . Transforming themselves quite quickly into a facade of industrial democracy, they carry out the routine functions of formal confirmation of plans, they willingly identify themselves with other "socio-political organizations" [a familiar euphemism

for the party and associated organizations], at times they become the terrain for contests between (the latter) and the administration of the enterprise. The crews get nothing useful from them.[43]

Not surprisingly, in view of the character of most of the councils, public opinion polls reveal widespread indifference to them. The already numerous surveys on the subject—as always, a topic of great interest to Polish sociologists—suggest that "people's interest in the self-management councils is very weak and clearly in decline," as the Polish Sociological Association's summary puts it.[44] In one widely noted study prepared by the Central Committee's Institute of Fundamental Problems of Marxism-Leninism, fewer than 30 percent of the workers surveyed reported that they were familiar with the "rights, possibilities, and tasks of self-management," could say what issues their employee councils were concerned with at the time, or could name more than a few of the council members.[45] In personal conversations workers from several major enterprises told me that they had no idea how their "representatives" had been "elected."

Those councils that are genuinely independent and effective, however, have far more symbolic and political importance than their numbers suggest, for they constitute small islands of real, albeit limited, working-class autonomy—remainders, and therefore reminders, of the heady days of Solidarity's legal existence. Some outspoken veterans of the 1981 movement are boycotting the self-management institutions altogether under present conditions, but Lech Wałęsa and the Solidarity underground leadership, who have so far discouraged any involvement with the new officially chartered unions, have publicly endorsed participation in self-management in certain circumstances.[46] At some plants slates of activists more or less clearly identified with Solidarity traditions have swept to victory in enterprise elections. In a few cases—most notably Huta Warszawa, the Warsaw steel works that has become a bastion of support for the independent union—these councils have raised broad challenges to the plans of appointed management and its ministerial superiors, and even taken stands on a variety of public issues. More often, the active councils play a quasi-trade-union role, exposing management abuses, defending mistreated individuals, and bargaining over the distribution of wages and bonuses. The workers' council at the Elana fiber plant in Torun has at least twice taken the initiative to recreate a new version of something like the old Network by calling meetings of representatives of self-management at large enterprises from all over Poland, but each time the authorities have ordered plant management to forbid any such convocation.

These independent councils help to sustain the morale of Poland's weary workers, and in the country's still volatile political situation they may yet play a significant role in the reconstruction of a mass movement capable of forcing change upon the regime. The social forces that turned to self-management in 1981 have hardly disappeared, and the grievances the self-management movement attempted to address—the frustration and resentment that political mismanagement of the economy engenders—are all the more acute today. As an ideal, self-management retains significant popular support: one recent independent survey of employees in heavy industry found that fully 87 percent of the sample supported the introduction of "full workers' self-management." (Only 56.25 percent, by contrast, favored an enhanced role for the church, and 78.1 percent supported truly free elections to the Sejm.)[47] Many of the numerous political groupings that have sprouted in the underground in recent years have incorporated self-management into their platforms.[48]

But an ideal, no matter how broadly accepted, rarely inspires large-scale political activity unless its supporters sense both a need and an opportunity to realize their vision. With the Polish economy losing ground again after several years of slight relative improvement, and the economic reform (such as it was) being eroded by a resurgent bureaucracy, the problems self-management purports to remedy obviously remain. But the chances of the new workers' councils accomplishing much in rebuilding Polish industry seem slight. It was Solidarity that created the space in which the self-management movement was born, and Solidarity's backing that gave it its political muscle. With Solidarity driven into the margins, the councils now stand alone, facing the determined efforts of ministers, managers, party officials, and leaders of the new unions to undermine their autonomy and limit their scope. Without the protection of a union with the will, strength, and independence to stand up to the authorities, there is little likelihood that the surviving councils can fulfill the hopes that many Polish workers for a time vested in the idea of self-management. But for now, some of the councils are helping to keep the struggle alive. There will surely come a time when the Polish working class will find the strength to return to the offensive, and it may well be that self-management will again have a place on their banners.

Notes

1. In a major survey conducted in December 1980 researchers from the Polish Academy of Sciences examining popular "visions of the social order" found 57 percent of their sample "positively in favor" of a system of "full self-management of enterprises," and another 28.7 percent "rather in favor." See Lena Kolarska and Andrzej Rychard, "Visions of the Social Order," Part 3 of "Polacy '80," in *Sisyphus* 3 (1982):207. (This issue of *Sisyphus*, a Warsaw sociological journal, was in English. Wherever possible, citations here will be to English-language translations of Polish materials.)

2. Międzyzakładowa Komisja Założycielska, *Aktualny Program Dzialania NSZZ* (Gdansk, September 5, 1980). A somewhat different translation appears in *Labour Focus on Eastern Europe* 4, nos. 1–3 (Spring–Autumn 1980):48–49. In the Gdańsk Agreements the references to self-management are in the section entitled "With regard to Point 6"; for one of the many available translations see A. Kemp-Welch, ed. and trans., *The Birth of Solidarity: The Gdańsk Negotiations, 1980* (London: Macmillan, 1983), 172. On the discussions that produced this part of the accord, see pp. 153–54 of the same volume for the comments of Tadeusz Kowalik (one of the "experts" who helped to negotiate for the workers) in his memoir on "Experts and the Working Group."

3. In Polish the same word (*samorząd*—literally, "self-rule") is used both for workplace self-management and for the more diffuse concept of self-government. Both translations will be used here, depending on the context. For a more detailed discussion of the dynamics that pushed Solidarity toward self-management in mid-1981, see Henry Norr, " Solidarity and Self-Management, May–July 1981," *Poland Watch* 7 (1985):97–122, and my book, forthcoming from Cornell University Press.

4. David S. Mason, *Public Opinion and Political Change in Poland, 1980–1982* (Cambridge: Cambridge University Press, 1985), provides a comprehensive review of the available survey data. On changing views of self-management, see esp. p. 96, table 4.4; p. 122, table 5.6; and p. 180, table 7.12.

5. The principal sources are *Tygodnik Solidarność*, the weekly paper the union began to publish in April 1981, and *AS* (Agencja Prasowa Solidarność), the press packets that a union agency issued every few days during 1981. The latter consists of protocols of leadership meetings, documents, reports on local events, studies by experts advising the union at the regional as well as national level, and excerpts from Solidarity's vast, fascinating, and so far little studied regional and factory press.

6. Thanks go to the International Research and Exchanges Board for the grant that made the trip possible.

7. See, e.g., Jan T. Gross's "Editor's Preface" to Jadwiga Staniszkis, *Poland's Self-Limiting Revolution* (Princeton: Princeton University Press, 1984), x.

8. See, for instance, the stories recounted by Henryka Krzywonos, the Gdańsk train-driver-turned-Solidarity-official, in Jean-Yves Potel, *The Promise of Solidarity* (New York: Praeger, 1982), 188–89.

9. Personalism, a movement associated with the French theologians Jacques Maritain and Emmanuel Mounier, has exercised enormous influence in Poland, despite the traditional conservatism of the Polish church. Not surprisingly, the Catholic groups and publications that were part of this trend were also those most directly linked to Solidarity. See Stefania Szlek Miller, "Catholic Personalism and Pluralist Democracy in Poland," *Canadian Slavonic Papers* 25, no. 3 (Sept. 1983):425–39; John Hellman, "John Paul II and the Personalist Movement," *Cross Currents* 30, no. 4 (Winter 1980–81):401–19; and Carl Marzani, "The Vatican as Left Ally?" *Monthly Review* 34; no. 3 (July–Aug. 1982):1–42, esp. 23–27.

10. The classic sources for the perspective that came to be associated with KOR are Leszek Kołakowski, "Hope and Hopelessness," *Survey* 17, no. 3 (80) (1971):37–52; Adam Michnik, "The New Evolutionism," *Survey* 22, nos. 3–4

(100–101) (1976):267–77; and Jacek Kuroń, "Reflections on a Program of Action," *Polish Review* 22, no. 3 (1977):51–69. Among secondary sources see especially Jacques Rupnik, "Dissent in Poland, 1968–78: The End of Revisionism and the Rebirth of Civil Society," in Rudolf L. Tokes, ed., *Opposition in Eastern Europe* (Baltimore: Johns Hopkins University Press, 1979), 60–112; Andrew Arato, "Civil Society Against the State: Poland, 1980–81," *Telos* 47 (Spring 1981):25–47; and idem, "Empire vs. Civil Society: Poland 1981–82," *Telos* 50 (Winter 1981–82):19–48.

11. Among Western sources, Albert Szymanski's *Class Struggle in Socialist Poland* (New York: Praeger, 1984) is an egregious example of this kind of interpretation of the political dynamics of Solidarity, although it does not focus specifically on the issue of self-management.

12. Excerpts of the draft program, introduced and translated by Marta Petrusewicz, appeared in *Socialist Review* 59 (Sept.–Oct. 1981):159–79. Full translations are available in Peter Raina, *Poland '81: Towards Social Renewal* (London: George Allen & Unwin, 1985), 172–97, and Roman Stefanowski, comp., *Poland: A Chronology of Events, February–July 1981* (New York: Radio Free Europe Research, March 5, 1982), 147–70. Raina's book, like his two previous anthologies of documents from the Polish opposition, is a valuable compendium; Radio Free Europe's periodic chronologies, along with its regular background and situation reports, also constitute a useful and generally reliable source.

13. Wojciech Arkuszewski and Piotr Rachtan, "Robotnik" (an interview with the bulletin's editors), *Tygodnik Solidarność* 2 (April 10, 1981).

14. From "Co dalej?" *Robotnik* 78 (Aug. 27, 1981), translated as "One Year After August—What Shall We Do Next?" *Labour Focus on Eastern Europe* 5; nos. 1–2 (Spring 1982):15–19.

15. Milewski, who happened to be abroad on Dec. 13, 1981, has since been the banned union's official representative in the West.

16. At the end of World War II there were only about 7,000 engineers in Poland. George Kolankiewicz, "The Technical Intelligentsia," in David Lane and Kolankiewicz, *Social Groups in Polish Society* (New York: Columbia University Press, 1973), 183. By 1980, according to official Polish data, there were 355,985 engineers of one sort or another working in the socialized sector of the economy. *Rocznik Statystyczny 1984* (Warsaw: Główny Urząd Statystyczny, 1984), 62; table 11(94). On the sociology and political history of the Polish engineering profession, see (besides Kolankiewicz, 180–232) Alexander Matejko, *Social Change and Stratification in Eastern Europe* (New York: Praeger, 1974), 163–69, and two recent, so far unpublished works by Michael D. Kennedy, "Professionals and Power in Polish Society" (Ph.D. diss., Department of Sociology, University of North Carolina at Chapel Hill, 1985), esp. ch. 5, and "Polish Engineers' Participation in the Solidarity Movement" (Sept. 12, 1985), a revised version of a paper presented at the 1985 annual meeting of the American Sociological Association.

17. Jean Woodall, *The Socialist Corporation and Technocratic Power* (Cambridge: Cambridge University Press, 1982), 147 and ch. 5, passim. On the slowdown in rates of social mobility, see Krzysztof Zagórski, "Transformations of Social Structure and Social Mobility in Poland," in Kazimierz Słomczyński and Tadeusz Krauze, *Class Structure and Social Mobility in Poland* (White Plains,

N.Y.: Sharpe, 1978), 61–80; and Walter D. Connor, *Socialism, Politics, and Equality* (New York: Columbia University Press, 1979), chs. 4 and 5.

18. An official document formalizing the *nomenklatura* and identifying the specific positions to be controlled by various levels of the party hierarchy was adopted by the Politburo of the ruling Polish United Workers Party (PUWP) in 1972. It was first published as an annex to Thomas Lowit, "Y a-t-il des Etats en Europe de l'Est?" *Revue Francaise de Sociologie*, 20, no. 3 (July–Sept. 1979):431–66. An English translation appeared in *Labour Focus on Eastern Europe* 4, nos. 4–6 (1982):55–56.

19. The text of the Network's draft appeared in *AS* 19:308–10. Excerpts are translated in the excellent anthology edited by Stan Persky and Henry Flam, *The Solidarity Sourcebook* (Vancouver, B.C.: New Star, 1982), 183–85. See also the discussion in Domenico Mario Nuti, "Poland: Economic Collapse and Socialist Renewal," *New Left Review* 130 (Nov.–Dec. 1981):23–36.

20. See Michael Poole's useful survey in "Theories of Industrial Democracy: The Emerging Synthesis," *The Sociological Review* n.s. 30, no. 2 (May 1982):181–207. Poole (182–85) locates the works of Paul Blumberg and Carole Pateman in a tradition of "developmental" or "educative" democracy that he traces back to John Stuart Mill.

21. These distinctions are drawn from Carole Pateman, *Participation and Democratic Theory* (Cambridge: Cambridge University Press, 1970), 67–73 and passim.

22. Nuti, "Poland," 30. See also George Kolankiewicz, "Employee Self-Management and Socialist Trade-Unionism," in Jean Woodall, ed., *Policy and Politics in Contemporary Poland* (London: Frances Pinter, 1982), 141.

23. *AS* 34:302.

24. Staniszkis, *Self-Limiting Revolution*, 21–22.

25. Alain Touraine et al., *Solidarité* (Paris: Fayard, 1982), 144.

26. A translation of this revealing document appears in *Uncensored Poland* (bulletin of the U.K. Information Centre for Polish Affairs) 11 (Aug. 4, 1981):12–15.

27. Józef Kuśmierek, "Why Now?" (speech at a Network meeting in June), translated in *Intercontinental Press*, Sept. 7, 1981, 878–79.

28. *AS* 28:304.

29. On the evolution of the union line in Wrocław (in this respect a microcosm of the whole union), see especially J. Koziński et al., "Konkurs na dyrektora," *Tygodnik Solidarność* 18 (July 31, 1981), and Jan Waszkiewicz, "Głodni ale samorządni" (Hungry but Self-Governing), *Tygodnik Solidarność* 21 (Aug. 21, 1981).

30. Arato in particular had developed this interpretation of the strategy of the Polish opposition and the significance of Solidarity. See n. 10 above.

31. In an unusual move the KKP, on Wałęsa's suggestion, had the transcript of its discussion published—see "O sytuacji w Kraju i Związku," a special supplement to *Tygodnik Solidarność* 19 (Aug. 7, 1981). Timothy Garton Ash, whose book *The Polish Revolution* (New York: Scribner's, 1984) is the best overall introduction to the Solidarity phenomenon, rightly perceives the pivotal character

of the KKP's July session—see 184-94. Extensive excerpts from the proceedings appear in French in *Les Temps Modernes* 445-46 (Aug.-Sept. 1983):406-26.

32. From the point of view of Western democrats, reluctance to come to grips with political differences within the movement was one of Solidarity's less appealing traits. Participants in the organization, however, defend this "solidarism" as a conscious and necessary response to the danger of fragmentation that their massive and socially variegated movement inevitably faced, especially given the unrelenting pressure of a hostile and manipulative regime. In part, of course, the avoidance of political debate was also a function of the immaturity of an organization that few had even dreamed of a year earlier and of the political inexperience of a generation raised in a system that made a mockery of the slogan of "socialist democracy." On a deeper level, however, Solidarity's solidarism may also mirror a surrounding political culture built more around moral values than articulated interests. See Staniszkis, *Self-Limiting Revolution,* 22, and Rudolf Jaworski, "History and Tradition in Contemporary Poland," *East European Quarterly* 19, no. 3 (Sept. 1985):349-62. Some critically minded Solidarity militants attempted to encourage political differentiation and the more open articulation of interests within the movement. See, e.g., Jan Lityński, "Dyskusja nad programem—czas zacząć się różnić?" *Robotnik* 75 (June 12, 1981).

33. Waszkiewicz, "Głodni" (n. 29 above).

34. Staniszkis, *Self-Limiting Revolution,* 73.

35. The phrase is from Edward Skrzypczak, the newly installed party chief at the large Cegielski works in Poznań, addressing the party's Extraordinary Ninth Congress—*IX Nadzwyczajny Zjazd PZPR: Stenogram z obrad plenarnych* (Warsaw: Książka i Wiedza, 1983), 615. Skrzypczak's attitude is all the more telling in that by all accounts he was in many ways a sincere reformist, who was removed from his local position and from the Central Committee shortly after the proclamation of martial law.

36. *Pravda,* Sept. 11, 1981.

37. *AS* 40:200-212.

38. Mason, *Public Opinion,* 180.

39. On the National Federation, and the "Lublin Group" of radical self-management activists that initiated it, see especially Jean-Yves Potel, "La revendication autogestionnaire dans la Pologne de Solidarité," *Sociologie du Travail* 3 (1982); "Interview with Henryk Szlajfer," *Intercontinental Press* (Sept. 7, 1981):876-78, and Zbigniew Kowalewski, "Solidarnosc on the Eve," *Labour Focus on Eastern Europe* 5, nos. 1-2 (1982):25-29. In my view the importance of this current, which had significant influence in only a few regions and enterprises, is sometimes exaggerated, especially by left-leaning Western observers.

40. Merkel, "Krajobraz przez bitwą," *Tygodnik Solidarność* 35 and 36 (Nov. 27 and Dec. 4, 1981).

41. Jerzy Osiatyński, Włodzimierz Panków, and Michał Fedorowicz, *Samorzad w gospodarczej polskiej 1981-85* (Warsaw: Polskie Towarzystwo Socjologiczne, Oddział Warszawski, 1985). Not having access to the report itself, I have relied on a digest published in *Tygodnik Mazowsze* 147 (November 21, 1985).

42. Christopher Bobinski, *Financial Times,* Sept. 24, 1985.

43. *Polska 5 lat po sierpniu* (Warsaw: Miedzyzakładowa Struktura Solidarności, 1985), 65—a report prepared for Wałęsa by a panel of anonymous but reputedly distinguished experts on the occasion of the fifth anniversary of the birth of Solidarity, includes an extended discussion of the self-management problem; excerpts appear as "La Pologne, Cinq Ans Après," *Autogestions* 22 (1985):30-40.

44. Osiatyński, Panków, and Fedorowicz, *Samorząd* (note 41 above).

45. Zdzisław Malak, "Samorząd—co o nim myślą?" *Polityka* 31 (July 30, 1983):4.

46. For Wałęsa's 1984 statement, and a taste of vigorous debate in the Polish underground press about the potential and limitations of the present self-management system, see "Three Articles on Workers' Self-Management," *Radio Free Europe Research—Polish Samizdat Extracts* 7A (Sept. 7, 1984); "A Chance for Self-Management: An Interview with Henryk Wujec," "The Position of the Steelworkers' Clandestine Committee on Workers' Self-Management," and "Self-Management: It Should Be Worth It," all in *Radio Free Europe Research—Polish Underground Extracts* 9 (June 14, 1985):3-13; and "We Decided to Give It a Try—A Conversation with an Activist in the Workers' Self-Management Council in Polfa," in ibid. 13 (Sept. 11, 1985):17-20.

47. Preliminary results of the poll are reported by Janusz Bugajski, "Polish Workers Express Their Opinion," *Radio Free Europe Research—Poland Situation Report* 16 (Oct. 11, 1985), from the summer 1985 issue of the underground journal *Obecność*. The survey encompassed workers at a number of major industrial complexes; the results reported so far are apparently based mainly on data from the Warski shipyard in Szczecin, but these are said to be representative of the whole panel.

48. Teresa Hanicka, "Political Groups in the Polish Underground," *Radio Free Europe Research—Background Report* 118 (Oct. 14, 1985), provides a convenient survey of eleven of the explicitly political organizations (as distinguished from the underground *union* bodies).

10

THE INSTITUTION OF DEMOCRATIC REFORMS IN THE CHINESE ENTERPRISE SINCE 1978

Jeanne L. Wilson

The People's Republic of China has undergone dramatic changes since the death of Mao Zedong and the convocation of the landmark Third Party Plenum of the Eleventh Party Congress in November 1978. Although not unchallenged, Deng Xiaoping's consolidation of political power in late 1978 has enabled him to launch a series of reforms that seek to enact far-reaching modifications in the social, political, and economic structure of Chinese society. Instituted in many instances as an explicit rejection of policies pursued during the Maoist era, the post-1978 reforms have given a high priority to goals of political institutionalization and economic modernization. Under Deng Xiaoping's guiding influence, the Chinese Communist Party has embarked on a course of internal self-criticism and rectification designed to purge the Party of Maoist sympathizers, dislodge the geriatric old guard, and elevate a younger, better educated generation of cadres to political leadership. Changes instituted in the economic organization of Chinese society have been extensive. The institution of the agricultural responsibility system in the Chinese countryside has been accompanied by the dismantling of collective production at the level of the production team in favor of a system of household contracting of production. Chinese experimentation with industrial reform, characterized by a decentralization of decision making and increased reliance on the market mechanism, received a go-ahead for nation-wide implementation at the Third Plenum of the Twelfth Party Congress in October 1984.

The efforts of the Chinese leadership to set China upon a new course have been accompanied by an increased interest in the concept of societal democratization. "Without democracy," according to Deng Xiaoping, "there can be no socialism."[1] Here too a series of reforms have been enacted, designed to set limits on the capricious display of political power and encourage a more pluralist expression of interests in Chinese society. Among the measures taken to strengthen Chinese democracy, the institution of forms of democracy within the workplace has figured prominently. The subject of this chapter is the Chinese experience with democratic management and the implementation of worker participation in the post-1978 period. The first section of the chapter deals with the theoretical rationale employed for instituting democratic management in the enterprise. The second section then turns to the application of forms of democratic management in practice. The third section examines noninstitutional forms of worker participation. The chapter concludes with a discussion of the Chinese experience with democratic management since 1978 in a historical and comparative context.

The post-1978 process of democratic reform in the enterprise is still in an incipient stage of development that has been marked by considerable fluctuation in policy initiatives and a certain inconsistency in application. Like the broader reform movement of which it forms a component, the attempt to institute forms of democratic management seems to have been guided less by the presence of a master plan than by a commitment to working out generalized goals through experimentation and practice. Nonetheless, an underlying aim of the Chinese leadership in enterprise democratization has been to redress a perceived imbalance between the democratic and the centralist aspects of democratic centralism by directing a greater emphasis to the democratic side of the equation. Current Chinese policy in no way evinces a loss of faith in democratic centralism as an organizational precept nor in the leadership role of the Chinese Communist Party (CCP) as the final arbiter of decisions. The Chinese leadership adheres to standard Marxist-Leninist doctrine in viewing the relationship between the CCP and the Chinese people as governed by a mutual correspondence of interest, at least in the long run. It is argued in this chapter, however, that the expression of interests and demands sanctioned and even encouraged by current policy is limited by the prevailing realities of political control. Short of a restructuring of the means by which power is distributed in Chinese society, the concentration of power in the hands of the enterprise Party committee imposes fundamental constraints on efforts to democratize the workplace.

Democratic Management within the Enterprise: The Rationale

Since 1978 the Chinese leadership has instituted a series of measures designed to enhance the operation of democracy in Chinese society. Attempts have been made to strengthen the socialist legal system, develop electoral forms of representation, institute forms of democratic management and "self-management" at the grassroots level, promote "inner-Party" democracy, and expand spheres of autonomy within Chinese society.[2] Seen in this light, the movement toward enterprise democracy constitutes one facet of a series of interrelated reforms. Nor is it possible to disassociate the Chinese leadership's reasons for pursuing democratic management from its broader goals for societal democratization. As with other policies of the current regime, the Chinese leadership's motivation for democratization has an explicit historical referent. Perhaps the most pervasive justification for the democratic reform movement is to establish political stability and prevent the reoccurrence of the political chaos of the Cultural Revolution. For Deng Xiaoping and his supporters, virtually all of whom were victims of political persecution during the Cultural Revolution decade, the attempt to ensure political stability is a paramount political concern. Democracy is seen as a means of preventing the overconcentration of power, cult of personality, arbitrary personal dictatorship, privilege, and corruption exhibited during the Cultural Revolution by placing limits on the uses of political authority. A second objective of democratization, with particular implications for the Chinese enterprise, has been to enhance Chinese modernization efforts. The present Chinese leadership appears to have accepted the assumption, commonly held in the West and in parts of East Europe, of a causative link between modernization and the expression of societal interests.[3] In this view, which may be seen as a variant of pluralism, the process of modernization necessitates an increasing specialization in the division of labor, which gives rise to and demands input from different societal interests and demands.[4]

The application of the Chinese leadership's goals for democratization to the enterprise reflects an accommodation to concrete circumstances of the enterprise environment. The Chinese leadership's concern to place limits on the authority exercised by the Party is expressed as an attempt to depoliticize the enterprise and to develop spheres of autonomy in enterprise operations. The objective of stimulating the expression of societal interests is tied directly to the aim of increasing productive output. The largely proletarian composition of the enterprise labor force, moreover, entails a special consideration of the relationship between the proletariat and its vanguard in socialist society. Specifically, three rationales for democratization within the enterprise can be distinguished as instrumental to the current leadership's goals: (1) the promotion of enterprise democracy as a means of underpinning regime legitimacy; (2) the promotion of enterprise democracy as a factor of productive efficiency; and (3) the promotion of forms of worker participation as a means of restructuring enterprise authority relations.

Enterprise Democracy and Regime Legitimacy

To the Chinese leadership, one rationale for the institution of workplace democracy is its functions in underpinning the legitimacy of the regime. The connections between regime legitimacy and enterprise democracy are both ideological and pragmatic, resting on a series of assumptions, some of which remain implicit, about the nature of the relationship between the workers and the state. In the ideological realm the CCP, as do all Communist parties, derives its legitimacy from its claim to act as the vanguard of the proletariat. The reconciliation of Marxist theory with Chinese reality has always been an awkward question in the People's Republic of China, given the peasant origins of the Chinese revolution and the still predominantly peasant composition of Chinese society and the CCP. Nonetheless, for all his glorification of the peasantry, not even Mao Zedong ever sought to sever the Party's theoretical links to the proletariat as the leading class of the revolution. The 1982 constitution designates the People's Republic of China as a "socialist state under the people's democratic dictatorship led by the working class and based on the alliance of workers and peasants."[5] The institution of democratic management serves to augment the Party's claim that the proletariat, in the final analysis, exercises a contributory role in formulating the affairs of state. Worker participation in the enterprise provides a necessary symbolic evidence of the status of the working class as the masters (*zhurenweng*) of Chinese society.[6]

Besides serving as a means of ideological justification, democratic management is also perceived by China's leaders to serve a legitimating function through increasing workers' support for the system. The current leadership has been candid in expressing its concern about the evidence of slackening political commitments among Chinese workers, especially young workers under the age of thirty-five who are estimated to make up 60 percent of the workforce. Among the many detrimental repercussions of the Cultural Revolution has been a decline in Party prestige, manifest in the workplace by an acknowledged difficulty in recruiting young workers into the Party.[7] In this context, democratic management is one of several strategies—the intensification of ideological education, and Party rectification being others—advanced to counter worker alienation.[8] It is hoped that the incorporation of workers into participatory roles will enhance workers' feelings of efficacy and strengthen their sense of identification with the system. Worker participation is seen to fulfill an integrative function in intensifying workers' loyalties to the state, thus serving to shore up regime legitimacy.

Enterprise Democracy as a Factor of Productive Efficiency

A second rationale for enterprise democracy, closely related to the perception of socialist democracy as a response to the needs of modernization, is the advocacy of enterprise democracy as a factor of productive efficiency. In this view the institution of forms of worker participation is presented as an objective demand of modernization. The development of the productive forces, which gives rise to increased specialization in the division of labor and complexity in the productive process, is seen as necessitating the implementation of worker participation in management. Enterprise democracy is perceived as an organizational requisite of the modern enterprise, which, despite token efforts taken toward its initiation in the capitalist world, is capable of being realized only under the nonexploitative conditions of socialism.[9] From the Chinese perspective, moreover, enterprise democracy is directly linked to productive efficiency. The institution of worker participation in management is seen as a means of harnessing workers' energies to the task of production. As noted by Su Shaozhi: "The important factor of raising labor productivity and developing productive forces lies in the initiative and creativity of the working people. Only with the realization of democratization, thus enabling the working people to become real masters in enterprises, society and state, can the initiative and creativity of the working people be brought into full play."[10] This perspective is reiterated in the 1984 Reform Decision:

> The well-spring of vitality of the enterprise lies in the initiative, wisdom, and creativeness of its workers by hand and brain. . . . In restructuring the urban economy, it is imperative to handle correctly the relationship of the workers and staff to their enterprises so that they are its real masters and can work as such at their jobs . . . . Under socialism there is unity between the authority of the enterprise's leadership and the status of the working people as masters of the enterprise and their initiative and creativity. This unity is a prerequisite for the proper effective exercise of their initiative.[11]

The Chinese analysis of enterprise democracy as a factor of productive efficiency is an amalgam that reflects the influence of several contributory sources. The current leadership's emphasis on worker initiative as a factor of productive efficiency represents a point of continuity between the Maoist and the present era in shared voluntarist assumptions about the innate creativity of the working masses. The Chinese conception of enterprise democracy as an integral component of socialist managerial practice, however, traces its ideological origins to Soviet-derived principles of scientific management. Despite criticisms made by Western observers of Taylorism as outmoded, Taylorism is defended in the People's Republic of China as a reputable managerial system that ensures "the best utilization of the workers' physical capabilities."[12] To the Chinese, as dedicated adherents to the practice of democratic centralism, there is no irreconcilable conflict between the emphasis on the role of the human factor and centralized leadership and strict labor discipline.

The Chinese analysis of democratization as a factor of economic efficiency, however, moves beyond the parameters of Soviet discourse—although the differences may be mostly a matter of degree—into the East European camp, including its émigré wing. Since Deng Xiaoping's consolidation of political power, major East European reform documents have been translated into Chinese and studied by Chinese reformers.[13] Reportedly, several East European émigré economists now living in the West—i.e., Ota Sik, Włodzimierz Brus—who had been influential proponents of democratic reforms in their own countries have been consulted by the Chinese for advice in instituting reform measures.[14] The influence of Brus is clearly evident, for example, in the writing of Su Shaozhi, director of the Institute of Marxism-Leninism and Mao Zedong Thought of the Chinese Academy of Social Sciences. In discussing the argument between Brus and Stanislaw Gomulka over the application of democracy within socialism, Su comes down squarely in favor of Brus's analysis of democratization as a factor of economic development. Although Su does not make use of the same vocabulary, his analysis follows Brus's acceptance of Harvey Libenstein's notion of "x-efficiency" as a factor of economic development. For Su, as for Brus, democratization of the enterprise is seen as a means of motivating employees in production.[15]

Although undoubtedly written with an awareness of their existence, Chinese writings are notably devoid of references to East European experiences with democratic management that have transgressed the boundaries acceptable to the Communist Party. Contemporary Hungarian practice in democratic management, for example, is presented as a successful example of workplace democracy; the establishment of Hungarian workers' councils in 1956 does not appear as an item for discussion on the Chinese reform agenda.[16] The Chinese evaluation of democratic management in any given European state is generally more closely tied to the state's foreign policy relationship with the People's Republic of China than to a measured assessment of objective factors of democratic management.[17] Nor do Chinese democratic reform discussions touch on theoretical questions of Marxist theory, which are of interest in certain East European circles. The Chinese debate about the possibility of the existence of alienation in a socialist society that developed after 1979, whatever its pragmatic utility in providing a justification for Deng Xiaoping's reform efforts, lacked a Marxist theoretical analysis linking alienation to relations of production within the workplace.[18] Rather, Chinese attention to East European theorizing about democratic management is mainly propelled by a pragmatic interest in its application as a factor of economic efficiency. East European ruling elites themselves may have no less utilitarian motives in advancing an expansion of forms of worker participation.[19] However, East European efforts to establish democratic management originated in the 1970s, partly out of a concern to identify the social prerequisites of conditions of "developed socialist society."[20] Chinese reformers have not hesitated to borrow from East European models, despite the obvious differences in levels of socioeconomic development. But in the Chinese interpretation, democratization is advanced not as a method for coping with the complexities of industrialized society but as a means of socialist construction.

Worker Participation and Reforming the Enterprise Leadership System

The institution of democratic reforms within the enterprise since 1978 has been integrally connected to attempts to restructure the enterprise leadership system. The key issue is the role of the Party in the enterprise. China's short-lived experiment with the Soviet-style system of managerial responsibility for enterprise operations was discarded in 1956 in favor of the Maoist-approved system, which allocated an operational control over the enterprise to the enterprise Party committee. The Third Party Plenum of the Eleventh Party Congress, in developing a critique of the abuses of political power in the People's Republic of China, singled out the operation of the Party within the enterprise as a target of special attack, noting the overconcentration of enterprise authority and the tendency of the Party committee to substitute for the enterprise management. What was a virtue in the Maoist era was now seen as a distinct liability. In contrast to the "politics in command" ethos of Maoism, the current leadership has stressed the desirability of professional management, technical expertise, specialization in the division of labor, and the development of spheres of autonomy in enterprise operations. The central theme in the ongoing debate over the reform of the enterprise leadership system has been the issue of managerial versus political authority in the enterprise distribution of power. Nonetheless, a consistent subtheme of discussion has argued the need to reform enterprise structures so as to provide institutional opportunities for workers to participate in the enterprise decision-making process.

By late 1978 the CCP leadership had announced its intention of restructuring enterprise authority relations, laying out some guidelines for the direction of future change. Criticisms of the Party's monopoly of power within the enterprise were combined with calls for the establishment of a system of managerial responsibility and increased attention to mechanisms of worker participation. Speaking to the newly resurrected Ninth National Congress of the All-China Federation of Trade Unions

(ACFTU) in September 1978, Deng Xiaoping called for the institution of enterprise elections, in which workers would elect their managers, and for the establishment of workers' congresses, representative meetings of enterprise staff and workers, as structures of worker participation.[21] By mid-1980, Chinese proposals to reform the enterprise leadership system had advanced to a format that envisioned a tripartite sectioning of authority between the workers' congresses, the management, and the Party. According to this scheme the workers' congresses would assume a policy authority to make decisions on enterprise policy, the management would exercise a command authority entrusted with the responsibility for overseeing the day-to-day details of enterprise operations, and the Party would take on a supervisory authority, retiring to the second line of enterprise operations and concentrating on political and ideological work within the enterprise. Each actor was portrayed as playing a functionally separate role, enjoying operational autonomy and a more or less equal status in enterprise operations. In its most liberal format, reform advocates went so far as to advocate the replacement of the "factory manager responsibility system under the leadership of the Party committee" with the "factory manager responsibility system under the leadership of the workers' congress."[22] Nor did the reform proposals remain a matter of rhetoric alone, as the "factory manager responsibility system under the leadership of the workers' congresses" was adopted at selected keypoint enterprises on an experimental basis during 1980.[23]

The suggestion that the workers' congresses replace the enterprise Party committee as the "highest structure of authority" in the enterprise represented, at least on paper, an attempt to effect a startling shift in the distribution of power in the enterprise. Although the all-important details of implementation were not worked out, Chinese reform proposals explicitly called for democratization of the enterprise by granting increased authority to the workers' congresses. Inspiration for the reform proposals was perhaps derived from Chinese interest in the Yugoslav model of self-management. The tripartite division of authority envisioned in the Chinese reforms bore a certain resemblance to the Yugoslav method of work organization, and Chinese suggestions for democratic reform coincided with a nation-wide movement to grant increased self-management powers to the enterprise.[24]

The year 1980, however, constituted a high-water mark for liberal advocates of reform in the People's Republic of China. The reform movement suffered a severe setback at a Party Work Conference in December 1980 when antireform forces in the Party, by now a broad coalition who ran the gamut with respect to political beliefs but shared a common discontent over the direction in which the reformers were heading, managed to halt the momentum of the reform movement.[25] Reform was not swept off the agenda altogether, but a period of economic "readjustment" was ordered, which placed a moratorium on reform efforts. In the aftermath of the conference the notion that the workers' congresses serve as the repository of policy authority in the enterprise was shelved. Issued in June 1981, the "Provisional Regulations Concerning Congresses of Workers and Staff Members in State-Owned Industrial Enterprises" by and large provided for the reconstitution of the workers' congresses in their pre-Cultural Revolution format, definitively subject to the authority of the enterprise Party committee.[26]

Set in the context of traditional assumptions of Chinese Communism, the democratic reform suggestions of 1980 appear highly iconoclastic, possibly the reflection of opinions held by a minority of progressive intellectual reformers but not a sentiment embraced by the mainstream of the political leadership.[27] The Chinese leadership's decision to reassert the primacy of Party controls over mechanisms of worker participation was wholly in accordance with long-standing Marxist-Leninist convictions about the relationship of the Party to the proletariat. But the Chinese leadership's decision to reject the 1980 democratic reform suggestions may also have been reinforced by the external influence of the Polish crisis. The debate over the reform of the enterprise leadership system, as it unfolded in 1980, was notable in its failure to discuss the role of the trade unions within the enterprise, and the few references made to the unions were uncharacteristically cryptic and tentative.[28] Although the reformers showed a preoccupation with differentiating spheres of authority in the enterprise, no mention was made of the possibility of instituting an operational autonomy for the unions. Despite the geographical and cultural distance separating China from Poland, evidence suggests that the Chinese leadership viewed the Polish situation as a lesson with direct implications for China.[29] After an initial period of discrete toleration, the Chinese leadership adopted a dim view of Solidarity, taking the orthodox Marxist-Leninist position that the concept of an independent trade union movement was nothing less than a contradiction in terms and an affront to the vanguard role of the Communist Party. The emergence of Solidarity, moreover, presumably strengthened the hand of those segments of the political leadership opposed to the democratic reform movement and may well have caused others, originally more sympathetic, to think twice about the wisdom of granting expanded powers to the workers. Although the workers' congresses differed from the unions in operating only as self-contained units at the enterprise level, without the potential for nation-wide mobilization, the Chinese leadership apparently found the concept of workers' congresses operating independently of direct Party controls too threatening to permit.

Despite the setback received in 1980, however, the reformist forces in the Party have gradually been able to regain the upper hand.[30] Although more conservative than the 1980 democratic reform proposals, "The Decision of the Central Committee of the Communist Party of China on Reform of the Economic Structure" promulgated in October 1984 reveals a continuing commitment to enterprise democratization. A key goal of the reform decision is to institute the depoliticization of the enterprise. The 1984 document lays to rest, at least in theory, the "factory manager responsibility system under the leadership of the party committee," replacing it with the "factory manager responsibility system." The differentiation of spheres of authority—in particular between the Party and the management—constitutes another critical aspect of enterprise operations. According to section 11 of the reform decision:

> Modern enterprises have a minute division of labor, a high degree of continuity in production, strict technological requirements and complex relations of co-operation. It is therefore necessary to establish a unified, authoritative and highly efficient system to direct production and conduct operations and management. This calls for a system of the director or manager assuming full responsibility. Party organizations in enterprises should actively support directors in exercising their authority, in giving unified direction to production and operations, guarantee and supervise the implementation of the principles and policies of the Party and the state, strengthen the Party's ideological and organizational work in enterprises, improve their leadership over the trade union and the Youth League organizations, and do effective ideological and political work among the workers and staff members.[31]

The description of enterprise authority relations laid out in the 1984 Reform Decision is best seen as an attempt to reconstitute the Soviet-style model that was only imperfectly adopted in the People's Republic of China prior to 1956. The extent to which the Reform Decision specifies a return to the Soviet-style model has perhaps been somewhat obscured by the predominant attention given to reform directives that sanction the partial dismantling of the planned economy through decentralization of decision-making powers and the introduction of market mechanisms along the lines adopted in Hungary. Nonetheless, the Chinese elaboration of the "factory manager responsibility system" is in reality the application of the formerly much maligned Soviet style system of "one-man management."[32] Despite the Soviet leadership's hostility to many of the changes adopted in China, there is nothing in that quotation that conflicts with the standard Soviet analysis of enterprise operations.[33]

Nor does the description of enterprise democracy delineated in the Reform Decision per se exceed the parameters of the Soviet-style model, although subsequent Chinese discussions have perhaps moved closer in practice to the East European variant. Enterprise democratization is essentially viewed as a process of continuing the depoliticization of the enterprise through the expansion of spheres of authority. Despite the twists and turns of Chinese policy since 1978, the current Chinese line on enterprise democratization conforms to the original guidelines laid out by Deng Xiaoping in his 1978 speech to the Ninth Congress of the ACFTU in identifying the workers' congresses, enterprise elections, and the trade unions as components of democratic management. Thus, since the beginning of the decade, the Chinese leadership's treatment of the question of the unions has also returned to Marxist-Leninist orthodoxy in acknowledging the indispensable function of the unions as a link between the Party and the proletariat. In fact, the current Chinese articulation of the trade union line is easily the most liberal of the entire post-1949 era, with unions urged to take the representation of the workers' interests as a primary endeavor. Present policy also acknowledges the legitimacy of a trade union operational autonomy. The revised trade union constitution unveiled at the Tenth Congress of the ACFTU in October 1983 noted for the first time the importance of independence in trade union work.[34]

To the Chinese leadership the promotion of enterprise democracy is seen as complementary to the institution of the factory manager responsibility system rather than in contradiction to it. The reform of the enterprise leadership structure is viewed as a means of strengthening Party, managerial, and mass work in their respective scopes, a process referred to as "strengthening in three respects" (*san jiachang*). As noted in an article in *Workers' Daily:*

> Enlargement of enterprise decision-making means enlarging the decision-making powers of the enterprise as a whole, including workers and not just enlarging the decision-making power of factory directors as individuals. Introduction of the factory manager responsibility system does not exclude worker participation in working out an enterprise's important decisions and in its democratic management.[35]

The Chinese leadership's current conception of enterprise authority relations has thus retained to a certain degree the tripartite division of authority central to the 1980 reform proposals. The question of the relationship of the Party to structures of democratic management, however, possesses few of the ambiguities currently besetting efforts to define the Party-managerial relationship.[36] The independent operational authority granted to factory management by the Reform Decision does not extend to structures of workplace democracy. For all the talk of autonomy, the workers' congresses and the trade unions are explicitly identified as subordinate to the enterprise Party committee, which maintains the leadership role of the Party.

Enterprise Democracy: Forms of Worker Participation in Practice

Observers of the Chinese reform movement have noted that Chinese attempts at democratization have tended to stress depoliticization, or the retreat of the state from society, over mobilizational efforts to increase mass participation.[37] The institution of democratic reform in the workplace, however, appears as a partial exception to this pattern in which the incorporation of workers into participatory roles has been advanced as a vital element of enterprise democracy. As mentioned, current policy identifies three principal formats by which workers are provided with opportunities to express their interests: workers' congresses, enterprise elections, and the trade unions.

The workers' congresses, as representative meetings of elected staff and workers, are seen as the fundamental means for incorporating workers directly into the enterprise decision-making process. Both state- and collectively owned enterprises in China are expected to establish workers' congresses. Scheduled to meet biannually, two key functions of the workers' congresses are to conduct investigations into enterprise operations and to exercise supervision over the enterprise management. The enterprise director is enjoined with the responsibility of presenting periodic work reports to the workers' congresses and responding to workers' comments and criticisms. In the past several years workers' congresses have increasingly been identified as the appropriate body to deal with such questions as housing allocation, wages, bonuses, work regulations, and the implementation of a punishment and reward system in the enterprise.

In contrast to the workers' congresses, which represent a reconstitution of a pre–Cultural Revolution organ, the institution of enterprise elections is essentially a Dengist innovation.[38] The implementation of elections to select enterprise cadres has been highly experimental in format, subject to considerable variation in application. Current policy suggests that collectively owned enterprises should universally hold elections in choosing their managerial leadership. State-owned enterprises, on the other hand, have been presented with the option of either electing or appointing managerial cadres, with some mechanism for soliciting worker and staff input in the selection process. Reform proposals have often attempted to differentiate between lower and higher levels of enterprise personnel, leaving open the alternative for direct appointments to managerial positions at the highest levels. The process of enterprise elections, moreover, needs to be coordinated with reform efforts to institute qualifying examinations prior to the appointment of managerial personnel.

Despite the specter of Solidarity, or perhaps because of it, the current Chinese leadership has chosen to concentrate upon the trade unions as a key structure for instituting enterprise democratization. As with the workers' congresses, each enterprise in China, whether state- or collectively owned, is expected to have an operational trade union. Trade union membership is open to all Chinese wage earners.[39] A substantial percentage of Chinese staff and workers, however, are not unionized, largely because trade unions are not universally established in the rural and collective sectors of the economy. As of the end of 1982, approximately 67 percent of the total Chinese wage-earning population belonged to trade unions.[40] Chinese unions are conceived, in accordance with the classic dictates of Leninism, as performing a transmission-belt function, linking the leadership to the workers in the enterprise. Unions are seen to serve as a conduit simultaneously representing the interests of the leadership to the workers and the interests of the workers to the leadership. Whereas production was identified during the Maoist era as virtually the exclusive focus of trade union activity, the present Chinese leadership has emphasized the democratic side of the continuum in defining the trade union's primary role as acting in defense of the workers' interests. The major purpose of the Sixth Executive Meeting of the Tenth ACFTU in July 1985 was to study ways by which the unions could promote democratic reforms in the enterprise.[41] In accordance with pre–Cultural Revolution practice, the responsibility for organizing the workers' congresses rests with the unions, which are also in charge of handling day-to-day administrative work when the congresses are not in session.[42] Reform proposals circulated in the past several years have also envisioned a larger role for the unions in enterprise management and urban administration, somewhat along the lines of the East European experience.[43] Although it might seem that Chinese unions are tied to democratic management more as representational bodies than as direct structures of worker participation, unions function in the Chinese view both "as an organ of democratic management and a participant in democratic management."[44]

The development of structures of worker participation in the enterprise is integrally tied to the progress of the enterprise reform movement. Chinese industrial reforms are still in a preliminary stage of implementation, and their final evolution cannot be predicted with any certainty. For the moment, however, the prospect of instituting meaningful forms of worker participation within the enterprise is constrained by two interrelated factors: (1) the movement toward decentralization sanctioned by the 1984 Reform Decision leaves significant managerial powers lodged above the enterprise level, and (2) the Party still maintains a leadership role over the implementation of forms of worker participation in the enterprise. These features, of course, are not unique to China but to a greater or lesser extent plague the implementation of worker participation in all socialist-style societies.

The reform of the Chinese urban economy set forth in the 1984 Reform Decision locates China, on the continuum of socialist economic forms, closest to Hungary. The Chinese Reform Decision does not have the goal of abolishing central planning but of combining methods of central planning with some reliance on the market mechanism as an indicator of scarcity values. The number of products subject to mandatory planning allocated by the method of material balances by the state has been reduced from 120 to 60; other products are expected to be regulated through the institution of guidance planning and the application of economic levers. As in the Hungarian case, moreover, the Chinese economic decentralization laid out in the 1984 Reform Decision falls short of a complete devolution of authority to the enterprise, leaving significant decision-making powers located above the enterprise level. The Reform Decision decrees that the enterprise is to operate as a "relatively independent economic entity."[45] To date, however, a significant beneficiary in the redistribution of decision-making authority has been the cities, which have sought to use their newly gained powers to impose their will upon individual enterprise.[46]

The partial decentralization of decision-making authority to the level of the enterprise, moreover, has not been accompanied by a coextensive effort to introduce forms of shopfloor participation in management. Although the functions and powers delegated to the workers' congresses appear extensive on paper, a closer examination of the workers' congress regulations reveals that all resolutions and proposals passed by the workers' congress are dependent upon the factory manager for implementation. Workers' congresses may put forward their own suggestions in cases of disagreement with the enterprise leadership, but they are bound by the principles of democratic centralism to abide by the final decision of the enterprise leadership. The infrequency of workers' congress meetings—twice a year—serves to substantiate the impression of an organization relegated to the sidelines of the enterprise decision-making process. Economic decentralization may be considered a necessary condition for worker participation, but it is not in itself a sufficient condition to guarantee the implementation of worker participation as a form of enterprise democracy.[47]

The major impediment to the institution of worker participation in enterprise management, however, is not the constraints—significant as they may be—imposed by central planning but the domination of structures of worker participation by the Party. The depoliticization of the enterprise is a central goal in the reform of the enterprise leadership structure, but it is uncertain how far the Chinese leadership will be willing or able to go in disengaging the control wielded by the enterprise Party committee. Deng Xiaoping's strategy to carry out a personnel change in the enterprise, bringing loyal supporters of the reform cause into the enterprise leadership, is a hopeful sign. The replacement of managerial cadres at the enterprise level has been a feature of administrative reform; the third stage of the Party rectification campaign has similarly aimed to evaluate the performance of Party members at the grassroots level, including the enterprise. As of December 1985 some 10,000 enterprises in China were reported to have instituted the factory manager responsibility system, signaling the Party's relinquishing of operational control over the enterprise.[48]

It seems, nonetheless, that Deng Xiaoping's political aim in the enterprise has been more to change Party personnel than to change the organizational basis of Party operations. Certain elements of Party organization remain intact and do not seem likely to be called into question. Democratic centralism, the existence of the "interlocking directorate," and the Party's prerogative to exercise a final say over personnel choices seem sacrosanct as fundamental principles of Leninism. Compared with the East European or the Soviet case, moreover, Chinese enterprise operations have been distinguished by the pervasiveness of political controls, exercised through informal as well as formal channels. Political organization in the Chinese enterprise has typically extended down to the workshop floor. The Party has monitored workers through such measures as the maintenance of dossiers, files kept on each enterprise employee, including a political evaluation, and the operation of enterprise small groups, which have served as a focal point for political study and the initiation of periodic criticism and self-criticism sessions.[49] The reform of the enterprise structure to allow the establishment of spheres of autonomy necessitates that the enterprise Party committee effect its own form of retreat from the shop floor and modify its traditional preoccupation with assessing forms of political behavior.

The envisioned depoliticization of the enterprise, however, is not viewed as incompatible with the maintenance of Party leadership over structures of worker participation. The revival of the workers' congresses since 1978 has been orchestrated under the guiding hand of the Party. A reading of the workers' congress regulations reveals an explicit commitment to the leadership role of the Party. The Party's control over workers' congress proceedings is virtually assured by placing Party members—"leading cadres of the enterprise Party, administrative, trade union, and Youth League organizations," according to article 11 of the regulations—on the workers' congress presidium.[50] The operation of the interlocking directorate, moreover, has acted to ensure that the chairman of the workers' congress be a concurrent member of the enterprise Party committee. Delegates to workers' congresses are selected under the watchful eye of the Party, which has sought to cull out potential troublemakers. By interjecting its personnel in key roles within the workers' congress structure, the Party has thus been able to control the agenda of workers' congress proceedings.

Problems with the implementation of the workers' congress system have been readily acknowledged in the Chinese press, where workers congresses have often been criticized for lapsing into a sterile "formalism." Excerpts from a series of letters from workers published in the *Zhejiang Workers' News,* for example, bear testimony to the domination of the congresses by the enterprise leadership structure. Workers complained that "they had sent their representatives to meetings only to raise their hands," that "workers are allowed to hold congresses only when they serve the needs of the leaders," that workers' representatives were "not selected by workers but designated by leaders," and that the presidium of the workers' congress had become "a joint meeting of Party branch secretaries."[51] Such problems, however, are blamed on "bureaucratism" and improper adherence to regulations rather than conceived as a symptomatic reflection of the enterprise distribution of power.

The same mechanisms of control that operate to subordinate the workers' congresses to the Party may similarly be seen at work in the Party's interactions with the trade unions. The recent sanctioning of a limited trade union independence arises out of a recognition of the trade union's need for autonomy if it is to fulfill its designated role to defend the workers' against injustices perpetuated by the enterprise leadership. Nonetheless, the trade unions' ability to act even as a semiautonomous actor within the enterprise structure is fundamentally constrained by the network of ties binding it to the Party. The trade union constitution establishes the Party's leadership role over the unions, specifying the unions as organizations that have the duty to respect the Party line and uphold Party policy.[52] As with the presidia of the workers' congresses, Party members dominate the higher echelons of the trade union leadership within the enterprise, and the enterprise trade union chairman is usually a member of the enterprise Party committee. Nor are the informal ties between the Party and the trade union any less pervasive. Because the Party has controled ladders of career advancement in the enterprise, trade union cadres have found it a risky business to oppose political norms. Speaking out for the workers' interest has typically been a highly charged political act, liable to sound the death knoll for a cadre's career. As Kang Wenhua, the chairman of the Mukdan Trade Union Committee, has noted: "In the past we felt that to grasp production was safe; to grasp livelihood was dangerous. To follow the tide was safe; to independently take responsibility for developing movements was dangerous. To be responsible to the leadership was safe; to be responsible to the masses was dangerous."[53] The traditionally low status of the trade union in the enterprise, moreover, does not augur well for the trade union's prospects in carving out its own independent niche in the enterprise hierarchy.

Although recent trade union policy proclamations have unceasingly stressed the need to strengthen trade union operations, preliminary evidence suggests that the enterprise reform movement has either failed to address certain long-standing problems of the trade union's role or has had unintended detrimental consequences for the unions. A December 1985 editorial in *Workers' Daily* acknowledged that "since the implementation of the economic reforms, more and more problems have affected the trade union movement."[54] Neither the Party nor management has demonstrated a consistent commitment to the task of trade union institutionalization, rather showing a reluctance to relinquish certain functions that were incorporated into the management's sphere of operations during the Cultural Revolution.[55] In carrying out the reform of administrative personnel, the enterprise leadership has been prone to transfer capable people out of the trade union to other departments and to use the trade unions as a sort of final resting spot for surplus cadres. Speaking to this problem, the Party secretary of Hunan Province, Liu Zhengwei, noted that the overall quality of trade union cadres was actually being lowered as a result of administrative readjustment as older cadres with a low cultural level were being transferred into the trade union.[56] Evidence also suggests that the movement toward economic decentralization has made the trade unions more vulnerable to the whims of the enterprise leadership while weakening the vertical links connecting the enterprise trade union to higher levels of the union organization.[57]

Workers' opportunities to exercise a voice in the selection of enterprise leaders are also constrained by the leading role of the Party. Electoral slates in the People's Republic of China have moved from one candidate per position to allow for a choice among candidates. Preparation of the slate of selectors for leadership posts, however, takes place under the supervisory guidance of the enterprise Party committee, making it extremely unlikely that a non-Party-approved candidate would appear on the ballot. Judging from the East European experience with limited choice elections, personality is likely to become a factor in differentiating between candidates.[58] Individual candidates may also conceivably take different positions on how to implement policy, with significant implications for enterprise employees. But the basic policy line, set from above, is not a matter open to debate.

Noninstitutional Forms of Worker Participation

The limited opportunities for workers to raise demands through structures of workplace democracy raise the question of how, if at all, Chinese workers seek to pursue their own interests. Interest articulation is by no means absent in the Chinese enterprise, but the domination of the Party over institutional structures of worker participation has left workers prone to developing strategies based on informal, or, more rarely, illegal means. Nonetheless, the Party's domination over the network of enterprise authority relations shapes the pattern of behavior open to workers. The Party's ability to control the dispersal of rewards and punishments in the enterprise, which is accentuated by the reliance of workers on the enterprise for the provision of such scarce resources as housing and the delivery of social services, has led to a situation that Andrew Walder has labeled "organized dependency."[59] Walder's research has emphasized that organization in the Chinese enterprise, far from conforming to Weberian ideals of impartiality, is highly personalized, characterized by the development of vertical ties of interaction linking subordinate to superior. Workers are enmeshed in a network of personal connections that encourages the growth of patron-client relationships. For the Chinese worker the cultivation of a cordial personal relationship with a superior is usually the most effective way of pursuing one's interest. This behavior, which often includes the bestowal of special gifts and favors, is generally considered in the West a form of corruption. It constitutes, however, a primary example of political participation in its focus on the distribution of scarce resources within the enterprise, although it may not fit in very well with Western assumptions about the scope of participatory behavior. The portrayal of the Chinese enterprise as a network of connections in which personal loyalties reign supreme runs contrary to the Chinese Communist analysis of organizational activity as well, which stresses, no less than Weber himself, the predominance of institutionalized rules of conduct. But the propensity of Chinese workers to pursue their self-interest under the protective guise of patron-client relations has certain advantages for the Chinese regime. The highly personalized structure of ties in the Chinese system acts to ensure that workers will seek to gain rewards on an individual basis. As long as Chinese workers remain atomized, pursuing their interests independently of one another, the threat to the regime is minimal.

The convergence of formal and informal mechanisms of political control within the enterprise serves as a powerful deterrent to the unsanctioned collective expression of worker interests. But the Party's capacity for exercising control and ensuring compliant behavior among workers is, of course, incomplete. Expressions of worker discontent exist, ranging from such frequent individual behaviors as absenteeism and the illicit use of sick leave to less usual collective forms. Probably the most commonplace collective expression of worker interest in China takes the spontaneous form of the work slowdown. But strikes are not unknown and constitute yet another form of worker participation, albeit one that is not sanctioned by the regime. In an interview with foreign journalists in 1983, Chinese trade union executive committee member Wang Jiachong acknowledged the existence of strikes in China, although he declined to give specific details.[60] Some Chinese workers, inspired by the Polish example, have also sought to raise demands through establishing independent trade unions. State president Li Xiannian was reported to have acknowledged the existence of Lech Wałęsa sympathizers in the People's Republic of China in the midst of an attack upon Solidarity as an example of "sham trade unionism" (*jia gonghui zhuyi*) delivered at the Tenth Congress of the ACFTU in October 1983.[61] Scattered reports, moreover, have indicated attempts to establish Solidarity-style trade unions in China, with no notable signs of success.[62]

A significant challenge to the Chinese leadership is the need to redirect illegal forms of worker participation into acceptable channels. The Polish crisis poses the same problem to the Chinese leadership as to its East European and Soviet counterparts, namely, how to defuse worker antagonisms and integrate workers into the system. Mao Zedong's rather uncharacteristic reaction to worker disturbances in Poland and Hungary in 1956 was to enact a policy of liberalization and partial concessions, which failed because of the escalation of demands beyond the Party's boundaries of acceptable discourse. The current leadership, far more ideologically predisposed toward such a course in any case, has similarly emphasized liberalization as a response to the Polish crisis. Despite the Chinese leadership's original hesitation over the role of the unions at the height of the Polish crisis in 1980, it presumedly subsequently decided that increased participation within the system was preferable to the increased potential for labor unrest outside it. Given the experience of the 1950s, when the unions were twice condemned for "syndicalism" and "economism," this was a decision that was most likely thought to involve risks.[63] A fear of the trade union's potential capacity for nation-wide mobilization is evident in the guidelines issued by the Second Session of the Tenth Congress of the ACFTU in December 1984, specifying that "national, transregional, and transindustrial mass activities should by all means be discouraged."[64] The current leadership, no less than with Mao Zedong, faces the issue of striking a balance between the forces unleashed by liberalization and the maintenance of control.

The tensions engendered by the Chinese leadership's attempt to expand the boundaries of legitimate participation are also illustrated by the issue of strikes. The right to strike, which was first installed, at Mao Zedong's behest, in the Chinese constitution of 1975 and retained in the constitution of 1978, was eliminated in the 1982 constitution.[65] Like the removal of the "four big freedoms" from the constitution in 1980, the right to strike was castigated as an example of extensive democracy verging on anarchism. Nonetheless, a rather quixotic discussion on the status of the right to strike exists in the People's Republic of China. In early 1984 ACFTU chairman Ni Zhifu stated in an interview:

> In socialist China, we don't approve of strikes to solve problems. It only harms the interests of the working class in the end. The state, the enterprise, and the workers have no fundamental conflict of interest. Workers can use democratic methods to solve their problems and uphold workers' rights. They have no need to strike.[66]

Ni, however, proceeded to qualify his impeccably Leninist analysis by suggesting that workers might legitimately be driven to strike in situations in which working conditions were intolerably dangerous and management deaf to workers' exhortations. The strike, according to Ni, could be viewed as an extraordinary measure used in a case of last resort to combat bureaucratism. The responsibility for organizing the strike and serving as an intermediary between workers' and management would be that of the trade union. The quasi-legitimacy accorded to worker collective action directed against a recalcitrant management is reiterated in the resolution of the Second Executive Session of the Tenth Congress of the ACFTU, which states that "trade unions should support workers in exercising their rights to boycott those who direct production in violation of regulations."[67] As a practical matter, the prospects of the trade union's organizing the workers to strike against management appear remote.[68] But the discussion of the right to strike is of considerable theoretical interest in its implicit recognition of the existence of conflicting interests in Chinese society.

Besides efforts to expand the basis of worker participation, the Deng Xiaoping leadership has sought to head off labor unrest through making improvements in the workers' standard of living. As elsewhere, evidence points to the primacy of economic variables as the key determinant of worker support for the state in the People's Republic of China. The current leadership has staked its main claim to legitimacy among the working class on its promise to deliver in the economic sphere. Seen in this light, the often repeated promise of the Dengist leadership to raise the standard of living of Chinese workers is not simply altruistic. The Chinese leadership's own understanding of the causal relationship between economics and regime legitimacy is exemplified in Li Xiannian's reported remark to Simone Weil in 1980 that China would face a situation like that in Poland unless economic reform efforts were successful.[69]

Since coming to power in 1978, the Deng Xiaoping regime has instituted a series of measures, including wage rises and the reinstatement of piecework and bonuses, designed to counter the legacy of falling wages inherited from the Maoist era and to improve the workers' standard of living.[70] At the same time the economic reform movement poses a threat to certain institutionalized expectations held by Chinese workers about the nature of the relationship between workers and the state. The announced intention of the state to do away with the state guarantee of employment for urban dwellers, to abolish the system of permanent job security, to widen wage differentials, and to eradicate the complex system of urban price subsidies infringes upon the "social compact" forged between the state and its workers since 1949, with its system of welfare benefits and institutional guarantees that a generation of workers has come to identify as virtual perquisites of socialism. The attempt to abolish worker benefits long espoused as examples of the superiority of the socialist system runs the risk of creating widespread disaffection among Chinese workers.[71] The considerable challenge for the Dengist leadership is to convince the majority of workers that the sacrifices demanded by the reforms will be exceeded by increased material benefits, and that the disadvantages accruing from the institution of reform measures in the short run will be more than compensated for by a rise in the standard of living in the long run.

In the initial stages, at least, the implementation of certain reform measures has run up against obstacles at the grassroots level that reflect shared worker and managerial opposition to directives transmitted from above. Examples include the tendency toward egalitarianism in the payment of bonuses, foot-dragging in enacting the floating wage system, in which wages are to be linked to output, a reluctance to fire workers, and a widespread tendency to use retained profits on bonuses and welfare projects of benefit to workers rather than plowing profits back into capital investment projects. These practices, which reflect a process in which original reform directives have been transmuted in practical application, might be considered to represent an accommodation to demands raised by the workers. The resistance of Chinese workers to market-oriented reforms finds parallels in the reform experience of other socialist states, notably Poland and Hungary. The Chinese system, however, differs significantly from that in East Europe and the Soviet Union on one key point, i.e., the structure of the labor market. Whereas East Europe and the Soviet Union face a labor shortage, China has a vast labor surplus. In a labor market characterized by scarcity, workers in East Europe have been able to use the threat of the withdrawal of their labor power as an effective tool in negotiating with the higher authorities.[72] Whether Chinese workers possess the resources to bargain successfully with higher authorities over the future course of the reforms is uncertain.

Conclusions

Much of the content of current regime policy on enterprise democracy can be seen as a deliberately formulated reaction to the perceived inadequacies of Maoist practice. Mao's conception of democracy within the enterprise placed an emphasis on mass movements and the institution of schemes by which workers would take part in management and managers would labor on the workshop floor, thereby breaking down the division of labor. Mao placed little value on institutional structures of worker participation, and the workers' congresses and the trade unions were among the first casualties of the Cultural Revolution, abolished at its onset in 1966.[73] The Dengist leadership is at odds with fundamental precepts of Maoism on such issues as the position of the Party in the enterprise, the establishment of separate spheres of authority, the application of representative forms of democracy, and the role of the trade unions. Deng Xiaoping's drive to depoliticize the enterprise and to develop the preconditions for the limited expression of interests within the workplace strikes at the very heart of the Maoist model.

Despite its innovative features, the post-1978 Chinese experience with workplace democracy is by no means lacking in historical antecedents. The current leadership's conception of enterprise democracy traces its ideological lineage back to the years of the early and mid-1950s, prior to the launching of the Great Leap Forward. Trade unions predate the establishment of the People's Republic of China, and the workers' congresses were first instituted in Chinese factories in 1949. The closest analogies to the current situation, however, are to be found during the Hundred Flowers period of 1956–57. Proposals were formulated that envisioned a redistribution of enterprise authority, with increased powers delegated to the workers' congresses, and an operational independence for the trade union was advocated as a prior condition of defending the workers' interests.[74] The movement to democratize the enterprise was stillborn with Mao Zedong's launching of the Anti-Rightist Campaign in June 1957. But it is evident that, far from being relegated to the dustbins of history, the discussions of enterprise democracy from the Hundred Flowers era served as a source of inspiration to the Deng Xiaoping leadership in planning democratic reforms after a hiatus of twenty years.

Thus, although the democratic reform movement carried out since 1978 contrasts sharply with the goals and values of the Maoist era, it exhibits strong underlying continuities in Chinese thought and practice in the early to mid-1950s. Similarly, current Chinese policy on enterprise democracy, far from appearing notable, fits rather imperceptibly into the general range of behavior exhibited by other Communist states. The Chinese attempt to institute democratic reforms to allow for a greater range of expression of enterprise interests parallels attempts previously undertaken elsewhere in the Communist bloc. Even the Soviet Union constitutes a model of sorts to China, in its advocacy of managerial responsibility and the relative absence within the Soviet enterprise of the informal mechanisms of political control—such as the small groups—that have helped to maintain the Party's domination over the Chinese enterprise. Chinese efforts to grant the trade union an operational independence, to institute representative structures of worker participation, to hold limited choice elections, and to encourage forms of interest articulation within the enterprise correspond to the democratic reform agendas of some East European states. As elsewhere in the Communist world, however, the Chinese leadership remains committed to a belief in Party leadership over Chinese society and to democratic centralism as an essential prerequisite for socialist organization. The democratic reform program of the Deng Xiaoping leadership places China on the liberal end of the continuum in a comparative socialist context. But Chinese policy is still located well within the boundaries of socialist-state behavior.

The question for the Chinese future is whether or not Chinese workers will be able to express diversified interests, raise demands, and exert influence over the enterprise decision-making process. As the Soviet example illustrates, this is a related but separate issue from the establishment of operational authority for the enterprise management. The East European experience with democratic reforms, instituted under conditions usually considered more conducive to the establishment of democracy—i.e., mature working class, an industrialized economy, in certain cases, a "democratic" tradition—strongly suggests that forms of pluralist expression, if they develop at all in China, will do so within circumscribed limits set by the Party. A vast expansion in the parameters of the dialogue over enterprise democracy since 1978 has in some instances pushed China to the edge of Communist discourse. The recent discussion about strikes, for example, is unusual in the Communist context. But the rhetoric of enterprise democracy has not been matched by a corresponding boldness in prescriptive application. The institution of workplace democracy has been characterized to date by the Party's careful attention to mechanisms of control, lest a dangerous element of spontaneity be injected that could cause workers' demands to get out of hand.

In the short run the key issue in the Chinese implementation of enterprise democracy is the extent to which the Chinese leadership can push through its projected policy of enterprise depoliticization. For all the leadership's promotion of the topic, it is unclear what depoliticization will actually entail in concrete application or how its implementation might be diluted with time. It is clear, however, that even the initial implementation of this reform has aroused the opposition of the enterprise Party committees, which fear, quite legitimately, that their powers are being stripped away. The success of enterprise depoliticization is also highly dependent on a number of political intangibles, i.e., how long Deng Xiaoping will live and whether his successors will be willing or able to carry on his reform policies. It does not seem likely that China will revert to a form of Maoism, but a leadership advocating a more conventional Marxist-Leninist approach to modernization is surely not out of the question. Substantial evidence exists—i.e., the "spiritual pollution" campaign of 1983, Standing Committee of the Politburo member Chen Yun's criticisms of the reform movement at the Fifth Plenum of the Twelfth Party Congress in September 1985—to indicate that at least a portion of Party members feel uncomfortable with the orientation of the reforms. However, if the Chinese leadership is able to restructure the role of the Party so that it no longer plays a direct part in day-to-day enterprise operations, the potential will exist for the development of spheres of enterprise autonomy. This is not to suggest that China will turn into a model of pluralism but to indicate that enterprise depoliticization constitutes a necessary, if not a sufficient, step toward the establishment of an environment in which workers can express their interests.

Notes

1. Wang Qianghua, Liu Jingrui, Zhang Yide, and Tao Kai, "Why Must We Thoroughly Negate 'Extensive Democracy'?" (*Guangming Ribao,* Sept. 13, 1984, 2), in *FBIS,* Sept. 20, 1984, K7.

2. For further discussion of the democratic reform movement, see Brantly Womack, "Modernization and Democratic Reform in China," *Journal of Asian Studies* 43, no. 3 (May 1984):417–39; William A. Joseph, "The Dilemmas of Political Reform in China," *Current History* (Sept. 1985):252–55, 279–80; David S. G. Goodman, "The Chinese Political Order After Mao: Socialist Democracy and the Exercise of State Power," *Political Studies* 33 (June 1985):218–35; and Harry Harding, "Political Development in Post-Mao China," in A. Doak Barnett and Ralph N. Clough, eds., *Modernizing China: Post-Mao Reform and Development* (Boulder: Westview Press, 1986), 13–38.

3. This assumption, for example, seems to underlie the institution of the New Economic Mechanism in Hungary. "Socialist democracy," Janos Kadar told the Ninth Party Congress of the Hungarian Socialist Workers' Party in November 1966, "meant the better allocation of spheres of authority." Quoted in Robert M. Bigler, "The Role of Bureaucrats and Experts in the Planning and Implementation of Hungary's New Economic Mechanism," *East European Quarterly* 18, no. 1 (Spring 1984):93.

4. H. Gordon Skilling refers to "quasi-pluralistic authoritarianism" as a potential characteristic of Communist regimes. See H. Gordon Skilling, "Group Conflict and Political Change," in Chalmers Johnson, ed., *Change in Communist Systems* (Stanford: Stanford University Press, 1970), 215–34. For discussions about the potential for pluralism in the Chinese political context, see Harding, "Political

Development in Post-Mao China," 13–38; and Andrew Nathan, *Chinese Democracy* (New York: Alfred A. Knopf, 1985) 224–32.

5. "Constitution of the People's Republic of China," *Beijing Review* 52 (Dec. 27, 1982):12.

6. Premier Zhao Ziyang noted, for example, in his speech to the Second Session of the Sixth National People's Congress, that "we must give full expression to the role of the worker masses as masters of the house. This is an important characteristic of our socialist enterprises that must not be overlooked." Quoted in Zhang Youyu, "Workers' Participation in Enterprise Management Should Be Allowed, So That Socialist Enterprises Can Be Run Well" (*Gongren Ribao,* Aug. 24, 1985, 1) in *JPRS-CEA-85-008,* Oct. 2, 1985, 93.

7. The problems of recruiting young workers into the Party are discussed in Yu Yannan, "Jiachang Dang Xiang Gongren Chunzhongde Lianxi," *Hongqui* 23 (Oct. 1982):25–29. Yu recounts the case, for example, of the Nanjing Radio Factory, in which only 9 of the 10,023 young workers who had joined the factory workforce since 1976 had chosen to become members of the Party. Yu also notes such problems as a shortage of Party members on the workshop floor and the existence of production teams without any Party members because of the need to transfer new Party members directly into managerial positions to replace retiring cadres. A more positive account of the recruitment of young workers into the Party is presented in "Jiji Youzhan Youxiu Qingniangong Ru Tang," *Gongren Ribao,* June 30, 1985, 1, in which 48 percent of the total Party membership at the Beijing Number One Shoe Factory is reported to consist of young workers under the age of thirty-five.

8. In an attempt to rectify problems of political disaffection, the Party introduced a program in 1983 to intensify ideological and political work among employees in state-owned enterprises. One of the key measures of the program specifies that young workers under the age of thirty-five in state-owned enterprises are to be given paid leave for two weeks a year, on a rotating basis, to attend full-time study courses on patriotism and communist thought. The formal document is presented in "Zhonggong Zhongyan Fachu Quanyu Pizhuan Guoying Qiye Zhigong Sixiang Zhengzhi Gongzuo Gangyao (Shixing) de Tungzhi," *Xinhua Yuebao* 465 (1983):78–85.

9. See, for example, Jiang Yiwei, "Lun Shehuizhuyi Qiye Guanlide Jiben Tezheng," *Jingji Guanli* 11 (1980):14–22; and Zhang Youyu, "Workers' Participation in Enterprise Management," 94.

10. Su Shaozhi, "Economic Development and Democratization," *Selected Writings on Studies of Marxism* 8 (Mar. 1981):5–6.

11. "Decision of the Central Committee of the Communist Party of China on Reform of the Economic Structure," *Beijing Review* 27, no. 44 (Oct. 29, 1984):6.

12. "Lu Dingyi on Workers' Role in Enterprises" (*Guangming Ribao,* Dec. 15, 1984, 1), in *JPRS-CEA-85-006,* 15–17. For a discussion of the application of Taylorism in the Soviet Union, see Don Van Atta, "Why Is There No Taylorism in the Soviet Union?" *Comparative Politics* 18, no. 3 (Apr. 1986):327–38.

13. See Nina P. Halpern, "Learning From Abroad: Chinese Views of the East European Economic Experience, January 1977–June 1981," *Modern China* II, no.

1 (Jan. 1985):77-109; and Nina P. Halpern, "China's Industrial Economic Reforms: The Question of Strategy," *Asian Survey* 25, no. 10 (Oct. 1985):998-1012.

14. H. G. Kosta, "China on the Road to a Market Economy?" RAD Background Report/226 (China), *Radio Free Europe Research*, Dec. 30, 1984, 1-8.

15. Su Shaozhi, "Economic Development and Democratization." Also see Włodzimierz Brus, "Political System and Economic Efficiency: The East European Context," *Journal of Comparative Economics* 4(1980):40-55; and Stanislaw Gomulka, "Economic Factors in the Democratization of Socialism and the Socialization of Capitalism," *Journal of Comparative Economics* 1 (1977):389-406.

16. Su Shaozhi's discussion of W. Brus's conception of enterprise democracy significantly fails to mention Brus's characterization of "Kadarism" as a system of limited economic decentralization instituted in the absence of structures of workers' self-management. See Brus, "Political System and Economic Efficiency," 48-55.

17. This point is developed in Halpern, "Learning From Abroad," 77-109.

18. See, for example, Wang Chang-ling, "The Debate About 'Alienation' Among Mainland Scholars," *Issues and Studies* 21, no. 3 (Mar. 1985):90-103; and Wang Ruoshui, "On Estrangement," *Selected Writings on Studies of Marxism* 12 (May 1981).

19. As a Hungarian study of the interrelationship between economics and politics concluded, "The progress of management therefore requires democratic ways in politics." See "Economics and Democracy," *New Hungarian Quarterly* 26, no. 97 (Spring 1985):121-22.

20. For discussions of democratic management under conditions of "developed socialism" in East Europe, see Jack Bielasiak, "Workers and Mass Participation in Socialist Democracy," in Jan F. Triska and Charles Gati, eds., *Blue-Collar Workers in Eastern Europe* (London: Allen and Unwin, 1981), 88-107; and Daniel Nelson, "Romania: Participatory Dynamics in 'Developed Socialism'," in ibid., 236-52.

21. *Zhongguo Gonghui Dijiuci Chuanguo Daibiao Dahui* (Beijing: Gongren Chubanshe, 1978), 4.

22. See, for example, Tian Fang, Qi Dong, Liu Xun, Yun Zhen, and Zhen Ji, "Zhongqing Shi Kuangda Qiye Zizhuchuan Shidiande Chubu Diaocha," *Jingji Yanjiu* 3 (1981):28-35; "Shixing Zhigong Diabiao Dahui Lingdao Xiade Changzhang Fucizhi," *Jingji Guanli* 4 (1981):42-44; Ma Hong, "Guanyu Gaige Gongye Qiye Lingdao Zhidude Tantao," *Renmin Ribao*, Nov. 20, 1980, 5; Jiang, "Lun Shehuizhuyi Qiye," 14-22; and Wang Mengkui, "Qiye Lingdao Zhidu Zhongde Yige Wenti," *Jingji Yanjiu* 1 (1981):37-44.

23. See "Shixing Zhigong Daibiao Dahui," 42-44; "You Zhidaihui Guolun Jieding Qiyede Zhongda Wenti," *Renmin Ribao*, Nov. 20, 1980, 1; and Tian Fang et al., "Zhongqing Shi Diaocha," 28-35.

24. By 1980 an estimated 6,600 enterprises had been granted increased self-management authority in enterprise operations. For discussions of the influence of the Yugoslav model on Chinese reformers, see Kosta, "China on the Road to a Market Economy," 1-8; and Halpern, "Learning From Abroad," 77-109. As illustrations of Chinese interest in the Yugoslav system, see *Nansilafude Shehuizhuyi Zhizhi Zhidu He Jingji Fazhan* (Shanghai: Renmin Chubanshe, 1979); Meng

Yunjeng, "Nansilafude Shehuizhuyi Zhidu," *Jingji Yanjiu* 12 (1978):53–59; and Pang Chuan, "Nansilafude Zizhi Zhidu," *Jingji Guanli* 7 (1980):13–18.

25. For a discussion of the politics of the reform movement, see Carol Lee Hamrin, "Competing 'Policy Packages' in Post-Mao China," *Asian Survey* 24, no. 5 (May 1984):487–518.

26. "Provisional Regulations Concerning Congresses of Workers and Staff Members in State-Owned Industrial Enterprises," in John L. Scherer, ed., *China Facts and Figures Annual 1982* (Gulf Breeze, Fla.: Academic International Press, 1983), 28–31.

27. Kosta asserts that no one in the leadership could be found to advocate worker self-management for the Chinese system patterned after the Yugoslav model. Kosta, "China on the Road to a Market Economy," 1–8.

28. See, for example, Wang Mengkui, "Qiye Lingdao Zhidu," 37–44; "Shixing Zhigong Daibiao Dahui," 42–44; "Women Xhi Zenyang Kaihao Zhigong Daibiao Dahuide?" *Jingji Guanli* 5, (1980):33–35; and "Jingji Tizhi Gaige Xuyau Jinyibude Yixie Wenti," *Jingji Guanli* 8 (1980):28–30.

29. After meeting with state president Li Xiannian in July 1980, then president of the European parliament, Simone Weil reported that she had been told that China would face a crisis similar to that in Poland unless current economic reform efforts were successful. See He Shen, "Solidarity Union of Poland and China" (*Zheng Ming*, no. 10 [Oct. 1, 1981] 26–29), in *JPRS* 79689, Dec. 1981, 72. For additional discussions of the impact of the Polish crisis on Chinese politics, see Tony Saich, "Workers in the Workers' State: Urban Workers in the PRC," in David S. G. Goodman, ed., *Groups and Politics in the People's Republic of China* (Cardiff: University College Cardiff Press, 1984), 164; Nathan, *Chinese Democracy,* 41, 204, 206, 230; and Harding, "Political Development in Post-Mao China," 22.

30. For a discussion of the leadership struggles waged over reform, see Hamrin, "Competing 'Policy Packages' in Post-Mao China," 487–518.

31. "Decision on Reform of the Economic Structure," 6.

32. For discussions accentuating the positive benefits of "one-man management," see Wang Mengkui, "Qiye Lingdao Zhidu," 37–44; Ma Hong, "Quanyu Gaige Gongye," *Renmin Ribao,* 5; and Xiao Liang, "Implementing the Plant Director Responsibility System Is a Major Reform in the Leadership System of Enterprises" (*Renmin Ribao,* Mar. 17, 1986, 5), in *FBIS,* Apr. 1, 1986, K7.

33. For a discussion of Soviet perceptions of the Chinese economic reform movement, see Gilbert Rozman, *A Mirror for Socialism: Soviet Criticisms of China* (Princeton: Princeton University Press, 1985), 80–85, 129–36; and Marshall I. Goldman, "Soviet Perceptions of Chinese Economic Reforms and the Implications for Reform in the USSR," *Journal of International Affairs* 39, no. 2 (Winter 1986):41–55.

34. "Zhonggong Gonghui Zhangcheng," *Renmin Ribao,* Oct. 24, 1983, 3.

35. Zhang Youyu, "Workers' Participation in Enterprise Management," 94.

36. The question of the role of the Party in the enterprise is the topic of voluminous discussion in the Chinese press. For examples, see Xiao Liang, "Implementing the Plant Director Responsibility System," K6–K10; Cao Zhi, "Improve and Strengthen the Party's Leadership in Enterprises" (*Red Flag* 14 [July 16, 1985]:13–17), in *JPRS-CRF-85-019,* 21–29. For an example of an article

defending the system in which the Party secretary retains operational control over the enterprise, see Wu Hanzhou and Yang Jian, "The System of Factory Directors of Enterprises Owned by the Whole People, Concurrently Serving as Party Secretaries" (*Jingji Guanli* 12 [Dec. 5, 1985]:27–31), in *FBIS,* Feb. 19, 1986, K8–K15.

37. See, for example, Womack, "Modernization and Democratic Reform in China," 417–39; Joseph, "Dilemmas of Political Reform in China," 252–55, 279–80; and Hong Yung Lee, "The Implications of Reform for Ideology, State and Society in China," *Journal of International Affairs* 39, no. 2 (Winter 1986):77–89.

38. Elections were held in the Chinese enterprise on occasion before the ascension of the current leadership but never for the selection of high-level leadership cadres.

39. For a discussion of criteria for trade union membership, see *Gonghui Gongzuo Wenda* (Beijing: Gongren Chubanshe, 1981), 11–15; and *Zhongguo Gonghui Zhangcheng Jianghua* (Beijing: Gongren Chubanshe, 1984), 33–42.

40. In units in which a trade union was organized, 73,310,000 staff and workers out of a workforce of 85,866,000 were reported to be trade union members at the end of 1982, a membership rate of 85.3 percent. But with a Chinese urban workforce of 112 million at the end of 1982, approximately 27 million Chinese worked in units without a trade union organization, or approximately 23 percent of the total Chinese wage-earning population. Xue Muqiao, ed., *Almanac of China's Economy 1983* (Hong Kong: Chinese Economic Yearbook Limited, 1983), sec. 1, p. 39. In 1981, 85 percent of Chinese trade union members were estimated to work in state-owned enterprises, with the remaining 15 percent of trade union membership drawn from the collective sector of Chinese industry. Saich, "Workers in the Workers' State," 161. A current aim of trade union policy, however, is to increase union membership through the establishment of unions in collective enterprises and in rural areas and through the recruitment of contract workers who were often deliberately excluded from joining the trade union in the past.

41. "Tuijin Qiye Lingdao Zhidu Gaige Ba Qiye Minzhu Guanli Yinxiang Xin Jiduan," *Gongren Ribao,* July 15, 1985, 1.

42. The trade union's responsibilities for overseeing the workers' congresses, however, have given rise to confusion over differentiating between the functions of the unions and the workers' congresses. See, for example, "Tuijin Qiye Lingdao Zhidu Gaige," 1; Guo Feng, "It Is the Common Duty of the Party, Administration and Trade Unions to Do Well in the Democratic Management of Enterprises" (*Gongren Ribao,* June 12, 1985, 3), in *FBIS,* June 27, 1985, K16.

43. See, for example, Tong Chengmin, "A Discussion on Questions Concerning Urban Trade Unions Participating In and Discussing Government Administration" (*Gongren Ribao,* Feb. 27, 1986, 1) in *FBIS,* Apr. 1, 1986, K10–K13; and Xiao Tuo, "Inherent Attributes of Trade Unions and Their Participation and Discussion of Government Administration" (*Gongren Ribao,* Feb. 27, 1986, 4), in *FBIS,* Apr. 1, 1986, K13–K15.

44. "Tuijin Qiye Lingdao Zhidu Gaige," 1.

45. "Decision on Reform of the Economic Structure," 6.

46. For a further discussion of this question, see Jan S. Prybyla, "The Chinese

Economy: Adjustment of the System or Systemic Reform," *Asian Survey* 25, no. 5 (May 1985):568; Christine Wong, "The Second Phase of Economic Reform in China," *Current History*, Sept. 1985, 278–79; and Dorothy J. Solinger, "Industrial Reform: Decentralization, Differentiation, and the Difficulties," *Journal of International Affairs* 39, no. 2 (Winter 1986):113–14.

47. William N. Dunn and Josip Obradovic, "Workers' Self-Management and Organizational Power," in Josip Obradovic and William N. Dunn, eds., *Workers' Self Management and Organizational Power in Yugoslavia* (Pittsburgh: Center for International Studies: University of Pittsburgh, 1978), 11.

48. "Shixing Changzhang (Jingli), Zerenzhi Hui Buhui Yingxiang Gongren Zai Qiye Zhongde Zhurenweng Diwei?" *Gongren Ribao*, Dec. 20, 1985, 2.

49. Andrew Walder discusses the mechanisms of Party control in the enterprise in "Work and Authority in Chinese Industry: State Socialism and the Institutional Culture of Dependency" (Ph.D. diss. University of Michigan, 1981); "Participative Management and Worker Control in China," *Sociology of Work and Occupations* 8, no. 2 (May 1981):224–51; "Organized Dependency and Cultures of Authority in Chinese Industry," *Journal of Asian Studies* 43, no. 1 (Nov. 1983):51–76; and *Communist Neo-Traditionalism: Work and Authority in Chinese Industry* (Berkeley: University of California Press, 1986).

50. "Provisional Regulations," 30.

51. "Workers' Congresses 'Only Nominal' Power Organs" (*China Daily*, Sept. 4, 1983, 4), in *FBIS*, Sept. 7, 1983, K18.

52. *Zhongguo Gonghui Dishici Chuanguo Daibiao Dahui Zhuyao Wenjian* (Beijing: Gonren Chubanshe, 1983), 51.

53. Kang Wenhua, "Dang Zhongyan Ban Gonghui Zhichule Zhengquede Fangxiang," *Gongren Ribao*, May 2, 1983, 1. In some cases, apparently, the trade union cadres who dare to stand up to the management in defense of the workers' place themselves in more than a precarious political situation. According to an exposé in *Workers' Daily*, when the assistant trade union chair at a Zhongqing glass factory expressed his opposition to the factory leadership's abuse of the workers' rights(in this case the factory leadership had illegally appropriated wage raises for itself while ignoring the workers), the assistant factory manager beat him up, sending him to the hospital. See "Gonghui Ganbu Luo Shaohua Dizhi Puji Zhong Waifeng Zaodu Da Fuchangzhang Ma Zhongjie Yi Quanmou Sidong Shou Daren Bei Chezhi," *Gongren Ribao*, July 16, 1985, 1.

54. "Gonghui Yao Jiji Can Zhengyizheng," *Gongren Ribao*, Dec. 20, 1985, 1.

55. The issue of the adminsitration of labor insurance benefits, officially a function of the unions, has been a particularly contentious issue. For a discussion of the question of distinguishing a distinct trade union sphere of responsibility, see "Resolution of the All-China Trade Union Federation" (*Xinhua*, Dec. 27, 1984), in *JPRS-CEA-008*, 118–26.

56. "Bixu Gaibian Gonghui Ganbu Yuebai Yueda de Qingkuang," *Gongren Ribao*, Mar. 24, 1984, 2; also see "Buyao Suibian Chaodiao Gonghui Ganbu Zuo Qitade Shi," *Gongren Ribao*, Apr. 23, 1983, 3; "Buyao Ba Nianlao Tiruode Ganbu Anpai Dao Gonghui," *Gongren Ribao*, July 22, 1983, 2.

57. It was reported, for example, in an article in *Workers' Daily* in early 1983 that some enterprise leaderships were using their newly granted powers to abolish

the trade union as an enterprise structure, merging its duties with other administration departments and transferring trade union cadres to other positions throughout the enterprise. See "Buyao Suibian Choudiao Gonghui Ganbu," 1.

58. See Alex Pravda, "Elections in Communist Party States," in Guy Hermet, Richard Rose, and Alain Rouguie, eds., *Elections Without Choice* (London: Macmillan Press, 1978), 169–95.

59. Walder, "Work and Authority in Chinese Industry;" "Organized Dependency and Cultures of Authority," 51–76; and *Communist Neo-Traditionalism*.

60. Elizabeth Chang (Paris *AFP* in English, Oct. 17, 1983), in *FBIS*, Oct. 20, 1983, K9.

61. "Mudi Zai Yu Guanliao Zhuyi Duihang Gongren Keyi Anqian Liyou Bagong," *Zhongbao*, Feb. 20, 1984, 1.

62. See Michael Parks, "Chinese Leaders Fear Loss of Control," *Los Angeles Times*, Nov. 19, 1981, 1; "Gongren Keyi Bagong," 1; Harry Bernstein and Michael Parks, "Labor Unions Emerging as a Major Force in China," *Los Angeles Times*, Dec. 29, 1980, 1; He Shen, "Solidarity Union of Poland and China," 72–80; Takashi Oka, "China Gives Workers a Voice to Prevent Solidarity-Like Movement," *Christian Science Monitor*, Oct. 21, 1983, 10; Kenneth J. Hammond, "Rise and Fall of a Chinese Version of Solidarity," *New York Times*, Feb. 18, 1982, 24. An additional discussion of this topic, with further references, can be found in Nathan, *Chinese Democracy* 41, 204, 206, 230; and Saich, "Workers in the Workers' State," 161, 164.

63. During the so-called first trade union crisis of 1950–51 the trade union leadership clashed with the Party leadership on the issue of the trade union's right to exercise a limited operational autonomy in defense of the workers' interests. Despite a purge of the trade union leadership, the unresolved conflict resurfaced during the "second trade union crisis" of the Hundred Flowers period of 1957, ending once again in a thoroughgoing purge of the trade union apparatus.

64. "Resolution of All-China Trade Union Federation," 126.

65. The constitutional right to strike notwithstanding, it should be noted that Mao Zedong did not hesitate to dispatch the People's Liberation Army to quell the strikes that erupted in China in 1976.

66. "Gongren Keyi Bagong," 1.

67. "Resolution of All-China Trade Union Federation," 123.

68. Nor did Ni provide any concrete illustrations of legitimate forms of collective action in Chinese factories, although he did indicate two cases—including the highly publicized Bohai Oil Rig disaster, in which twelve workers died—as examples of managerial negligence. See "Gongren Keyi Bagong," 1. In a 1983 interview, then ACFTU executive committee member Wang Jiachong was reported as stating that strikes could be supported by unions in exceptional cases, such as those involving industrial safety. According to Wang, such strikes had already taken place in the People's Republic of China, although he declined to provide concrete examples. See Chang, K10.

69. He Shen, "Solidarity Union of Poland and China," 72.

70. Average urban wages declined an estimated 19.4 percent between 1957 and 1977. Andrew Walder, "The Remaking of the Chinese Working Class, 1949–1981," *Modern China* 10, no. 1 (Jan. 1984):22–24.

71. For reports of worker unrest stemming from the reforms, see Jim Mann, "Reforms Stir Worker Unrest in Chinese Factories," *Los Angeles Times,* Oct. 19, 1984, sec. 1A, p. 1; and K. C. Tsang, "Prospects for Increased Protests Over Reforms" (*South China Morning Post,* June 24, 1985, 10) in *FBIS,* June 25, 1985, W1.

72. See Charles F. Sabel and David Stark, "Planning, Politics and Shop-Floor Power; Hidden Forms of Bargaining in Soviet-Imposed State Socialist Societies," *Politics and Society* II, no. 4 (1982):439-76. Csaba Mako and L. Hethy noted that the growing demand for labor has provided workers with the ability to secure wage rises in Hungary. Csaba Mako and L. Hethy, "Worker Participation and the Socialist Enterprise: A Hungarian Case Study," in C. Cooper and E. Mumford, eds., *The Quality of Life in Western and Eastern Europe* (Westport, Ct.: Greenwood, 1979), 296-326.

73. By 1966, however, workers' congresses were virtually moribund, and the unions similarly exhibited few signs of vitality. Neither structure had ever fully recovered from the debilitating effects of the Great Leap Forward.

74. The concept of the establishment of separate spheres of enterprise authority is evident in the suggestion that the workers' congresses "share equal status with management." Lai Ruoyu, chairman of the ACFTU, went so far as to argue the necessity for the trade unions to develop an "independence" from both management and the Party. See *Survey of China Mainland Press,* no. 1423, 1956, 10; quoted in Paul Harper, "Political Roles of Trade Unions in Communist China," (Ph.D. diss., Cornell University, 1969), 277.

11

WORKER PARTICIPATION, DEPENDENCY, AND THE POLITICS OF REFORM IN LATIN AMERICA AND THE CARIBBEAN: JAMAICA, CHILE, AND PERU COMPARED

Evelyne Huber Stephens

Workers' participation schemes, such as producer cooperatives, hold considerable attraction for advocates of development models with higher degrees of equity and democracy than pure dependent capitalist or state-socialist development models. Participatory forms of organization of production satisfy the criteria of equity, participation, and decentralization, and such reforms are not ruled out by the context of scarcity of resources. Nevertheless, participation schemes broader than isolated experiments have been rare occurrences in Latin American and Caribbean countries, and successful ones have been even rarer. The frequently heard facile argument that the lack of participation schemes in these countries is due to the low level of development and thus to low qualification, education, and ability of the labor force to participate in decision making is flatly contradicted by the Chilean experience, which shows that these factors are not unsurmountable obstacles. Rather, the following analysis points to two different important reasons for the scarcity of successful workers' participation reforms in Latin America and the Caribbean: (1) the impact of dependency on the class structure and power relations in society and thus on the relative weakness of forces favoring the development of participation schemes, and (2) the limitations of the ability of state elites to simply legislate participation schemes as vehicles for the promotion of their overall political project.

In contrast to West Europe where the principal driving forces behind workers' participation have been unions and labor parties,[1] the origins of participation schemes in the dependent capitalist societies of Latin America and the Caribbean are mostly to be found in the initiative of state elites with a reformist political project, whose coming to power was not primarily due to union support. The class structure (i.e., the small size of the industrial working class and the large pools of urban and rural surplus labor) and the industrial structure (i.e., the large number of small enterprises) have tended to prevent unions from acquiring sufficient organizational strength to be the major promoters of workers' participation. The unions have been unable to wrest participation rights directly from employers or to provide a sufficient political support base to elect governments with the mandate to legislate such rights on their behalf. Thus the nature of participation schemes has been shaped by the governments' overall political projects, and the development and consolidation of the schemes have been largely dependent on the governments' strength and capacity to implement their reformist projects as a whole. And this capacity has been limited by the constraints of dependency.

Governments committed to reformist political projects have promoted workers' participation schemes for a variety of reasons. First, governments have done so for ideological reasons. Participation schemes are important elements in two types of reform ideologies, the democratic socialist one and that promoted by the progressive wings of Christian Democratic parties. Progressive Christian Democratic doctrine, with its roots in Catholic social thinking, is not opposed to private ownership in principle, but it emphasizes social responsibility of employers, integration of workers into the enterprise, and some notion of social justice. It also advocates the creation of intermediary institutions between the individual and the state in order to facilitate cooperation among human beings as members of the society and to provide opportunities for the full development of human abilities.[2] Thus the concept of workers' participation in decision making in enterprises and co-ops fits into Christian Democratic inspired reformism as well as democratic socialism. It conforms to the goals of equity, participation, and decentralization, which are central to both ideologies, although to varying degrees. Second, the traditional importance of the role of the state in these societies has served as a facilitating factor, as have other reform policies. The state in Latin America has traditionally played a very strong role in all aspects of labor relations,[3] which suggests in a quite obvious way the option of reshaping these relationships in a participatory direction through governmental action. Furthermore, land reform, a high-priority item on the agenda of any government with a serious reform commitment in Latin America and the Caribbean, has offered the option of establishing cooperatives on expropriated estates, where the need to maintain economies of scale and/or considerations of equity have ruled out subdivisions of the lands. Third, state elites have frequently regarded participation schemes as excellent vehicles for social transformation, insofar as they would promote egalitarian, solidaristic, and participatory attitudes and behavior among their members. These attitudes and behavior would constitute the essential base for active popular support for the larger process of social transformation and for the government initiating and implementing this process.

However, experience indicates that even in periods of strength, reformist governments cannot simply legislate the establishment of participatory forms of organization of production and rely on them to function as carriers of transformation. Rather, as the following comparative analysis of initiatives for workers' participation in Jamaica, Chile, and Peru will show, such reforms are fragile creations indeed and cannot run ahead of the overall process of transformation in the society. In fact, they can even have counterproductive effects on the overall process of change in the desired direction. Besides unity of the state elite, a sustained effort at implementation, and bureaucratic capacity to carry the implementation through, reactions of organized forces (particularly unions and political parties) at the enterprise and the national level are important.

The structure of the design itself has some importance, although the same design can have different effects depending on the involvement of organized forces. Designs that emphasize the experience of direct participation in decision making rather than simply in election of representatives have a greater potential to generate involvement of workers and support for the larger process of change. Furthermore, channels for communication and participation at higher levels are crucial for linking the members of participatory enterprises and co-ops to one another and to the government, and for involving them in planning and policy making in the process of social transformation.

Ultimately, the consolidation of participatory forms of organization of production depends on the governments' ability to maintain a degree of stability in the macroeconomic situation, since economic crisis conditions weaken reformist governments and parties as well as unions, and thus the crucial forces supporting participatory schemes. The tenure of reformist governments is particularly susceptible to the repercussions from austerity policies imposed by the International Monetary Fund (MF) in balance-of-payments crises. Furthermore, even governments committed to participation are likely to abandon promotion of such schemes under pressures from the IMF, particularly its insistence on policies designed to cultivate business confidence. The layoffs and drastic deterioration of real wages, which invariably result from IMF stabilization policies, absorb labor's attention and relegate the defense of participation schemes to secondary importance. Thus in order to understand the origins, development, and effects of workers' participation and self-management schemes, one has to understand the political base and the political project of the government and the constraints on the government resulting from the structures of a dependent economy and society.

The Political Base and Project of the Governments

Jamaica

Participatory reforms were promoted by the People's National Party (PNP) government of Michael Manley, which came to power in 1972.[4] The PNP in 1972 was a largely nonideological, middle-class dominated party with cross-class electoral support. In the 1972 election 52 percent of the unemployed and unskilled, 61 percent of manual wage labor, 75 percent of white collar wage labor, and 60 percent of business, managerial, and high-income professional people voted for the PNP.[5] Despite its mass party structure, there was little grassroots involvement; lower-class followers were tied to the party through patronage.[6] Like its rival, the Jamaica Labour Party (JLP), the PNP had a union affiliated with the party, which provided help in election campaigns but was not the decisive support base. The PNP-affiliated National Workers Union (NWU) and the JLP-affiliated Bustamente Industrial Trade Union (BITU) had an exclusively economistic orientation and were not the source of major policy initiatives of the parties when in government. The union leadership in these two dominant blanket unions, as well as in several smaller unions, was predominantly of middle-class background and co-opted from the outside. Union leaders that had risen through the ranks were extremely rare, which further reduced the autonomous strength of the union movement.

Even before 1974, when the PNP officially revived its socialist heritage of the 1940s and declared its commitment to the pursuit of a democratic socialist development model, the government started to implement a set of policies consistent with such a model. These policies included state sector expansion, reduction of dependency through trade diversification, increased domestic food production, a renegotiation of relationships to the transnational bauxite-aluminum corporations, redistributive fiscal and wage policies, social and cultural policies aimed at inclusion of the lower classes, and a nonaligned foreign policy. By the 1976 elections these policies, together with the PNP's rhetorical style and close relations to Cuba, had caused a trend toward class polarization and political realignment. The bourgeoisie had turned against the government virtually in its entirety, and the PNP suffered heavy losses in the business, managerial, and professional group as a whole (down from 60 percent PNP in 1972 to 20 percent in 1976) and among the white-collar employees (from 75 percent to 57 percent), but it was able to offset these losses with gains among blue-collar workers (up from 61 percent in 1972 to 72 percent in 1976) and the unemployed and unskilled (from 52 percent to 60 percent).[7]

By the end of 1976 the government found itself confronting a severe balance-of-payments crisis. Jamaica's traditional trade deficit was aggravated by declining export volumes and prices in 1975 and 1976. Capital flight as well as a press campaign in the United States that negatively affected tourism further contributed to the balance-of-payments pressures. Thus in its second term, the government had to accept IMF agreements, the second of which was extremely stringent. The resulting rollback of living standards and deep recession rendered the population susceptible to a vicious delegitimization campaign of the opposition and led to a massive defeat of the PNP in the 1980 election, with 41 percent of the vote against the JLP's 59 percent share.

Chile

Workers' participation was introduced by Salvador Allende's Unidad Popular (UP) government during its tenure in office from 1970 to 1973. The UP was a coalition with an explicit socialist ideology and a strong union base, but it was also dependent on cross-class electoral support. A 1970 survey in greater Santiago showed that Allende received 60 percent of his support from industrial workers, 10 percent from those employed in personal services, 17 percent from office and sales employees, and 14 percent from professional, managerial, and entrepreneurial groups.[8] Despite mass party structures and the dominance of ideological politics at the national level, grassroots politics at the local level had a heavily clientelistic character as well.[9] Unions in Chile were clearly more politicized than in Jamaica; union leaders had a stronger ideological outlook, and the political education of the base was more developed.[10] This was partly a result of the Labor Code of 1924, which had made all labor federations illegal and thus virtually forced the unions to align themselves with prolabor political parties in order to be able to generate collective action on a larger scale than the enterprise. Within the Central Unica de Trabajadores (CUT), which had been formed in 1953, the unions close to the UP parties were dominant, but the unions close to the Christian Democrats received 27 percent of the vote in the 1972 elections to CUT,[11] and they were very strong in the rural sector. Yet despite their strong political ties, the orientation of Chilean unions was also predominantly economistic in the sense of putting direct material benefits of members above the struggle for socioeconomic transformation.

From its accession to power, the UP embarked on its path of democratic socialist transformation in a much more radical way and at a much faster pace than the PNP ever did. More enterprises were nationalized, large agricultural estates expropriated, and the wage/price policies effected a more rapid and substantial increase in the buying power of the lower classes. The effects of these policies, together with deliberate attempts of the internal and external opposition to damage the economy, resulted in severe inflationary and balance-of-payments pressures and in shortages and disruptions in production. These economic dislocations in turn contributed to class polarization and the growth of the militant disloyal opposition and popular countermobilization in support of the government. The resulting threat to the economy and to public order, reinforced by growing civilian calls for military action and by U.S. encouragement of such action, shifted the internal balance of forces in the military from the constitutionalists to the interventionists, preparing the way for the 1973 coup.

Peru

Various forms of participation were introduced by the Peruvian Revolutionary Government of the Armed Forces under President Velasco, which seized power in 1968.[12] The military's main concern was with integral security, which they perceived to be threatened by the structures of the dependent economy and exploitative society and by the weakness of the civilian government. Thus they embarked upon a set of structural changes in economy and society that were designed to bring about economic strength and national integration, the prerequisites for integral security. These changes included reduction of dependence, expansion of the state sector, land reform, social programs for the urban lower classes, support for popular organization under tutelage of the state, and redistributive and participatory reforms for labor.[13] To the extent that members of the military government were ideological, the majority held some variety of communitarian ideas, highly averse to the idea of class struggle, and they hoped that the reforms would weaken class-based organizations. A few younger officers close to Velasco and some important civilian advisers had a socialist conception of the desirable social order, however, and were able to exert some influence on the reform process in its first six years.[14]

Initially the government enjoyed a high degree of autonomy from civil society, but by about 1973 opposition from the dominant classes had strengthened and started to narrow the government's room for action.[15] At the same time, pressures from popular forces increased. The Peruvian labor movement as of the late 1960s was divided into two major confederations with close links to Apra, Peru's only mass party, and to the Communist Party; there also were a small Christian Democratic confederation and several independent radical unions. The unions close to Apra and the radical unions opposed the military government, whereas those close to the Communist Party supported its reform policies. Thus the government sponsored its own central union organization to compete with the other confederations. This, together with the effects of other reform policies, caused a dramatic increase in unionization; the number of unions doubled between 1968 and 1975, with the Communist-linked confederation remaining the strongest.[16] The result was a heightened level of mobilization capacity of the unions and increasing militancy in strike action.

By 1975 severe balance-of-payments problems resulting from a high debt burden and declining export volumes and prices called for the beginning of ever more stringent austerity policies. The coup replacing Velasco with Morales Bermudez in 1975 marked the transition to the Second Phase of the process, which (despite official proclamations to the contrary) involved not only a stop but a partial rollback of the reform process. Under the stabilization programs negotiated with creditor banks in 1976 and with the IMF from 1977 on, opposition to the government from all social classes rapidly mounted, and in 1978 the military initiated the process of withdrawal from government with elections to a Constituent Assembly, which ended in the presidential and congressional elections of 1980.

The Role of Participation in the Reform Project

Jamaica

In the conception of Michael Manley, who decisively shaped the PNP's political project, workers' participation in decision making in enterprises was one institutional form contributing to the widest possible participation of the mass of the Jamaican people in the process of transformation toward a more egalitarian society, overcoming the stark class and race divisions characterizing Jamaica.[17] This process was to redistribute material resources as well as power and thus required increased participation of the lower classes in politics, in the process of production and the benefits from production, and in the social and cultural life of Jamaica. In the political arena, the PNP attempted to achieve this by turning the party into a real mass party, emphasizing political education and promoting grassroots involvement in the party's policy-making bodies. In the cultural arena the government launched a variety of initiatives to stimulate and put greater value on indigenous cultural expressions. In the economic arena it emphasized job creation through the expanded state sector, along with the establishment of cooperatives on sugar estates owned by the government, strengthening of workers' rights vis-a-vis employers, and plans for workers' participation in decision making in public and private enterprises. Higher levels of popular participation, organization, and assertiveness in all these areas were to bring about a shift in the balance of power in society, thus facilitating and reinforcing the redistribution of material resources.

The establishment of cooperatives on the sugar estates, besides transferring power and resources to the sugar workers, had a great symbolic significance, as it eliminated one of the most visible legacies of slave society and the colonial economy. A reform of labor relations in the private sector became important because the mixed economy was to be a permanent feature of the Jamaican democratic socialist model. In many enterprises labor relations were characterized by authoritarianism and even disdain on the part of employers, and hostility and a propensity to spontaneous militancy on the part of workers.[18] Arrangements for workers to participate in decision making in the enterprise were to put the two sides on a more equal footing and to establish relationships of mutual respect and cooperation. Workers' participation, then, was a goal in itself as well as an element in the process of transformation, intended to shift the power balance in enterprises, thus contributing to shifts in the society at large, and to generate attitudes of solidarity among workers and cooperation between employers and workers.

Chile

For the UP, promotion of popular participation in the economic, political, and cultural spheres was to perform the same mobilizing and transformative functions as for the PNP. However, the UP's commitment to a faster and more far-reaching process of transformation resulted in some important differences in approach. Since the social area, consisting of fully and majority state-owned as well as state-administered enterprises,[19] was to rapidly become the dominant sector in the Chilean economy, workers' participation schemes were only introduced there, not in private enterprises. In the rural sector, on the expropriated land of large private estates, the UP attempted to establish more inclusive forms of agrarian reform enterprises than traditional co-ops. The government was hampered in these attempts, however, by its inability to change the reform legislation passed by the Christian Democratic government of Eduardo Frei (1964–70).[20]

As on many other issues, there were disagreements among the UP coalition parties on the importance of workers' participation in the enterprises in the social area. For most of them, workers' participation was a goal worth pursuing in itself because of its democratic and egalitarian qualities, as well as an instrument to mobilize workers and strengthen the popular base for the construction of a democratic socialist society. The Communist Party, in contrast, advocated a more statist model of economic organization as well as a more controlled process of popular mobilization.

Peru

The approach of the majority of the Peruvian military government to popular participation emphasized incorporation of peasants, workers, and the urban poor into participatory institutions and into organizations linked to the state. Redistribution of resources and transfer of certain decision-making rights to popular classes through the establishment of agrarian producer co-ops, urban squatter organizations, and workers' participation schemes were to be guided from above and to bypass existing class-based organizations in order to weaken them. This, in turn, would reduce the potential for class struggle at the bottom. The land reform, which eliminated the economic power base of the old oligarchy, would also reduce this potential at the top and thus facilitate the achievement of national integration.

Workers' participation in private and state enterprises was designed with both political and economic goals in mind. By reconciling interests between employers and employees and by increasing investment and productivity, it was to strengthen the enterprises and the national economy; by making unions superfluous, it was to weaken them both at the enterprise and at the national level. Officially, the government denied that its workers' participation reform was intended to weaken unions, but it did insist that the reform was to overcome antagonisms between labor and capital. Unofficially, the government clearly hoped that its reforms would constitute a noncoercive tool for the weakening of unions and would thus be compatible with its policy of cooperation with existing unions, which it pursued to reduce labor militancy.

However, the radical faction in the government had a different conception of the political project and the role of popular participation in general and workers' participation in particular. They saw the reforms as tools to strengthen popular organization and mobilization, thus modifying the balance of power in society in favor of the popular classes and pushing the government's reform course to the left. They regarded workers' participation in private enterprises as a step in a gradual movement toward socialization and full workers' control. They saw existing popular organizations that had the same goals as allies in this process, rather than as competitors, and they collaborated with them in practice. By 1974 it became clear that the radical faction was on the decline in the internal power struggle. Yet up to that point its activities had contributed to real gains in strength of popular organizations, as well as to a hardening of opposition of the bourgeoisie, through the introduction of ambiguities into the reform designs and through the encouragement of and assistance to popular organizations pressuring for more far-reaching reforms.

Designs of Workers' Participation Schemes

Jamaica

In 1975 the PNP government appointed a commission composed of experts and representatives from the private sector, labor, and the government bureaucracy to study the issue of workers' participation and come up with suggestions for Jamaica. The commission looked at experiences in other countries and carefully studied the solicited submissions from unions and employers. In 1976 it presented to the Cabinet a report that suggested the establishment of workers' participation schemes in both public and private enterprises employing more than 40 workers. Works councils composed of half worker and half management representatives were to be in charge of personnel and social affairs. In enterprises with more than 100 workers, an Economic Committee was to be consulted on all major economic developments in the enterprise and was to have the right to full financial information. The unions were to be included insofar as some of the worker representatives would be elected by the workforce and some appointed by the unions. The commission also recommended worker representation on the board of directors, one-half in public sector enterprises and one-third in the private sector. Finally, the commission emphasized that after a period of careful study of various pilot projects, legislation would be needed on the subject, since one could not rely on voluntary action on the part of employers.[21]

Manley's budget speech in May 1977 contained outlines for the establishment of participation schemes that followed the commission's recommendations, but with two important modifications.[22] First, the position and functions of the unions were differentiated more explicitly from those of the works councils, and the commission's recommendation that the unions democratize their own operations was omitted. Questions of remuneration, working hours, and individual worker grievances were to remain the exclusive responsibility of the trade unions. Within the guidelines, detailed structures for participation would be the subject of collective agreements between unions and employers. Second, the number of worker representatives on the boards of directors was preliminarily limited to two seats in both private and public sector enterprises, to be changed after a revision of the Company Law.

Chile

The UP government, in collaboration with CUT, elaborated a set of guidelines for workers' participation schemes in enterprises belonging to the social area.[23] The guidelines provided for an administrative council as highest authority in the enterprise, composed of five worker representatives, five state representatives, and a state-appointed administrator. The worker representatives were elected by a general assembly that was to meet monthly and was charged with supervising the participation of various groups in the enterprise. At the level of production departments, section assemblies were to meet monthly, elect representatives to a production committee, and oversee operations in their section. The presidents of all the production committees in an enterprise belonged to a coordinating committee, which was the main channel for communication with the administrative council. The scheme, then, combined opportunities for direct participation in decisions about matters of daily concern on the shop floor with participation of worker representatives in decisions at the top enterprise level. The unions were assigned an important role in the participation scheme insofar as the union commission, composed of the leaders of all the unions in an enterprise, was to preside over the general assembly and participate in the coordinating committee.[24] Unions were also responsible for educating workers about the participation schemes. However, in order to maintain an organizational differentiation between the unions and the workers' committees and assemblies, union leaders themselves could not run for election to the administrative councils or the production committees.

Peru

Workers' participation in Peru was introduced by legislation in 1970 for all industrial manufacturing enterprises with six or more workers or roughly $250,000 gross annual income. The next year the legislation was extended to the fishing, mining, and telecommunications sectors, covering public as well as private enterprises. It provided for the establishment of an Industrial Community (CI) in every enterprise, composed of all employees from janitor to manager, except those with a share in ownership. The enterprise was required to give 25 percent of net profits before taxes to the CI every year, 10 percent in cash to individual employees, and 15 percent to the CI as a collectivity in the form of shares newly issued or sold to the CI by existing shareholders. Initially, the CI was entitled to one representative on the board of directors of the enterprise, and its representation was to grow in accordance with its share in ownership.

Ownership by the CI was to grow up to 50 percent, at which point the CI and the owners would jointly manage the enterprise. The exact arrangements for that point, in particular the question of how to solve deadlocks, were left unspecified in the law and in official interpretations, as a result of diverging conceptions of the whole political project by the different factions in the government. An early draft of the legislation supported by the radical faction had actually not set the 50 percent limit and had thus contained the potential for private enterprises to gradually come under majority worker ownership and management.

Under the CI as legislated, workers were not given any participation rights in decision making in the enterprise. The general assembly was in charge only of electing its officers and representative(s) to the board of directors, of deciding what to do with the collective income of the CI from its shares, and seeking ways to improve enterprise operations in collaboration with management. The general assembly was specifically barred from dealing with any personnel issues. In accordance with the intention of the majority in the government to weaken existing unions, union officials were barred from holding office in the CI or acting as representatives of the CI in dealings with employers or the state bureaucracy.

Clearly the CI legislation was in no way satisfactory to the radical faction in the government. As an alternative, they promoted the project of a Social Property Sector, to be composed of collectively owned (by all the workers in the sector) and fully worker self-managed enterprises. After consultation with many groups and advisers familiar with worker self-management schemes around the world, legislation establishing this sector was decreed in 1974.[25]

The Functioning of Workers' Participation Schemes

Jamaica

The participation schemes in Jamaica, never got beyond the planning stage except for a few experiments in public sector enterprises. The main reasons for this were the predominantly negative reactions of the unions to the proposals, followed by the government's loss of political initiative and room to maneuver because of the economic crisis. As expected, employers strongly objected to the idea, and their leverage vis-à-vis the government was strengthened by the IMF's involvement beginning in 1977.

The unions' reaction was motivated in part by partisan political reasons (in the case of the BITU), and in part it was a result of their rather authoritarian structure and their lack of ideological vision and education. Officially only the Union of Technical, Administrative and Supervisory

Personnel (UTASP) offered opposition, forbidding any of its delegates (i.e., shop stewards) to participate in training schemes.[26] All the other unions paid lip service to the goal of workers' participation. Unofficially, however, the unions were concerned about a possible erosion of their power by losing influence over their members at the workplace. Relationships between rank-and-file members and the middle- and top-level leadership in many unions have been neither close nor based on strong trust, which is one of the factors underlying the phenomenon of frequent wildcat strikes in Jamaica.[27] Thus the availability of alternative channels for the direct articulation and defense of workers' interests might well have weakened the position of these outside leaders. The BITU, true to its particularly undemocratic and paternalistic tradition,[28] cautioned extensively about the lack of education and preparation of workers and emphasized the need for extensive training prior to any significant legislative initiatives in the area. The NWU and the Jamaica Association of Local Government Officers (JALGO) were the only major unions supporting the concept, but for the NWU it was just one among many goals and not one with high priority. The University and Allied Workers' Union (UAWU), headed by the general secretary of the communist Workers' Party of Jamaica, also supported the project but with the clear implication that participation was only a step toward full workers' control. As a result of their apprehensions and hesitations, the unions (other than JALGO and the UAWU) served as brakes on the process, rather than as pressure groups mobilizing workers in support of it.

Employers were virtually unanimously opposed to the introduction of workers' participation, particularly to any legislation on the issue. Reactions ranged from mild and pragmatically argued to quite rabid and principled opposition. An example of the former is the statement submitted by the Grace Kennedy Corporation to the commission set up by the government.[29] The company cautioned about the problem of "translating the worthy idea of worker participation into an effective operating reality," and it pointed out that it already had initiated a number of programs for active involvement of the workforce, such as group discussions held by supervisors to solicit and "discuss plans and ideas for completing assigned task [sic]" and others. The All-Island Cane Farmers Association's submission provides an example not only of the more strident opposition to workers' participation but also of the authoritarian and disdainful attitude of a large portion of Jamaican employers. The association explained its opposition to workers' participation with an analogy to military organization. The worker was regarded as equivalent to a foot soldier and management to the "commanding sector" of the army; given the limited training of the footsoldier-workers, they would naturally be ill-equipped to give advice on operations outside of their ambit of operations; at most, they

342 Worker Participation, Dependency, and the Politics of Reform

might make suggestions as to the techniques that would make their tasks easier and more productive and pleasant. Reynolds, the Jamaican subsidiary of a U.S. aluminum company, categorically objected to workers' participation on the grounds that "we cannot accept the right of a worker to decision-making that belongs to ownership." Finally, the Citrus Company of Jamaica argued that the concept was ill defined and warned that "producer democracy which is not compatible with consumer freedom and entrepreneurial rewards is doomed to create fertile grounds for a new tyranny."

In 1977 the government set up a Worker Participation Unit in the Ministry of Labor that was in charge of organizing participation schemes, studying them, and making suggestions for improvements where needed. However, within the following years, the impetus behind the project largely dissipated. In February 1978 eight of fifteen field organizers trained for the Worker Participation Unit were laid off, and in June 1978 new guidelines concerning participation in the public sector were issued, along with the universal restriction that only experimental schemes were to be set up, and on a purely voluntary basis.

The layoff of these field organizers was an immediate result of strong union objections to the personalities and political inclinations of the people chosen and trained. But the scaledown of the project as a whole was largely a result of the economic crisis, which absorbed the energies of the top-level political directorate. This meant that the only force that could have overcome union as well as employer opposition was otherwise occupied. Even if there had been more union support for workers' participation, the 1978 agreement with the IMF, with its premium on the cultivation of private sector confidence, would have made a compulsory introduction of workers' participation against the strong employer opposition virtually impossible.

Thus the only two participation schemes with any significance that were ever established were in the public sector, at the Jamaica Broadcasting Corporation and Jamintel. Some boards of the utilities moved in the direction of accepting worker representatives. In the government-owned sugar factories, works councils were set up for joint consultation at the lowest level, in questions of working conditions and social services. In contrast, not a single participation scheme approximating the guidelines was experimented with in the private sector.

Chile

In Chile the speed of implementation and the successful development and functioning of participation schemes varied considerably. There was no central administrative apparatus exercising control over state enterprises that was capable of enforcing implementation of the guidelines. Therefore the establishment and promotion of participation schemes were dependent on local initiatives from administrators, union leaders, and party activists. The unions showed different reactions to the guidelines. Some of them, in a similar fashion to Jamaican unions, manifested considerable reluctance because they feared losing influence; bureaucratic and paternalistic behavior existed among parts of the Chilean labor movement, just as in Jamaica.[30] Furthermore, political splits in the labor movement resulting in union rivalry and partisan political competition within enterprises obstructed the development of the participation schemes in many cases. However, in contrast to Jamaica, there were more ideologically motivated unions that were supporting workers' participation, seeing it as part of the larger process of transformation. In addition, the UP parties themselves had more ideologically committed cadres at local levels, including in the factories, that were able to promote the participation schemes, bypassing obstructionist union leaders where necessary.

By June 1972 some type of participation scheme was in operation in 76 percent of the enterprises in the social area.[31] The crucial variables determining the degree of actual involvement of workers in decision making were the degree of labor mobilization and consciousness, the political ideology and attitude of worker leaders toward participation, and the composition of political party support in the enterprise.[32] Where workers had an experience of struggle, for instance in strikes and militancy before or during the transfer of the enterprise into the social area, or where unions and political parties had reached workers with political education about the process of social transformation and the workers' role in this process, workers had a higher propensity to actively participate in decision making and in supervising the implementation of decisions. Where union and sectional leaders were supportive of participation and of the wider process of transformation, the schemes were also more intensely used.

In contrast, where Christian Democratic influences were strong among leaders as well as workers, the levels of participation were lower.[33] This was also true for enterprises with strong Communist influence. Though the latter was less a matter of partisan political motives than in the case of the Christian Democrats, the Communist Party was only lukewarm toward participation, because it favored a more centralized, state-directed model of organization in the social area and was more skeptical toward popular mobilization at the national level. Where worker involvement and leadership support was strong, however, the government-appointed administrator and members of the administrative council tended to be receptive, disseminate information, and collaborate with the various committees, which in turn increased the importance of these committees and further heightened the level of participation. In the case of reluctant administrators, the workers had the opportunity to mobilize pressure and enlist the help of those sectors in the government committed to workers' participation to get the administrator replaced.

Where actual workers' participation in formulation, execution, and evaluation of decisions at the various levels in the enterprise was high, it had a favorable impact on enterprise performance as well as on workers' attitudes.[34] Since the elimination of the traditional hierarchical system of authority was accompanied by the creation of a new democratic, participatory system of authority, peer pressure came to substitute for the previous disciplinary powers of supervisors. Since the new work experience under these participatory structures increased workers' sense of dignity and responsibility, work motivation and effort increased. The result was lower absenteeism, a decrease in strikes, and an increase in innovations in the enterprise and productivity. Furthermore, enterprises with higher participation levels also tended to have higher investment ratios.[35]

The effects of high participation levels on egalitarian and solidaristic attitudes and behavior also manifested themselves in more egalitarian and collective structures of remuneration. Wage differentials between different categories of employees were reduced, and individual piece rates were replaced by collective incentive systems. There was also strong emphasis on an improvement of collective social services, such as medical facilities, day-care centers, and recreational facilities.[36] In short, in enterprises with a dominant political and union presence supportive of the process of transformation, workers were mobilized into utilizing the new channels for collective decision making, and this experience in turn fostered egalitarian and solidaristic behavior.

Peru

Union reaction to the participation reform in Peru was also initially cautious—not in the least surprising, given the implicit co-optative intention of the reform. However, experienced union leaders at the enterprise and at higher levels soon realized that the CI could actually strengthen their position if they became actively involved in defending the rights of the workers as members of the CI. In many cases much of this activity had to be unofficial because of the legal exclusion of union leaders from CI positions and from the handling of CI affairs, but in other cases leaders resigned from their union positions to run for CI positions.[37] Employer opposition was virtually universal and intense, and all kinds of evasive maneuvers were used to foil the impact of the legislation. First, employers attempted to delay the establishment of the CIs, and where the workforce was unorganized, the CI was frequently not established at all until the Ministry of Industry launched an enforcement drive. Where the workforce was organized and informed about the legislation, however, the union often became the driving force behind the establishment of the CI.

Once the CI was established, serious conflicts erupted as employers started to use evasion tactics and workers attempted to assert their rights. For instance, accounting tricks were used to reduce the amount of declared profits, new enterprises and partnerships were created to which profits were channeled, information was withheld from the CI, and the CI representatives were ridiculed at board meetings. Naturally, the workers with most experience in confronting employers and enlisting the help of the state bureaucracy, namely union officials, played the leading role in the defense of CI rights, notwithstanding their formal exclusion from CI affairs. The only formal recourse for the CI to insist on its rightful share of profits and on its other rights in the face of employer intransigence was to claim to the Ministry of Industry, which was in charge of supervising the implementation of the legislation. However, the ministry had neither the bureaucratic capacity to perform this function on its own initiative nor the sanctioning power to force enterprises to comply with the law where CI complaints were followed up on and verified. Thus it took strong direct worker pressure on the enterprise and on the ministry to get involved in forcing recalcitrant employers to grant the benefits to the CI. This, of course, only served to strengthen the position of the unions in the unionized enterprises. In nonunionized enterprises the experience of conflict over the CI legislation, combined with the demonstration effect from CIs in unionized enterprises that successfully defended their rights, led to the formation of new unions.

The CI, then, did not redistribute decision-making rights, nor did it smooth labor relations; on the contrary, it intensified the conflict of interest between labor and capital.[38] Accordingly, it did not result in any attitudinal or behavioral changes among the workers regarding work effort, as the conflict over the distribution of the results of work efforts became highly visible and there was no change in their daily work experience. Participation for rank-and-file workers was restricted to attendance at the twice-yearly general assembly of the CI and the election of a council and a president as executive organs of the CI. The main activities of the CI centered on the supervision and disposition of its collective financial assets. The CI lacked the right to participate in managerial decisions at any level but the board of directors, where its representatives could make suggestions, but acceptance of these suggestions was left to the discretion of the board and management. Furthermore, the CI was officially barred from dealing with any labor relations questions, which remained the preserve of unions. Thus there was no direct experience of participation in decision making about work organization that could have changed workers' attitudes, but the CI did strengthen solidaristic attitudes indirectly via the experience of highly visible conflicts with the employers, which reinforced traditional union solidarity.

There were exceptions to the general pattern of conflict. In some highly profitable enterprises with a relatively small workforce in which management complied with the legislation, the CI did have the desired co-optative effects.[39] The profits distributed to the workforce were very large compared with prevailing remuneration levels, and thus the workforce became concerned with maximizing enterprise profits. This entailed not only labor peace but also an effort to keep the workforce small by hiring temporary workers rather than full-time permanent workers to replace those leaving. In other words, a spirit of group egoism emerged in these enterprises, putting group interests and solidarity above class interests and solidarity.

Effects on Labor's Strength and Support for the Government

Jamaica

Since the project never got off the ground, the strength of labor was not affected one way or the other, nor did the government gain or lose much labor support because of its initiative in this area. At best, one can speculate that it managed to increase its support base slightly among the members of JALGO, while at worst it might have heightened suspicion among members of other unions mediated by their leaders' hostility toward the project.

Ironically, workers' participation had a highly indirect negative effect on support for the government. In one of the very few cases where participation developed to a certain extent, at the Jamaica Broadcasting Corporation, though on a largely informal experimental basis, it strengthened the influence and visibility of the UAWU and thus indirectly of the communist Workers' Party of Jamaica. Through participation in hiring decisions, employees with UAWU ties managed to significantly influence the composition of the newsroom staff and thus the presentation of news and special reports. The Workers' Party took a position of "critical support" for the government, pursuing a strategy of "collaboration of all progressive force." Thus the UAWU's gains could have been, at best, a mixed blessing for the government. In reality its influence on the newsroom of the public broadcasting station, which in Jamaica has traditionally been perceived as the government's mouthpiece, probably did more damage than good to the government's credibility and wider popular support in 1980 because of the radical slant given to the news presentations and analyses.

In terms of opposition among employers, the workers' participation project contributed at most marginally to their alienation. This is not to say that it would not have provoked strong opposition had it been implemented; but since it was not, it never became nearly as important as other factors in generating opposition against the government. None of the business leaders interviewed in 1982 even mentioned the project when asked about the reasons why they or other members of the business community had turned against the government.[40] Their attention in 1976, when the commission report on worker participation was presented, was absorbed by the rapidly deteriorating economic situation and by the heightened political polarization and mobilization visible in the election campaign. By 1977, when Manley presented the guidelines, there was little support left to lose for the government among the bourgeoisie. With very few exceptions, the business community had turned to strong opposition against the government by the 1976 election. Furthermore, the business community never felt immediately threatened by the project because they (correctly) perceived that the project was not a high priority item on the government's agenda.

Chile

By strengthening solidarity among the workers, the successfully functioning participation schemes in Chile also strengthened the mobilization capacity of labor. The demands for participation at higher levels of economic policy making from the participants in these schemes also indicate a heightened level of understanding of and support for the larger social transformation project. One can reasonably conclude that this support translated into support for the government carrying out the project. However, there is a question as to the importance of the independent contribution of the participatory experience to union solidarity and support for democratic socialism. As Espinosa and Zimbalist show,[41] experience in solidaristic struggles and ideological orientations of workers and their leaders were the factors determining the successful functioning of the participation schemes to begin with. Thus one should conclude that the participation schemes had a reinforcing effect on labor strength and governmental support where these factors were present already, rather than generating them where they were not.

Since the participation schemes did not directly affect private employers, this project per se did not involve high costs to the government in the form of increased business opposition. It was the process of incorporation of enterprises into the social area itself, preceding the introduction of workers' participation, that fundamentally threatened the bourgeoisie. However, the workers' participation project did have an indirect effect on business opposition to the UP government, insofar as it reinforced labor solidarity and militancy and thus sharpened the perception of threat on the part of the bourgeoisie.

Peru

The introduction of the CI, by heightening the visibility of the conflict between labor and capital and of the utility of unions in protecting labor's interests, contributed directly to the increase in unionization and thus the growing strength of the labor movement. The government's reactions to these developments further reinforced labor mobilization and ultimately militancy. The CI provided not only the motivation but also the organizational shelter for establishing unions at the level of industrial establishments.[42] The CI assemblies brought workers together, thus reducing fears of individual reprisals from employers for signing membership lists. Such fears were further reduced and unionization efforts facilitated by the Law on Stability of Employment, decreed by the government in 1970 to thwart employer opposition to the CI. Employers threatened mass firings and the government responded with this law, which stated that after an initial trial period of three months, an employee could be fired only for serious misbehavior.

The experience with the limitations of the CI also gave rise to demands for an expansion of participation rights at the enterprise level and at higher levels of economic policy making. To put some collective pressure behind these demands, as well as behind the efforts to enforce the CI rights already given, some CIs in enterprises with a strong union tradition initiated the formation of a national organization linking individual CIs together. These efforts were supported by SINAMOS, the government's agency for national mobilization, and they culminated in a national congress of CIs where—contrary to the official position of SINAMOS—quite radical resolutions were passed that called for transformation in the direction of full workers' control.[43] After a change in its top leadership in 1974, SINAMOS took a more interventionist and decidedly more conservative position, and it managed to effect a split in the national organization of CIs, bringing one faction closely in line with government policies. However, the other faction, around the CIs that had originally promoted the organization, remained the more influential and visible one, and the actions of SINAMOS only reinforced the determination of the members of this faction to act in a collective fashion.

Similar developments occurred in the union movement. The government decided to set up a new central union organization sponsored by SINAMOS to compete with the three existing union confederations, in the hopes that it would eventually eclipse the others and prevent unwanted labor militancy. Because of the manipulative tactics used in setting up the new confederation (such as co-optation and intimidation of existing unions into joining) and its obvious subservience to the government, it never made any inroads into the hold of the other confederations, particularly the one close to the Communist Party, on the key industrial sectors. Rather, the whole attempt strengthened solidarity among the existing unions and provoked militancy in defense against intimidation and co-optation attempts.

The CI, and related activities of SINAMOS, strengthened support for a process of social transformation and for the radical faction into the government, but not for the class-conciliation project advocated by the mainstream in the government. The resulting process of mobilization led to a significant increase in strike action, motivation for which was reinforced by the deteriorating economic conditions. The shape of strikes got shorter and larger, indicating the growing use of protest strikes, many of which were directed at the government as well as employers.[44] With the onset of the Second Phase and its economic austerity policies, militant labor opposition against the government of Morales Bermudez mounted, and with the purge of the radical officers from the government in 1976, the last rallying point of support for the government was eliminated. Despite the government resorting to repressive measures, such as the selective declaration of states of emergency, the deterioration of real wages under the IMF policies continued to galvanize labor into militant action. The heightened capacity for solidaristic action manifested itself in Peru's first successful national strike in 1977 and several others in the following years.

In contrast to the workers' participation reforms in the other two countries, the CI was a major contributing factor in the opposition of the bourgeoisie to the government. Nationalization in Peru was directed predominantly at foreign capital and thus posed no real threat to the national bourgeoisie. Although the CI did not constitute a direct threat either, in the sense of a potential loss of control over the enterprise in the short or medium run, the uncertainty about the long run and the very idea of having to share ownership with the workers and having to accept worker representatives on the board was highly offensive to most employers. Accordingly, they not only attempted to circumvent the CI at the enterprise level, they also continued to pressure the government for a weakening of the legislation. The Law on Stability of Employment was the second major issue of contention, solidifying the determined opposition of the bourgeoisie against the government of the First Phase. The CI also had an indirect effect on bourgeois opposition by way of increasing labor mobilization and militancy, which the bourgeoisie blamed on government encouragement. During the Second Phase, then, under pressures from the bourgeoisie supported by the IMF, government policy shifted in a distinctively antilabor direction and the most opposed pieces of legislation were suspended or changed.

The Decline of the Workers' Participation Project

Jamaica

The abandonment of the workers' participation plans in Jamaica was clearly linked to the economic crisis. The crisis fully absorbed the attention of the government. Furthermore, the budgetary austerity imposed by the IMF greatly reduced the government's capacity to pursue any of its reform policies. In the case of the participation project, austerity meant that financing for the "unproductive" activity of selecting and training new field organizers and implementing programs for worker education to prepare them for a participation in decision making on enterprise organization and operations would be obstructed. The IMF's insistence on restoration of business confidence did not allow for any additional policies resolutely opposed by the business community.

Essentially, the austerity policies forced a near general arrest of the reform process, and the resulting drastic decline in Jamaican living standards ultimately brought about the decisive defeat of the government in the 1980 elections. Thus the economic crisis prevented the consolidation of the democratic socialist reform project. In order to understand this failure, the reasons for the balance-of-payments crisis of late 1976 need to be explained. They are to be found in the weakness of Jamaica's dependent economy on the one hand and certain policy mistakes and omissions on the other hand. In the 1960s Jamaica ran a balance-of-trade deficit, financed by the inflow of investment into bauxite-alumina and tourism. When the investment cycle in these industries was completed in the early 1970s, the country was faced with an immediate severe balance-of-payments problem, because it was highly dependent on imports of all kinds, from food and energy to raw materials, capital, and consumer goods. This problem was then aggravated by the increases in oil prices as well as in prices of non-oil imports. The crisis was precipitated by the decline in bauxite-alumina and sugar exports in 1975–76, and by a simultaneous decline in tourism revenues caused by an adverse press campaign in the United States and the cessation of commercial bank lending to the government.[45] The illegal flight of capital, which appears to have picked up considerably in 1975 and 1976, also contributed to the crisis.

Notwithstanding the importance of these results of dependency, however, part of the reason for the decline has to be sought in the government's lack of an economic plan in accordance with its overall transformation project and in its consequent neglect of policies promoting a slow reorientation of the economy toward greater self-reliance and diversification of external economic relations.[46] In the crisis situation of early 1977 an alternative, non-IMF emergency economic plan that contained such suggestions was elaborated. It emphasized promotion of agricultural production to reduce reliance on food and raw material imports and to create employment, establishment of Community Enterprise Organizations (a form of socially owned self-managed enterprises), support for small businesses, and the search for trade partners and sources of finance outside the traditional metropolitan channels.[47] However, given the severity of the crisis at that point and the consequent dislocations in the traditional manufacturing sector resulting from the restriction on imports of industrial inputs envisaged by the plan, the government anticipated a strong political backlash, not only from the bourgeoisie but also from parts of the labor movement. Thus it decided not to take this risk and to accept an IMF package instead. Arguably, if this type of plan had been adopted earlier and some of the distributive expenditures in the more favorable economic circumstances of 1974, for instance, had been redirected toward such a plan, the blance-of-payments problem might have been alleviated, the implementation of the IMF dictates avoided, and the chances for success of the whole transformation process increased.

Chile

The reason for the demise of the workers' participation project, of course, was the coup against Allende. The coup was triggered by the high degree of political polarization and intense mobilization on both sides, which in turn was partly a result of the severe deterioration of the economic situation.[48] As in Jamaica, the economic deterioration had its roots in the vulnerability of Chile's dependent economy, particularly the high import dependence on food, capital, and intermediate goods, the export concentration on copper, and the high foreign debt accumulated by previous governments. But the much faster pace of change pursued by the UP government, together with the stronger politically motivated internal and external pressures, rendered the foreign exchange crisis, the shortages, and the disruptions of production much more acute than in Jamaica. Moderation in the pace of change, in particular in the takeover of enterprises and in redistributive wage-price policies, could have alleviated the strains on the economy, and it could have opened the way for the political compromise necessary to stem the process of rapid polarization.[49]

Peru

Workers' participation in Peru also fell victim to the economic crisis, insofar as the crisis aggravated internal splits in the government over the decision whether to adopt austerity policies in 1976. This forced decision resulted in the purge of the remaining radical officers from leading positions and a decisive shift to the right in the government's composition and policies. The first package of severe austerity policies was negotiated with and implemented under the supervision of private banks, but by 1977 the banks insisted on an agreement between Peru and the IMF.[50]

The project of the Social Property Sector was the first casualty of austerity. There were simply no more funds made available for the execution of plans and already elaborated concrete projects for socially owned, worker self-managed enterprises. Accordingly, only a very small number of such enterprises ever started operating.[51] The CI legislation was changed in 1977, with a new upper limit of 33 percent on the share of ownership and thus seats on the board of directors that the workers could attain. Furthermore, collective ownership by the CI was transformed into individual share ownership of its members. Also, the Law on Stability of Employment was suspended, to great acclaim from the bourgeoisie. As in Jamaica, the key emphasis under the IMF austerity programs was on business confidence, and the price for this confidence was the repeal of legislation that had strengthened the position of labor in the enterprise. The labor movement, despite its gains in mobilization capacity, was not strong enough to block these rollbacks of labor rights. Furthermore, the decline in real wages and the threat of unemployment were so strong that they were the central subjects of all protest action; the importance of the CI paled by comparison.

Also parallel to Jamaica, the economic crisis was caused by a combination of a long-term trend and short-term precipitating factors, both related to Peru's dependent economy, and of policy mistakes. Peru's major raw material exports, except for mining, were undergoing a secular decline in the 1960s and 1970s,[52] causing a shortfall in foreign exchange revenues. Furthermore, beginning in 1973 the anchovy catch declined drastically, the 1975 world recession depressed mining exports, and in 1976 it became clear rather suddenly that the expected discoveries of commercially viable oil deposits in the jungle area would not materialize. This was particularly detrimental to Peru's balance of payments, because in anticipation of the oil revenues, the government had borrowed heavily from commercial banks to finance ambitious capital-intensive development projects whose capacity to generate or at least save foreign exchange was low or nonexistent in the short and medium run.

To summarize, then, the decline of workers' participation in the three cases was a result of the failure of the governments to consolidate their larger project of social transformation; a failure manifesting itself in either the fall of the government or drastic policy changes. In all three cases, this failure was closely linked to the economic crisis that either precipitated the fall of the government or forced it to implement IMF austerity policies. The economic crisis, in turn, was a result of dependency on the one hand and policy mistakes and omissions on the other hand. Problems with export production and prices combined with high import dependence for energy, food, and industrial inputs, and with a high accumulated foreign debt brought about the critical foreign-exchange shortages. In the case of Chile, the rapid redistribution through wage-price policies and state sector expenditure aggravated the shortages by greatly increasing demand for imports of food and industrial inputs. In Peru and Jamaica redistribution and increases in state sector expenditures, though still significant, were slower, but crucial mistakes were made in the financing and the pattern of expenditure. Both governments borrowed heavily from commercial banks, and neither one made a concerted effort to reorient the economy toward greater self-reliance or to channel resources into small-scale production geared toward a wider distribution of productive assets in the society. Thus neither government laid the basis for protecting its economy from severe disruptions resulting from the certain cut-off of external financing in case the government decided to reject IMF austerity policies.

Conclusion

The comparison of the different experiences with workers' participation in Jamaica, Chile, and Peru showed how the conception of the participation schemes was shaped by the nature of the larger political projects of the governments, and how the schemes developed in accordance with the trajectory of the overall projects, namely with the governments' (in)ability to strengthen their support base and consolidate their reform policies. Comparison established that the governments' failure was closely linked to the economic crises, which not only resulted in a halt of all significant reforms but also critically weakened the governments' support base and strengthened the militant opposition instead. Finally, comparison showed how the economic crises were largely due to a combination of constraints of dependency and inappropriate policies.

However, in further exploring the reasons for the inappropriate policies themselves, the economic crises, and the following rapid erosion of the governments' support base, one has to look more closely at power relations in the society. The low initial strength of the political movements supporting the governments and their projects, and the insufficient progress in strengthening these movements directly, obstructed (1) the prevention of the economic crises and the rejection of the IMF austerity policies and (2) the preservation of the reform processes. In Jamaica the divided, nonideological labor movement and the nonprogrammatic party, with little grassroots involvement, little ideological unity, and little ideological understanding at the mass and elite levels, hampered the government's ability to chart and follow a clear path of change and did not provide a strong organizational base to generate support for this process. Thus opportunities for solidifying the process economically by, for instance, promoting small-scale, self-reliant, collective forms of production were neglected, and more traditional distributive expenditures were emphasized instead. When workers' participation was put on the agenda, the lack of union support deprived the government of leverage to overcome employer resistance, particularly once the presence of the IMF strengthened the employers' position. Efforts to build a real programmatic mass party were made and significant progress was achieved, but not enough to provide the support base needed for a significant deepening of the reform process in the crisis conditions of 1977.

In Chile the level of political understanding in the labor movement and the UP parties was higher, but the partisan political splits among the unions and the significant internal disagreements in the UP coalition also weakened the government. Most importantly, the organizational strength of the UP parties was insufficient to widen the UP's electoral base to include a majority of the population; consequently, the UP had control over the presidency only, not Congress. The government's approach to this problem was to put primary emphasis on rapid social transformation in the assumption that this would automatically strengthen its support base, and it rather neglected direct organization and unity-building efforts. As the experience with workers' participation demonstrates, this assumption was not correct. The reforms functioned successfully and had the desired effects on mobilization in support of the UP's transformation project predominantly where supportive unions and party activists were present to begin with. As in Jamaica, the organizational weakness of its support base induced the government to rely on greater distributive expenditure than the economic situation warranted and thus contributed indirectly to the economic problems. The lack of ideological unity in the movement hampered a moderation in the pace of change and a political compromise when the economic crisis and political polarization had achieved such alarming proportions that the danger of an imminent coup became obvious.

In Peru the military government was initially without an organized support base in the society, and the attempt to build such a base by incorporating popular groups into state-sponsored organizations failed, mainly because the existing unions resisted these attempts. The government's hope that the CI would lead to class conciliation and the withering away of existing unions, thus facilitating its incorporative attempts, was not borne out. On the contrary, the CI contributed to labor mobilization and militancy and the growth of independent unions. The internal disunity in the government contributed to the failure of the incorporative project, in that the radical faction tacitly encouraged mobilization and autonomous action on the part of labor organizations, and the conservative faction insisted on more direct controls and intervention, thus increasing labor's propensity to defensive reactions. The radical faction on its part was not strong enough to consistently promote the growth of independent unions and build a unified support base among these unions for its own conception of the reform process. Thus they could not mobilize nearly enough popular pressure to win in the internal power struggle over the direction of the process in 1976.

The comparison of the three cases also showed that the introduction of participation schemes did not necessarily generate support for the governments' reforms and strengthen the labor movements. Rather, the development and effects of the participation schemes depended on the presence and reactions of unions. In Jamaica the unions were hostile or indifferent to the project, which was one of the reasons why it was never implemented and remained largely without any effect. In Chile participation functioned successfully in enterprises where unions were active and supportive of the project, and in these enterprises the experience with participation reinforced these positive attitudes and strengthened solidarity and support for the government's larger project of social change. In Peru, in enterprises where strong unions were present, they were capable of defending the rights of the CI against evasion tactics of employers. The experience of conflict over the CI strengthened these unions and also facilitated unionization efforts in other enterprises through a demonstration effect. This heightened strength of labor, however, only strengthened support for the conception of the transformation process held by the radical faction; in contrast, from the point of view of the mainstream project, the workers' participation reform had outright counterproductive effects.

The design of the participation schemes itself had some importance in their potential development and effects. The emphasis of the design on the experience of direct participation in decision making at all levels in the enterprise in Chile increased work motivation and performance, as well as egalitarian and solidaristic attitudes. In contrast, the CI in Peru did not provide for any real participatory experience in decision making on matters of production. It only increased conflicts over the distribution of the fruits of production, and thus did not cause any changes in work performance. Isolated examples in Peru demonstrated that schemes with an emphasis on ownership and profit sharing could have integrative effects, but only in highly profitable enterprises that had an employer willing to grant the CI its share, a small workforce, and a weak or absent union tradition. However, the scarcity of such cases underlines the impossibility for a government to bring such integration about on a sufficiently large scale to carry out a successful class-conciliation project on the national level.

The key, then, to the successful development of workers' participation schemes in Latin American and Caribbean countries is the ability of reformist governments to reduce the constraints of dependency on their overall process of transformation and to strengthen the political movement supporting the process. Rather than relying on the legislation of participation schemes to generate and strengthen this support, parties and unions have to be strengthened directly through legislative and material support for organizational activities and for unification efforts. Political education also has to extend to unions as well as to the party grassroots and other popular organizations. Political education is as important for the successful development of participation schemes as technical education about enterprise operations.

If reformist governments are to lessen the constraints of dependency and strengthen their organizational support base, they must first achieve ideological unity at the leadership level. Leaders must have a common vision of a desirable social order and of the strategy to achieve it if they are to send unambiguous signals to society about the direction of the process and so develop of a coherent economic plan to reduce the vulnerability of the dependent economy. In such politically and economically supportive environments, workers' participation schemes can develop and contribute to the progress of transformation.

Notes

Acknowledgments: The field work in Jamaica in 1981–82 and in Peru in 1975–76 on which this article is based was supported by fellowships from the Joint Committee on Latin American Studies of the Social Science Research Council and the American Council of Learned Societies and by a Fulbright Research Award for the American Republics. While in Jamaica, the author greatly benefited from an affiliation with the Institute for Social and Economic Research at the University of the West Indies, Mona. All of these institutions deserve thanks; none of them bears any responsibility for the views expressed in this article. The Jamaican research was part of a larger project, in collaboration with John D. Stephens, on the Manley government's attempt to pursue a democratic socialist development path. Thanks are also due to Carmen Sirianni and John D. Stephens for the helpful comments offered on earlier drafts of this chapter.

1. Evelyne Huber Stephens and John D. Stephens, "The Labor Movement, Political Power, and Workers' Participation in Western Europe," in Gösta Esping-Andersen and Roger Friedland, eds., *Political Power and Social Theory* 3 (Greenwich, Conn.: JAI Press, 1982).

2. For a discussion of progressive Christian Democratic doctrine and its philosophical roots, see Brian H. Smith, *The Church and Politics in Chile: Challenges to Modern Catholicism* (Princeton, N.J.: Princeton University Press, 1982); for specific attention to its conception of workers' participation, see Peter T. Knight, "New Forms of Economic Organization in Peru: Toward Workers' Self-Management," in Abraham F. Lowenthal, ed., *The Peruvian Experiment: Continuity and Change under Military Rule* (Princeton, N.J.: Princeton University Press, 1975), 357-61. Alfred C. Stepan, *The State and Society: Peru in Comparative Perspective* (Princeton, N.J.: Princeton University Press, 1978), develops the concept of organic statism to analyze the reform approach of the Peruvian military government, which was heavily influenced by Christian Democratic reformist thinking.

3. See Stanley M. Davis and Louis Wolf Goodman, *Workers and Managers in Latin America* (Lexington, Mass.: D.C. Heath, 1972), esp. 205-40.

4. The discussion of the Jamaican experience is based on field research on the Manley government carried out in 1981-82. For analyses of the socioeconomic and political background and the whole experience of the Manley government, see Evelyne Huber Stephens and John D. Stephens, *Democratic Socialism in Jamaica: The Political Movement and Social Transformation in Dependent Capitalism* (Princeton, N.J.: Princeton University Press, and London: Macmillan, 1986), 373-411; "Democratic Socialism in Dependent Capitalism," *Politics and Society* 12, no. 3 (1983); "Democratic Socialism and the Capitalist Class: An Analysis of the Relation between Jamaican Business and the PNP Government," *Social and Economic Studies* (forthcoming); "Bauxite and Democratic Socialism in Jamaica," in Peter Evans et al., eds., *States versus Markets in the World System* (Beverly Hills, Cal.: Sage, 1985).

5. Carl Stone, "Jamaica's 1980 Elections: What Manley Did Do; What Seaga Need Do," *Caribbean Review* 10, no. 2 (Spring 1981):40.

6. On the importance of patronage in the Jamaican political system, see Carl Stone, *Democracy and Clientelism in Jamaica* (New Brunswick, N.J.: Transaction Books, 1980). On Jamaican unions, see Ralph Gonsalves, "The Trade Union Movement in Jamaica: Its Growth and Some Resultant Problems," in Carl Stone and Aggrey Brown, eds., *Essays on Power and Change in Jamaica* (Kingston: Jamaica Publishing House, 1977); and Michael Manley, *A Voice at the Workplace* (London: Andre Deutsch, 1975).

7. Stone, "Jamaica's 1980 Elections," 40.

8. Brian H. Smith and Jose Luis Rodriguez, "Comparative Working-Class Political Behavior: Chile, France, and Italy," *American Behavioral Scientist* 18, no. 1 (Sept.-Oct. 1974):59-96.

9. Arturo Valenzuela, *Political Brokers in Chile: Local Government in a Centralized Polity* (Durham, N.C.: Duke University Press, 1977).

10. Alan Angell, *Politics and the Labour Movement in Chile* (London: Oxford University Press, 1972).

11. Juan G. Espinosa and Andrew S. Zimbalist, *Economic Democracy: Workers' Participation in Chilean Industry 1970-1973* (New York: Academic Press, 1978).

12. The discussion of the Peruvian experience is based on field research on the workers' participation reforms in the industrial sector carried out in 1975-76. For a detailed analysis of dynamics between labor, capital, and the government, see Evelyne Huber Stephens, *The Politics of Workers' Participation: The Peruvian Approach in Comparative Perspective* (New York: Academic Press, 1980). For a summary statement highlighting the political implications, see Evelyne Huber Stephens, "The Peruvian Military Government, Labor Mobilization, and the Political Strength of the Left," *Latin American Research Review* 18, no. 2 (1983):57-93.

13. Two excellent collections of essays that cover the various reform areas and the reasons for the demise of the government and its political project are Abraham F. Lowenthal, ed., *The Peruvian Experiment: Continuity and Change under Military Rule* (Princeton, N.J.: Princeton University Press, 1975), and Cynthia McClintock and Abraham F. Lowenthal, eds., *The Peruvian Experiment Reconsidered* (Princeton, N.J.: Princeton University Press, 1983).

14. See Liisa North, "Ideological Orientations of Peru's Military Rulers," in McClintock and Lowenthal, *The Peruvian Experiment Reconsidered,* for a discussion of the different ideological tendencies within the military government.

15. Peter S. Cleaves and Henry Pease Garcia, "State Autonomy and Military Policy Making," in McClintock and Lowenthal, *The Peruvian Experiment Reconsidered.*

16. Stephens, *The Politics of Workers' Participation,* 176-83.

17. Michael Manley, *The Politics of Change: A Jamaican Testament* (Washington, D.C.: Howard University Press, 1975).

18. Stone still found these attitudes to be important in his work attitudes survey carried out for the Jamaican government in 1982. See Carl Stone, *Work Attitudes Survey; A Report to the Jamaican Government* (Brown's Town, Jamaica: Earle Publishers, 1982).

19. Integration of private enterprises into the social area through "intervention" or "requisition," followed by state administration, was legally possible if labor conflicts or economic problems obstructed the normal process of production. By September 1973 the social area was composed of 420 enterprises, approximately 260 of which had been intervened in or requisitioned; see Espinosa and Zimbalist, *Economic Democracy,* 47-48.

20. See Stefan deVylder, *Allende's Chile: The Political Economy of the Rise and Fall of the Unidad Popular* (Cambridge: Cambridge University Press, 1976); and Cristobal Kay, "Agrarian Reform and the Transition to Socialism," in Philip O'Brien, ed., *Allende's Chile* (New York: Praeger Publishers, 1976).

21. See "Report of the Advisory Committee on Worker Participation," Kingston Library, Kingston, Jamaica, 1976. The report also includes the submissions from unions and employers on which the following discussion is based.

22. This speech was reprinted in *Jamaica Daily Gleaner,* May 25, 1977.

23. Unless otherwise noted, the entire discussion of the workers' participation schemes, their structure and functioning, relies on Espinosa and Zimbalist, *Economic Democracy.*

24. In Chilean enterprises, there were mostly two types of unions, one for blue-collar (*obreros*) and one for white-collar (*empleados*) workers; in addition, there could be employees belonging to professional unions. Frequently, the various unions had different political affiliations.

25. See Knight, "New Forms of Economic Organization in Peru."

26. The fact that this particular union was strongly opposed to workers' participation is not surprising at all. Well-functioning shopfloor workers' participation makes many supervisory functions superfluous and thus threatens the status as well as the jobs of supervisory personnel. In other countries, similar types of unions have also offered resistance to the introduction of participation schemes.

27. This was repeatedly pointed out by knowledgeable analysts of the Jamaican labor movement as well as by participants in labor relations in interviews carried out in Jamaica.

28. The founder and leader of the BITU, Alexander Bustamente, was President for Life and was empowered to appoint the executive committee as well as the leading officers of the union.

29. See "Report of the Advisory Committee on Worker Participation."

30. Espinosa and Zimbalist, *Economic Democracy,* 55, 77.

31. Ibid., 53.

32. Ibid., 183.

33. Party strength was measured by the percentage of the vote given by the workforce to the candidates with respective party affiliation in the 1972 CUT election; see ibid., 99ff.

34. Ibid., 138ff.

35. Ibid., 148–57.

36. Ibid., 140–41.

37. The original law made this possible by simply prohibiting simultaneous exercise of leadership functions in CI and unions.

38. For a similar view, see Giorgio Alberti, Jorge Santistevan, and Luis Pasara, eds., *Estado y clase: La comunidad industrial en el Peru* (Lima: Instituto de Estudios Peruanos, 1977).

39. See Luis Pasara, "Comunidad Industrial y Sindicato," 217–8, and Jorge Santistevan, "El Estado y los Comuneros Industriales," 319–23, both in Alberti et al., *Estado y clase.*

40. Stephens and Stephens, "Democratic Socialism and the Capitalist Class."

41. Espinosa and Zimbalist, *Economic Democracy,* 99–114.

42. Under Peruvian law, unionization is restricted to the establishment level; thus companies with several branches or centers of production have several unions.

43. Luis Pasara, "El Congreso de Comunidades Industriales," in Luis Pasara et al., *Dinamica de la Comunidad Industrial* (Lima: Desco; Centro de Estudios y Promocion del Desarrollo, 1974).

44. Stephens, *The Politics of Workers' Participation,* 195–204.

45. Norman Girvan, Richard Bernal, and Wesley Hughes, "The IMF and the Third World: The Case of Jamaica," *Development Dialogue* 2 (1980):134–45.

46. Pointing to these policy mistakes and omissions is not to suggest that they were obvious or could easily have been corrected. Rather, many of them had their roots in the preconditions encountered by the PNP, in particular the nonprogrammatic nature of the party, the split nature of the labor movement, and the limited capacity of the state apparatus. See Stephens and Stephens, *Democratic Socialism in Jamaica*, 270–319.

47. George Beckford et al., *Pathways to Progress: The People's Socialist Plan* (Morant Bay: Maroon Publishing House, 1985).

48. It is impossible here to cite even the most important part of the voluminous literature on the UP government and the reasons for the coup. Sergio Bitar, *Transicion, socialismo y democracia: la experiencia chilena* (Mexico, D.F.: Siglo veintiuno editores, 1979); Arturo Valenzuela, "Chile," in Juan J. Linz and Alfred Stepan, eds., *The Breakdown of Democratic Regimes* (Baltimore: Johns Hopkins University Press, 1978); and Frederico Gil, Ricardo Lagos E., and Henry A. Landsberger, eds., *Chile at the Turning Point: Lessons of the Socialist Years, 1970–1973* (Philadelphia: Institute for the Study of Human Issues, 1979), are among the most useful sources because of their nondogmatic analyses and the wealth of information presented.

49. Arguments concerning the dangers of the "maximalist" approach to a democratic socialist transition and the utility of a more gradualist path are developed in Evelyne Huber Stephens and John D. Stephens, "The 'Capitalist State' and the Parliamentary Road to Socialism: Lessons from Chile" (paper delivered at the Latin American Studies Association Meeting, Bloomington, Ind., 1980. Similar conclusions are drawn in Bitar, *Transicion,* a carefully substantiated analysis of the UP's experience.

50. Barbara Stallings, "Peru and the U.S. Banks: Privatization of Financial Relations," in Richard R. Fagen, ed., *Capitalism and the State in U.S.-Latin American Relations* (Stanford, Cal.: Stanford University Press, 1979).

51. Martin J. Scurrah and Guadalupe Esteves, "The Condition of Organized Labor," in Stephen M. Gorman, ed., *Post-Revolutionary Peru: The Politics of Transformation* (Boulder, Colo.: Westview Press, 1982), 128–29.

52. Rosemary Thorp, "The Evolution of Peru's Economy," in McClintock and Lowenthal, *The Peruvian Experiment Reconsidered,* 41.

ABOUT THE CONTRIBUTORS

CHRISTOPHER S. ALLEN is Assistant Professor of Political Science at the University of Georgia, and was a postdoctoral research fellow at the Harvard Business School in 1984–86. He is currently examining the role of employer associations, trade unions, and regional governments in the formation of West German industrial policy. Recent publications include "The Federal Republic of Germany," in Mark Kesselman and Joel Krieger, eds., *European Politics in Transition* (Lexington: D. C. Heath, 1987); and "Germany: Competing Communitarianisms," in George C. Lodge and Ezra Vogel, eds., *Idealogy and National Competitiveness* (Boston: Harvard Business School Press, 1987). With A. Markovits, he was the coauthor of the German portion of *Unions and Economic Crisis: Britain, West Germany and Sweden* (London: George Allen and Unwin, 1984).

ROBERT E. COLE is Professor of Sociology and Business Administration at the University of Michigan. He is a long-term student of Japanese work organization and is the author of *Japanese Blue Collar* and *Work, Participation and Mobility*. Most recently, he has edited *The U.S. and Japanese Auto Industries in Transition*. He is currently completing a book on the diffusion of small-group activities in industry in the United States, Japan, and Sweden. He is also conducting research on organizational strategies for quality improvement.

ELLEN COMISSO is Associate Professor of Political Science at the University of California, San Diego. She is the author of *Workers' Control Under Plan and Market* (New Haven: Yale University Press, 1979), a study of Yugoslav self-management. Her most recent work is as an editor and contributor to *Power, Purpose and Collective Choice: Economic Strategy in Socialist States* (Ithaca: Cornell University Press, forthcoming), originally published as a special issue of *International Organization* (Spring 1986).

GIUSEPPE DELLA ROCCA conducts research on labor in Milan, Italy. His work has been devoted particularly to the study of the social impact of technical-scientific progress. He has written widely on the relationship between the changes in the labor market and industrial relations. His books include *Potere e democrazia nel sindacato* (Roma: Edizioni Lavoro, 1979) and *Sindacato e organizzazione del lavoro* (Milano: Franco Angeli, 1982).

ROBERT HOWARD is a Cambridge, Massachusetts, writer and the author of *Brave New Workplace* (New York: Elisabeth Sifton Books/Viking Press, 1985). A *summa cum laude* graduate of Amherst College, Howard has studied sociology and history at the University of Cambridge in England and the École Normale Supérieure in Paris, France. His articles on work and technology have appeared in a variety of magazines, including *The New Republic, The Nation, Mother Jones,* and *Technology Review.*

ANDREW MARTIN is a political scientist on the staff of the Center for Technology, Policy and Industrial Development at the Massachusetts Institute for Technology. He is also an associate of the Harvard University Center for European Studies, where he codirected a study of union responses to economic crisis in five European countries and was responsible for the section on Sweden. This and several other publications reflect a long-standing interest in the Swedish labor movement and political economy, but his main concern has been the comparative politics of economic policy in the advanced industrial countries, and he is currently working on the dynamics of interdependence among those countries.

HENRY NORR is a Visiting Lecturer for Russian and East European Studies at Stanford University, and is completing a book on self-management in Poland for Cornell University Press. Before specializing in Soviet and East European studies, he worked as a printer, machinist, and community college teacher. His articles on work and workers in the Soviet bloc have appeared in *Soviet Studies, Survey, Poland Watch,* and *Socialist Review.*

GEORGE ROSS is Professor of Sociology at Brandeis University and Senior Associate at the Center for European Studies at Harvard. He is author of *Workers and Communists in France* (Berkeley: University of California Press, 1982); *Unions, Change and Crisis: France and Italy,* volume 1 (London: George Allen and Unwin, 1982), with Peter Lange and Maurizio Vannicelli; *The View From Inside: A French Communist Cell in Crisis* (Berkeley: University of California Press, 1984), with Jane Jenson; *Unions, Change and Crisis: the United Kingdom, West Germany, and Sweden* (London: George Allen and Unwin, 1984), with Peter Gourevitch and Andrew Martin; and coeditor of *The Mitterand Experiment: Continuity and Change in Socialist France* (Cambridge, U.K.: Polity Press, 1986).

LESLIE SCHNEIDER is an associate of the Harman Program on Technology, Public Policy and Human Development in the Kennedy School of Government, Harvard University. She also serves as a consultant on technology management and work organization to a variety of public and private institutions in the United States and Europe. Dr. Schneider has recently written about some of the most advanced efforts to include workers in the design and implementation of new workplace technological change. She is a coeditor of *Systems Design: For, With and By the Users* and *Women, Work and Computerization: Opportunities and Disadvantages* (both published by North-Holland in Amsterdam).

CARMEN SIRIANNI teaches sociology at Northeastern University in Boston and is a research fellow at the Center for European Studies at Harvard. He is the author of *Workers Control and Socialist Democracy: The Soviet Experience* (London: Verso/NLB, 1982), and has coedited two previous books for Temple University

Press: *Work, Community, and Power: The Experience of Labor in Europe and America, 1900-1925,* with James Cronin (1983), and *Critical Studies in Organization and Bureaucracy,* with Frank Fischer (1984). In 1985-86 he was a National Endowment for the Humanities Fellow and member of the Institute for Advanced Study in Princeton, where he prepared *Of Time, Work and Equality,* to be published by Basil Blackwell's Polity Press in Cambridge, U.K. He is coeditor of the Labor and Social Change series of Temple University Press.

EVELYNE HUBER STEPHENS is Associate Professor of Political Science at Northwestern University. She is the author of *The Politics of Workers' Participation: The Peruvian Approach in Comparative Perspective* and the coauthor of *Democratic Socialism in Jamaica: The Political Movement and Social Transformation in Dependent Capitalism,* as well as of several articles on reformist political movements and governments in Latin America and West Europe. Her current research deals with the role of government-sponsored accommodations between labor and capital in the consolidation of democracy and in the pursuit of socioeconomic reform in Latin America and the Caribbean.

JEANNE L. WILSON received a Ph.D. in political science from Indiana University and is currently an Assistant Professor of Political Science at Wheaton College in Norton, Massachusetts. She is the author of several articles on Chinese labor policy. At present, she is working on a comparative study of Chinese and Soviet labor.

INDEX